Democratic Education for Social Studies

An Issues-Centered Decision Making Curriculum

A volume in
International Social Studies Forum: The Series
Series Editors: Richard Diem and Jeff Passe

International Social Studies Forum: The Series

Richard Diem and Jeff Passe, *Series Editors*

Democratic Education for Social Studies: An Issues-Centered Decision Making Curriculum (2007)
   Second edition by Anna S. Ochoa-Becker

Democratic Education for Social Studies

An Issues-Centered Decision Making Curriculum

Second Edition by
Anna S. Ochoa-Becker

First Edition by
**Shirley H. Engle
and Anna S. Ochoa**

INFORMATION AGE
PUBLISHING

Greenwich, Connecticut 06830 • www.infoagepub.com

Library of Congress Cataloging-in-Publication Data

Ochoa-Becker, Anna S.
  Democratic education for social studies : an issues-centered decision
making curriculum. – 2nd ed. / by Anna S. Ochoa-Becker.
      p. cm. – (International social studies forum the series)
  Rev. ed. of: Education for democratic citizenship, by Shirley H. Engle and
Anna S. Ochoa. New York : Teachers College Press, c1988.
  Includes bibliographical references.
  ISBN-13: 978-1-59311-590-6 (pbk.)
  ISBN-13: 978-1-59311-591-3 (hardcover)
  1. Citizenship–Study and teaching–United States. 2. Civics–Study and
teaching–United States. 3. Social sciences–Study and teaching–United
States. I. Engle, Shirley H. Education for democratic citizenship. II.
Title.
  LC1091.O27 2007
  300.7'1073
                                                                2006036220

CONTENTS

PART I

A Rationale for an Issues-Centered Decision Making Curriculum for Citizens of a Pluralistic Democracy in a Global Age

PART II

A Curriculum for Democratic Citizenship Education

ACKNOWLEDGMENTS

Many colleagues, graduate students, student-citizens, teachers and mentors have made contributions that gave support to this book. While I will surely overlook some, I will try to identify those without whom the new version of the Engle-Ochoa book would not have been written.

Especially valuable was the partnership created with Professor Shirley H. Engle, now deceased. Together, we agreed to the principles that constituted the original version of this book. We were very pleased that the book was cited frequently in the social studies literature.

Deep thanks go the Office of the Dean of Faculties at Indiana University when it was headed by Dr. Moya Andrews. Her office provided funding for a research assistant that helped enormously. Both Dr. Helen McCain and Michelle Henderson served in this capacity. Both were committed to the thesis of the book and gave of their time and effort above and beyond the requirements for which they were reimbursed.

My colleagues at the School of Education and the Social Studies Development Center at Indiana University, Bloomington also deserve my very sincere thanks. The stimulating climate of the academic setting that they created and that I had the privilege to experience, certainly heightened the quality of my thinking as well as my writing.

Jim Becker, a global educator (my well informed and thoughtful husband) who read and reread draft chapters, earns my deepest thanks and appreciation.

Professor Richard Diem, Past President of the National Council for the Social Studies, who served as editor of the Social Studies Series for Information Age Publishing and provided feedback that was very useful. It was a pleasure to work with him. He is a scholar and teacher who not only knows the field of social studies education but has had extensive experience in it.

Taking a long view, I must thank the future teachers, graduate students and student-citizens who gave me the grounding and experience that

Democratic Education for Social Studies, pages ix–x
Copyright © 2007 by Information Age Publishing
All rights of reproduction in any form reserved.

shaped the professional commitments that are addressed. The young citizens for whom I served as teacher at the middle and secondary levels for eleven years and for a shorter time, those very young citizens at the elementary level were indispensable in shaping the views I hold regarding the nature of social studies education. My fellow educators at Grand Blanc Middle and High Schools in the Flint, Michigan area, my professors at Wayne State University in Detroit, the University of Michigan in Ann Arbor, Michigan and the University of Washington in Seattle, Washington must also be recognized even in this very general way. Some were more than colleagues; they were mentors as well.

Among the many books that sparked interest and excitement, none surpassed the works of Maurice Hunt and Lawrence Metcalf (1955, 1968) with their boldness in opening the closed areas of public discussion and the school curriculum with concomitant emphasis on values and citizen decision making. These had been issues that were deemed too controversial to teach or to discuss publicly. Their book was recommended to me by a new "change of career" teacher, Jack Stone at Grand Blanc High School. The message of these authors not only stimulated my thinking, it also affirmed some embryonic ideas of my own. Seldom have I read an academic book that was so compelling that I could not put it down until I read the last page. Their thinking has guided my career and the direction taken in the principles advanced in the first and second versions of this book.

To other friends and colleagues such as Dr. Carole Hahn, Professor Susan Klein, Dr. Mark Previte, Dean Richard Wisniewski and especially to those of whom I have not made specific mention, my sincerest appreciation extends to them as well. To Eric Garabant, my computer guru, I owe more thanks than I can express in this statement.

Finally, I cannot overlook the powerful experiences and background that my parents brought to my life. As educated and privileged political refugees, who fled the Communist takeover in the Soviet Union and emigrated to Canada, where I was born, they communicated an appreciation for freedom and equality that was intense and contagious. Despite their permanent separation from family and social standing, I never heard, any form of complaint about their lives in Canada—which were quite modest and their occupations menial. Would I have become so very attached to democratic principles without the background and family climate they created? I doubt it! To them, the deepest thanks of all.

Any mistakes, significant omissions or errors are, of course, mine.

—Anna S. Ochoa-Becker
Bloomington, Indiana

PREFACE

A fundamental goal of schools in this democratic nation, is to educate citizens so that self-governance can flourish. The purpose of this book is to improve school curricula designed to strengthen the capacity of the people to govern themselves. This Issues-Centered Decision Making Curriculum proposes to accomplish this goal by emphasizing knowledge of significant social conditions and controversial issues, reasoned commitments to democratic values with emphasis on the expansion of social justice, as well as to the development of intellectual and political abilities needed by young citizens to address the challenges of the new century.

Many educational reforms, past and present, do not address the nature of curriculum needed for effective citizenship. The testing and accountability movement do not do so. Charter schools and voucher plans do not do so. In the 1960s a host of social studies curriculum projects, collectively labeled the New Social Studies and funded by the federal government, were tried in selected schools, but were soon replaced by a narrow textbook-bound curriculum in most school districts.

In the first edition of this book published in 1988, Shirley Engle and I offered a broader and more democratic curriculum as an alternative to the persistent back-to-the-basics rhetoric of the '70s and '80s. This curriculum urged attention to democratic practices and curricula in the school if we wanted to improve the quality of citizen participation and strengthen this democracy. School practices during that period reflected a much lower priority for social studies. Fewer social studies offerings, fewer credits required for graduation and in many cases, the job descriptions of social studies curriculum coordinators were transformed by changing their roles to general curriculum consultants. The mentality that prevailed in the nation's schools was "back to the basics" and the basics never included or even considered the importance of heightening the education of citizens. We certainly agree that citizens must be able to read, write and calculate but these abilities are not sufficient for effective citizenship in a democracy.

Beyond proficiency in these basics, Engle and I emphasized that young citizens must learn to address, with a high level of competence, the questions and issues that concern the welfare of this pluralistic nation and this increasingly interdependent world. Our well-being and our survival are at stake. Both the public and educators need to view a more democratic form of citizenship education as basic too! No citizen is born with the understandings and abilities for self-governance. Schooling for all citizens is the most salient way that citizens can and must learn about the dynamic nature of this democracy that needs to be responsive to the expanding diversity and complexities in this nation as well as its role in the global community.

This version of the original work appears at a time when young citizens, teachers and schools find themselves deluged by a proliferation of curriculum standards and concomitant mandatory testing. In the '90s, virtually all subject areas including United States history, geography, economic and civics developed curriculum standards, many funded by the federal government. Subsequently, the National Council for the Social Studies issued the Social Studies Curriculum Standards that received no federal support. Accountability, captured in the No Child Left Behind Act passed by Congress, has become a powerful, political imperative that has a substantial and disturbing influence on the curriculum, teaching and learning in the first decade of the 21st century. Ringing in my ears as I write, are the words of an outstanding local teacher who had been told "heads would roll if test scores do not improve." I was amazed to hear the quiver in her voice when she publicly shared her concerns. When such a dedicated and competent teacher agonizes over mandated testing, a wakeup call for all educators is in order. This educational environment that emphasizes measurable learning with such intensity that it minimizes the amount of attention paid to broader ideas and to the development of thoughtful, informed citizens. This narrow view has the potential to reduce young citizens and the adult citizens they will become to nonthinking, nonparticipating puppets of a system where thoughtful self-governance was the goal. The destructive view that frightened this dedicated teacher was dramatically affirmed view when a consultant hired by a large metropolitan school district met with several faculty from Indiana University about school reform. He set the context of the meeting by stating: "We [the school corporation] want to prepare young people to be efficient and capable workers so let's not be concerned with their values or their intellectual abilities, those will be taught on the job." This abrogation of the central responsibility of democratic schooling was, for all of us, alarming. To be more honest, we saw it as immoral. Do we really want our schools to have such limited goals and do we really want to abandon the original purpose of schooling to provide an education for all of its citizens that would enable their ability to govern themselves. Such a limited curriculum where our goals are to teach young children to read, write and calculate without any serious regard for their broader understandings, values and abilities, disappointingly, it suggests an abandonment of any commitment to what a democracy should be.

The schools alone cannot do what an Issues-Centered Decision Making curriculum seeks to do. The schools need help. Not only financial help, but help from families, from significant others, and from community organizations. Moreover, the schools in this democracy must be held responsible for doing everything they can to educate thoughtful and informed citizens who care about the quality of life for themselves and others and who have a sense of what it takes to make a democracy function.

This Issues-Centered Decision Making Curriculum would involve young citizens searching for answers to the following kinds of challenging questions: Was the war in Iraq justified? Should the United States have emphasized diplomatic rather than military efforts, prior to the Iraq war? Should we have sent a larger military force? Should cooperation of other nations been a priority? What is pre-emptive war? What values should guide our decisions to intervene in other nations? Was a preemtive war justified in relationship to the War in Iraq? Was sufficient military equipment available to men and women placed in harm's way? A similar set of probing questions should guide learning related to historical contexts such as the Westward Movement, the Great Depression, the Civil War or Vietnam. Wrestling with such questions, having strong discussions in classrooms and participating in projects that draw on the thinking and creativity of young citizens is much more consistent with the demands of democratic citizenship than textbook-based instruction that requires that young people memorize its single view of history even though we know they soon forget the information they memorized. Asking young citizens to support their answers with reason and evidence is not only more challenging, it is one of the very important abilities needed by democratic citizens. Instead of memorizing the information in textbooks, this curriculum builds the foundation for a heightened quality of democratic citizenship and a more highly confident citizen. Teachers and student-citizens can generate probing questions about such persistent issues such as those related to the tension between security and freedom, what form of welfare assistance is appropriate or the importance of equality of opportunity. Historical issues as well as contemporary and future-oriented issues such as cloning, expanding stem-cell reseach and euthanasia should also receive attention. More recently, issues such as the conduct of stem cell research, abortion and cloning have grown out of medical, sociological and technological research and how we resolve these issues will impact the future. Such questions and the search for understanding in order to make decisions that can be justified are the intellectual grist of highly competent citizens of a strong democracy. Our citizens must have intellectual challenges and the schools must do all they can to realize such goals. The present social studies curriculum evident in many schools gives almost exclusive attention to historical topics and emphasizes memorization of textbook material. Many, if not most young citizens find this curriculum uninteresting. Their predispositions see the present and future timeframes to be especially important. How can we continue with textbook dependent programs when we realize how little of it remains in memory? By proceeding with such curricula, we reduce the potential that young citizens can bring to issues that confront them and the world they live in.

This new version is both an update and a revision. Originally published in 1988, it is overdue. Professor Engle died and I developed some chronic health issues. These events delayed completion of this volume. The new version includes scholarship that is more recent and represents some changes in this author's thinking. Whether Shirley Engle would have agreed with these changes is unknown, but he was not one to ignore new evidence or new reasoning out-of-hand. This volume gives stronger emphasis to social justice, diversity and global perspectives, to school and classroom climate and to an alternative meaning to the concept of democratic citizenship that guides this curriculum.

Many of our colleagues found the original version worthy. It was very well received and to this day, remains one of the more frequently cited references in the field of social studies education.

I have tried to maintain as many of Shirley Engle's words as possible and have missed, deeply, the opportunity to interact with his intellect. As those who knew him are well aware, once he accepted an idea as intellectually worthy, Shirley became robustly passionate about its importance. He never stopped believing that the social studies curriculum could be sronger, more democratic and more useful to our young citizens than it is. Without question, his spirit permeates this work.

—Anna S. Ochoa-Becker
Bloomington, Indiana

PART I

**A RATIONALE FOR AN ISSUES-CENTERED
DECISION MAKING CURRICULUM FOR CITIZENS
OF A PLURALISTIC DEMOCRACY IN A GLOBAL AGE**

CHAPTER 1

DEMOCRATIC IDEALS

Implications for Social Studies Curricula

"The stakes are too high for government to be considered a spectator sport."

—Barbara Jordan,
The first African American woman
to be elected to the Texas Senate

INTRODUCTION

This chapter sets the context for the Issues-Centered Decision Making Curriculum presented in this book. With deep and consistent commitment to democratic principles, this curriculum has the potential to create stronger citizens for a strong democracy. It emphasizes the values of social justice that democracy entails. Fairness equity, equality, freedom and justice need stronger application if minorities and other marginal peoples are to receive all the benefits that this democracy claims to embrace. Self-governance is the bedrock of this democracy. It fails if its citizens do not participate. Currently, it shows signs of weakness when judged by the numbers who vote (only a minority actually cast ballots) or the numbers of people who do not have equal opportunity or by the obstacles that face far too many of our citizens. Self-governance is an imperative; citizens who are uninformed, who lack complex thinking processes, who lack commitment to democracy and its social justice values as well as those who lack social and political abilities will spell its demise unless they receive stronger education for their role as citizens.

Democratic Education for Social Studies, pages 3–27
Copyright © 2007 by Information Age Publishing

*   *   *

In this book, the goal of social studies education is incontrovertibly linked to the democratic ideal. Social studies, at its best, is that part of general education that specializes in the preparation of effective democratic citizens.[1] Such citizens are not only patriotic, loyal, and law-abiding. They are citizens deeply dedicated to democracy and are seriously concerned with the improvement of their pluralistic society and its role in the global community. They must be informed, thoughtful and constructive critics of public policies and practices committed to improving the quality of human lives.[2] Political analysis, decision making and political activity are hallmarks of the kind of citizens a strong democracy needs. Such behavior represents serious concern for the common good and reflects a strong desire to improve public issues that threaten to reduce the quality of life, the expansion of social justice to all citizens, and the potential of democracy.

Our citizens should have a commitment to improve the quality of democracy and the human condition. Authentic expressions of citizen criticism and political interest are not acts of disloyalty. Quite the contrary, they have a very strong attachment to democratic principles that they hope to stretch ever closer to the democratic ideal. Such citizens focus not only on their own self-interest. They can see beyond their immediate circumstances and while they have a strong commitment to improving their own lives, they are concerned with improving the lives of all citizens and strengthening democracy. In this sense, democracy, and certainly a strong democracy, requires a heightened idealism and a dedicated acceptance of democracy's values among its citizens.[3]

Particularly in this democracy, citizens need to embrace a framework of social justice that emphasizes such values as acceptance of diversity, equality, fairness, freedom, and the common good. The effective democratic citizen, therefore, is a constructive critic of the state who is willing and able to participate in its betterment and who vigorously supports its very fundamental democratic principle that citizens can govern themselves (Torres, 2004). As used here, the phrase, "strengthening of democracy" refers to improving democracy's policies and practices so that they are more consistent with democratic principles and hold more promise to expand practices associated with social justice. The characteristics of democratic citizens will receive more attention in Chapter 2, The Citizen We Need in a Democracy.

Social studies programs can take many forms in behalf of educating citizens, social science disciplines as content for study, controversial issues to be thoughtfully considered, understood and decided upon and/or participation in school and community projects.[4] However, it is imperative that educators evaluate these various forms in terms of the quality of their service to democracy and in particular, to the principles of self-governance and social justice. What follows is an elaboration of democratic principles that are integral to social studies programs in this democracy.

Around the world, many nations are struggling as they take initial steps to develop democratic institutions (Bahmueller & Patrick, 1999; Friedman, 1999). The democratic ideal and its rhetoric are exceedingly popular. Indeed, it is common for nations that are extremely authoritarian to use the language of democracy to describe themselves, despite obvious contradictions between democratic principles and their social and political realities. Called by Thomas Jefferson, "the Great Experiment," democracy may take many forms, but its appeal is to basic beliefs that transcend these differences.

The words of Gunnar Myrdal (1944), the distinguished Swedish economist, summarize ideals that continue to guide social studies education in the preparation of citizens for a democratic society. In his book, An American Dilemma, he identified the essential ideas that he called "The American Creed." These ideas include respect for the dignity of each individual human being, a belief in human perfectibility, a recognition that equality of opportunity applies to all people and a deep commitment to certain inalienable rights such as freedom, equality, and popular sovereignty. From these ideas flow still others, such as a government based on the consent of the governed, respect for the decisions made by the majority and as importantly and respect for the right of minorities to assert their views. Myrdal includes freedom of speech and the press, tolerance of racial and religious differences and by implication, a commitment to making decisions using dialogue and reason, rather than violence or arbitrary authority as inherent in the American Creed. Myrdal saw these values as deeply rooted in English Common Law and the Enlightenment. He underscored these principles as the driving force in our War for Independence, in the Preamble to the Constitution, in the Bill of Rights as well as in the constitutions of the various states. Myrdal concluded these values came into play continually in the lawmaking process, in Supreme Court decisions and in political life at all levels.

However, despite widespread acceptance of these values, there have always been disharmonies as the Creed applied to particulars practices and events. Just as recent debates regarding affirmative action and diversity have revolved around questions of excellence as well as fairness and equity of treatment, so throughout our history has there been a continuous discussion over the meaning of democracy, freedom and equity and their implementation when applied to specific cases.

Particularly bothersome and persistent has been the conflict between two essential democratic values: freedom and equality. The application of both of these values is essential to expanding social justice in this democracy. However, the exercise of one person's freedom may well mean the denial of equality to another. These values are in persistent tension with each other as the affirmative action issue well illustrates. The continuous debates between opposing views across this nation's history, with both professing democratic ideals, rage along this uncertain line. Even today, there are countless and constant violations of the rights of individuals across this pluralistic nation and across the planet.

As affirmed by Eric Foner (1998) in *The Story of American Freedom*, the value of freedom is not a fixed ideal, nor does it have a single, exacting definition. Rather, it is constantly shaped by the varied and changing beliefs of all its citizens as they struggle to improve the conditions and address the pressing issues of their times. Foner argues that freedom is a concept that is central to the identity of this nation and its peoples. Especially meaningful is Foner's recognition that those persons, who are society's marginal people, help to clarify the meaning of freedom by revealing its limitations and identifying the peoples whom freedom eludes. Thus, the meaning of freedom becomes sharper as its absence in the lives of some citizens becomes evident. Importantly, Foner argues that freedom and diversity are linked inextricably. Intrinsic tensions and connections between these values set the context and reveal the tension in which citizens will decide which of these values prevails in their particular time and space. Prior to the 1960s and the Civil Rights Movement, it was acceptable for restaurant owners to display "whites only" signs to announce clearly that African Americans were not welcome. This action revealed a higher priority for the freedom of property owners to do as they pleased, rather than being responsive to the principle of equality. The Federal Civil Rights Act of 1964 prohibited discrimination in voting, public accommodations, public facilities and public schools by placing the emphasis on expanding the value of equality to a greater number of people. However, even to this day, in many places where bigotry prevails, law enforcers have often ignored such illegal transgressions. The tensions between these two values are both intrinsic and persistent.

Tragically, across time, they persist and citizens, by their actions or lack of action, will decide where the future will be on an issue so very central to the health of democracy. Without question, democracy's citizens must have both the commitment and the capacity to address these tensions in a way that heightens democratic ideals. In essence, this persistent issue provides a major challenge to social studies educators responsible for the education of citizens for a democracy that addresses the values of social justice. Overtime the insights of Reinhold Niebuhr (1971) also emphasize the need for citizens to engage in continuous negotiation generation after generation, in order to negotiate the tensions and controversies resulting from the contradictions that reside within these values. Niebuhr's observations continue to apply to contemporary conditions:

> A democratic society differs from the traditional societies of the ancient and medieval periods by at least three characteristics. First, it invites the free play of political opinion and social forces and arms its citizens with ultimate authority over the government by giving them the right to vote.... Second, democratic societies do not, and cannot, compel cultural and religious

uniformity.... Third, Western democracies allow free competition between economic forces on the theory that justice can be achieved through the free market. Thus, we are brought to the real issue of consensus in a democratic community. The problem concerns the measure of consensus operating within the very differences of opinion and interest that have free play within society. Here is the core of the problem. For, if the differences are too wide, the party conflict may become so acrimonious that each side will accuse the other of disloyalty to the common good. If there is no consensus below the level of political conflict, contradictory moral and religious convictions may also destroy the unity of the community. (pp. 1–4)

Niebuhr's insights regarding the tension regarding the unity of this nation on one hand and the diversity of its people on the other, provides a penetrating look at continuing and inescapable issues that confront democracy's citizens. The sharp divide over the role of religion in public policies and practices as seen between the values of Christian evangelicals as contrasted with those who value the separation of church and state, poignantly illustrates Niebuhr's point. Social studies educators bear the responsibility to prepare our citizens to participate thoughtfully and actively in such significant dialogues, so very central to the quality of this democracy.

In the last decade, the concept of communitarianism has gained salience—a response to the extremely isolated and disconnected lives that too many people live. My informal discussions with elementary teachers have often emphasized that young children must learn how to live responsibly and respectfully as members of a community where they are able to build connections with others. To this end, in one local elementary school, fifth graders spend a week early in the school year with their teacher at a nearby recreational camping facility to give teachers and students, in a community, experience that breaks down some authority barriers and builds a sense of community. Academically, qualities such as caring and community represent newer curriculum frameworks (Anderson, Nickels, & Crawford, 1994; Noddings, 1992a, 1992b, 2002).

Moreover, the work of Benjamin Barber (1998), a political scientist who has writes extensively about democracy and the challenges it faces, underscores the need for "a place for us" which he conceptualizes as the space between "the opposing poles of government and the market, or the state and individual, or contract association and community" (p. 38). He emphasizes the need for civility and connection and the ways that we can and should build a stronger sense of community by reclaiming our connections with others, which Barber reminds us was a deep tradition in the early days of the Republic. The best hope for strengthening democracy lies neither in the indoctrination of shaky truths nor in painting over the problems and issues that plague us but rather with the nurturing of citizens who, with open eyes and minds, have an opportunity to become acutely aware of the importance of expanding social justice principles in this democracy. Our citizens must have the facility to make intelligent political judgments that address controversial issues facing their communities, their society as well as the planet.

Each generation of citizens needs to consider how democratic principles manifest themselves. At times, we have had presidents who increased the power of the presidency using procedures such as executive privilege, presidential appointments and personal influence in order to expand the power of this office. Furthermore, at times the Supreme Court assumed a more activist posture that, in effect, took on the force of public policy. Examples are found in such cases as *Brown v. Board of Education*, the school integration decision and *Roe v. Wade*, which is permissive of abortions and others. Such cases represent the power that the Supreme Court can exercise. Democratic citizens need to be aware that assumptions of power by any branch of government need careful scrutiny to ensure that such changes preserve the principle of checks and balances and enhance the common good.

While deeply committed to democratic principles with emphasis on expanding social justice, the position taken in this book recognizes that in this country and others, democracy has faced and will continue to face serious problems. The town meeting model of democracy, suited to an agricultural society in our early history is no longer useful or workable. A large and growing population eventually made the town meeting version of democracy dysfunctional. The United States Constitution provided for a republic as a form of government that permits the people to govern themselves through elected representatives rather than by direct citizen participation. Today, given the size of this nation's population, approximately 300 million people (Population Reference Bureau 2006), the burden of representation that loads on 435 Congressional representatives is excessive. Each represents over 500,000 citizens. This ratio of 1/500,000 clearly borders on the dysfunctional. Furthermore, for all citizens, the challenge of deciding among candidates for congressional seats and other elected positions requires more sophistication than ever. No single candidate is likely to agree with all of a given citizen's positions. It takes thoughtful scrutiny to weigh the agreements against the disagreements to determine whether a specific candidate is the citizen's best choice or not. The scope and complexity of domestic and global issues faced by our citizens is indeed challenging in ways that earlier generations did not need to consider. However, the preparation of citizens who recognize their persistent responsibility to be informed and to engage themselves with the amelioration of these issues must be at the center of the work of social studies educators at all levels.

Citizens and those who educate citizens need to recognize that technology makes it virtually possible for citizens to vote directly from their homes for candidates for public office. Even more dramatic, future advancements may allow citizens to vote directly for proposed legislation at any level of government from their homes or publicly available computers. While the latter development may or may not be desirable, citizens should recognize that these possibilities could eliminate the need to have elected representatives. Furthermore, under such circumstances, the possibility of diminishing the republic as a form of government emerges, a condition that should give all citizens considerable pause. While such developments await wider technological applications, the possibility is not beyond our reach. Having the technological capacity to eliminate the need for legislative bodies at any level of government is highly challenging, it will take a wise, well-informed and thoughtful citizenry to decide whether such new directions serve the cause of strengthening the quality of democracy.

It is disappointing to those concerned with the vitality of democratic principles that the majority vote, when examined carefully, is really a minority vote, because such a large number of citizens do not vote. Furthermore, too many voters are uninformed and some are misled by slick media presentations. Such media-based efforts as political advertising to promote candidates for public office have made it essential for political parties and their candidates to raise inordinate amounts of money in order to make a respectable run for the office. In the 2004 election, all candidates seeking the presidency spent over a billion dollars. (Federal Election Commission, 2005). Therefore, only candidates who can attract large donors have any chance of being successful. Furthermore, this condition causes special interest groups to invest heavily in full time lobbyists to secure the votes of elected lawmakers. The rhetoric in favor of campaign finance reform is voluminous, but efforts to ameliorate the role of wealth in determining the outcomes of elections have been very resistant to change. In 2002, after years of persistent effort, a Campaign Finance Reform Act became law. However, it fell short of insuring that candidates could avoid their dependence on huge amounts of money to pay for costly television and newspaper advertisements. While the Act limits the amount of money candidates can accept, it is legally possible for donors to route funds through nongovernmental organizations (NGOs) that can use these funds to pay for ads in behalf of their organizational goals that they connect to their preferred candidates. While this Act has symbolic value, it hardly prevents big money from continuing to buy elections. Obviously, well–funded special interest groups wield much more power than do ordinary citizens—a tragic development for a democracy that has struggled to test the viability of self-governance for well-over 200 years.

Furthermore, we know that the rights of minorities and of marginal peoples are not evenly protected, to say the least. Despite legislation and court decisions, minorities, marginal people and women still face highly inequitable conditions. Educational opportunities, employment opportunities, health care, housing and child care are distributed inequitably among these populations. Social studies educators should understand that in a pluralistic society we must have a multicultural curriculum that raises the challenging and controversial issues that diverse populations face (Bennett, 2005; Banks, 2005a, 2005b; Gay, 2005).

In her well-known book, *Comprehensive Multicultural Education,* Bennett, (2005) identifies the following practices that can help educators give serious attention to pluralism.

- Recognize racial history and its impact on oppressors and victims.
- Examine our own attitudes, experiences, and behaviors concerning racism.
- Understand the origins of racism and why people hold racial prejudices and stereotypes.
- Understand the differences among individual, institutional, and cultural racism.
- Be able to identify images in the language and illustrations of books, films, television, news media, and advertising.
- Be able to identify current examples of racism in the immediate community and society as a whole.
- Identify specific ways of combating racism.
- Become anti-racist in our own behavior. (p. 100)

Social studies educators at all levels can integrate such perspectives and practices in the study of many kinds of controversial issues that they address in their classes in order to sensitize student-citizens to the persistent presence of pluralism in their lives. Whether the issue is pollution, war or crime, it is desirable for young citizens to examine the differing impacts such issues have on minorities and marginal peoples as well as to examine the international or global implications.

Citizens of this democracy are concurrently citizens of their nation, members of the human species and inhabitant of Planet Earth. Being a member of the human species does not carry any official rights and responsibilities. However, the more intense our relationships become with peoples elsewhere on the planet, international businesses and nations make it unavoidably clear that our best interests, the interests of all peoples who make the planet their home, and the interests of subsequent generations will be served only if all people treat the planet, its resources and its inhabitants with respect and care. Citizens must be assertive regarding the distribution of society's benefits to those who have lived on the margins for far too long. Without the vigor and dedication of its citizens about such issues, democracy will flounder and democratic principles will lose meaning.

Internationalization means increasing cross-cultural contact. It has both positive and negative aspects. It takes the form of increasing numbers of international students, tourists and a much higher volume of contacts and communication with peoples of different cultures. Today's technology makes issues and events occurring anywhere on the planet immediately available in all of our living rooms. Furthermore, these events or issues deeply influence our lives. The worldwide impact of the explosion in Chernobyl and the international AIDS crisis are only two of a myriad of examples that illustrate the global impact of planetary conditions. World trade is one of the more controversial aspects of internationalization that is helping some people in some nations and exploiting others for cheap labor. All of these developments call for a curriculum that gives more attention to issues that do not respect national boundaries.[5] Terrorism and the events of 9/11 make this matter poignantly clear. However, environmental issues, world hunger, the spread of disease whether AIDS, Mad Cow disease or the West Nile virus and improving the standard of living for all must also be addressed more vigorously.

We also know that international policies and practices are seldom subject to the will of the people. Most citizens know very little about global affairs and do not discern the subtle, but significant relationships between local and global issues. For example, it is doubtful that many, if not most, citizens could explain, much less justify, why the United States sent troops to Haiti in 1993 or know why the United States decided to have a military presence in Bosnia in the early 1990s. Frequently, actions in various global trouble spots are in direct opposition to the interests of democracy. Contradictory to democratic self-governance, a small number of people and corporations often direct the international policies of the United States rather than the broad base of our citizenry. Furthermore, most citizens are not sufficiently cognizant of world affairs to play an intelligent and knowledgeable role. Citizenship education programs not only can, but also must do all they can, to develop democratic citizens who are informed about global issues, who see the relationship between local and global issues and also are willing and able to make their voices heard.

However, with all of its problems, democracy still offers the best hope, when compared with other political systems, for preserving the basic dignity of all human beings and the betterment of the human condition. The educational perspective advanced in this book is that if our democracy has problems, and it certainly does, the solution to them lies not in authoritarianism, but in more effectively conceived democratic institutions. For the sake of all peoples, if democracy is to work better and if self-governance is to succeed, education must prepare its citizens to promote democracy's welfare.

Democratic citizens must realize that the conditions under which democracy must work is dramatically different from those prevailing in the early days of this nation. Technology and its appropriate use is a significant issue itself. Undoubtedly, the future holds much more change. Thus, the responsibilities that citizens of a democracy are called upon to shoulder are vastly more complicated than they were two hundred years ago or even in the early 1900s when social studies as a unified curriculum was formally conceived in 1916 (Nelson, 1994).

Technology has produced an upheaval in the ways that people live, work and play. Importantly, it has changed the ways that people relate to one another. The reduction of face-to-face discussions and the increase in bureaucratic communication does little to heighten the sense of community or interpersonal connectedness that contributes to enhancing social conditions in a democratic society. The wars in which democracies have participated and the economic and social displacements that followed have placed a tremendous strain on the maintenance of free democratic institutions. Many venerable institutions, such as the family, marriage, the work place and certainly, the government itself, (including schooling at all levels), serve as strong examples of technological adaptation. Inevitably, citizens will need to insure that these institutions respond to unknown future conditions. Democracy's citizens will need to generate creative responses to strengthen democracy in this postmodern society. Most of our pressing environmental problems such as global warming and toxic waste did not even exist or were not recognized as issues as recently as fifty years ago. In the future, citizens will continue to face new issues that they have not addressed previously. By emphasizing the study of issues and paying serious attention to enhancing intellectual processes, heightening their tolerance for ambiguity and preparing young citizens for change, social studies curricula can be of great value to strengthening democracy.

It is clearly impossible to teach the next generation of citizens every piece of information they may need to know. However, it is very possible to have them learn how to examine compelling issues and develop the intellectual power that will help them address the challenging matters of their times. Wiggins (1989) captures the essence of the debate:

> Given the pain of necessary curriculum deletion, critics retreat to rigid ideology to ensure that someone else's canon is cut. The traditionalists demand complete cultural literacy; the progressives deify "thinking" and multiple points of view. The former see themselves as the guardians of rigor, standards and disciplinary knowledge; the latter see such views as elitist, narrowly pedantic, unmindful of non-traditional knowledge and modern epistemology. Alas, "literacy" is frequently reduced to memorized lists or cultural hegemony, and "perspective" ends up being my perspective, that is egocentrism (p. 45).

Currently, the demands for compliance with curriculum standards as measured by mandatory testing are guiding teaching, learning and the curriculum in too many social studies classrooms in a manner consistent with Wiggins' description of the traditionalist agenda. Sadly, the emphasis too often is on memorization rather than higher level thinking and on so-called facts found in social studies textbooks or derived from curriculum standards or the teacher's lecture. Such practices represent goals that have little relationship to expanding social justice or heightening the quality of democratic citizenship.

Individual civic responsibilities have not only vastly increased in number over just a few years, but they have changed in kind as well. In today's world, some of our very important relationships may well be with people we will never see, rather than confined to those in our immediate communities or within our nation. While we can illustrate our extended broad reach in many ways, it is especially poignant to those who have lost loved ones in Bosnia, the Persian Gulf, Afghanistan, and/or Iraq. Moreover, fundamental democratic values such as freedom, equality and justice have taken on new meanings in a world of instant communication, economically powerful multinational conglomerates and the threat of terrorist movements that are not identified with a particular nation but with transnational networks whose locations are elusive.

Dramatic changes evident in the United States by reviewing the history of labor unions, which came into existence barely a hundred years ago and were until recently bulwarks of power. They are now struggling for their very survival in the face of the high tech revolution. Furthermore, the two party system that has dominated the political process for well over 200 years is in sad disarray because of the power in the hands of special interests. Political party discipline is rapidly becoming unenforceable (Kornbluh, 2000), a condition that challenges the two-party system. Word of mouth as well as face-to-face relationships and party loyalties, where political decisions were once made, are now seriously compromised by the mass media. The public has less influence on policy outcomes than ever before. When the public is less involved, the quality of self-governance is threatened.

In a survey of eligible voters, David Thelen (1996) found that citizens believed that public officials were not interested in what people like themselves thought. Furthermore, the credibility of leaders in education, the clergy, the professions and the press has been badly compromised by the mass media and the growth of special interest morality over concern for the common good. Thelen's findings do not bode well for the health and vitality of a strong democracy.

Among the forces and trends that diminish democracy, the practices and policies of our capitalistic economy deserve serious attention by citizens. Given the persistence of glaring poverty in a land of plenty and the widening gap between the rich and poor, it is baldly clear that some practices associated with free enterprise have contributed to conditions that are not dissimilar to those in some of the world's poorest countries. In such nations, where a minority of very wealthy elites hold disproportionate power and control, the poor become more and more plentiful as well as more and more hopeless. The widening gap between the rich and the poor in the United States is cause for considerable citizen concern.

The principles and practices that characterize democracy differ substantially from those associated with capitalism. Democracy is idealistic as well as positive about the potential of human beings. It embraces a premise of respect for each individual. Capitalism, characterized by the goal of financial success and the accumulation of wealth, is highly competitive. In this society, these two contrasting systems have struck an accord. Sometimes, the government imposes restrictions on corporations and businesses through such mechanisms as taxes, child labor laws and anti-trust legislation. At other times, government agencies and legislative bodies have also tried to strengthen the nation's economy by providing assistance to small businesses, manipulating interest rates and attracting new businesses with favorable tax conditions. Corporations have provided employment for many people and have included health and retirement plans as benefits to their employees. The foundations that many corporations have created sponsor research, provide scholarships and engage in a wide range of activities that have improved this society. Some corporations have also abused their power as a number of recent corporate scandals demonstrate. Tragically, their employees have lost their benefits as well as their jobs. Furthermore, the divide between social classes and between the haves and have-nots, has deepened. These two systems, the one political, the other economic, are at once compatible and at the same time, are at odds with each other. Too many citizens seem to be all too willing to sacrifice the values of democracy for gains in their economic well being and social class status. Individuals who are obsessed with the accumulation of wealth demonstrate the extremes of capitalism that they make visible by buying luxury cars, building multi-million dollar homes and earning seven figure salaries. Among the citizenry, the widening gap between the wealthy and most citizens creates instability and lack of confidence in the system. To be sure, even the founding fathers held property rights as sacred, including their slaves whom they viewed as property. However, today, the dominance of self-interest and property rights reveals itself as we observe fellow citizens who may not vote or participate in public life, but are highly energized when there is any threat to their property value or the possibility of an increase in taxes. The intensity of their self-interest is obvious as these same individuals appear at zoning board meetings to defend their property values but they are conspicuously absent when schools, halfway houses and increased pay for public employees need support.

All of us want a healthy economy that provides jobs, job security and allows a comfortable style of life. However, abuses of wealth and power are all too evident. Unfortunately, some of our corporations in they daily practices have been little concerned with issues such as the expansion of equal opportunity, sound environmental practices or severe health issues such as AIDS and Black Lung disease. On occasion, some corporations have even opposed the efforts of government to remedy such conditions that continue to threaten the well-being of all of us. Furthermore, in a pluralistic democracy in a global age must not only persist in its traditional values, but it must develop new institutions and new values, that are at one and the same time, both compatible with traditional values, yet are also responsive to dramatically changed and novel conditions in order to sustain itself in a complex and challenging world.

Certainly, it is of far greater importance to teach young citizens to make intelligent and justifiable decisions independently than it is to tell them what to think. Blind indoctrination is futile, if not immoral, and is contradictory in a democracy. We must stop exhorting youth to be so-called "good" citizens, according to our personal view of "good," and instead help them to ask probing questions about their own values and those of others. We must engage ourselves, teachers and students alike, actively and directly in the difficult task of reconsidering our behavior as individuals, as teachers and as a community in light of the traditional values we may have taken for granted or even ignored in the past. The training ground for civic competence lies in the process of engaging our student-citizens in the understanding of issues that confront them, their society and the planet. The curriculum proposed here faces many challenges. However, they are challenges that strong teachers and administrators have mounted despite restrictive community climates. Examples of more open and democratic teaching were evident even during the red scare of the McCarthy era in the 1950s, a difficult time when some teachers bravely took to teaching about comparative political systems rather than restricting their curriculum to the evils of communism. Currently, the demands currently imposed so widely by mandatory testing, restrict and narrow the social studies curriculum stand as a barrier to the broader and more significant goals associated with democratic citizenship. Still, it seems necessary to say that social studies educators are evading their responsibility if they stop short of such engagement.

A unique contribution of democracies, including that of the United States, has been to keep the debate over the meaning of justice, freedom and equality open and free of the violence and brutality that characterize autocracies whether of the right or the left, even those that claim they are democratic. It stretches credibility to the breaking point to conceive of democracy being imposed on people by armies, secret police and death squads. Yet, the U.S. and its few supporters in the coalition have used these characteristics blatantly. Furthermore, the United States government relied on military force rather than emphasizing diplomacy as a step toward democracy. Neither are such practices as intellectual harassment, secrecy or deceit consistent with democratic principles. Our citizenry must be prepared to demand that such practices not affect their lives or the offices of our government at any level.

Concerns over terrorism directed at targets in the United States have made clear the agonizing dilemma that exists between national security and civil rights. Recently, the civil rights of individuals from other nations who are being detained without legal charges are in question, the rights of those persons to speak to lawyers privately has been suspended and the enactment and enforcement of the Patriot Act, all seriously challenge democracy's concern with widening civil rights in favor of national security. This national crisis confronts all citizens who care deeply about democratic values and maximizing equity and fair treatment for all.

This conception of democracy and its issues is central to the purpose of social studies in the education of citizens Its purpose is not to impose any particular form of democracy on young people or to intrude itself in such a way as to preclude the consideration of any other point of view, however abhorrent it may be. Rather, the dialogue must be kept open. Its role is to help children and youth acquire the knowledge and intellectual abilities needed to participate productively in meaningful dialogue and to enable young citizens to take an intellectually sound and active part in the improvement of issues that society faces. Citizens in a democracy must be able to judge the credibility of various claims of truth. They must be able to exercise independent judgment about both personal and public affairs. We therefore applaud the following statement from Robert Hutchins (1982) on the aim of a democratic society. The position he takes is that the education of citizens improves by seizing every opportunity to keep talking about questions worth talking about with as much intelligence as can be mustered. It follows logically from this statement of purpose that controversies, rather than fixed knowledge and values, must play a central role in social studies education. As Hutchins (1982) explained:

> I think that the only thing it is possible to do in a democratic country on any subject is to keep talking and to seize every opportunity to talk. I recently ran across a letter from Thomas Jefferson to John Adams. Jefferson, at the age of 70, wrote to John Adams, aged 78. Jefferson said more or less these words, "I state my difference with you not because I wish to begin a controversy, when we are both too old to change opinions over a long life of experience and reflection. I state my difference with you only because we ought before we die to explain ourselves to one another. (Back Cover)

In these few sentences, Jefferson captured the aim of a democratic society. Thus far, in this chapter, both the potential strengths and problems of democracy have been given attention, the case for an open and democratic curriculum was made and the central role of social studies that aids and abets continuing dialogue around public issues emphasized.

Now, we turn to a survey of democratic values. The listing is admittedly idealistic and there will be those who will be incensed because it lacks realism or even because it is in conflict with their own private beliefs-those, for example, who for ideological or selfish, bigoted reasons, may argue that all people should not have equal opportunity, after all. Nonetheless, this list will afford a basis for argument as the reader examines an Issues-Centered Decision Making Curriculum that is more responsive to the needs of democracy.

A basic value of democracy is respect for the dignity of the individual. This value includes the protection by the state of the life and general well being of the individual as well as the protection of individuals in their right both to dissent from their group and the right to exercise influence public affairs as a member of a minority group. A single citizen can ignite an issue by a well–written letter to a local newspaper. This individual may also protest along with others who share common interests regarding the well-being of society. Increasingly, various government policies and practices have honored group rights that apply to culturally distinctive or marginal groups, to women, to persons with alternative lifestyles, to handicapped persons and other marginal peoples. Affirmative action, class action suits and laws such as the Civil Rights Act of 1964 are a few poignant examples of more enlightened government policies in the United States. Nonetheless, we have a long way to go.

A prominent feature of democracy has been the continuing struggle of people to improve their lives and to distribute opportunities, economic well being and their understandings as widely as possible. Improvement comes about through the exchange of ideas which democracy not only allows, but also protects. In a democracy, it is theoretically possible for a single individual or one small group to persuade the entire nation to change its course. As Margaret Mead wisely observed: "Never think that an individual or a small group cannot change things; it is the only thing that ever has" (Institute for Cultural Studies, 2006)

It is impossible to think of democracy without the protection of the right to dissent. Indeed, democracy's strength resides in the exercise of this right. Dissent provides the opportunity to examine existing policies and practices that may no longer be viable and may no longer support democratic principles. Respect for each individual also implies acceptance and respect for human differences as found in both individuals and groups and most importantly, respect for the rights of others to express their feelings and opinions even when they are deviate from existing norms or those held by more powerful citizens. In schools, this concern for individuals and groups means that teachers take the experiences and questions of young people seriously and never ignore them. More broadly, respect for the individual and groups runs counter to all kinds of discriminatory and prejudicial behavior that applies to culture, race, religion, gender and lifestyle Furthermore, respect for all citizens makes less likely the use of compulsion and force in human affairs and increases the use of reason and dialogue as more effective ways to make decisions.

A second tenet of democracy is the right of individuals and groups to participate in decisions important to society as a whole. Without such participation, respect for the individuals and groups is meaningless and democracy unworkable. In our contemporary, populous and pluralistic society, political participation includes the right to vote and to have that vote count. However, in the presidential election of the year 2000, the credibility of the election results was severely challenged in the state of Florida.

Such undocumented failures to count all ballots and to provide clear and understandable voting protocols that each voter could easily follow are probably, not confined to the state of Florida. While there are many ways that citizens can use to call attention to their concerns, it is imperative that each person must have the right to vote in a democracy in a manner that is straightforward and easily understood and verifiable.

Participation embraces the right to fair representation through the mechanisms of the political system (committees, councils, legislatures, executive officials and the like). Public participation takes place in the workplace, social and governmental units including the educational system and wherever decisions regarding social policies and practices are made. In a democracy, all citizens must have an equal chance to influence decisions that shape their lives. While each citizen should be able to exercise these rights, policy makers and those in authority must recognize that each individual is unique and that this uniqueness matters. Too many of our citizens do not possess the abilities, the understandings or the confidence to take advantage of these rights as effectively as their more privileged fellow citizens do. An older woman who is minimally literate, an eighteen year old who has been a consistent victim of abuse, a young adult of color who has been profiled by police authorities or a Latino high school student who must drop out of school to help support the family are unlikely to participate equitably with others in public affairs. The extent that these citizens default or are unable to exercise their rights because they do not start at the same baseline as more privileged citizens, is the extent to which democracy and democratic rights are really not functioning as rights at all. These rights elude the grasp of those who have felt oppression and those who are poor and powerless (Bloom, 1998).

A third tenet of democracy is the right as well as the responsibility to inform ourselves about public affairs. All citizens must have equitable access to education and information. The widest and most open distribution of information to all people is a democratic necessity making the education of citizens an imperative. A democratic society cannot live up to its name without it. Yet, both educators and citizens must recognize that we do not achieve dependable knowledge merely by having information disseminated in schools or by the media. Information, by itself, has little meaning. To be useful, we must analyze it, review and relate it to our framework Therefore, of equal importance to information, is the development of intellectual acuity that enables citizens to collect, sort, verify and apply knowledge in ways that are meaningful to them and applicable to the issues of their time. In this Curriculum, intellectual processes and their development are as important as the understanding gained. As Thomas Jefferson (1819) so succinctly put it, "A nation both ignorant and free, never was and never will be."

Educators need to remember that neither knowledge nor wisdom comes full blown out of books, lectures or television programs. Rather, citizens must process information in their minds and apply their understandings to real life situations. This intellectual process is unique to every individual. Without question, the development of intellectual acuity and the processes involved are as important in the context of democratic education as the information itself, perhaps even more so. It is these intellectual processes whereby information becomes meaningful. As the characteristics of a democratic education are spelled out, attention to intellectual processes with an emphasis on higher level thinking must be an integral and very significant dimension of the social studies curriculum. We have research that tells us that we can teacher young people to think in more complicated ways—to conceptualize, to generalize, by example, by modeling, by specific practice in different thinking processes. Teachers need to provide every opportunity for their young citizens to expand their thinking abilities.

Fourth, democracy assumes an open society in the sense that the possibility of changes and improvement are taken for granted. Democracy is never completed. There are no final solutions nor unquestionable answers. Instead, strong democratic citizens constantly strive for improvement and a belief that it is possible to improve the quality of life for all. In this respect, democracy is antithetical to authoritarian systems that deny variations except those preferred by ruling elites who often reduce the importance of new information and new interpretations. They usually insist on the strict obedience of the citizen to the governing class. The strength of democracy lies in its openness, its responsiveness to new information as applied to new conditions and its fostering of critical questioning that carries respect for dissent in its wake.

Democratic citizens must not only recognize the tension between self-interest and the common good, they also need to be disposed to modifying the relative weight given to each of these concepts as these are applied to public affairs. In this nation, acquisitiveness and accumulation of highly visible signs of wealth is extremely important to a number of citizens. Wealth is equated with power. We only need to look at the excessive salaries that are paid to professional athletes, entertainers and chief executive officers of corporations to observe the excess of wealth possessed by a few. At the same time, members of some groups are struggling for a small piece of the pie. Capitalism thrives on the desire of individuals to satisfy their needs. It assumes that self-interest and competitiveness energizes their efforts. These values, when carried to extremes as they sometimes are, debase human beings and diminish the expansion of social justice that is so integral to democratic principles and practices.

In the workplace, such values drive some individuals to compromise their coworkers in order to increase the chances for their own advancement. In the family, these values often lead to both adults working at full time jobs to afford what they want, to pay for college, travel and the like. Owners of property insist that they have the right to do anything they wish with what they own. Only in the last 50 years, did civil rights legislation prevent owners who served the public from discriminating among their customers on racial grounds.

Fifth, democracy assumes some independence of the individual from the group. Since the vitality of a democracy depends on citizens who exercise independent judgment, their education is not merely a matter of accepting unquestionably the ways of the group. While such conditions might exist in dictatorial systems, an open society encourages individuals to be autonomous from their own group and autonomy requires some understanding of the origins of group differences and the nature of cultural and social biases, including those of one's own group. Such understanding requires the broadening of experience and perspectives beyond the local and the immediate. It suggests an expansion of viewpoints that range from the parochial to the cosmopolitan. Furthermore, citizens of a democracy must be allowed room for doubt, even for their most cherished beliefs. They must be encouraged to question and to be constructively critical. They need to be able to withstand their own socializing process. At the same time, an important responsibility of education in a democracy is the countersocialization of youth. Countersocialization involves learning to be a thoughtful critic of society rather than an unquestioning citizen-soldier who is obedient and acquiescent to authority. Countersocialization entails an acceptance of criticism and dissent and sets democracy apart from authoritarian systems. Social studies educators must remember that serious questioning is highly valued by democracy especially when done by seriously thoughtful citizens. This value makes the system work.

A sixth tenet is the principle of equality of opportunity for all people. This tenet is asserted boldly in the 14th Amendment, enacted over a hundred years ago in the aftermath of the Civil War. Since then, the integration of black military personnel during World War II, the Brown Decision, the march to Selma, Alabama, Martin Luther King's letter from the Birmingham jail, the 1983 march on Washington, the legal and educational work of the Southern Poverty Law Center among other significant efforts and events, represent the expansion of social justice. Many individuals and groups exercised their responsibility as citizens to create a more equitable environment for all peoples of this nation.

Social studies educators recognize that we still have a long and difficult way to go. Each generation will face such challenges and social studies educators have the professional responsibility to foster the capacity of student-citizens to address complex and controversial issues that they are essential to strengthening democracy. In this very significant way, social studies educators help create the future.

If these tenets are principles essential to a democracy, then it is very important that those engaged in the education of democracy's citizens understand that the democratic citizen is a new and different breed, very unlike the docile and obedient subjects that have inhabited many societies throughout history. This new breed of citizen requires an education that provides both the knowledge and abilities that empower citizens to be thoughtful, assertive, proactive as well as able to demonstrate the ability to function fully in an open society.

In the matter of cultural transmission and habit formation, the contrast between democracy and autocracy is baldly evident. In an autocracy, habit formation is cultivated by blind conditioning with little or no reflection by citizens. In such settings, these practices apply to virtually the totality of citizenship education. *Subjects*, which is a term that is an appropriate descriptor of so-called citizens in an autocracy, are expected to be unquestionably loyal and obedient creatures of habit. In sharp contrast, habits represent a minuscule part of the characteristics of democratic *citizens* and furthermore, habit formation must be tempered with reason. Habits, in a democracy, are held with much tentativeness and once learned, they may be questioned and modified. A reasonable thinking person is one who alters her or his view as they hear new evidence that may cause them to shift positions. What we believe while in high school does not necessarily predict our subsequent beliefs as adults. Without a doubt, an informed, reasonable and active citizen who understands that change is not only possible but likely is exactly what democracy needs.

This discussion does not mean to suggest that democratic citizens are less committed to democracy than their counterparts are to autocracy. Indeed, their commitment may be even stronger because it has reason on its side. Citizens of a democracy are more likely to stand by their commitment to broad principles that they have accepted voluntarily, openly and without coercion. In a democracy, citizens should be able to make adjustments for new conditions and new knowledge without threatening the underlying democratic foundations of society. Citizens of a dictatorship are more likely to find social change disorienting, since there is little or no room under dictatorship for reasoned adjustment.

While democratic citizens usually exhibit attitudes and behavior friendly to democracy and are strong in their commitment to democratic principles, somewhat paradoxically, they must possess countersocializing characteristics such as the willingness and ability to criticize and question social norms, their own values as well as public policies and practices. Furthermore, democratic citizens, often stand out against the crowd and identify the issues of their times in their broadest perspective. In addition, they seek rational solutions to controversy in contrast with arbitrary solutions that are all too easily forthcoming in an autocracy. If citizens realize these expectations, educators need to provide the strongest and most engaging preparation for citizenship.

The education of the very young in all societies is a process of socialization. From parents, significant adults, peers, the media and teachers, young children learn how to behave, what to believe, what to honor and respect and what to fear. Indeed, their socialization includes almost everything they need to know to fit into society. Children learn all of this, as if by osmosis, from the very beginning of life without children doing any deliberate thinking about it. From a Piagetian perspective, socialization occurs during the pre-reflective years, before children enter elementary school. This process encourages their conformity to the folkways and norms of society. Small children learn such important matters as political bias and attitudes toward social and cultural differences without substantive reasons for holding such beliefs. Stereotypes, prejudice and discrimination have their roots in socialization.

By the time children enter kindergarten, they have been carefully taught— a condition that any seasoned kindergarten teacher can describe in rich detail. To this teacher, who is a very significant person in children's lives, the work of broadening each child's perspective is a daily challenge. In an autocracy, this process of socialization continues into adulthood. The expectations are that citizens will be patriotic and conforming. In such societies, absolute authority receives emphasis by the continued use of the socializing process into adulthood, through such methods as censoring the media and very specifically prescribing the content of education, both of which spread propaganda in schools. The practice of revising their history textbooks with new interpretations favorable to the selected values of the established class is not uncommon.

In comparison to the lifelong socialization process that is part of the education of citizens under dictatorships, educators in a democracy must expose young citizens to educational situations that liberate them from the dead weight of socialization. At the earliest possible ages, children need to engage in developing reasons for beliefs that they earlier accepted on faith. When they reach the ages when rational thought is possible, certainly by the time they reach middle school, careful attention should be paid to developing their intellectual capacity for independent thought, constructive social criticism and problem-solving.

In a democracy, the education of citizens must involve both socialization and counter-socialization. Its citizens must possess the habits and commitments necessary to democratic survival, such as a deep respect for all individuals and a genuine commitment to democratic values. However, democratic citizens hold these values in a reasoned way. Educators can foster this reasoning process in the education they provide for student-citizens. Moreover, its citizens must be both willing and able to engage in constructive criticism to improve their communities, the broader society and even conditions across the planet. The responsibility for each of these characteristics sits squarely on the shoulders of citizenship educators and school administrators. The future strength of democracy is dependent on the quality of their efforts to educate the young.

Since socialization processes may be merged almost imperceptibly with those that represent countersocialization, especially with young children at lower grade levels, there is the danger of not noticing the differences. For instance, some teachers might use content from the social sciences to cultivate a positive attitude of respect for others among student-citizens, when such content better serves as a springboard for investigation and thereby serve as an instrument of countersocialization in a democracy. Or, on occasion, teachers of young children may transmit fictional versions of a family (recall the Mary, Dick and Jane Readers that presented a stereotypical family that dominated elementary school readers for decades) instead of promoting questioning abilities that could lead to a broader and more differentiated understanding of what a family can be. In history classes, there are numerous opportunities to ask whether there are other versions of a particular event. The teacher might deliberately provide a contrasting version of the same event followed by questions such as: "How does it happen that there are two versions of the same event? How can we know which version is correct?" Could there be other versions? In turn, the discussion following such questions could lead young people to more challenging questions: "What is the nature of evidence? Or proof?" Or, take for another instance. How can children who have been reading poetry or historical prose about wars for freedom might be challenged by questions such as "What does freedom really mean? How can we know when we have freedom? What are the limits of freedom?"

At this point, an operational definition of social studies, one consistent with the nature of democratic citizenship, is in order. Social studies is concerned exclusively with the education of citizens. In a democracy, citizenship education consists of two related yet contrasting parts: socialization and countersocialization. Socialization occurs primarily, but not exclusively, with preadolescents. However, as student-citizens demonstrate increased intellectual capabilities, socialization is no longer appropriate. At this level, countersocialization must begin and teachers must nurture independent and critical thought. Countersocializing emphasizes questioning the validity of claims to truth made by the media, by their teachers, by their textbooks or by their peers. Here, teachers need to pay particular attention to involving young people in the examination of pressing and controversial issues. The social sciences and history along with literature, art and journalism and other relevant fields of study combined with the first hand experiences of student-citizens, can and should serve as the basis for examining truth claims from these disciplines.

Following this discussion of the democratic ideal, it is necessary to reiterate that democracy has never worked perfectly, if indeed it ever can. However, democracy distinguishes itself by making it possible to recognize existing issues and to work toward their resolution. We must all recognize that throughout the development of democracy and even today, the freedom to pursue private and corporate gain often runs counter to civic justice and the general welfare. As Robert Reich (1983), former Secretary of Labor, has stated,

American democracy has operated throughout its history with two cultures: the one private, later corporate, business culture that claimed for itself the responsibility for investment, productivity, and economic growth; the other, the civic culture that claimed for itself the responsibility for the equitable distribution of welfare among our citizens, including health, education, public services, environmental protection and the like. The two cultures are frequently in conflict. The government has tended to throw its weight to the first one and then the other of these interests. The challenge for a democracy is to combine economic growth and social justice. (p. 67)

Reich (1992) further predicted:

We are living in a transformation that will arrange the politics and economics of the coming century. There will be no national products, no national corporations, no national industries. There will be no national economies, at least as we have come to understand the concept. All that will remain within borders are the people who will comprise a nation. Each nation's primary assets will be its citizens' skills and insights. Each nation's political task will be to cope with the centrifugal forces of the global economy which tear at the ties binding citizens together, bestowing even greater wealth on the most skilled, while consigning the less skilled to a declining standard of living. As borders become more or less meaningless in economic terms, those citizens positioned to thrive in this world are tempted to slip the bonds of national allegiance, and by doing so disengage themselves from their less favored fellows. (p. 3)

Reich's predictions represent his view of economic and political changes, not his preferences. Informed citizens must examine them in the same way. Whether we prefer what may happen in the name of globalization or not, we will experience what he calls "centrifugal forces of the global economy" and so will the young citizens whom we prepare for citizenship in a global age.

Disharmony regarding the very uneven distribution of wealth is a central persistent issue. The possession of great wealth by some serves to limit the distribution of equitable resources for others. Due to political advantage, individual initiative, inheritance or just luck, some people are much wealthier than others. Once achieved, wealth gives those who possess it the advantage of gaining even more. Along with wealth goes power and influence that permits individuals or corporations to command a high level of responsiveness as they pursue their self-interest in the marketplace as well as in the halls of government. They also have easier access to higher levels of education and to the best that the culture offers. The wealthy usually come to control the means of production as well as the distribution of knowledge. By financing and controlling research, by owning and controlling the media, and by the use of financial resources to pay lobbyists who promote legislation in their behalf, the wealthy have a larger say in the control of schools and what they teach (Apple, 1982; Kozol, 1992). Acts by government or its representatives in a democracy have sometimes restrained the wealthy by such measures as progressive taxation and free public education. However, it is democracy's persistent task to insure social justice with an emphasis on equity for all people in the face of an elite whose level of wealth gives them a disproportionate advantage.

Shall we treat them all alike? Or, shall we honor and be responsive to their differences? The term, difference stands in place of the liberal concept of universality that emphasizes individuality and individual rights. Bloom (1998), argues compellingly that despite its liberal values, the preoccupation of democracy with the concept of universality has not been able to remedy the plight faced by marginal peoples. Bloom advocates a philosophy that includes a politics of difference and multicultural feminism that attends to the challenging conditions faced by marginal people. Furthermore, it is only through the vigorous influence of organized groups who represent minorities or marginal peoples, that progress regarding equity and equality of opportunity occurs. The challenge of minimizing the increasing difference between the haves and have-nots will also undoubtedly energize large groups who, understand the issues, can articulate their needs and take action in effective ways.

Lastly, the promise of democracy for openness and vigor in dealing with society's issues conflicts with the tendency of the culture to reproduce itself with all of its rigidities, inconsistencies and inequities intact. This situation exaggerates the fact that the socialization process is largely a silent process. It lies in the domain of things taken for granted, in the habits of the culture including many no longer appropriate, but never questioned. By parents, teachers and significant others, these habits are easily transmitted easily by example, by gesture and even by the raising of the eyebrow. Conformity can be a comfortable state especially when it glosses over gross inequities and controversy. Nonetheless, the message of this book rests on the very strong belief that, despite its shortcomings, democracy is the best possible vehicle for ameliorating these problems. Given the very strong endorsement that this book gives to social justice and democratic ideals, social studies education that ignores these matters is not only unreal and without credibility for both student-citizens and citizens, but hypocritical and immoral as well. The sensible solution for social studies educators is to take an approach that faces the issues directly and treats them with intellectual honesty, reason and compassion as they prepare democratic citizens.

CONCLUSION

This chapter presents the democratic principles, with emphasis on those values that relate to social justice—fairness, equity, equality, freedom, due process are balanced with concern for the common good. These values underlie this Issues-Centered Decision Making Curriculum. Furthermore, the tenets of democracy serving as the foundation of the proposed curriculum are identified. The concepts of socialization and countersocialization are introduced and they are basic to learning and teaching at all grade levels. (See Chapter 3 for a more complete discussion). Chapter 1 serves as the start of a rationale for this curriculum—one that is concerned with the quality of education received by our young citizens so that they care enough, are dedicated enough and are sufficiently able informed, thoughtful and active enough to be the citizens of a pluralistic democracy in a global community. Our democracy needs strengthening by citizens who are able to govern themselves. They must be able to enjoy the privileges of a humane political system and rise to the issues that confront it in both domestic and global spheres. Not a small task for social studies educators at all levels, early childhood through college.

NOTES

1.   Social studies is the curriculum area that assumes major responsibility for preparing democratic citizens in the nation's schools. At the same time, citizenship education is a broad goal that applies to the entire school. In this book the terms, *social studies* and *democratic citizenship education* are used interchangeably. The single verb "is," with what appears to be a plural subject, "social studies" may strike the reader as an error of agreement. However, the curriculum offered here, is a unified, integrated and interdisciplinary area of study. Therefore, I view the term, "social studies" as singular. Consequently, this area of the curriculum is especially concerned with social conditions and issues, however controversial and challenging they may be—particularly those needed to expand and enhance the social justice concerns of people whose lives are limited in terms of education and/or opportunity. To improve this democracy, our citizens must be not only aware but also concerned about its betterment and willing to act in behalf of its improvement.

2.   Social and political criticism is a hallmark of democratic citizenship. Engaging in such constructive criticism is not the same as being negative or identifying only the weak aspects of our system. Instead, the kind of criticism we strive for is patriotic. Such citizens love this country enough to address its weaknesses with a view to how it may be improved. A strong democracy requires such vigilant citizens who are informed, thoughtful, questioning, and reasonable in making decisions that apply to public affairs that can be justified in terms of democratic values.

3.   While complex and controversial issues are central to this Issues-Centered Decision Making Curriculum, obviously young citizens cannot solve these very challenging issues. However, they can engage in an analysis of issues, a consideration of possible solutions and undertake actions that might improve some aspect of the issue. Examples are found in their neighborhood, community or by writing letters and/or speaking to public officials or news media personnel among others.

4. In this book, social studies is not seen as a separate set of subjects that are taught in school, but a unified field whose goal is to strengthen the capacity of young citizens to be effective adult democratic citizens. Each of the school subjects that are identified as school social studies offerings such as United States History, Government, Civics, World History, Economics, etc., should be focused on this goal.

5. The terms *international* and *global* do not carry precisely the same meaning. International is a term that literally means between nations, while global is more comprehensive and recognizes the importance of interactions among peoples, groups, cultures, countries, and organizations. It embraces the term, international, but also attends to the increasing interconnectedness of people, places, and cultures as well as events and issues across the planet. Global conditions have local implications. The worldwide AIDS epidemic is evident in countless local communities across the planet. Furthermore, local conditions have global implications. Higher unemployment in a given community may be related to the capacity of other nations to manufacture products at a lower cost because they pay their workers less. Throughout history, social change has often occurred because of contacts with new and different cultures that result in new developments in music, the arts, technology, as well as social behavior.

CHAPTER 2

THE CITIZEN WE NEED IN A PLURALISTIC DEMOCRACY IN A GLOBAL AGE

*Democratic education . . . shapes the education of future citizens which
in great measure forms their moral character. Because democracies must rely on the
moral character of parents, teachers, public officials, and ordinary citizens to educate
future citizens, democratic education begins not only with children who are to be taught
but also with citizens who are to be their teachers.*

—Amy Gutmann, 1999. (p. 49)

INTRODUCTION

The social studies curriculum has as its purpose the preparation of thoughtful, knowledgeable and active citizens in order to sustain and improve our pluralistic democracy in a global age. The term 'global age' is deliberately included in this statement of purpose for two reasons. First, it embraces the significance of expanding diversity both across the planet as the term, pluralism does within our own society. Secondly, it recognizes closer and increasingly frequent connections between and among peoples, cultures and nations as well as the powerful influence of multinational organizations and the technologies of rapid communication and transportation. Pluralism is virtually everywhere and virtually everything that is local has a global connection. Both adult citizens and young citizens need to understand and act on these prevailing conditions.[1]

Democratic Education for Social Studies, pages 29–64
Copyright © 2007 by Information Age Publishing
29

For educators engaged in citizenship education at every level, for the sake of our student-citizens, our children and grandchildren, for the purpose of strengthening social justice as well as the quality of citizen participation in our democracy, both global dimensions and pluralism must, without question, play a significant, explicit, and visible role in social studies. To do otherwise is to shortchange our young citizens who will undoubtedly live with these conditions and who must be prepared to address the issues that their generation will face. The school, with all of its many challenges, is still the agency that must take citizenship education as its major goal although it is not the only agency influencing the quality of democracy's citizens. Today, a quality curriculum for democratic citizens must recognize and give serious attention to social, cultural, economic and political developments because they make enormous differences in the personal as well as the public lives of democracy's citizens.

The following questions require serious attention by educators at all levels. What is it that such citizens will need to do? What values, what knowledge and what abilities will they need? Answers to such questions vary with contemporary conditions as well as the unknowable and largely unpredictable future. However, it becomes increasingly clear that the curriculum that educators use not only needs to represent the past but should also attend to contemporary issues and possible future issues.

The discussion below includes an identification of educational implications for democracy, diversity and global developments that are persistent and likely to affect individuals and groups of citizens in the future. However, the thoughtful reader will recognize that due to the uncertainty of the future, citizens of all ages can only speculate and identify trends that may (or may not) continue into the future. After all, it is the uncertainty of the future that demands rigorous and continuous rethinking by social studies educators. In a continuous and constant way, they must appraise the nature of the content and processes needed to strengthen the capacities of young citizens so they can better address the issues of their times. This statement identifies the very essence of the complex, but exciting challenges, that educators at all levels, kindergarten through college, face as they design and implement intellectually demanding citizenship education programs for student-citizens and future teachers.[2]

In this context, it is important that the reader recognize that the point of view expressed in this book rejects any attempt to assume an essentialist position regarding the knowledge used in this curriculum. Particularly, to identify discrete factual bits as essential to the curriculum is foolhardy. To ask students to memorize the names of capital cities, whether the capital of Turkey or Saudi Arabia, without providing a context that gives these facts importance and meaning is to engage in counterproductive learning. On the other hand, if student-citizens are pursing inquiry into the issues related to the Middle East crisis, knowing the names of these capitals is likely to be useful and learning about these issues would provide a context (Freire, 2001). Educators must address the following question continuously. Why should student-citizens know this fact or this piece of information? Furthermore, their reasons should contribute to deeper understanding of the world around them rather than simply assume that such facts be learned as knowledge for its own sake. In a democracy, we desperately need citizens who have understanding of how democracy and how the world works and individuals who have thought about how aspects of it can be improved and strengthened. Knowledge for its own sake is not a valid rationale for the subject matter that is used.

It takes little reasoning to conclude that knowing the specific name of the capital of Saudi Arabia contributes little, if anything, to a meaningful understanding of the issues that plague the Middle East. The reasoning underlying this Issues-Centered Decision Making Curriculum proposed in this book collides head on with such essentialist educational practices in social studies programs. Teaching and learning that focus young people on facts without explicit awareness of the reason for learning this information preempts the use of classroom time that could otherwise engage their intellect regarding the controversies and complexities of their community, their nation and/or their planet. Instead, providing young citizens with intellectual experiences regarding real world problems and pressing issues that relate to their welfare, that of their fellow citizens as well as the other residents of the planet is not only very much more valuable than memorizing such information, but it also confronts student-citizens with the same intellectual challenge faced by thoughtful democratic citizens. This proposed curriculum rests on the assumption that effective democratic citizenship is strengthened if, instead of learning specified facts, classroom time is spent engaging student-citizens in thinking deeply about the causes, the manifestations and the possible solutions to challenging issues that are likely to threaten their personal welfare as well as the welfare of others and the planet. At the same time, citizens cannot understand any controversial issue without involving related facts. When we learn facts in context, they take on significance and we are much more likely to remember them. Learning to access factual data as needed to illuminate the study of a particular controversial issue is very important given technological advancements. The use of the Internet has become as important as library searches. However, none of us can commit all facts to memory. Facts are far more easily remembered when they contribute to understanding and learning facts merely to pass tests or merely to appear knowledgeable and informed is not meaningful.

WHAT IS CITIZENSHIP IN A DEMOCRACY
AND A GLOBAL AGE?

In a narrow sense, a citizen is a legally recognized member of a state or nation. However, the goals advocated in this curriculum aim at not only maintaining, but also strengthening democracy. However, in this curriculum democracy is not confined to our relationship with the nation-state. In this chapter and throughout this book, the reader will explore an alternative, broad conception of citizenship that includes the wide scope of relationships that people encounter in their lives.

Citizenship is a matter of identities, relationships, privileges and responsibilities. In the global village in which we live and in the foreseeable future, our primary relationship is with the human species. Lee Anderson points out that we are members of many groups in which we have we have relationships, privileges and responsibilities. At a time when individuals, organizations, institutions, multinational corporations as well as nations have increasing contacts with each other and a greater frequency of relationships with peoples, organizations, institutions, multinational corporations and nations across the planet (repetition intended), the importance of a comprehensive response in the schooling experience of future adult citizens of a democracy is imperative. We live and are likely to continue to live in a global community and share a common fate with all people elsewhere on the planet and consequently this proposed curriculum gives explicit attention to global issues including pluralism and diversity. Taking this view will better prepare our student-citizens to live in a global village or as some would say "this troubled planet." It makes a great deal of sense to accept Anderson's view. The quality of life in Zambia, Australia as well as the United State is of concern to all of us. Moreover, global issues will not be resolved unless multiple nations and peoples cooperate in both finding and implementing a solution. The potential damage of Mad Cow disease, the poignant tragedies associated with AIDS, the nuclear power accident in Chernobyl and the threatening dynamic of terrorism are the responsibilities of peoples in other places on Planet Earth. Accepting our relationship to other peoples and other cultures with different languages implies that school programs should give attention to understanding those cultures— their interesting differences but also their profound similarities. Student-citizens should also have the opportunity to learn a second language.

We also derive our identities (and they have become multiple identities) from many other groups created by human beings. People have created nation-states. For many people their relationship with the state is their primary relationship. Educationally speaking, if this relationship was our only concern, it would confine the curriculum to enhance the abilities of student-citizens related to voting in a democracy. Can the schools insure that they will be more informed and more able to make justifiable decisions regarding the votes they cast? However, voting is not the entire role of citizens in a democracy. Nor is voting the only citizen activity to which young citizens might bring the values of freedom, fairness and equity. While we cannot require our student-citizens to accept any set of values, we can model them and verbally support them as values that are important to democracy and to teachers personally. Moreover, there are many sub units to the nation-state: provinces or states, counties, cities, neighborhoods, religious institutions, places of employment, families and friendship groups.

The emphasis in this definition is on the *relationships we have with other human beings in all settings from interpersonal to the public.* This definition values the application of democratic principles to all our own interactions between individuals when engaging in dialogue with others. It connects democratic behavior by citizens with the social justice demands of individuals and groups who legitimately cry out for equity or restitution. The insistence of Martin Luther King to improve the opportunities for African Americans calls for restitution by Native Americans in return for the lands taken from them as well as demands for opportunities for women who should earn the same compensation when they do the same jobs that men do. These represent the tip of the iceberg as conditions needed in this democracy to fulfill its promise of social justice. This definition of citizenship embraces all of our relationships within our immediate families, our communities, within our workplace, within schools, within social membership organizations, within relationships with our neighbors, friends, family and of course, within our relationships in the public sphere from local to global. In a democracy, the rights of individuals are paramount. These include the right to express oneself, to participate in governance, to equal protection of the laws, to the right of free association and the right to fundamental democratic freedoms related to religion, speech and the press. With these rights among others, come responsibilities that include respect for others, respect for the law, the exercise of the franchise and the responsibility to be concerned not only to enhance self-interest, but also for the common good. In this context of having loyalties to multiple units, situations give rise to tensions and conflict. A Catholic girl decides to date a fellow from an atheist family, or your parents are Christian missionaries based in Taiwan, their daughter who is a teacher refuses to promote religion in her classroom. Tensions of this sort can lead to major rifts among families, religions and friends.

Social justice and democratic citizenship are too complex, too demanding and too precious to leave to chance. Certainly, democratic citizens must be informed, thoughtful and persistently analytical as they examine social issues, causes and candidates that shape the conditions of their times. Informed citizens are very aware that people can both exercise influence and be influenced by others not only within our own nation but also from across the planet. The power and increasing number of multinational corporations and nongovernmental organizations (NGOs) that play a strong role in the formation of domestic and international public policy call for a broader definition of citizenship to guide the nature and of future citizenship education programs realistically. It is here that global perspectives and pluralism need strong representation.

Such a broader conception is provided by Lee Anderson (1990) for educators. His view of citizenship is present in his expansive rationale for global education. He posited the following changes that are currently evident and likely to persist into the future. His conception applies to the preparation of citizens.[3]

Lee Anderson (1979, 1990) attempted to define citizenship in a global age as follows.

> Citizenship refers to the decisions, judgments and actions through which individuals link themselves, knowingly or unknowingly, deliberately and inadvertently to the public affairs of the groups of which they are members. In the case of small, face-to-face groups, the links between an individual and the group's public affairs are often direct and immediate. In the case of large impersonal collectivities, it is aggregative processes that link individuals to the public affairs of large groups.... Citizenship may be self-conscious and deliberate or unknowing and inadvertent, but in any case, individuals cannot escape from their citizenship in the network of human groups that make up their social universe. Knowingly or unknowingly, each of us make decisions, reach judgments and take actions that personally or systematically involve us and in turn others, in the shaping and sharing of human values in social contexts that range in size, intimacy and complexity from families to large, remote, and complicated collectivities such as the city of Chicago, the State of Illinois, the United States of America. (pp. 337–339).

Especially noteworthy in Anderson's statement is the idea that the concept of citizenship applies inescapably to all of our relationships. His commentary implies that we have rights and responsibilities in all of these settings. For citizens of a democracy, it leads to the conclusion that in most contexts, we should apply democratic principles to all our relationships in which we participate, not only to those that exist in the public sphere. In this broader conception of citizenship that Anderson posed, democracy embraces many, if not all facets of life. In effect, whenever and wherever citizens make decisions that affect others, whether in the workplace, in voluntary organizations, in the family or in friendship groups, the democratic political system will be stronger when its principles apply in the multiple settings in which all of us participate. Certainly, it is not realistic to think that democratic policies and practices apply only in the context of public affairs if they do not also pervade, to the greatest extent possible, the rest of our lives. Democracy, in effect, must become a habit that citizens apply consistently in all of their relationships in multiple settings where diversity, equity and freedom receive attention to the greatest extent possible.

We know that some young children are socialized by parents and teachers only in ways where they must conform and obey with no room for questions, some are ignored in major decisions that affect them, some are expected to be seen and not heard and/or some are victims of child abuse and violence. It is not reasonable to expect that the school can be very successful in transforming their habits to ones that are principled, civil, respectful of others and democratic. No government agency, no organization and no school can mandate democratic behavior among its members. Such coercive efforts are contradictory to democratic principles of freedom of choice and freedom of expression. However, all agencies, whether the workplace or less formal social organizations, can lead by example and by modeling to heighten concern for addressing issues of social justice and influence the development of democratic norms in the family, the school, the workplace and organizations that have social, economic and/or political purposes. In the case of the school, its personnel should model democratic behavior and respectfully demonstrate acceptance of cultural differences. Importantly, social studies teachers can address experiences on the playground and identify those tensions that occur among young people as starters for understanding and solving interpersonal issues and making decisions to improve them. The seeds planted in these early years make early childhood and elementary educators extremely important.

Moreover, even citizens acting alone can influence and ameliorate society's challenging issues. One citizen can have an impact, albeit minimal, on a wider context. If an individual independently decides to buy a car with low fuel consumption out of concern for the world's supply of dwindling oil resources, without being required to do so by law, he or she is performing an act of citizenship that demonstrates concern for fellow human beings. If this many citizens choose to act in the same way, it can profoundly affect the welfare of other people, not only in this nation, but across the world. Such collective actions can develop social norms that, on occasion, can even assume the force of law. Clearly, not only the public decisions that citizens make but also, their personal decisions and actions are instrumental in building a stronger democracy and heightening social justice.

Citizenship, therefore, transcends the affairs of the state. Most citizens are members of a myriad of groups and organizations that extend beyond the immediate purview of the state and all are inhabitants of the planet. However, the largest group we all belong to is the human species. At a time when human beings have the capacity to destroy each other as well as our civilization, when individuals, organizations, multinational corporations as well as nations have worldwide impact, the effectiveness of citizens and the quality of their relationships to each other is much more than an academic issue. It is, without question, this relationship that determines whether the world will be more peaceful or not, whether people across the planet will live decent lives or not and whether the citizens of nations that are more developed and wealthier will understand the importance of strong and positive relations with those who they now see as different as not different at all. Repeating Anderson, "First of all, we are members of the human species." Yet we are the only species that engage in murder of our own kind, mass killings and even consideration of the use of weapons that can destroy the entire human species and the planet.

The fundamental strength of democracy lies in the respect it affords to the rights of all of its citizens. Democratic citizens must hold such respect for others in order to improve the conditions of all citizens who value and want to heighten social justice. To such ideals, the conduct of social studies programs designed to promote enlightened self-governance is dedicated.

In sum, Anderson's definition of citizenship serves as a beacon for the curriculum proposed here. We may not always think of ourselves as citizens across this multiplicity of contexts, but to the extent that we apply democratic principles with an emphasis on equity and freedom in these various settings, we cannot help but strengthen the fiber of democratic life here at home.

Increasingly, globalization facilitated by technology, has made and will make dramatic differences in our lives and global forces will influence the policies and practices of this democratic nation. Many authors, many articles and many books have addressed these developments in recent years. Globalization has both positive and negative connotations (Becker, 2002). In less developed nations, there is a pessimistic view that identifies globalization as the dominance of wealthy nations that are likely to exploit nations that are poor. Many of our citizens, observe corporations exporting jobs to nations where workers receive less pay than our workers receive, are seriously concerned about unemployment and joblessness at home. They view globalization as a threat. Furthermore, many citizens do not fully understand the concept of globalization. Even experts bring together different facts and opinions and have found little consensus.[4]

Some, like Benjamin Barber (1992), a political scientist dedicated to democracy, view globalization as a threat to democracy as it universalizes the world economy and moves toward a single international market. From his perspective, globalization undermines the sovereignty of nations and reduces their capacity to regulate public affairs within their own borders. He is especially concerned that democratic nations will no longer be able to protect individual rights. Since there is no international organization with sufficient power to protect individual rights, globalization is a threat to the traditional rights of United States citizens that are intrinsic to maintaining a democracy. Barber (1995) finds global capitalism challenges conventional morals and values in much of the world and that often results in additional threats to democracy as well as the resurgence of ethnic and tribal groups and that sometimes increases the chances of their violent reactions in defense of their traditional values. His perspective is captured in the following words: "The world is coming together economically, but it is falling apart politically at the same time." He sees capitalism and fundamentalism on the rise, but neither of these trends have any interest in fostering democracy. Yet, he still finds that democracy may be our only hope.

From a contrasting perspective, Thomas L. Friedman, the New York Times journalist, who has addressed the impact of technology on the future especially as it relates to globalization, is quite optimistic. Regarding these trends that undoubtedly will be part of our future, Friedman sees technology providing people with access to knowledge they have never had before. No longer will knowledge be limited to the wealthy and powerful. In his book, The World is Flat (2005), he asserts that technology that gives all individuals regardless of their roles, status or wealth, access to the same levels of knowledge and therefore, the gap between ordinary people and those in power starts to wither away. In the future, people with more powerful roles or people with wealth are much less likely to control access to knowledge that they may not want the regular citizenry to have. Such practices have been the case with totalitarian governments, but democratic governments have exercised control as well. However, the current state of technology makes most knowledge much more available to anyone who is able to use a computer. Friedman calls this more democratically oriented aspect of technology a 'flattener' in that it widens and makes more equitable the base of the public's knowledge. As knowledge becomes available to more and more people, the power of hierarchy whether in corporations, governments or other institutions diminishes since they no longer have the capability to keep important knowledge in the hands of a few people at the top of the hierarchy. This trend is not minor. It reduces the importance of hierarchies and increases the power that all people have creating greater equity among all citizens according to Friedman.

In contrast to Barber, Friedman reports on efforts in India and China to use the technological skills that some of their young people have acquired to improve their standing in the world economy. Bangalor in India and Dalin in China are examples of two cities whose efforts in this regard are vigorous. They are centers that U.S. firms use extensively and these young nationals work for them—a practice that results in unemployment at home. However, these workers are not only improving their own standard of living, they are strengthening their national economies. They are making better wages than their parents are. Friedman sees this development as a 'flattener' as well. It creates a condition of greater equity between rich and poor nations. The more these young people improve their lives over those of their parents, the more satisfied and productive they will be as citizens and as participants in the global community. However, whether or not Barber is right or Friedman is right (and they are not the only contrasting viewpoints), these developments, globalization and technology appear to be irreversible. Globalization and technology will continue to alter our lives as well as the character of our democracy. Democracy's citizens need to be as familiar as possible with such trends that will have impact, not only within the United States, but they will be evident across the entire planet.

When emphasis is given to globalization, technology and their future development in this Issues-Centered Decision Making Curriculum, it is not intended that they be cast in either a favorable or an unfavorable light. However, it is strongly suggested that young citizens not complete their social studies course or programs without substantial attention to the study of worldwide phenomena that intensify and alter, in yet unknown ways, their relationship with peoples of differing cultures and developments across the planet as well as the quality of lives they will live. Not to do so, is greatly shortchanging our young citizens and is abandoning concern for the quality of their future. In addition, over time democracy, as we know it, could be substantially changed.

Citizens of all ages need to recognize how we are already very interconnected and interdependent with peoples, cultures, nations, multinational corporations and the rest of the planet. Many serious and significant issues that are both public and controversial cross international boundaries and cannot be improved or solved by any one nation acting alone. Poverty, the environment and the spread of communicable diseases such as AIDS, small pox or Mad Cow disease are a few challenging examples. Improving such global conditions that are not national, calls for a very high level of multinational cooperation and requires the development of cross-cultural understanding and competence among citizens.

For citizenship educators, globalization along with technology, have very serious implications as they prepare young citizens to understand global conditions and define their values regarding these world wide developments. We must help them gain abilities to access significant knowledge, but every bit as important are the abilities needed to analyze it carefully, test its creditability and apply it wisely.

From another perspective, citizens of this democracy should realize that some citizens in this nation have applied the concept of civil disobedience in order to heighten social justice (Atkinson, 1937). At the peak of the Civil Rights Movement, Martin Luther King spent time in jail in Birmingham, Alabama. From his jail cell, he wrote a letter to his fellow pastors in the South. In this letter, which has been quoted and reprinted thousands of times, Dr. King (1963) made it perfectly clear that he was fully aware that the law required that he be jailed and that he willingly submitted to that consequence. In this situation, he valued a society of laws even though laws made by human beings can be, and in this case were, seriously flawed and inhumane. He emphasized that his actions followed a higher moral law that placed the dignity of human beings and the gaining of rights for African Americans above the laws that the white establishment had previously created. Reflecting his philosophy of civil disobedience as espoused by Mahatma Gandhi, King made the distinction about laws that are higher in value than laws made by human beings. More recently, protest marches and the actions of environmentalists using full-time tree-sitting as a strategy to block land wanted for development multiple housing is similar to a situation faced by a pharmacist who was fired recently because she would not dispense abortion-inducing medication and that would contradict her religious beliefs. She too appealed to a higher law from her perspective. Importantly, these examples, while very controversial, illustrate the strong posture a single citizen or a group concerned with problematic issues can take in behalf of their values. The principles underlying civil disobedience recognize that citizens will honor the law and accept its punishment, even though they find the law it upholds and the practices it permits reprehensible.

Civil disobedience receives some attention here because its use is more, rather than less frequent today than it has been in the past. Importantly, a major principle of civil disobedience disavows the use of violence. Both young and adult citizens need to examine the many facets of civil disobedience and consider the conditions under which it may apply. People are not perfect nor are all acts of civil disobedience deserving. In some cases, this strategy may cause more harm than good as is true of any political strategy citizens may choose to use.

DEMOCRATIC EDUCATION: THE CURRICULUM

Citizenship education for a democracy must include far more than knowledge of government, its structure, organization or procedures. Instead, the strongest attention in social studies programs is teaching that nurtures, but does not require, a reasoned commitment to democratic principles with emphasis on equity, freedom and self-governance. Social studies educators must develop deep understanding of how these principles apply to every aspect of life—personally, socially and publicly. Above all, the democratic citizen must be a vigorous thinker, a competent decision maker and an active participant who supports equitable conditions for all peoples and honors freedom to the greatest extent possible. Furthermore, democracy depends on the expertise, experience and skills held to varying degrees among its citizens. This dependency invokes the possibility of a meritocracy that creates a tension with equality of input among all citizens. In order to decide if a bridge is built, engineers who have the necessary training to assess the location involved, are needed. This decision that requires specialized knowledge should not be made by a majority vote. Most people do not have the expertise to make a sound judgment in this instance. Therefore, it makes sense to rely on the expertise of engineers, not a vote of the people. However, the hope for a stronger democracy and the realization of a higher level of social justice lies in widely distributed, intelligent participation of citizens from all walks of life. Many citizens need to hold such concern for social justice in order to expect any expansion in the use of fairness, equality and equity as values that enhance social justice.

Some political scientists take the position that democracy works best when only an elite minority of the population participates in making public policy. Of course, that idea contradicts the very essence of democracy. The position taken here rejects this conclusion because it violates the dignity of individual citizens and violates self-governance. To give up on the non-elite would be tantamount to creating a condition where the few rule the many (i.e., an oligarchy) and one that denies the rights democracy ascribes to individuals, to social justice and to the over-arching principle of self-governance. This elitist position is undemocratic. If our student-citizens experience a strong citizenship education program, more citizens will have the capacity to become more informed, more thoughtful and more involved. This is the broad challenge that faces social studies educators. A democratic system and a social studies program fail if they do not empower less advantaged and marginal people to participate more fully in the society as a whole.

Democracy is not a matter of subservience to power or blind loyalty to the state. Rather, it entails a willingness to be responsible for the democratic nature of the state as well as other settings where citizens participate and engage in decision making. At its best, democracy vigorously embraces the principles associated with equity and social justice. Decision making abilities, along with all of the knowledge and intellectual processes that go into the making of decisions, are at the center of democratic citizenship as well as the education that should be received by its citizens (Engle, 1960).

AN ISSUES-CENTERED DECISION MAKING CURRICULUM: AN OVERVIEW

This curriculum for democratic citizenship education divides into four interrelated parts: knowledge, a reasoned commitment to the democratic ideal, intellectual processes, and political competence. Intellectual processes involve higher level thinking that is interpretive, analytical, creative. It should lead to making reasoned and evidence-based decisions by evaluation a wide range of alternatives. Young citizens, who not only reconsider the past but also understand contemporary issues as well as the trends and possibilities that reside in the future will undoubtedly contribute more to the quality of this democracy than those who only study the past.

Knowledge

Democratic citizens require a broad liberal education. An education that is confined to vocational or career education will not do. Nor will piecemeal excursions into a few academic areas that are unrelated to the issues that citizens face. In today's increasingly interrelated and diverse world, piecemeal treatment of pressing and complex issues will certainly fail. It is imperative that citizens gain the widest possible perspectives on domestic and global affairs if they are to contribute to the ordering of these affairs and make reasoned decisions to facilitate the improvement of human lives, at both personal and public levels. The knowledge needed by democratic citizens to understand the complex and controversial issues of their world is as complex and controversial as the issues themselves. Such knowledge is set in broad contexts, is interdisciplinary in nature, is always tentative and is subject to changing evidence and interpretations. It honors the personal experiences of teachers as well as those of student-citizens. Furthermore, educators must understand that knowledge needed for democratic citizenship is not packaged conveniently between the two covers of a textbook or the time it takes to deliver a teacher's lecture. Finally, not all citizens need know the same pieces of information regarding the issues they face, nor do they need to possess precisely the same abilities, attitudes and values. Even to hope for such common results from any curriculum is to violate basic assumptions of free choice and of individual opinions and their expression. This emphasis on common results (everybody must learn the same thing) negates democratic education. Due to their idiosyncratic experiences, citizens will always differ from each other and there is not much teachers or other significant adults can do to alter that reality. The differing interests, talents, knowledge and diverse opinions that citizens hold create a mosaic that a democracy should never suppress. Democracy is one form of government that accommodates and requires such variance and respect for diversity. These divergences need both affirmation and encouragement. Mandatory testing when applied to social studies influence the teacher, the curriculum and the learner to focus on a set of common results that are likely to rely on memory, not on rational understanding.

However, the role and responsibility of citizens requires that they do what they can to contribute to their society and to the welfare of the human species across the planet. Citizenship educators at all levels should heighten their capacities to strengthen democracy and social justice. Democratic citizens should be able to see their nation, state, locality and their individual lives as the foundation of their political and social relationship to the world. Too many citizens do not understand such compelling issues regarding the environment, judicious use of resources, cultural issues, poverty, crime and the population explosion sufficiently well to discuss them intelligently, much less make sensible decisions and take action that might help to minimize them.

Deep understanding of these matters cuts across domestic and national boundaries and depends on a wide range of fields of study. For instance, to facilitate deep understanding of the earth and the development of living things on the earth, these fields will include, but go beyond, history and the social sciences and include many other fields such as biology, climatology, ecology and physical anthropology. Obviously, not only the social studies curriculum, but also the science education curriculum could share in the study of earth–people relationships. However, the overarching goal in this curriculum is in deep understanding, in the context of democratic and social justice principles, (particularly equity, fairness, due process and self-governance). It is the informed relationship between humans and their environment as well as reasoned public policy that we need to protect and preserve the environment. It is very important that the curriculum focus on giving young citizens the chance to examine the issues that always draw on a multiplicity of disciplines for comprehensive understanding. A single discipline will not suffice. Such issues include addressing the challenging issues of managing scarce natural resources, population distribution and control, curbing pollution, poverty, prejudice, discrimination as well as equity issues related to civil rights, affirmative action and equal opportunity. In studying such issues, organizations and institutions related to these issues deserve examination. The educational goal is that young citizens shall become progressively more involved in complex and controversial issues that relate to earth–human relationships and to their own lives as they advance through their years of elementary and secondary education. Social studies educators must help student-citizens identify and build the knowledge base that applies to the issue(s) they are studying. They need to emphasize that the effective use of accumulated knowledge and insights drawn from many disciplines as well as the personal experiences of citizens need to be organized in ways that facilitate understanding of critical issues in a democratic fashion because it is the ability to combine these multiple perspectives that is vital to democratic citizenship.

Secondly, young citizens in a democracy need to understand how institutions, (economic, governmental, cultural, legal as well as the family), work. While examining institutions, they need to appraise the extent to which they practice democratic principles including those entailed by equity. Most importantly, the institutions and ideas that characterize democracy such as separation of church and state, a free press, equity, equality of opportunity and freedom of expression must receive attention so that the next generation of citizens can support, preserve and strengthen these aspects of democracy. Young citizens need opportunities to become knowledgeable regarding issues that have challenged these values in the past and examine their current and future development. Certainly, present day democracy is not a final product; it is a work in progress. Rather, it is in a stage in the development of this democracy that is continually evolving. Its development in the past is based on the tentative resolution of conflicting and complex issues and undoubtedly, in the future it will be hotly contested, fought over and even died for. Democracy and its principles of social justice are probably the last best hope for humanity on earth. They are not without persistent challenges and young people should be involved in a curriculum that encourages constructive criticism and improvement of the human condition.

The study of past, present and future issues organize the knowledge that citizens need to know, combine and apply in this curriculum. Understanding significant issues entails multiple and often, competing perspectives. It is interdisciplinary. It draws on content from a wide range of sources, some as far a field as poetry, fiction and philosophy, but the study of issues in historical context can be especially instructive. The *Dred Scott* decision, the Scopes Trial, the execution of the Rosenbergs, the McCarthy hearings, the Civil Rights Act, the Brown decision, *Roe v. Wade*, the *Baake* decision, and the Patriot Act among others represent pivotal points in the development of ideas that impacted this democracy, sometimes expanding freedom and equity and at other times limiting such central democratic values. That history which reveals the limited rights and welfare of less powerful groups such as minorities, women, children and alternative lifestyle individuals must receive strong attention in social studies programs to broaden the perspectives that young citizens hold regarding equity issues and the politics of difference in the United States (Zinn, 2002; Zinn and Arnove, 2004).

Importantly, historical study needed by citizens is markedly different from what ordinarily passes for historical learning. Much too often, historical study stops short of the real study of events in depth and is little more than the memorization of a single version of chronology and historic items of dubious importance. Instead, the study of history proposed here is analytical in nature. It goes broader and deeper in the search for the reasons behind events and highlights past crises and controversies for explanation.

It examines the values and value dilemmas embodied in our institutions and their effects on powerless groups and individuals. Often, investigations into such issues expressed in fiction, art and music that are areas that should be consulted along with historical accounts and accounts from differing points of view. Such classic works in literature as *The Grapes of Wrath*, *Tom Sawyer*, the poetry of Langston Hughes and *Gone with the Wind* represent the beginning of a long, long list of literature from which teachers and young citizens can choose to read and interpret together to deepen their insights of the impact history has had on many of its citizens. Such studies are described in Chapter 7, The Framework of the Curriculum.

A curriculum based on the examination of controversial issues begs the following questions: What issues deserve emphasis? Are some issues more important than others are? How should they be studied? An Issues-Centered Decision Making Curriculum requires that the issues studied be of interest to young citizens. This criterion implies that the issue has relevance and application to their lives. Such interests are sometimes sparked by a school or community event. An environmental protest, by reading a engaging and potent novel such as *To Kill a Mockingbird* that highlights social and racial exclusion or *The Runaway Jury* that takes on the tobacco industry for its role in promoting cigarette smoking despite the industry's knowledge of its injury to people are possible beginnings. *Across 5 Aprils is* a novel that can be used as early as the fifth grade to make the point that war sometimes challenges families in terms of loyalty and commitment as two brothers choose to fight on opposing sides of the Civil War. However, an issue for class study may emerge from the experience of a member of the class or a controversy in the school setting. Censorship of the student newspaper, the selection of a minority homecoming queen or fights between students from different schools at athletic events can serve as launching pads for animated classroom study and dialogue. Since controversial issues demand intensive study and investigation, interest levels need to be as high as possible to sustain the involvement of the class. Some may argue that issues related directly to the planet's survival such as the use of nuclear power, environmental issues and resource use deserve priority. Others will argue for issues surrounding peace and war. The highest priority in this curriculum is to use issues that are interesting and engaging to young people although teachers must be aware of connecting specific issues that they raise to larger issues that characterize the community, the society or the planet as a whole. Teachers must make sure the issues increase in significance and importance. Trivial issues should not consume class time. However, in order to motivate young citizens, we may start with the immediate issues of personal interest and then expand the study to broader issues that are more complex and effect wider populations. Furthermore, across the curriculum, it is prudent to make sure that issues from the past, present and future are studied. Some educators argue that only issues that are persistent across time are legitimate foci for classroom study. However, current practice in social studies classes is preoccupied with the past at the expense of consideration of the present and the future. Some argue that we cannot teach about the future because we do not know what it will be like; others, including this author believe that, if as citizens we do not know what kind of a future we might like, we put ourselves in a position of being its passive recipients, even its victims. Instead, we must prepare youngsters to take responsibility for issues set in both the present and the future. New issues are continually emerging; stem cell research, cloning, expanding nuclear power, terrorism, higher levels of poverty, the widening gap between the rich and the poor in the U.S. and across the planet as well as the power of the media. These issues can attract the interests of young people by an appropriate news clipping, a film or an exciting guest speaker. A class circle where young citizens can share their interests and identify or respond to possible issues for study is another start-up possibility. Regardless of the sources used, the interests of student-citizens must be tapped if this curriculum is to reach its potential (Van Sickle, 1996).

Thirdly, democratic citizens need to understand the nature of social and cultural differences across time and across the planet. They must not confuse differences in social practices or differences in skin color with right and wrong, superior or inferior, friend or enemy. The need for deep understanding and respect for social and cultural differences increases with the growing interdependence of people on this planet. Democracy, once confined primarily to Western Europe, is now spreading across larger parts of the world. Consequently, the acceptance and understanding of both social and cultural differences and similarities has become an even greater imperative. Citizens need to understand that all cultures came to their present state through forces that operated in their own history. Any culture, whether found in the People's Republic of China, the United Kingdom or nations of Islamic tradition is not the result of historical accident. Rather, these cultures represent the results of their own history. Of equal importance is the recognition that the people of other nations and cultures probably see us in ways that are different to how we see ourselves. In fact, young and adult citizens could profit from reading accounts of U.S. policies and practices in the foreign press and thereby learn more about the views others hold of the United States and why.[5]

Democratic citizens need to see social and cultural differences as explainable and reasonable regardless of the differences that they may demonstrate from their own. Educators need to model and address the importance of respecting differences and encourage student-citizens to apply these perspectives to their personal as well as their public decisions. Similarly, teachers must do what they can to refute secular fanaticism that looks upon different peoples as enemies targeted for destruction. Open and accepting minds are among the hallmarks of democracy as well as social justice and citizenship education programs need to do all that they can to cultivate these orientations.

This emphasis on the significance of understanding and acceptance of cultural differences calls for the study of both domestic and world cultures. student-citizens should conduct such studies in depth and seriously examine our institutions and the extent to which they support or impede cultural diversity, equality, equity, freedom and democracy. Certainly, the perspectives of sociology and anthropology can facilitate such understanding. Educators must not confine the study of cultures to the cosmetic (at times manifest by the insertion of photographs of visibly different peoples in textbooks) or be satisfied with learning materials where the study of other cultures appears only as a special unit. In this pluralistic society and the global community, concern for cultural diversity in the United States and across the planet should permeate all issues under study.

The tension between the individualism that is central to democracy and our membership or affiliation with ethnic, racial, gender and/or life style groups is real and persistent. The agonizing descriptions that gays provide of their "coming out" to their friends and family illustrate very powerful tensions as have the protests in behalf of advancing civil rights or the demise of affirmative action. Maxine Greene (1978) makes this point so very aptly:

> ...my concern is as much with persons and their life worlds as it is with equity and the social system. I am as interested in personal emancipation as I am in equality and justice. At one, I am aware that traditional liberal reliance on a morality based on human rights has not resulted in equal opportunity for many, many individuals—namely females and members of minority groups, who continue to suffer from disadvantages that are undeserved. I want to develop an approach to equality and justice that rests on a conception of individual inviolability and critical self-consciousness, one that takes into account the way inequity and exclusion actually afflict individuals struggling to define themselves in the world. I want to try to develop an approach that allows me to move back and forth between the objective arrangements made by the social system and the experience people have with opportunities, both provided and withheld. (pp. 126–127)

In this statement, tied as it is to the highest of ideals, Greene provides us with a moral compass. While fulfilling both of these goals is not completely attainable, it steers citizens in a direction that fully honors human dignity and is concerned about justice applied to social, racial and ethnic groups as well. Few of us can match the eloquence of Maxine Greene, but in a democracy, citizens must find ways of shaping a society that is more inclusive, more caring and more concerned about equality for all people while at the same time honoring the importance of the individual. Greene's words speak both to the importance of the individual and concurrently, to the importance of groups of marginal people who too often have experienced our social system at its worst.

Fourthly, democratic citizens need to be aware of the challenges human beings have faced across time in the struggle for reliable knowledge, of how human beings have gradually developed canons of objectivity and reliability and the way they have become aware of their limitations. Across time, we have come to recognize the strong part played by subjectivity in the construction of knowledge and the significant uniqueness of each individual's perception and values. Democratic citizens need to see science as a way of thinking and a way of reaching and verifying certain kinds of conclusions and recognize that human interests and subjectivity influence scientific investigations as well as they adhere to the stringency of the scientific method. Democratic citizens respect science and the scientific method and have high regard for its standards of openness and honesty. Furthermore, they understand and appreciate the role of evidence and the nature of proof in dealing with perplexing public questions. They respect facts supported by evidence and are able to distinguish them from conjecture. At the same time, they must understand the limitations of science, recognize that scientific conclusions are not always correct, certainly not always final and are always subject to revision and even substitution. They need to become aware that moral and ethical questions do not fit neatly into the scientific mold. As they make decisions, they should appreciate the contributions that derive from religion, philosophy and aesthetics as well as how scholars judge reliability and validity in these fields. In short, they must be aware of the contributions and usefulness of many fields of study and the multiple perspectives that can give richer meaning to the issue at hand.

Understanding the nature of knowledge with all of its complexities as well as recognizing many ways of knowing (Belenky, Clinchy, Goldberger, & Tarule 1997; Gardner, 1993) should receive emphasis when teaching young citizens. However, the problem of dependable knowledge is so central to democracy that it demands special emphasis. Meaningful study of history, the social sciences and the humanities supplemented by units of study in epistemology through which secondary school students can grasp the nature of knowledge and the different ways it is constructed all require curriculum implementation. Some concentrated attention in the secondary curriculum to epistemology can help young citizens understand the complexity of the problem of knowing with all of its tentativeness and help them to apply these understandings to conclusions presented by the media as well as to issues facing citizens. For example, if one individual assumes that knowledge is divinely inspired and another finds it to be socially constructed, it is virtually impossible for them to share the same perspective on any controversy.

However, knowing involves much more than understanding the canons of proof. Citizens must also be able to access knowledge. Reliable knowledge is of little use unless it is open to all. While advancing technology is helpful in this regard, young citizens need to treat information drawn from the Internet with the same critical orientation afforded to any other sources. Furthermore, democracy must not tolerate the denial of knowledge or of alternative perspectives. Democratic citizens need to understand how central to the development of democracy has been the struggle for such principles as freedom of the press to investigate and report its findings and the freedom of speech to spread one's opinions, even when these opinions are contrary to authorities who hold power. The constant vigilance that should characterize democratic citizenship requires that citizens be on the alert for instances where those in authority pressure the media to withhold, distort and/or manipulate information. Furthermore, we must remember the degree to which commercial media are dependent and beholden to their advertisers—some of whom are large corporations whose financial support the networks need to function. Public radio and public television are alternatives that rely on federal funding as well as that of the public. Therefore, they are more independent in their programming.

Citizens also need to understand the differences between ways of knowing, whether these are faith-based, intuitive, scientific or folkloric in nature. Belenky et al. (1997) have addressed gender differences and ways of knowing and have advanced the premise that thinking takes contrasting forms in male and females. For educators, the following words from Belenky and her coauthors provide insight for classroom practice.

> "...educators can help some women develop their own authentic voice if they emphasize connection over separation, understanding and acceptance over assessment and collaboration over debate; if they accord respect and allow time for the knowledge that emerges from first hand experience; if instead of imposing their own expectations and arbitrary assignments they encourage students to evolve their own patterns of work based on problems they are pursuing." (p. 229)

The thinking presented above by Belenky and her colleagues displays considerable parallel with various aspects of this Issues-Centered Decision Making Curriculum. For classrooms to engage in collaborative work, for young female as well as male student-citizens to pursue issues of their own choosing and for teachers to understand that student-citizens have valuable experiences to share that can help guide what is studied in the classroom is very consistent with procedures embedded in the proposed curriculum.

Likewise, the work of Carol Gilligan (1993; Gilligan et al., 1997) reported that the values women hold are distinct from their male counterparts. Historically, women have been defined in terms of the way they fit into the male life cycle and male values assumed dominance. Gilligan argued for research that independently examines female development. In her studies, she found that women appear to place emphasis on caring, responsibility to others and attachment as contrasted with their male counterparts. Through literature and through history, Gilligan found that the male places more importance on individual achievement and visible success as values. Her work strongly suggests the need for more attention to the development of women on their own terms. Such emerging research can contribute a great deal to our understanding of the human intellect and the influence of alternative socialization experiences for males and females.

Citizens need to understand that knowledge may be denied them in a number of ways. Censoring books intended for study in school or in school libraries, control of what the press may investigate and publish either by government censorship or by those rich enough to own newspapers and television stations and who are therefore able to manipulate news coverage to supply sensational and entertaining content over hard news in order to increase profits. Vigilant citizens must be alert for evidence of stonewalling by government officials when requests are made for information. In short, social studies educators need to do everything they can to help young citizens become sophisticated users of knowledge. They must understand the difference between scientific truth and truth revealed in other ways that may also deserve consideration.

The problem of access to knowledge needs the attention of young citizens as they pursue issues in history and other social studies classes. Accounts of the struggles, that have been undertaken so that the right of the people to know is preserved, require classroom attention. Books such as *Inherit the Wind* (Lawrence & Lee, 1955) about the Scopes Trial on the teaching of evolution, serves as a fine example. Other examples are found in the activist posture taken by librarians and some members of the press to maximize freedom of inquiry for the public at large. In particular, such organizations as People for the American Way, the American Civil Liberties Union and the American Library Association and their active Office of Intellectual Freedom are extremely important in preserving these freedoms when they are threatened. Teachers need to expose young citizens to these very significant efforts in behalf of protecting openness in this democracy. The freedom to read, to inquire and to express one's views are precious freedoms that democratic citizens must never take for granted.

Further, social studies teachers need to work cooperatively with the Language Arts or English Departments in planning what books classes will read. Over time, books used in literature classes or elsewhere in the curriculum have been challenged by parents or community members. Targets have been such classics as Huckleberry Finn, The Scarlet Letter and a host of others. Such classic pieces of literature persist only because of the efforts of vigorous advocates for intellectual and political freedom.

Fifthly, and most importantly, democratic citizens need to appreciate the struggle of people to be just, civil and fair in their relations with each other. They need to understand the central role that such values as freedom, equality, justice, fairness, concern for the common good and due process occupy in a democracy. Attention to such values requires much more than textbook definitions. Instead, values need examination in terms of how they apply to human lives. The meanings and uses of these values are not simple. They have diverse meanings and a host of issues about how they come alive in a democratic society. Moreover, as in the case of freedom and equality, they sometimes find themselves in competition with each other. If our successor generation is to preserve these values, they must have a deep understanding of how they influence the nature of this society. Each generation of citizens will define and apply these values in different contexts and often with different meanings. Democratic educators must not impose them on the young. They must honor the democratic value of freedom of thought and speech and consequently they should not use doctrinaire methods to shape young minds. Democratic educators must place their faith in the weight of the arguments that embrace the reason and/or evidence that support such values, fully recognizing that their application is sometimes flawed and imperfect. Democratic citizens must be responsible for their own ethics and morality and be able to justify their decisions and actions respecting the public good on a continuing basis.

As suggested above, the history of democratic institutions affords many examples of value issues over which citizens have taken issue and in some cases, have fought and died.

The humanities highlight additional examples. Persuasive cases for particular values are found in both classic and contemporary literature. The following books, among many others, offer a few useful examples: *Plunkett* (Riordon, 1963), a novel that poignantly reveals the workings of the Tammany Hall political machine; *On The Beach* (Shute, 1957), a novel that takes the reader to an imagined view of survival after a nuclear disaster; *The Diary of Anne Frank* (Frank, 1958), an account by an adolescent that presents the horrors of hatred and prejudice at the time of the Holocaust or *Nectar in a Sieve* (Markandaya, 1954) that depicts the challenge of women's lives in mid-20th century India.

The study of history contributes substantially to the understanding of controversial issues. Indeed, history teaching organized around the issues that became evident in different historical periods is encouraged by this curriculum. The depth of understanding around a given issue, which is far more important than the amount of material covered, is so important that special units of study need inclusion throughout the curriculum. A capstone course that would focus on our most bothersome and most significant issues is a serious curriculum change that deserves consideration. For example, protection of the environment, nuclear proliferation, persistent prejudice and discrimination, the attainment of a more peaceful planet, world hunger and poverty are all issues of great magnitude, persistence and significance. It is impossible for the curriculum to address all of them. However, it is possible for the school to provide an opportunity for the concentrated study of selected issues. (See Chapters 5 and 7)

Artistic works often present the travesties and triumphs of human beings visually. These insights can deepen understandings of controversial issues. During the Spanish Civil War, Picasso created a compelling rendition of the horrors of civil strife titled Guernica that presents with dramatic imagery the devastation human beings can perpetrate against each other. Similarly, Arthur Miller's play, *The Crucible,* serves as a forceful and dramatic presentation of issues that juxtapose individual freedom and social conformity. There is no end to the availability of such literature, art and music that can heighten the significance of controversial issues and challenges to the human condition.

While teachers may expose young citizens to value analysis in literature, art and music, the problem of what to value and what to value most is of such overwhelming importance that a special capstone effort is called for in social studies classrooms. The following questions need examination: What should I value? What should I value most? How can I decide which value is most important? What reasons or evidence support my values? Such a program is detailed further in Chapter 7 on Curriculum.

Finally, democratic citizens need to be fully aware of the major issues that confront society and be knowledgeable about them. They need to know about the conditions that led to these issues and be familiar with bodies of information that relate to them. They need to know what the issues are as well as to identify the values that they applied to resolving them. Their classroom experiences should provide an opportunity to think and talk about some of these issues in a thoughtful manner and to clarify and justify where they stand (Ross, 2001).

Commitment to the Democratic Ideal (Values)

Basic among the characteristics of the democratic citizen is commitment to the democratic ideal. Democracy in the United States is, without question, among the best of social systems because it honors respect for each individual regardless of creed, color, ethnicity, gender or religious belief.

This means that all human beings deserve treatment that is caring, understanding, civil, compassionate and equitable. Furthermore, each individual has the right as well as the responsibility to be knowledgeable and to participate along with others in making decisions and taking action that concerns their society and the global community. When citizens remain passive, uninformed and disinterested in public affairs, they deny democracy the vitality and strength it requires for its maintenance, growth and improvement. In addition, they deny themselves by not participating in the creation of policies and practices that may improve their lives. Moreover, by not actively participating, they place additional burdens on those who do.

Such citizens, in effect, break the fundamental social contract between the citizen and the state in a democracy. Susan Adler, (2001) a Past President of the National Council of the Social Studies, said it well:

> ...even in a democracy, where diversity and differences of opinion and free speech should not only be expected but also welcomed, many people equate being a good citizen primarily with obeying the rules. (p. 3)

Adler argues that we should welcome disagreement, but she finds too often citizens comply and agree rather than enter into an argument that can be stimulating and illuminating. We need to recognize that diverse viewpoints require expression. All of us can agree to disagree. As importantly, diverse viewpoints deserve to be valued. It is this kind of dialogue, one characterized by diverse views, that expands our awareness and stretches our intellect. The more we invest intellectual energy in understanding diverse ideas, the sounder the decisions we make are likely to be.

It is possible to view the passive behavior of citizens not only as lack of responsibility but, in an ethical sense, as an act of disloyalty that in some cases, weakens the democratic fiber of society and reduces the potential influence that individuals and groups have in promoting conditions that better their lives and strengthen democracy. Social studies educators must dedicate themselves to fostering citizens who are not only informed and concerned, but are willing to participate in behalf of strengthening the democratic ideal (Mosher et al., 1994).

Young people can learn, even early in their formative years, to respect these principles through examples set by adults in their lives as well as through stories and simple histories that celebrate these ideals. Later, as young adolescents, they should come to a more reasoned understanding of democracy that permits them to bring meaning to such democratic ideals as freedom of choice, equity, openness to new ideas, protection of minority rights and opinions, freedom of the press, freedom of religion, freedom to disagree and freedom to speak one's mind without fear of reprisal. In contrast to autocratic practices, democracy depends on the participation of individuals who are able to make decisions that influence their lives. Citizens, who have tasted freedom and who have experienced being partners in the affairs of the state, are likely to feel more compelled to choose democracy, whatever its shortcomings, over any other form of social organization and governance. However, the democratic citizen must make this choice openly, freely and without coercion.

Intellectual Processes

The intellectual development needed by democratic citizens greatly exceeds the abilities that often are commonly labeled social studies skills. Intellectual abilities are far more complex than map skills, library skills, note taking skills and the like. Although these skills are useful, they do not substitute for intellectual strength. The focus here is to apply the intellect to make meaning, to expand comprehension and to connect to the decision making process. Such abilities are crucial in the context of democratic education. Indeed, how we make meaning of information, the grounds we choose to draw conclusions, how we analyze and prioritize values and how we evaluate and justify decisions are very complex processes. These intellectual processes are integral to the content of a democratic curriculum (Parker and Rubin, 1966; Engle, 1960). They are on a par in importance with the subject matter or knowledge component discussed above. These processes are best learned when student-citizens examine controversial issues and when the application of these processes is needed and relevant.

The focus in this Issues-Centered Decision Making Curriculum is on applying the intellect to make meaning to enhance understanding, to expand comprehension and to support decision making and political action that can make democracy stronger. Higher level thinking abilities are crucial in the context of democratic education. Indeed, how we make meaning of information, how and on what basis we draw conclusions, how we analyze and prioritize values, how we evaluate evidence and justify our decisions, how we decide whether or not to take action in behalf of our values and concerns and how we determine the manner in which we will take action constitute challenging, but very necessary ways of thinking and doing for citizens of a democracy. These intellectual processes are also a body of content that serves as an integral part of this curriculum (Parker & Rubin, 1966). These processes, in and of themselves, constitute curriculum content that parallels the importance of the knowledge component of social studies. Experience by student-citizens in understanding issues and making substantiated decisions is essential for citizens in a democracy. Indeed, we all learn best when the application of content and processes are needed and relevant.

The following material identifies the intellectual abilities needed for strong democratic citizens and includes hypothetical examples to make the matter as clear as possible:

1. Being able to identify complex issues and cast them in a broad perspective, identifying points of controversy as well as the underlying values which may be in conflict.

   Hypothetical example #1: If the issue under study relates to the persistent Palestinian-Israeli conflict and controversy has arisen with respect to the amount and kinds of foreign aid the U.S. provides to Israel, student-citizens need to examine U.S. policies and practices regarding aid to Israel across time. Our aid to Israel as compared to that of other nations and the impact of providing aid to Israel as one of the actors in this tense and sometimes violent relationship are conditions that need serious consideration. Are other nations providing aid to Israel? Should they? Why? Should we continue aid to Israel? Should we also help the Palestinians? In what ways? Why? The class should also examine this issue recognizing that there is a substantial Jewish population in the United States that has a strong stake in the role the United States assumes with Israel. However, they should be familiar with Palestinian viewpoints and their rationale for a homeland in the Middle East as well. The point is to bring the broadest possible perspective to the issue so student-citizens understand the controversy as comprehensively as possible in a balanced way.

   Such issues are not easy to understand and teachers need to present them so that student-citizens understand their broader context including the religious issues as well as the role of the United States in facilitating the creation of the State of Israel in the Middle East in 1949. The intellectual abilities involved in this process are challenging and very significant. Student-citizens are not likely to bring such broad perspectives to the issue initially, but if presented with examples, they learn this more comprehensive way of examining issues easily by experience.

2. Being able to select and access relevant information about the issue from a variety of fields of study and from sources that present competing and contrasting points of view. Student-citizens need to investigate these sources and make meaning out of the information they present with a view to applying knowledge they find to their understanding of the issue and the proposed recommendations they generate to ameliorate the issue. As student-citizens examine sources they need to make careful judgments about their credibility.

   Hypothetical example #2: Prior to the investigation of the issue, the teacher with the cooperation of the school librarian can identify the print and nonprint resources (including relevant websites) related to the issue under study. Beyond school and local libraries, the use of the Internet as well as visual and human resources that can illuminate the issue should be identified. Both teachers and student-citizens should be involved in creating criteria (identifying the values) that apply to the issue at hand. All sources used deserve careful and critical scrutiny to estimate their credibility as accurately as possible. Is the author an expert? Is the author an eyewitness? Is the description sufficiently detailed? Is it accurate? Are there other sources that confirm it? Is the report, article or document timely? Is it too old to be credible? Are there more recent works? These kinds of questions are crucial. When information becomes available on websites on the Internet, it is not believable until such questions have been asked and answered.

3. Being able to create a future scenario of likely consequences regarding any proposed solution to an issue and to identify the criteria (values) by which these consequences should be judged.

   Hypothetical example #3: Solutions to issues require testing. One way to do that is to develop a detailed description (a scenario) of how the solution might play out, what challenges exist, what values it would represent and what impact it would have on all parties involved. Here, student-citizens should identify the criteria (values) by which consequences should be judged. Peace might be one value. Would the proposed solution increase the chances for a peaceful Middle East? What reasons and/or evidence would support this conclusion? Student-citizens should speculate about what the policy of the United States might have been if a large number of our citizens were of Palestinian background. Improved relations between nations might be another value. Would this solution improve the relationship between Israel, the Palestinian authority, the other Middle East nations, the United States and its allies?

4. Being able to make reasoned judgments where the evidence is conflicting or where there is a conflict of values.

   Hypothetical example #4: Examining the credibility of sources is a persistent intellectual task of democratic citizens. However, sorting out which statements have the strongest evidence can be very challenging. Citizens need to learn to examine the credentials of authors, analyze points of view, detect bias and identify evidence and/or reason that support contrasting claims. They also need to justify values, which always involves a process of prioritization. Relevant questions for class consideration are: Which values apply here? Why is it that these values should guide the search for a solution? Which values are most important? Why are these values most important? Are there other values that are relevant to this issue? What are other values that any of the actors bring to this issue? Are they worth consideration? Why or why not? Do we have relevant values that compete with each other? How can we resolve or minimize that tension?

5. Being able to understand the perspectives of people who hold different views or different cultural perspectives regarding an issue. What reasons and/or what evidence support their conclusions? Do these reasons or this evidence deserve consideration?

   Hypothetical example #5: While developing such abilities, teachers might ask the following questions to guide student-citizens to consider the perspectives of all relevant actors related to the issue. How might each actor or actors respond and react to the proposed solution? Do any of these perspectives deserve to influence the solution? If so, what reasons and what evidence support that solution? Are these values consistent with your priority of values? How? How do they differ?

6. Being able to choose or create a solution which, though less than ideal, is politically viable and moves in the desired direction.

   Hypothetical example #6: Based on the materials student-citizens read that take positions on this issue, do they also provide evidence and/or reasons? Some may feel that the level of foreign aid to Israel requires reduction and others may feel the level of aid needs to be increased or balanced with aid to the Palestinians. Other points of view are, of course, possible. Not all student-citizens in a given classroom are likely to hold the same point of view. The abilities involved here apply to the question of how much foreign aid is needed from the United States and in what form it should be given. Continually, student-citizens should engage in a serious examination of pertinent evidence, reason and values. Sometimes, abilities that support conflict resolution and compromise need to be introduced—if emotions run high Otherwise, class members may agree to disagree—that is to practice civility in the context of a group divided in its views. (For materials that provide details of conflict resolution and cooperative learning see the following sources in the References. Kreidler, 1997; Sadalla, Holmberg, & Halligan, 1990; Slavin, 1995).

Political Abilities

Being willing and able to exercise political influence that supports justifiable decisions and being able to organize and sustain the involvement of supporters is of paramount importance if efforts to influence social change are to follow. For far too long, the schools have not provided opportunities for community participation in the form of service learning or social action. We must not shy away from providing such opportunities any longer if we wish to do a better job improving the quality of democratic citizens. Experience counts. In this case, student-citizens need to consider the kinds of actions that they are able to take that might be most effective such as letters sent to newspapers, letters to and/or meetings with legislators, supportive organizations and the like. Making placards, engaging in peaceful protests or putting on a play that illustrates the issue and raises the awareness of other students, teachers and parents are all possibilities. There are many others. Certainly, reading, writing and speaking abilities are involved. The opportunity to bring about some improvement in local, national or global conditions is a never to be forgotten enterprise. Young citizens deserve to have this kind of experience during their school years in order to be more participatory adult citizens.

The public often considers voting to be the sine qua non of democratic citizenship. Though very important, the argument that is advanced here is that voting is but one of several ways that strong democratic citizenship is manifest. Involvement in public affairs at any level, individual to global, can take the form of letter writing, participating in community and neighborhood meetings, applying democratic procedures to one's interactions in the workplace, in the family and in volunteer work of many kinds. All of these practices can help strengthen democracy. Benjamin Barber in his insightful book, *A Place for Us* (1998) argues for using the 'space' between government and the economy to create a more civil society. Barber asserts that any two people, the basic human group, in concert with each other and using interactions that are consistent with the democratic ideal, hold the potential, depending on how respectfully and democratically they treat one another, to contribute to a civil and more intellectually alive society. Democratic citizens must realize that the actions they take, however small and seemingly insignificant, can contribute to the quality of our democratic system. Barber's concept of the space we have between government and the economy views is not inconsistent with Anderson's (1990) desire for democratic relations to function in all the settings where decisions are made. Anderson's call for democratic relations between people in all the settings where they have contact with others may assume the existence of Barber's space for civility. These two authors seem to agree that our democratic system (they both view it as a system) is sufficiently open and has room for improvement.

Despite the many ways of exercising political influence, our citizens must see voting as deserving serious attention. It is the most fundamental of rights afforded to citizens of a democracy. Any political system that denies this right to its citizens is not a democracy at all. It is a sham. Furthermore, voting rights, as less powerful groups have realized, are the starting point of political influence with respect to gaining equitable benefits in the society. In this regard, it is significant that African Americans did not gain the right to vote until 1870 after the legal abolition of slavery. Even in the present day, there are still locations where racists inhibit African Americans from voting. Furthermore, women did not gain that right until 1920. For marginal groups sidelined by society, earning and using voting rights is essential to creating a social and political environment that has any hope of becoming more equitable and democratic.

If citizens choose not to vote, they lose their stake in public affairs. Furthermore, if they vote but, are not informed, if they mindlessly reflect the messages of slick media presentations or simply vote as their friends and family do, they are treating this hard won right of democratic peoples with great disrespect. Sadly, across the last century, the percentage of eligible voters who actually cast ballots has continually declined. More recently, some presidential elections were decided not by majority vote, but only by a plurality. In the presidential election of the year 2004, the voting turnout was lower than ever with 64 percent of registered voters (not all citizens) turning out to vote. Moreover, the state of Florida had a severe challenge to the efficiency and honesty of their elections in the year 2000 elections.

Exercising the right to vote is not a simple matter. It is not enough to know how to mark a ballot. Seldom are the issues that accompany any election of candidates, completely clear. Candidates may be hard to sort out. Some may share positions with the views of a particular citizen, but reveal a few major exceptions. The citizen may see attractive positions on different sides and be forced to make fine distinctions between candidates that force the identification of priorities. The citizen's final decision may entail compromise, weighing a wide range of positions and prioritizing values.

To be informed, responsible voters, citizens need to read as widely as possible and discuss the controversial issues at length with family, friends, co-workers and other relevant people. They must be able to detect bias and assess the credibility of the sources to which they have access. Without being taught about these matters, the citizen easily becomes a victim of those who try to manipulate public opinion. Citizens should ask the following kinds of questions of what they read, see, and hear. How do I know that this statement is true? Do I have all the facts I need? Am I being manipulated by high priced advertising, by politicians or by the media? What criteria should I use in selecting a candidate? Is that criteria something I can defend?

Citizens who want to be responsible voters must weigh a host of competing factors, distinguish what is accurate from what is not, identify the salient issues of their time and perhaps, suppress their own self-interest because attention to the common good is so important. None of us are born with these complex and significant predispositions and abilities. They have to be carefully taught. Fostering such abilities regarding issues, elections and politics is a major focus of social studies education. Furthermore, political influence is probably best learned as it is practiced. There is no substitute for that experience. While student-citizens can and should read about the roles of social activists such as Jane Adams, Martin Luther King, Caesar Chavez, Susan B. Anthony, Ralph Nader, Cornel West, Betty Friedan or see films that portray social action in process, neither reading nor viewing have the same power as active experience provides.

In this regard, it is useful to reflect on a vignette presented by Newmann et al. (1977) in which a single individual is walking along a desolate beach and hears a call for help from someone swimming alone. Unfortunately, the beach walker cannot swim. Therefore, no matter how much he or she may want to save the swimmer, which is certainly the moral position, his or her morality is rendered moot because of the lack of necessary skills. Thus it is, with many citizens in our democracy who do not exercise influence in public life because they lack the necessary experience, the confidence and abilities. Our schools and their social studies programs need to do more, much more than they presently do, to prepare student-citizens for more vigorous participation in public affairs. Otherwise, citizens compromise the principle of self-governance and become disempowered citizens.

In a highly populated and pluralistic society such as ours, a higher percentage of diverse ethnicities, religions, social and economic interests as well as organized interest groups have become increasingly influential in political life. Examples are:(e.g., the National Rifle Association, the National Association of Manufacturers, the American Enterprise Institute, the National Organization of Women, the American Civil Liberties Union, Planned Parenthood, the religious right and a host of others). Many active citizens belong to one or more such groups through which they make their voice heard in the press, in Congress and at local and state levels. While such groups are certainly legitimate, the dangers of self-interest at the price of the common good, deserves the constant attention of democratic citizens. That potential resides in special-interest groups that can become overly zealous and can compromise the welfare of the whole across time. For example, until recently, cigarette manufacturers prevailed. Only in the last decade have citizens demonstrated sufficient concern and judges and juries have made decisions that assigned penalties to the manufacturers of tobacco products. While democratic citizens may work with interest groups of all kinds, they must also learn to weigh, temper and balance their decisions and actions in keeping with their concern for others, for society as a whole and for the global community. Democracy, we must all remember, fails to the extent that not all of its people receive fair treatment and it fails to the extent its citizens are uninformed, thoughtful, dedicated and active in public affairs.

However, despite decreasing voter participation, volunteerism in this nation is at a fairly high level (Thelen, 1996). Many people give of their time to work in soup kitchens, read to persons who are blind, visit the elderly, serve as school patrols, tutor young children, participate in neighborhood crime watch programs, deliver Meals on Wheels, help in hospitals and the like. Such voluntary reaching out to others without pay is at the root of strengthening a sense of community. Engaging in such efforts help us feel that we belong, that we are useful and we care.

SCHOOL AND CLASSROOM CLIMATE

Schooling has the potential to contribute to the development of a commitment to democracy in at least two ways. To date, these have not been fully realized. First, in schools that have enlightened administrators and teachers who are willing to work at building a democratic curriculum, student-citizens are able to learn about the struggles associated with the emergence of democratic systems. Democracy is a political system that evolved after centuries of autocracy took a variety of forms. Whatever the form, autocrats did not treat their subjects with the respect and dignity that characterize the democratic ideal. Secondly, schools hold the potential, too often unrealized, to provide an example of democracy in microcosm in how the school functions as a community guided by democratic principles. School and classroom climate needs to demonstrate democratic qualities where all school personnel participate in creating a democratic model; one that provides a fitting environment for operating a social studies program devoted to heightening democracy.

There is substantial research to support school efforts of this kind. One educational intervention is directed at the overt curriculum and the second speaks to the hidden or covert curriculum (Massialas, 1996). Research reported by Lee Ehman (1980) and Hahn (1996; 1998) reveals a connection between school and classroom climate and the political attitudes of adolescents. The significance and power of classroom climate is strongly supported by research that found positive correlation, though not causal, between exposure to social issues and a sense of citizen duty (Hahn, 1996). Classrooms where there was an open climate seem to generate a higher level of political interest, political trust and a higher sense of civic duty. These conclusions are highly plausible and deserve the focused attention of citizenship educators.

Moreover, in a recent study of schools in 30 nations, open classroom climates were associated with a higher level of curriculum knowledge as well as intention to vote as adults (Torney-Purta, Lehmann, Oswald and Schulz, 2001).

School rules, like society's laws, should be reasonable. Student-citizens should participate in making or revising them and should understand the reasons behind them as well as their consequences. The process of school governance should never be coercive or arbitrary and the capacity of young citizens to participate in their own governance should not be over-looked. As important as a democratic school and classroom climate are, very few schools and very few teachers have been responsive to this research. Many, if not most, of our schools and social studies classrooms have not tried it. Schools and classrooms, teachers and administrators must demonstrate respect for the rights of minorities as well as minority views or both democracy and social justice will dwindle into mediocrity.

Hahn (1996) completed a careful review of research that is instructive for citizenship educators. She summarized as follows.

> Student in such classes [when an open classroom climate exists] as compared to students without that experience, are more likely to develop 1) an interest in the political world, 2) a sense that they and citizens like themselves can have some influence on political decisions in a democracy and 3) a belief that citizens have a duty to be actively involved in politics. Further, they are likely to report feelings of being integrated into, rather than feeling alien-ated from, the school culture. (p. 32)

A democratic school and classroom climate may be as important as the formal curriculum. Perhaps even more so. School personnel, administra-tors, teachers and other adult personnel need to make moves to develop a democratic climate if they want student-citizens to not only follow what we say but also learn from what we do.

CONCLUSION

The thrust of this chapter has been to present an overview of the four major components of an Issues-Centered Decision Making Curriculum in order to increase the likelihood of providing alert, active and caring citi-zens who are willing to give of themselves to create a more just and more vigorous democracy. Such a curriculum must integrate the knowledge needed to expand understanding of controversial issues, promote but not mandate a commitment to the democratic ideal, develop intellectual abili-ties such as analyzing issues, values, making decisions and provide opportu-nities to develop and use political abilities that are not only useful but necessary for democratic citizens. Just as importantly, this curriculum needs the creation of more democratic school and classroom climates which support the goal of gaining commitment to democratic principles by young citizens who must not only be knowledgeable, but who can bring this knowledge to bear in resolving issues and improving conditions that are evident in their various communities. Understanding controversial issues is much more than the mastery of specific bits of information often drawn from textbooks and it is much more than traditional specific skills. In this discussion, the use of the term, abilities rather than skills, is intended to communicate the holistic nature of these intellectual processes. There is no linear recipe for resolving controversy. Rather, it is a synthesis of many kinds of knowledge and intellectual processes applied to making sound decisions and taking action to improve the quality of life for all citizens in a pluralistic democracy in a global age.

Democracy is not merely an enlightened way of governing. It is, even at its best, a system that requires constant attention to what is right, equitable, and just. Every social issue has moral and ethical dimensions and learning to deal with these dimensions is every bit as important as learning to deal with the knowledge base that provides understanding of them.

It is the position of this book that the education of citizen decision makers requires the continuous inclusion in their schooling of real life issues that require the making of informed and defensible decisions. The building of a strong democracy as practiced by student-citizens in their classrooms and schools is a major ingredient of citizenship education in a democracy.

This chapter started with an insightful quote from Amy Gutmann, a serious scholar of democracy and democratic education. She reminds educators that we are not the only ones responsible for educating the next generation of citizens. Indeed, if we do not have the support of parents, neighbors, preschools, television, as well as social and religious organizations we cannot expect to make much headway. Nonetheless, this chapter concludes with the continued hope that education can heighten the quantity and quality of citizen participation. It can empower the less powerful and deepen democratic participation among all classes of citizens. However, we will not do so by covering more of the textbook nor by delivering new and better lectures or by repeatedly testing. Social studies educators can be more effective by engaging young citizens in issues and decisions that are of interest to them and ones that can be connected to broader and more complex controversies. We must listen carefully to the thoughts of student-citizens whose ideas and issues of interest are useful in guiding the content in this curriculum. Certainly, educators must not deny existing research. Together with student-citizens teachers. administrators and other adults that are employed by the school need to create school and classroom climates that model democracy's principles.

NOTES

1. As a former classroom teacher (13 years in Grades 4–12), I felt very uncomfortable as I wrote that it could be concluded that because young citizens rated social studies as their least favorite subject and because they remembered very little of what they were taught, that it is easy to come close to the conclusion that students as well as teacher were wasting their time. I am sharing this discomfort because that statement applies to me as well. It took me three difficult years to abandon the social studies textbook as the complete curriculum. Prior to that time, I gave reading assignments and expected my classes to memorize textbook material so they could pass the test when we finished the chapter. My point is that research confirms the poor attitudes that young citizens persistently report regarding social studies and that should be reason enough to change what we do. The purpose that guides social studies—stronger citizens for a stronger democracy—is too important to do more of the same. We must be open to changes that hold promise of raising the level of our results.

2. Social studies is the curriculum area that assumes major responsibility for preparing democratic citizens in the nation's schools. At the same time, citizenship education is a broad goal that applies to the entire school. In this book, the terms social studies education and citizenship education are interchangeable. The singular verb "is," follows the plural subject, "social studies." On its face, this usage may appear to be grammatically incorrect. However, social studies in the context of the democratic curriculum offered here, is an integrated, interdisciplinary curriculum. The term, social studies refers to the broad purpose of social studies—the preparation of informed, thoughtful, and active citizens for a democracy and whatever offerings the school has in social studies should have this purpose as their goal. Social studies should be taught in a holistic interdisciplinary manner and should be especially concerned with preparing the next generation to be thoughtful, informed, and active citizens of a democracy that is still growing and becoming.

3. The definition of citizenship used here is a departure from the one used in the original book done with Engle where we confined citizenship to a relationship with the nation-state. Engle and I discussed this matter at length. At the time, we had both read Anderson's work and thought it was too broad and beyond the power of the school and this curriculum. We kept the narrow definition. In the intervening years, heightened concern regarding very challenging issues that cross national boundaries and require cross-national cooperation for their solution combined with the increasing contacts that peoples around the world have with each other through rapid transportation and technological advances in communication, made the Anderson definition more appealing and applicable. The need to relate to diverse peoples who represent different cultures, customs, and beliefs but still share profound human similarities as members of the human species has become increasingly important. These views represent my thinking as I emphasized multicultural and global understandings in this curriculum. I still agree that the school cannot do it all and it does not have influence over the practices of other agencies or families and friends. However, it should do everything it can. These other influences also have responsibility for the development of the young. The extent to which they have norms

and practices that support democratic values is the extent to which they are cooperating with the goal of the school and its social studies program. "It takes a village to raise a child" is a statement that captures this message. Whether Engle would have agreed is unpredictable.

4. The terms *international* and *global* do not carry precisely the same meaning. International is a term that literally means between nations, while global is more comprehensive. It embraces the term, international, but also attends to the increasing interconnectedness of people, places, economic forces, health issues, and cultures as well as events and issues across the planet. Global conditions have local implications. The global AIDS epidemic is evident in local communities across the planet. So is Mad Cow disease, acid rain, and terrorism. Furthermore, local conditions have global implications. Higher unemployment in a given community may be related to the capacity of other nations to manufacture products less expensively. Throughout history, social change has often occurred as a result of contacts with new and different cultures that result in new developments in music, the arts, as well as social behavior.

5. The *World Press* is a unique journal that reports world news but also prints excerpts from newspapers of other nations that carry the views of those nations toward the United States particularly in cartoons and editorials. It is suitable for the middle school and secondary level and school libraries should subscribe. The Stanley Foundation, 209 Iowa, Muscatine, Iowa 52761. Phone: (563) 264-1500. www.stanleyfoundation.org

CHAPTER 3

SOCIALIZATION AND COUNTER SOCIALIZATION FOR A DEMOCRACY

"The teaching problem...olves equipping young people with the ability to identify alternatives, and to see possibilities in the situations the confront."

—Maxine Greene, 1978, p. 50

INTRODUCTION

This chapter emphasizes two concepts, socialization and counter-socialization as well as the relationship between them. These concepts and the processes associated with them guide the learning experiences that are used across this Issues-Centered Decision Making Curriculum. This chapter explains and exemplifies these concepts at K–12 grade levels.

*   *   *

The concepts of socialization and counter-socialization are central to this Issues-Centered Decision Making Curriculum. They deserve emphasis. The first concept is *socialization* which is the process of learning the existing customs, traditions, rules and practices of a society. The second is *counter-socialization* which involves expanding the individual's ability to be a rational and reasoning decision maker—citizen attributes that contribute to strong self-confidence, stronger citizens and to a strong democracy.

Democratic Education for Social Studies, pages 65–100
Copyright © 2007 by Information Age Publishing
All rights of reproduction in any form reserved.

SOCIALIZATION

Every society inducts young children into its customs, values and behaviors as a way of continuing existing cultural traditions and practices. The manner by which children learn these traditions constitutes the socialization process whose goal is to encourage conformity and thus ensure the continuity of the society. Parents, teachers, peers and the media serve as major agents of socialization (though socialization of young children may not be their primary role).

In essence, socialization is a conserving process. It transmits traditions and values that are common place in the experiences of the community and the larger society. However, it does not explicitly prepare the next generation for the unknown future and the changes it might bring. With the emphasis on tradition, the practices related to socialization foster conformity to existing cultural values, behaviors and practices. In and of itself, socialization seeks to strengthen social cohesion—a condition important to all societies. While socialization entails the means by which children learn to fit into the existing social order, it is not concerned with developing individuals on their own terms by emphasizing their intellect, their creativity, their uniqueness or their independence. Yet, these qualities deserve strong attention in a changing pluralistic, global setting where controversy and social change call for continuing dialogue and negotiation among reasoning and reasonable citizens.

Socialization is not, by nature, deliberative or reflective. It does not encourage individuals to question, to analyze, to examine values, to make creative decisions or to support their views with reasons and evidence. Instead, it is more doctrinaire. Moreover, it is unavoidable. Young children, who lack the intellectual strength to thoughtfully deliberate, will be socialized to whatever values and practices they experience. The process is unavoidable. It relies on emotion and authority to gain its ends. Those who implement the socialization process in a major way, early childhood educators and parents, very easily leave their marks, be they positive or negative, on very young children who are easily influenced by positive and negative rewards. By offering children rewards or recognition or the embarrassment, hurt or pain of punishment, socialization practices manipulate their behavior in order that they will learn to conform to adult expectations (Amadeo, 2002).

COUNTER-SOCIALIZATION

Socialization is an inescapable dimension of citizenship education and is the means by which young citizens initially learn the traditions of their society. However, in a democracy, *counter-socialization* emphasizes creative and independent thinking as well as social criticism that is based on reason and evidence. These abilities are fundamental to improving the quality of democratic life in a changing pluralistic society whose continually increasing connections with the rest of the world creates a future of persistent issues and challenges. Since counter-socialization leads student-citizens to have a critical deliberating mindset, it is essential that each generation of citizens develop the intellectual abilities to think seriously about problematic conditions that plague this society as well as the complex conditions in their communities and across the globe.

This broad context requires that the socialization process must be balanced with counter-socialization. Counter-socialization is a learning process that is designed to foster independent thought and social criticism that is crucial to political freedom. It promotes active and vigorous reasoning. Moreover, it includes a reappraisal of what has been learned through the socialization process. Some of those values that were learned in a mindless way, as if by osmosis, need to come under thoughtful scrutiny as young people develop their intellectual capacities. Importantly, the counter-socialization process does not necessarily imply rejection of what has been learned early in life. Rather, it calls for a thoughtful reassessment of ideas, learned early in life, by which young citizens can reach their own defensible conclusions as they face an unknown future where traditional values will warrant reexamination. Citizens who have engaged in a thoughtful and critical analysis of their beliefs and who recognize the complexity of public issues and public opinion are more likely to contribute effectively to the issues of their day and to live a meaningful and active democratic life.

THE RELATIONSHIP BETWEEN SOCIALIZATION AND COUNTER-SOCIALIZATION

When selecting appropriate content (content, as used here includes both subject matter and intellectual processes) and methods for educating democratic citizens, the ability and maturity of learners are persistent and significant concerns. At young ages, children are especially manipulable and are easily influenced by the use of emotion whether used by teachers, parents or textbooks. Often, rewards and punishments are used by authority figures to gain the compliance of young children. From one perspective, children can be seen as victims of those who attempt to influence them. Their limited intellectual ability gives them no other choice. Their susceptibility to the influence of adults requires that educators give very careful attention to the nature of their socialization. Since children cannot escape this process, their teachers need to be especially careful to use both content and methods that respect the integrity of young minds and ones that are as consistent as possible with democratic values.

Even in a democracy, socialization is the dominant learning process during the early years of schooling. Parents, siblings, teachers and other significant adults play critical and high profile roles. For the most part, children will accept and learn values and behaviors to which they are exposed, quite unthinkingly. Consequently, the goals that provide direction for the socialization process are very important. During these impressionable early years, the content and methods used should be guided closely by democratic ideals and by teachers who recognize the very powerful influence they have on the minds of very young children (Helivig, 1998).

To illustrate the importance of content and methods that young people experience in family settings, it is useful to examine a description of a family (hypothetical, but based on a family known to the author). This family consists of one female parent with two children that illustrates how content and methods, even in the less formal family setting, influence the knowledge gained as well as the thinking and behavior learned by children. This family includes a son, 15, and a daughter, 5, with a single, divorced mother who works full time at two different jobs to make ends meet. The father has visitation privileges that include selected weekends and two weeks in the summer. The son is a strong figure with a lot of athletic prowess and is a capable (almost all A) student. He enjoys his little sister and plays and roughhouses with her as older brothers often do. The mother is educated, holds a Masters Degree and is a very responsible parent. She engages in continuing discussions with her children and expresses her love for them in no uncertain terms. She listens to them carefully and treats what they say as important. At dinner, an important meal in this household where everyone is always present, she deliberately mentions events in the news and asks the children what they think of them. She encourages their expression of opinion and sometimes pushes their thinking to provide reasons for their conclusions. She also encourages joint family projects. The father, however, is controlling, directive and somewhat unpredictable. He clearly prefers interaction with his son rather than his younger daughter. It is also clear that he is affirmed by his son's successes, be they athletic or academic. However, he provides little opportunity for personal expression. The five year old daughter, a kindergartner, is both curious and outgoing. She often shares daily experiences at the dinner table. She adores and enjoys her brother but loses some of her spontaneity in her father's presence. Not all children have so much love and so much interest by only one parent to expand their intellectual process.

Analyzing this family from the standpoint of democratic socialization leads to the observation that these children function as young citizens on a continuing basis. The have never been in serious trouble. They help with home chores and get along with each other without any challenging difficulties. It seems reasonable to predict that they are likely to become responsible adults. They also have considerable opportunity to converse, to share ideas about a wide range of current affairs, to learn from each other and to express themselves. In addition, they engage in cooperative activities. These experiences, taken together, are positive aspects of their socialization and bode well for their performance as caring members of the community and citizens of a democratic society. Their father's influence is not as favorable. However, the fact that their exposure to him is restricted to small allocations of time reduces his influence on the children. Nonetheless, their experiences with their father are not supportive of developing their attitudes or abilities in ways consistent with democratic principles. This family ,particularly this mother, is contributing to the citizenship responsibility of the school. Unfortunately, such a positive family environment is not experienced by all young citizens.

Teachers are not the only actors that influence democratic socialization. Furthermore, schools cannot control how parents socialize their children. However, teachers need to become as aware as they can of the home environments of those they teach. Importantly, teachers can create classroom environments that reflect democratic values and foster democratic practices in young children. When they meet with parents, they can suggest television programs that children should watch and suggest ways that parents can involve them in discussions about the news. These are very important years and the opportunity for democratic socialization should be maximized. While young children have limited intellectual abilities that support the use of socialization practices, it should also be emphasized that even in the elementary years, a foundation for counter-socialization can be laid (Skeel, 1996). Even first graders have printed simple letters to the editor of their local newspaper urging adults to recycle—an action that suggests they know the importance of recycling and its usefulness to the community.

Young children develop their capacity to think and make decisions in the context of their lived experiences. Broken friendships, families moving, parents fighting, older siblings picking on them are all issues that are important to young children. Opportunities to learn how to handle these situations can be part of the early years of schooling. Despite the fact that initial efforts at counter-socialization can begin during the early grades, the socialization process dominates the shaping of early values and behavior of young children.

With the onset of early adolescence, intellectual abilities gradually expand and young citizens can begin to test ideas, raise questions, examine evidence and reach justifiable conclusions. Furthermore, in many, but not all cases their ability to read complex material is evident. Counter-socialization needs to become the dominant mode of learning during this period. At this age level, learning becomes more complex because young citizens can generate and assess alternatives, predict consequences and provide explanations, create informed guesses and support their views with reasons and evidence. Though not as experienced as adult citizens, they now possess the intellectual abilities needed to become effective democratic citizens.

In sum, even in a democratic system, student-citizens should be socialized to democratic attitudes and behaviors during the early years of schooling. Citizenship educators need to guide those early learning experiences in terms of democratic ideals (Niemi, 1990; 1998; Niemi & Sanders, 2004). At the same time, the process of counter-socialization needs to begin to the extent that the intellectual abilities of young children will permit during the middle school years. Student-citizens can now benefit from opportunities to both raise and investigate questions of interest to them and to the larger society. They can read novels and dramas such as *Inherit the Wind* (Lawrence & Lee, 1955) which dramatizes the Scopes Trial and addresses the matter of censorship, *On the Beach* (Shute, 1957) that highlights nuclear war and its aftermath or, *All Quiet on the Western Front* (Remarque, 1929) that raises significant issues about war. These books raise serious issues for adolescents to consider and discuss in their classrooms.

Such literary encounters with controversial matters set the stage for higher level thinking and decision making around both personal and public issues. Due to the increasing maturity and intellectual capacity of adolescents, there can be no justification for the continuation of socialization during the adolescent years. Current practices in both elementary and secondary schools often place undue emphasis on content and methods that rely on rote memory and unreasoned loyalty. Several research projects across the last few decades have verified this observation (Goodlad, 1984; Hahn, 1996). Social studies programs have been found to be very dependent on textbooks. Teachers, too often, employ a lecture-recitation mode that denies the opportunity for intellectual development that is so necessary in the education of democracy's citizens. The following examples illustrate existing socialization practices at the elementary and secondary levels.

Elementary School Level

Example #1

In most, if not all, elementary schools, national holidays are an important focal point at every grade level. They are part of the social studies curriculum. Columbus Day, Halloween, Thanksgiving, Christmas, the birthdays of Washington and Lincoln, Valentine's Day and even Easter are visibly evident on bulletin boards, in student arts and crafts activities, class parties, exchanges of greeting cards and gift exchanges. Recently, a memorial day in honor of Martin Luther King Day has been set aside. Taken together, these several holidays form the traditional holiday curriculum. They receive attention in elementary classrooms on an annual basis. This practice constitutes a substantial portion of the social studies program in a number of elementary schools. Beyond ritualistic celebrations of these events, the history and the meaning of these holidays receives little attention. However, celebrating these holidays is used to socialize children so that they display loyalty and honor historic heroes. Lincoln and Washington are often glorified as people who had no human failings. In this context, myths are often perpetuated. Children are still too often told that Columbus was "responsible" for the discovery of America which is a so-called fact that totally ignores the presence of Native Americans who were already here when Columbus arrived. Indeed, Columbus, it is claimed, was the first white man to come to this continent although there are such competing possibilities as Leif Erickson and Eric, the Red and the Columbus encounter was important to future explorers and subsequent exploration and settlement in the Americas. The careful reader will notice that two of the holidays listed above, Christmas and Easter are Christian and there is little celebration of Hanukah or the special days of other religious groups. Recently, some citizens have raised questions about the attention given to special Christian days.

Richard Shenkman (1988) in *Legends, Lies, and Cherished Myths* points out that no one seems to know when the first Thanksgiving took place, since Pilgrim records only refer only generally to 1621 and the day was not celebrated as a family feast nor was it an annual Pilgrim event. More recently it has been found that for Native people it was not a time of thanksgiving and that they regarded Squanto as a traitor for cooperating with the Pilgrims. Shenkmen also states that Santa Claus is probably the most familiar and the most misunderstood figure of all. The name is strictly American since in Europe he was always St. Nicholas and even the date of his arrival varied. In Europe, it was December 6th not the 25th. Unfortunately, the opportunity to gain more meaningful understanding of these holidays is lost in most elementary school celebrations. At each elementary grade level, children are repetitively engaged in activities that cultivate blind, unthinking respect for individuals who were not perfect people despite the fact that they may have made significant contributions.

These activities perpetuate myths about the glories of the nation's heritage without much meaning or reflection. Most related activities make overt use of children's emotions as well as rewards in the form of parties and games that serve to manipulate young minds. Certainly, it is not being suggested that national holidays be ignored but at the same time they should represent the wide range of diversity and include Hanukkah, Ramadan, Cinco de Mayo and the holidays that represent the diverse traditions of the diverse peoples of this society and the planet. As importantly, the meaning of these holidays needs to be clarified so that they are more than an occasion for classroom parties.

Furthermore, holidays associated with religions should be treated as efforts to teach about religion, but not to promote any particular religion. In communities that are homogeneous in terms of religion, it may seem natural or appropriate to engage in activities that support that particular faith, but social studies educators, as all public school educators, must respect the separation of church and state that serves as a major democratic principle.

Example #2

U.S. History is taught at the fifth, eighth, and eleventh grade in most school districts across this nation. In almost all cases, the textbook is the dominant source of knowledge, followed closely by teacher lecture. It is fair to say that whatever knowledge young people acquire in school about their nation's history comes from those two sources. The following passage from one current fifth grade history textbook illustrates how a textbook can socialize young people by subtly manipulating the perceptions they gain of historical events:

> It was late December when the Pilgrims landed at Plymouth Rock. They began at once to build homes, storehouses, and a common house which was used for meetings and prayer. Building in winter was a difficult task and many settlers were already weak from the journey. They did not have enough of the kinds of food that would have kept them healthy. By spring, about half of the original 102 colonists had died.
>
> During the winter the colonists met a Pawtuxet (pahTUHKSit) Indian named Squanto (SKWAHN toh). He was able to speak English with them because he had been captured seven years earlier by an English explorer. Squanto had been sold into slavery from Spain. After a time, he escaped and returned home.
>
> With Squanto as interpreter, the Pilgrims made friends with the Wampanoag (wahm puh NOH ahg) Indians and their leader Massasoit (mass ah SOYT). The Wampanoag and the settlers made a treaty, promising peace between the two groups. In the spring, the colonists planted the seeds they had brought with them. Soon, however, the colonists found that these seeds grew poorly in the New England climate. Squanto was able to help again. He introduced them to plant the seeds in small hills and to use fish as fertilizer to help the corn grow (Scott Foresman, 2003, pp. 168–175).

While some Native People, like Squanto, developed strong ties with the English, many others did not. In addition, this passage makes no mention of contrasting accounts that suggest that the English sold some of the Indians to Spain as slaves or that some Pilgrims were known to have dug up Indian graves for the corn, wheat and beans that had been buried with the dead. Furthermore, no mention is made of the fact that Squanto's collaboration with the Pilgrims was seen as an act of disloyalty by some Native Americans and not as a day of celebration but as a day of mourning.

In sum, important information is excluded from this textbook passage creating a distorted view of history. It fails to present the perspective held by the Native People toward the Pilgrim settlement. It paints an overly generous picture of the Pilgrims and ignores the tragic manner in which their settlement affected the lives of the Native People. Inadvertently or not, such textbook material presents simplistic and questionable generalizations as if they were indisputable.

Student-citizens who are asked to memorize such information acquire an unrealistic view of historical events. Since alternative accounts are not provided, they cannot possibly know that what they have read and memorized is distorted or incomplete. Learning that depends on this kind of material asks young citizens to accept such conclusions blindly, without analysis and without justification. Indeed, relying on such limited and distorted information is doctrinaire since it emphasizes information that casts Pilgrims in a totally favorable light. At the same time, it excludes information that would have the learner recognize that the treatment Native Peoples received at the hands of the Pilgrims was also characterized by indignities that historians have also recorded.

Textbooks are watered down versions of history. Sometimes they are referred to as tertiary sources as compared to primary and secondary sources that serve as the base of historical scholarship. Usually, although the textbook will not explicitly say so, publishers take a centrist, pro-establishment view of history that seldom presents competing interpretations nor does it open historical questions to the scrutiny of young citizens. Before the textbook is published, publishers and authors make many decisions about what to include and what to exclude. These decisions are based on the values that seem to prevail among the public since publishers want to sell as many copies of their textbooks as possible.

These examples of traditional socialization practices influence the young citizen's understanding in an unreflective manner. They foster blind patriotism by avoiding or ignoring alternative perspectives that are necessary for a more comprehensive view of these events. In addition, these examples fail to stimulate intellectual activity on the part of the learner. Student-citizens are seldom asked to compare and analyze alternative views of historical events, to question the grounding for claims made as truthful and are not asked to draw and defend conclusions. The opportunity to point out the tentativeness of historical knowledge is seldom taken. Such learning may be fitting in a dictatorship where only one interpretation of history is advanced, but it flagrantly contradicts the values that should guide democratic education. Learning about this nation's history can be studied in a much more open and less distorted manner.

Unlike totalitarian nations which are prone to rewrite their history to fit changes in their power structure, democracies need not perpetuate myths or half-truths to cultivate a loyal citizenry. Furthermore, democracies do revise their views of key actors in history (e.g., Lyndon Johnson and John Kennedy, both of whom have altered images based on recent scholarship. Many examples of reinterpretation of historical events are available such as the Japanese Internment or the Vietnam War resulting from changing ideologies or recent scholarship. People of all ages can learn that key historical actors recorded significant accomplishments despite their shortcomings. If reason and civility are to be nurtured, democratic education must involve student-citizens in an honest search for truth that is grounded in evidence and reason rather than myths and half-truths that are promoted to enhance loyalty to the state. Obviously, what is fitting for a particular age group must be considered but we must address history as honestly as possible. To continue the kind of practices illustrated in the two examples above is both dishonest and contrary to democratic ideals.

To this point, the concepts of socialization and countersocialization have been presented. The discussion will now turn to the implications for both *content and methods* at both the elementary and secondary levels.

Elementary Level Content

Socialization has been presented as a significant mode of learning during the early elementary grades. Importantly, preliminary efforts at countersocialization can also begin during the latter part of the elementary grades. Selecting content requires an identification of appropriate subject matter and an understanding of the ability levels of children. Importantly, in an Issues-Centered Decision Making Curriculum, content includes both subject matter and intellectual processes that are appropriate for young children. Subject matter can take a variety of forms. Most common topics such as the family, the city, or the Revolutionary War are used in the elementary grades often in an expanding environments framework. Such topics are evident in elementary social studies textbooks and these topics guide the social studies curriculum in many elementary classrooms.

There are other ways to identify subject matter that can take the form of questions that represent the interests of young citizens as well as questions that the teacher poses for students to consider. Using questions focused on controversy is more consistent with the values underlying democratic citizenship education and with this social studies curriculum Several scholars who have done extensive work in elementary schools have argued that from grade 3 forward, children can begin to pursue questions related to social issues. (Dunfee, 1970; Skeel, 1988; 1996).

Any topic, question or issue can be taught from a variety of perspectives. For example, the family can be presented in a narrow and monolithic fashion. That is, children may learn that a family consists of a mother, father, and one or more children. However, if this narrow perspective is taken, children are likely to learn that alternative family patterns such as a single parent with a child, an older sister with a young sibling, are somewhat peculiar and are not seen as real families. A major risk with such a narrow perspective is that the child's own family may not fit the model presented and thus this treatment of the concept of family may alienates some students–citizens from the subject matter at hand. In contrast, from a wider perspective, children can learn that families can take many diverse but viable forms. The point being emphasized here is that the perspective taken regarding the subject matter is terribly important and teachers need to think about this matter very carefully. It permeates the topic or issue and is crucial to fostering democratic citizenship as the subject matter itself. It is this perspective that is likely to leave images in children's minds.

To foster socialization consistent with democratic goals, the content, which entails both subject matter as well as intellectual processes, needs to have the following characteristics:

1. Content needs to emphasize persistent democratic values such as freedom and equality.
2. Content needs to incorporate the ideas of diversity and pluralism wherever possible including diverse ideas about history, about families, about cultures, and about truth claims.
3. Content needs to be presented in honest ways and it is especially important to illustrate that there really are many points of view and many interpretations.
4. Certainly, higher level thinking and decision making need to be encouraged wherever possible.
5. Content should emphasize that all of us are first of all members of the human species that inhabits the planet, Earth. After that, we are citizens of nations.

Furthermore, teachers cannot avoid teaching values. Presenting subject matter from a broad, diverse perspective reflects a value for a wider and more complex base of intellectual thought. Such a stance by teachers contributes to broadmindedness and openness that are qualities central to democracy and therefore, are important to cultivate in our young citizens.

Conventionally, the subject matter selected for the elementary grades in the nation's schools revolves around the following sequence of topics, with some variations:

Grade 1 Home, School, Families
Grade 2 Community Helpers
Grade 3 Local Community
Grade 4 The State They Live In
Grade 5 U.S. History
Grade 6 Old World, Western Hemisphere, Eastern Hemisphere

Although there are deviations and alternative to these topics, similar sequencing patterns still prevail in many schools. Teachers can view even these traditional topics in ways that meet the characteristics of this curriculum identified above. Such topics can serve as a basis for developing intellectual abilities that can be guided by thoughtful questions and dialogue in the classroom. Children can be engaged in explaining, hypothesizing, generalizing, reasoning, and making decisions. Persistent questioning is a powerful and significant process that all teachers have at their disposal to stimulate the thought processes involved in an Issues-Centered Decision Making Curriculum.

The following questions serve as examples of how conventional content can raise questions that stimulate the intellect of children. They are designed to accompany a children's story that compares a Japanese family with an American family:

1. Which of these groups of people is a family? Why do you think so?
2. How are these two families alike?
3. Can you think of reasons why they are alike even though they live in places that are very far apart?
4. How are they different?
5. Can you think of reasons why they are different?
6. Can you think of a way to solve the problem that the family in the story is facing?
7. Of the several solutions suggested, which solution do you think is best? Why?

Within limits, young children are able to respond to such questions and if they have the experience of doing so, they will have the opportunity to develop habits of thinking that expand their intellectual capacities. They also begin to experience intellectual diversity as they listen to their classmates present ideas different from their own. If teachers call attention to the nature of different responses, they will contribute to the abilities our young citizens need for their role as democratic citizens. Even conventional topics can be turned into problematic situations and can serve the ends of an Issues-Centered Decision Making Curriculum at the elementary level.

Method at the Elementary Level

Teaching methods used with elementary school children need to minimize the use of authority ("Do as I say because I am in charge") and emphasize the use of reason ("Why do you think we have a rule about not shoving others in line?"). The more children are rewarded for parroting ideas because the teacher or the textbook says they are true, the more likely it is that they will depend on external authorities rather than their own reasoning to arrive at answers on their own. Democratic education requires that the use of reason be encouraged wherever possible and that children be encouraged to provide reasons for what they think, what they say and what they do. If the people are to govern themselves, they our student-citizens must know how to think for themselves.

The section below addresses the teaching process as it applies to an Issues-Centered Decision Making Curriculum.

The Teacher as Role Model

The most important teaching practices reside in the example set by the teacher. The attitudes and behavior exhibited by teachers have a powerful influence over young children. To enhance democratic socialization, the teacher's behavior needs to demonstrate respect for reason, evidence, diversity and democratic values such as fairness, equality and equity. Openness to a variety of points of view and respect for competing views are all part of a teacher's behavior who is an authentic democratic model. Such teachers encourage children to ask "Why?" to generate their own reasons and explanations and to defend their decisions and points of view. Furthermore, if teachers regularly provide children with reasons, either for school rules or for the subject matter that they want children to learn, these young citizens are more likely to incorporate reason giving into their intellectual style. Teachers, who are willing to admit they do not know a particular answer or who question the presentation in the textbook, recognize that they are not the only source of classroom knowledge. They are serving as models of questioning. Teachers need to remember that young children see them as powerful models who set examples for them to follow. At very young ages, children are more likely to accept the validity of their teacher's behavior blindly and without reasoning. Later as adolescents, they can be encouraged to challenge the teacher's and the textbook's ideas. Teachers who are consistent and who treat young people in a respectful and caring manner are making a major contribution to the quality of the next generation of citizens. Moreover, since young children are influenced easily, elementary school teachers play an extremely important role in their development. Clearly, it is more desirable to socialize young children in the direction of democracy than to promote unthinking compliance. No textbook, specific technique or classroom activity can compare with the influence of the teacher as a role model.

Probing Questions

Probing questions (Table 3.1) represent a critical dimension of the democratic curriculum. Such questions ask children to think deeply about the meaning of terms (Is that what "being fair" really means?) and to provide reasons for claims they may make. If a child says "That is not fair!" that claim should be followed by a question such as "Why do you think that is not fair?" "What would be fair, if this is not?" Such questions can be used with disciplinary issues. Furthermore, questions from student-citizens need to be elicited and affirmed. Developing an independent thinker necessarily involves the capacity, the confidence and the creativity to ask questions and probe for answers. Teachers need to listen to children's questions carefully with a view to inferring the mindset of the learner. The ideas of young citizens must be listened to and taken seriously if an authentic Issues-Centered Decision Making Curriculum is to be realized. Questions from student-citizens can frame the beginning of meaningful classroom dialogue that is the hallmark of the democratic classroom (Wilen & White, 1991).

Table 3.1. Probing Questions

Kind of Question	Examples
Definitional Questions	For the purpose of our study how should poverty be defined?
Evidential Questions	Can you explain why you think education can reduce poverty? Are there other sources that agree with you?
Policy Questions	Can you create two possible ways that poverty may be reduced in our community? What are the strengths and weaknesses of your two suggestions?
Value Questions	What values are you hoping to promote with your two suggestons? Explain why those values are important.
Speculative	What if poverty disappeared? What would be the consequences?

Using Children's Literature

Without question, children's literature is among the richest of sources for the democratic socialization of young children. Reading and thinking about stories that reveal people from diverse backgrounds, people who overcame obstacles to succeed, people like *Thomas Paine* (Keane, 1995), who placed a very high priority on democratic principles, is especially valuable. This literature, which is very extensive, serves as a rich resource for democratic dialogue that enhances democratic socialization at the elementary school level. To illustrate further, the Caldicott winner, *Annie and the Old One* (1971) by Miska Miles portrays a young Navajo child coming to grips with her grandmother's impending death. In the hands of a sensitive teacher, this story can help children identify with the young girl's grief and provide a diverse view of how people perceive life and death from a different cultural perspective. *Giants for Justice: Bethune, Randolph and King* (1978) by Beth P. Wilson presents short biographies of three African American leaders and their struggle for civil liberties. Plentiful examples of children's literature are available for the purpose of democratic socialization (Tyson, 2002).

Open-Ended Dilemmas

Still other learning experiences that teachers can quite easily create are open-ended dilemmas which involve children in the decision making process. These dilemmas are unfinished stories where children are asked to think of ways in which the central issue of the dilemma might be solved. Subsequently, the children are asked to consider the consequences of each alternative and select the solution they believe is best. Most importantly, they are asked to provide reasons and evidence that support their choice.

An example of an open-ended dilemma actually used by a third grade teacher follows[1] "On a Saturday afternoon, you are in line to get into the movie house with a friend. You notice a five dollar bill on the ground. The line is moving and is quite long, and it is not possible to tell who dropped the money." Follow-up questions could take the following form:

- What is the problem in the story?
- Try to think of as many ways as you can that might solve the problem.

After a little time for thought, the teacher writes four to five responses from class members on the board representing a full range of alternatives from keeping the money, asking the cashier if anyone had said they had lost the money, to asking people in line if they had dropped the money. To make these dilemmas realistic and challenging, the teacher should have at least three possibilities in mind in case the class does not generate them. These alternatives should represent the continuum of solutions that support the two alternatives at the ends of the continuum and at least one should take a middle position. It should be made explicit that the class must consider a range of alternatives and the reasons or evidence that provides support. Teachers need to caution student-citizens about jumping to decisions in a hasty way and justifying their first instinctive response, without considering other options. Asking to think about what else could be done besides their first idea, is giving them an opportunity to create other alternatives and consider whether they are better than their first choice. The best alternative is the one with the best consequences for all parties involved.

- If we followed the first alternative (keeping the money) what would be the result? (Yes, you would have $5.00 you did not expect to have. You might also feel guilty since the money was not really yours. Is it worth it?)

A similar pattern of teacher questions and comments would follow each of the other alternatives.

After consideration of a full range of alternatives, the teacher asks: "Which of these alternatives is best? Why do you think so?" As each recommendation is made, the teacher invites the class to comment on the recommendation and encourages the class to talk to each other about the value of each alternative as contrasted with merely responding to the teacher. The point is to create a climate for civil discussion and to examine multiple ways of addressing the problem.

Teachers can create dilemmas about such areas of concern as fairness on the playground, friendship, loyalty, telling secrets, telling the teacher about the misbehavior of others and lying to avoid getting into trouble. In the third grade class mentioned above, the teacher presented one of these dilemmas on a daily basis. Such activities can stand alone or they can be integrated with the context of the social studies units. These dilemmas are exercises in examining values and decision making. A most important question is one that asks, "Why." This question calls for reasoning or evidence. To the greatest extent possible, these dilemmas should reflect problems of interest to young citizens. In fact, student-citizens need to be encouraged to create their own dilemmas. At the third grade level, the stories are quite simple. However, citizens of all ages can benefit from the kind of higher level thinking that is involved in open-ended dilemmas. When used with elementary school aged children, the use of dilemmas calls for independent thinking and represents the beginning of countersocialization practices even as early as the third grade.

Role Playing

The use of role playing offers still another way for children to engage in decision making on their own level. Given a problem that young children can understand, teachers can ask small groups (four or five) of children to act out alternative solutions. The open-ended dilemmas described above can provide the context for these role plays. Young children are given an opportunity to understand the roles of other individuals and thus broaden their perspectives about solving problems in different ways. Role playing can provide a strong beginning regarding counter-socialization. Children can compare the worth of different solutions, can engage in problem solving, decision making and sharing their experiences and reasons with their peers and their teacher (Shaftel & Shaftel, 1982).

Group Work and Cooperative Learning

Working in groups is not unusual in elementary school classrooms. Grouping for purposes of reading is virtually the order of the day in all elementary classrooms. Importantly, working in small groups is an experience consistent with democratic education. If we think about the adult activities we encounter in the family, friendship groups, the workplace, in social organizations, at public meetings and with neighbors, we find that participation in groups is relatively commonplace in our adult lives. Significantly, the ability to work in groups is especially consistent with an Issues-Centered Decision Making Curriculum whose goal is to build a stronger democratic citizenry.

Across the last few decades various forms of *cooperative learning* have been used quite extensively (Slavin, 1995). Research on cooperative learning tells us that it can yield very valuable results. Not only do children raise their academic performance in cooperatively structured small groups, but also if the groups are cross-racial and/or cross-cultural, the incidence of cross-racial and/or cross-cultural friendships increases. The positive experiences that young children can have with diversity on a face-to-face basis and at an improved level of academic performance are encouraged though this cooperative group process. The following items indicate some of the procedures involved in cooperative learning.

The teacher decides, preferably with class input, what is studied. Sometimes, this material often comes from the textbook because it is readily available. However, the resourceful teacher might create a three page packet that presents competing views on a particular issue of special interest to a particular class. The cooperative learning experience can proceed as follows:

- Both the size of the group and the diversity of the group are important considerations. To the extent possible, each group of four or five members should represent the diversity that exists in that particular classroom. Students with disabilities, culturally distinct students as well as males and females should be distributed as evenly as possible across the groups and represent the composition of the class to the greatest extent possible.
- Groups are given time to organize their work and to identify someone to chair the group. Assignments are decided upon for each person in the group and each group member is responsible for knowing everything possible about her or his assignment. In addition, each group member is responsible for teaching her or his assignment to the entire group until each person performs at a satisfactory level. Preferably, a packet the teacher has prepared is divided so that each person has an alternative interpretation or alternative solution to explain to the group.
- At the conclusion of group discussion, the teacher gives a test to each group. In each class, there can be a first place and second place group winner and the names of the winners are posted in the hall or foyer of

the school and/or printed in a school newsletter. Providing such recognition is particularly important (Palmer, 2001; Porro, 1996).

Conflict Resolution

Across the last decade, *conflict resolution* has been incorporated in a number of social studies classrooms. Its purpose is to involve children in learning experiences where they resolve conflicts in a civil and reasoning manner. As such, it makes a very valuable contribution to strengthening the capacity of citizens to handle conflict and controversy. One very useful source of materials is an organization called *Educators for Social Responsibility* (www.esr.org).

Classroom Dialogue. The quality of classroom dialogue is the sine qua non of democratic education. Exchanges of ideas among the members of the class can take many forms (Parker, 2001). Student-citizens can and should be asked to comment on what others say. They can agree, disagree or add information but encouraging an exchange of ideas is the goal. Competent teachers will encourage student–to–student responses and not limit the exchange of ideas to teacher–student interaction. To be able to express ideas effectively and persuasively in groups and public settings strengthens the capacity of citizens to be effective and to express themselves in the public arena.

Consequently, conflict resolution must not be ignored in elementary classrooms where children can be socialized to resolving conflicts in civil and reasoning ways (Kreidler, 1984).

Young children will often turn to the teacher as the legitimate authority in the classroom to resolve interpersonal matters. At such junctures, the teachers have a choice in the responses they make. For teachers advancing democratic education, these situations represent an especially important choice. Obviously, teachers can directly assume their classroom authority and direct children to comply with directive statements such as "Return that book, it belongs to Sam" or "Sally, it was not your turn. Therefore you cannot go out for recess." On the other hand, teachers can turn the matter into a question for the children to resolve. Here, the teacher may ask: "What happened?" of each child involved to gain insight into various perspectives. What would be fair in this situation is encouraging the children to identify possible alternatives and think about the possible consequences of these alternatives. In short, the teacher provides an opportunity for problem solving for young people rather than solving the problem for them. In this way, young citizens gain experience in addressing their own issues rather than depending on authority. These situations provide an opportunity to reason together, to be independent and to gain confidence in resolving issues with civility (Johnson & Johnson, 1996). All of these outcomes are consistent with the values at the base of an Issues-Centered Decision Making Curriculum.

The learning experiences described above are consistent with democratic principles and in particular, they provide a foundation for the subsequent development of countersocialization in later grades. The reader will note that the lecture–textbook–recitation mode is avoided in almost all of the learning experiences suggested because textbooks tend to provide a single interpretation of the events that are discussed. Such classroom activity usually contradicts the principles of democratic education by offering only one perspective and emphasizing learning as memorization rather than facilitating deeper understanding. Furthermore, the content in textbooks fails to engage the minds of student-citizens in any meaningful, active way.

As I write this chapter, I am also gravely aware that the current emphasis on mandatory testing does force the teachers to do what they can to increase the probabilities that their class will do well on these tests. While the testing tradition violates the creativity of teachers and reduces the time they need to respond to student interests or hold sustained classroom dialogue, I hope that dedicated teachers will find opportunities to incorporate some of the activities and the curriculum presented here.

Certainly, the classroom practices described above are not exhaustive of all possibilities. However, teachers can use these suggestions to engage the minds of young children and deepen their views regarding social studies content and values such as diversity, freedom, equity and equality. These practices involve children in higher level thinking, in examining values and in decision making.

Secondary Level: Middle and High Schools

Increasingly, with the onset of adolescence, practices that support democratic socialization need to be replaced with learning experiences that support counter-socialization. As the intellectual capacities of adolescents expand, the teacher's challenge is to develop these abilities to the fullest. Increasingly, the goal of counter-socialization needs to guide the selection of content (both subject matter and intellectual processes) and methods appropriate for a more full-blown democratic curriculum.

Content for Middle and High School

The central and critical goals of counter-socialization are to develop the ability of student-citizens to reason and to expand their capacity to engage in constructive social criticism, both of which are essential for strong democratic citizens. Consequently, the content and methods that are used must be tightly tied to that goal. Citizens are continually exposed to current affairs from television, newspapers, magazines and books, from politicians, fellow workers, friends and neighbors. They need to be able to process this information carefully for its veracity and with recognition that some of the information they receive may be self-serving in behalf of the source that advances it. In democratic societies, the quality of citizen participation is heightened in direct proportion to the number of reasoning, well informed citizens who can fully exercise their intellectual capacities and express themselves effectively both orally and in writing. It is here that the social studies curriculum can make its most meaningful contribution to the fabric of democratic life.

Two kinds of subject matter serve the purpose of counter-socialization. The first and most important subject matter in terms of democratic educa-tion is the study of significant controversial issues of the past, present, and/ or future. At each grade level, student-citizens need to study at least one such issue in-depth to the extent that their abilities allow. At the upper ele-mentary grades teachers can do much more than is currently done. The study of such issues most closely approximates the work of the democratic citizen. By studying such matters as poverty in our community, reducing crime in out city, reducing pollution, examining hunger and poverty on a worldwide basis or the ongoing threat of terrorism, student-citizens encounter the same challenges as those faced by adult citizens as they search for valid information, try to appraise its worth and try to decide what measures need to be taken and why. Studying controversial social issues entails an awareness of human diversity, of wide ranging and compet-ing opinions as well as of the dramatic changes that are continuous in our society and across the planet. Furthermore, an Issues-Centered Decision Making Curriculum, if treated with intellectual vigor, combines the need for reliable information, intellectual prowess and an examination of values. No other kind of subject matter has the same potential as complex and controversial issues for synthesizing these important dimensions of learn-ing and at the same time, contributing to the quality of citizen participa-tion (Ochoa-Becker, 1999).

A second source of subject matter is found in conventional topics and disciplines that are commonplace in the secondary social studies curricu-lum. These topics and disciplines include the study of history (U.S. and world) and government as well as some of the social sciences (sociology, economics, anthropology and geography). The curriculum advocated here would place controversial public issues at the center of social studies curric-ulum as an organizing concept. However, developing the intellectual abili-ties required of democracy's citizens can be done with conventional topics as well. It is acceptable for such conventional topics as the Roman Empire, the Age of Exploration, the Industrial Revolution, the institution of slavery or the Populist Movement to serve as a focus for intellectual and active involvement by student-citizens. When treated as questions to pursue, these questions provide an opportunity to identify relevant values, identify alternative perspectives, their consequences and make justifiable decisions. Classroom treatment of these topics must depart dramatically from conventional practice. In order to foster reasoning, the issues associated with these conventional topics must not be presented to young citizens as a body of fixed information. Rather, thoughtfully conceptualized, the study of these issues can serve center on a number of thought-provoking questions that can guide the teaching and learning process as well as the use of alternative perspectives and sources on these topics. Examples might be:

- What were the strengths and weaknesses of the Roman Empire? What might have been done to prevent Rome's fall? or
- Did the Populist Movement make a contribution to democracy? Why do you think so?

These are questions that require a subset of many questions to be well answered. Challenging student-citizens to create those questions (and answer them) is a demanding task that can lead young people to do some serious thinking.

Questions

Questioning is a very important process that teachers should master and be ready to use at any time, particularly when a class member shares an experience or an idea worth class examination. The five kinds of questions discussed below are ones that teachers need to apply to whatever subject matter they use.

Definitional Questions.   The first type of question calls for definition. For example, "What is slavery?" However, definitions provided by textbooks or the dictionary may be helpful but not sufficient, when the goal is to understand slavery as widely and deeply as possible. "We know that slavery exists when a person is legally owned by another in order to have the advantage of that person's labor without paying wages." While such a statement provides preliminary insight into slavery, it does not suggest the wide range of practices that slaves experienced at the hands of slave owners. Neither does it speak to the forms of slavery that are not supported by law or where laws are not enforced and citizens have no choice about their treatment or the harsh working conditions to which they are subjected. In order to probe student thinking, teachers can provide a case study example of coal mineworkers who are poorly paid and are forced to tolerate working conditions that are detrimental to their health. The class can be encouraged to think about whether this situation would fit as an example of slavery. Such case studies introduce shades of gray regarding the meaning of terms such as slavery and facilitate a broader view of this significant concept.

Evidential Questions.   Such questions require students to produce evidence to support their answers with evidence. In a unit on slavery, such questions as the following may be included:

- Why did slavery take root in the U.S.? How do we know this explanation is true?
- Where in the world did slavery originate? Where has slavery existed? How do we know?
- Slavery has existed in many places at many times. How are the conditions of slavery different? How are they alike? How do we know this to be true?
- What impact has slavery had on our society? What evidence do you have to support your answer?
- Has the Thirteenth Amendment totally solved the problem of slavery? What evidence can you find to support your answer?
- Is slavery totally abolished today? How can you find out? What evidence can you find to support your answer.

The manner in which student-citizens find answers (library research and Internet searches) to such questions is central to the process of countersocialization because it engages them in a demanding intellectual exercise where they are challenged to not only find answers but to identify evidence that supports their answer. This task involves logic and inference and also contrasts sharply requiring the memorization of answers from the teacher's lecture or the textbook. Very important abilities can be expanded as young citizens inquire into issues of importance to them, to their community, their country and to the world around them. Assessing the quality of evidence that supports their answers, finding documentation, appraising the strength of documentation, applying logic, raising political, legal and moral issues are all processes that contribute to the intellectual strength that young people will bring to their role as citizens.

Student-citizens need to consider a wide range of resources and persistently ask themselves whether the source provides sufficient evidence to support the answers given. This critical questioning attitude is at the heart of counter-socialization and is inherent to democratic education. The task of the teacher is to involve the class actively in a search for dependable evidence. Furthermore, as student-citizens present their answers, they need to defend their claims. "Why do you think your answer is right? Do other experts agree? What is the strongest evidence you have? Why do you think so? What is the weakest? Why?" These follow-up questions press student-citizens to evaluate evidence carefully and to recognize the tentativeness of the knowledge they have gathered.

Policy Questions.   Another type of question asks student-citizens to make decisions and to support their recommendation to ameliorate a particular controversial issue. For example, a teacher engaged in a unit on slavery might ask, "If you were Abraham Lincoln (or William Lloyd Garrison) what would you have done about slavery?" While this is a speculative question, it is a policy question that shaped both the history and future course of this nation at the time of the Civil War. Student-citizens are asked to take a stand and most importantly, to justify that stand with reasons and evidence in the face of alternative positions. In the process, they can experience the conflicts and competing views often evident in democratic life. In brief, it is here that their minds are being prepared for their role as a citizen of a democracy.

Value Questions.   While policy questions encourage involvement by student-citizens in an issue by taking a personal stand on the matter at hand, such questions also call for consideration of the ethical and moral dimensions of the issue. In this regard, value questions are needed. For example, the teacher might stimulate thinking by stating, "One result of the Civil War was that slavery was no longer legal in either the North or the South. Does the abolition of slavery justify the use of war and violence? Why or Why not?" Such questioning challenges the class to weigh the merits of freedom against the atrocity of war and loss of life and to appraise the consequences of maintaining or eliminating the institution of slavery. This task can trigger thinking about whether violence is ever justified and whether it is right to tolerate dehumanizing practices for any group of human beings. A follow-up question might be: "Does your answer change when you consider that Lincoln was trying to save the union?"

Speculative Questions.   The final type of question calls for creativity and imagination applied to the information, ideas and intellectual abilities young citizens have experienced. For example, a teacher may ask, "If slavery had never existed, how might race relations in the United States have been different?" This speculative question encourages broad and novel thinking about whether slavery set the stage for conflicts between races or whether these conflicts would have occurred anyway. Other speculative questions are "What would have happened if the South had won the war?" "Would the absence of slavery have minimized the chances of the Civil War, a war the South fought from a state rights perspective and that many Northerners viewed as a war to save the Union?" Certainly, the residual impact of slavery on the period since the Civil War needs to be considered. Such questions encourage a long-term view of history. What happens in one century can and does affect the next. Most importantly, such questions expand the intellect and engage the learner in a significant exercise that explores historic causes and effects across time. Speculative questions can help students make predictions about current policies and actions which were poignantly challenged by the recent war on terrorism, the devastation of human life in Rwanda and the persistent conflict in the Middle East.. Too often, social studies classes mire down in the past. However, citizens need to be able to think productively about the present and the future, about what is likely to happen and what they see as a preferred state of affairs.

If the issues raised by the kinds of questions identified above serve as grist for the study of conventional classroom topics, so that student-citizens can examine competing accounts of events, evaluate contradictory evidence and reach their own defensible conclusions, they will be learning how to function as democratic citizens. At every turn, student-citizens should be involved in the process of examining evidence that supports claims that are presented as true (truth claims) whether in the media, in textbooks or in personal conversations. Any of the conventional topics used in social studies classes can be subjected to these questions.

By calling for subject matter whose basis is found both in controversial social issues as well as in conventional topics and the social science disciplines, combined with learning experiences that are thought-provoking, rigorous and honest, this curriculum emphasizes that the content necessary for counter-socialization must approximate as closely as possible the issues that citizens face. This view of social studies programs is a far cry from the dry and descriptive narratives that student-citizens are often asked to recall and recite in social studies classrooms or memorize to pass tests. Moreover, this approach to social studies presents student-citizens with knowledge as it is, tentative, perplexed by questions, uncertain and subject to continuing reinterpretation.

Method for Middle and High School

As student-citizens mature intellectually, the functions of the teacher change. Certainly, during the middle and high school grades, teachers need to continue to serve as models of reasoning and participating citizens. However, it is very important that teachers behave in ways that recognize that their audience is also capable of independent thought. Unlike the unquestioning acceptance of young children, more mature adolescents have the capacity to question and challenge both the teacher and the textbook and these capabilities need to be expanded and encouraged. The education of democratic citizens requires that the critical responses of student-citizens be accepted and nourished. Therefore, teachers must not become defensive or angry when young citizens confront them with questions and competing points of view. Rather, such responses should be celebrated. They need to be probed, expanded and seen as opportunities to develop the reasoning power of future democratic citizens. At these ages, the teacher guides the counter-socialization process by stimulating independent, higher level thinking among young adults. The following approaches deserve serious attention as ways of enhancing counter-socialization with young people at these grade levels.

From Personal to Public Issues

In the social studies, a number of educators have taken positions that limit the controversial issues aspect of this curriculum to public, not personal issues. Arguments have been made that giving attention to the more immediate but more transient issues that are personal and important to young citizens, may be trivial and waste class time on the unimportant (Fred Newmann, 1991; Oliver & Shaver, 1966; and James Shaver, 1992). At the same time, it is also clear that despite the support of many educators from John Dewey (1933) forward to address issues that are part of the lived experience of students, there is virtually no evidence that such practices characterize social studies classrooms. In Dewey's words, "Education, in order to accomplish its ends both for the individual learner and for society must be based upon experience—which is always the actual life–experience of some individual" (p. 113). John Goodlad's research (1984) has certainly underscored the omnipresence of the lecture–memorize–recite mode where the teacher and the textbook determine the content. Some rethinking of the relationship between the use of public, private or personal issues is needed if any progress along these lines is to be made. Sophie Haroutunian-Gordon (1991) of Northwestern University has made an interesting contribution to this issue. Though an English educator (not social studies), she demonstrated that in a small class of inner city, African American adolescents, she was able to elicit a thoughtful discussion of Shakespeare's Romeo and Juliet by starting with matters that these young people actually face in their ongoing personal relationships. From that discussion she was able to lead them to consider the more persistent human concerns of love that is unfulfilled that makes this work of Shakespeare a classic. By drawing on the personal experiences of the class and listening carefully to what they said, she was able to expand their perspective on their personal matters and she also facilitated their comprehension of the connection between their lives and the statement made by time-honored literature. Social studies educators need to give more thought to ways of connecting personal to public issues. Otherwise, we are missing a rich opportunity to engage young citizens in the issues that challenge the quality of their personal and public lives.

While democratic citizenship education aims at encouraging citizens to be concerned with the common good, educators in this field need to realize that self-interest and the personal issues that young citizens face in an immediate way need to be addressed and used as jumping-off points to wider issues that impact the welfare of the entire society or the planet. In this wider context, student-citizens may need to consider the welfare of the entire society or the welfare of the peoples across the globe. For example, it would not be surprising to find that young citizens who are seventeen or eighteen (typically seniors in high school) might have some concern when an international crisis occurs that the draft might be reinstituted and they are likely to see themselves as likely candidates. Initially, the teacher in this case should be responsive to this personal concern. It is one that is authentic and one that can be linked to broader and deeper public issues. To begin with this teacher might involve the class in gathering information about the draft and the conditions that led to the institution of the draft at the time of the Vietnam War, the Korean War, World War I and World War II. A history of the draft would be especially useful here. Class members could talk to veterans who entered the armed services as draftees and those who volunteered. In addition, they could communicate with their Congressional representatives and Senators about the possibility of the draft. Such investigation would put them in a better position to estimate the chances of the draft applying to them and they would better understand what is involved in military service. A broader issue here is whether, in the interest of public security, a draft is needed. In this case, student-citizens can probe the extent to which a draft is needed and how large an armed force is involved. Furthermore, questions like the following may be useful. What role will draftees be likely to play? How likely is hand-to-hand combat? What opportunities does military service provide? What are the disadvantages? While teachers should have such questions in mind, they should also elicit questions from student-citizens. The challenge here is not to ignore what is important to members of the class, but to have an eye on widening the issue or identifying a similar issue to one of public policy. In this case, a broader question might concern national security. What does the United States need to do to provide for the security of our people so that we are as safe as possible? Why you think so?

Since stimulating the intellect of student-citizens is the overarching consideration during these adolescent years, the use of probing questions requires further discussion. Probing questions are open-ended. They do not have pre-determined answers. However, some answers are better than others if the student-citizen has evidence and/or reasons to support the answer. Neither do their answers lie in the teacher's lecture or in the textbook. Instead, probing questions are ones that trigger the reasoning process and student-citizens are called upon to organize the information at hand in order to arrive at their own independent, defensible answers. At this level, student-citizens are likely to generate answers that are more complex and teachers need to be more demanding than at the elementary level. The following kinds of questions, presented earlier in this chapter, need to be constantly evident:

- What does this mean? (*Definitional Question*)
- Why is that so? (*Evidential Question*)
- What if that had not happened? What might be the result? (*Speculative Question*)
- What should the government do? (*Policy Question*)
- How do you know that what you say is accurate? (*Evidential Question*)
- What reasons can you give for your belief? (*Evidential Question*)

For classroom purposes, examples applied to specific subject matter follow:

- Today we have the technology to minimize most of our problems with air pollution. Since the problem is one that can be improved, why do you think this has not happened?
- What if our government had no system of checks and balances? What do you think would happen to the way our country is governed?
- Our textbook says that the settlement of the West owed more to the endless toil of women than to those who fought Native People, fur traders or prospectors. What does this statement mean to you? Do you think it is true? Can you find evidence to support it?
- Terry, you have just said that you believe that every citizen should be allowed to own a handgun. For tomorrow, would all of you try to think about this proposal?

For every topic or issue selected for classroom study at the secondary level, teachers need to identify similar questions to stimulate thinking, guide classroom dialogue and serve as the basis of classroom projects. Teachers also need to ask student-citizens to contribute questions since asking penetrating and significant questions is an important characteristic of the democratic citizen. All of these questions have a tentative, uncertain nature. The answers to such questions cannot be determined beyond a shadow of a doubt. Likewise, citizens can never be totally sure that their positions are completely correct. They may not have voted for the right candidate or supported the right cause. A fair dose of humility and openness needs to flavor the views we hold as citizens. Those views may change on the basis of new findings and developments and reasonable people must be open to such possibilities. The recognition that ambiguity and uncertainty accompanies much of what citizens know and do is basic to minimizing the chances that student-citizens will develop dogmatic and authoritarian views. The best that any of us can do, teachers, student-citizens and adult citizens alike, is to reach conclusions and make decisions in a reasonable and informed way, knowing that all the facts are not in and that in the last analysis we might be wrong. Citizens who appreciate the tentativeness of knowledge and opinions are in a stronger position to participate responsibly in negotiating the citizen consensus required in a democracy.

Discrepant Points of View

Confronting student-citizens with discrepant points of view serves as a very important way that teachers can involve adolescents intellectually. If only one point of view is acceptable in a class discussion, there is no basis for probing or challenging ideas. Furthermore, if competing arguments are not presented, the initial point of view will prevail without thoughtful examination. More importantly, for democratic education, the opportunity for dialogue about controversial issues will be lost. The examples below illustrate the use of discrepant or competing ideas that influence the interpretation of historical events and serve as the grist of serious historical scholarship. Some people say the past never changes, but educators need to remember that honest scholarship means that interpretations are always tentative and subject to revision. In this way our view of the past does change.

The following example addresses the efforts of Commodore Perry and the "opening of Japan." The first example is drawn from a U.S. textbook. The second is translated from a Japanese history textbook.[2]

U.S. Version

Commodore Perry's trip to Japan was more successful than he had expected. He sailed into Tokyo Bay with four black warships on July 8,1853. It was the first time the Japanese had seen steamships which could sail despite the wind and current. Perry, aware that the Japanese might resent outside pressure, negotiated with the Japanese calmly and effectively. After he had given them gifts and asked them to trade with the U.S., he left. He realized they would need time to think about this request.

Perry returned with seven warships to find out the Japanese reply in February, 1854. With Japanese representatives in attendance, there was a feast and an exchange of presents aboard Perry's ships. The Japanese were delighted with the miniature telegraph and toy steam locomotive shown to them. According to the trip's official recorder, exchanging presents was very successful.

It was now sunset and the Japanese prepared to depart with quite as much wine in them as they could well bear. The jovial Matsusaki threw his arms around the Commodore's neck crushing...a pair of new epaulettes and repeating, in Japanese...these words, as interpreted in English: "Nippon and America, all the same heart." On March 31, 1854 they signed the treaty which opened Japan to limited trade, with the U.S.

Japanese Version

In June 1853, the American emissary, Perry appeared at Uraga with four warships. Perry brought a letter of friendship from the American President which sought the opening of Japan.

In January 1854, Perry came once again, this time with seven warships and he forcefully sought the acceptance of his demands. The feudal government was overwhelmed by the might of the Black Ships, and in March concluded the *Japan–U.S. Treaty of Friendship* (*the Kanagawa Treaty*) at Kanagawa. This treaty did not approve the opening of trade relations, but it did agree to the provision of supplies to American ships and assistance to shipwrecked vessels. It also promised to open the two harbors of Shimoda and Hakodate for those purposes. In addition, it gave unilateral most favored nation status to America. Thereafter, the feudal government concluded similar friendship treaties with England, Russia, and Holland.

The United States version is deceptively simple. It creates the impression that in less than a year Commodore Perry made two trips to Japan and was able to persuade the Japanese to sign a treaty in which they agreed to trade with the United States. The reader can be left with the impression that the Japanese were quite happy with these circumstances. On the other hand, the Japanese version suggests that Perry gained Japanese compliance by a display of power (seven black ships) and the use of force. Furthermore, the passage states that the treaty *did not* approve the opening of trade and is a blatant contradiction in the two accounts.

Which account is more accurate? Did Perry use force or didn't he? Did the treaty explicitly open trade between these two nations? Were the Japanese pleased with the treaty or not? Why do the two textbook accounts differ? How can we find out? These competing passages accompanied by probing questions raise doubt, challenge the intellect and confront the learner with alternative perspectives. Such questions can serve as the basis for serious classroom study, student inquiry projects and vigorous classroom dialogue.

Classroom Dialogue

Creating a classroom environment where student-citizens are challenged to probe, question, be skeptical of knowledge claims and where they can express their views on both controversial issues and learn how to support their views with values, reasons and evidence combine to be the most important and the most demanding tasks in implementing an Issues-Centered Decision Making Curriculum for both teachers and young citizens. Classroom dialogue is critical to counter-socialization. It must not be reduced to bull sessions where mindless points of view are expressed. Rather, strong classroom dialogue should have the following features:

1. An issue has been identified in concert with class members. To the greatest extent possible, these issues should represent expressed student interests. The identification of an issue may require negotiation with class members who may be of different minds about what issue they would like to pursue.

2. Once the main issue is identified, student-citizens and the teacher can participate in identifying the set of questions that would lead to a broader understanding of the issue and facilitate the examination of the worth of alternative points of view and their consequences in order to reach conclusions and make decisions that can be substantiated and justified.

3. The pursuit of understanding can take the form of library work, interviews with experts and relevant others, and searching the Internet. It is here that student-citizens need to be encouraged to be skeptical about factual claims, to evaluate evidence that supports them and to come to their own independent version of the truth. Working in cooperative learning groups (discussed earlier) can be particularly helpful here.

4. To create an environment where all participants feel safe to share their views without fear of embarrassment or ridicule is fundamental. At the same time both student-citizens and teachers need to advance ideas as thoughtfully and responsibly as they can. Class time is a precious commodity and warrants thoughtfulness on the part of all participants.

There are several patterns of classroom dialogue. The most common is an exchange between teacher and student. In this pattern, the teacher asks a question and the student answers it. Sometimes, the teacher will probe further by asking another question and the exchange may go on for a few minutes. How the remainder of the class responds to this interchange that involves one student and the teacher is very important to assess. Such exchanges can range in value from being interesting to the rest of the class and perhaps informative, to promoting boredom because they are not involved. The teacher can broaden such exchanges by directing a question at the class as a whole. "What do the rest of you think about what Pat and I said? Can you find any weaknesses in our thinking? Here, the teacher makes it clear that the teacher's views are subject to challenge as well.

Still another pattern is student to student dialogue. As soon as one student completes a comment, the teacher asks another student to respond. To the extent possible the teacher requests reactions from the class with a view of creating a setting where students respond and probe each other's reasoning. Recently, Maxine Greene thoughtfully reminded us that "teaching is a dialogue with class members, but the dialogue is slowly disappearing" (Greene, 2001). The important point that makes her definition of teaching, that affirms an Issues-Centered Decision Making Curriculum, is that it centers on an *exchange of ideas between students and teachers*. Exchange is the operative word in her definition and it is this term that entails interactive communication, not lectures and not preachments that represent one-way communication.

IMPLICATIONS OF SOCIALIZATION
AND COUNTER-SOCIALIZATION

Countersocialization represents a major task for schools and teachers. Moreover, educating citizens for a democracy presents a challenging and persistent dilemma. On one hand, democracy supports the value of freedom and freedom, in turn, allows and encourages diversity: politically, culturally and intellectually. Acceptance of diversity raises issues of equality and equity. On the other hand, all societies, including democracies, need some degree of conformity and consensus among their citizens. Political and social stability so require (Butts, 1989). Fulfilling the goals of freedom and diversity often compete. Freedom is often at odds with pressures for social and political conformity as illustrated by the lived experiences of peoples who have been and are subject to continuing oppression. The democratic experiment is indeed challenged to accommodate a wide range of views and practices evident among its culturally diverse citizens. It is these tensions that set the context for the continuing debate about how citizens for a democracy should be educated.

It is not surprising that stability and conformity compete with freedom and diversity in our schools and face the same dilemma as they do in the society at large. How can educators encourage divergent and independent thinking and initiative while at the same time managing a learning environment that is free from disruptive behavior and apply rules that restrict initiative and independence?

Learning requires self-discipline, opportunities to try and fail and an environment that stimulates intellectual capacities essential for quality participation in a democratic society. How can educators achieve a productive balance between a productive classroom environment and a classroom that is open to all ideas without unduly restricting the behavior of student-citizens in ways that violate democratic principles and practices? The teacher is a more experienced and more learned leader, but not the source of all knowledge and wisdom. Importantly, teachers are also learners who should display an enthusiasm for knowledge as they guide young citizens and participate in the search for knowledge that can be applied to controversial issues along with their classes. In brief, teachers need to respect the adage that "all of us is smarter than any one of us."

Can democracy be preserved and strengthened while educators make accommodation to pressure for conformity—pressures that often do not respect human differences and pressures that stifle the values of freedom and equality? These pressures may reflect the will of the people, but we must recognize that the will of the people is not always responsive to democratic values. A strong example brings an incident with first grade children to mind.[3] The mother of a white child called the teacher to ask her to break up the friendship that had developed between her daughter and an African American child. The teacher refused to comply. She told the parent that one of her goals was to have children accept each other and accept differences. The mother was livid but the teacher held her ground. Interestingly, at the end of the school year this mother called again. This time she thanked the teacher for the broadening experience she had afforded her daughter. Since the teacher stood firm in her respect for human differences, eventually the mother appreciated the stance that the teacher had taken and broadened her view. Such a happy conclusion is not common. However, education and schooling remain our most promising efforts to help citizens, both young and adult to appreciate and respect human differences. This task is fundamental to every public school in this nation.

Ongoing practices in this nation's schools favor values of consensus and conformity. When school personnel establish rules and punishments without involving students, they contradict democracy's values. By insisting, all too often, on compliance, without providing reasons or recourse, educators become models of authoritarian rather than democratic practices that not only contradict democracy's values, but also present an oppressive model of resolving conflicts. The presence of dress codes, rules about hair length and locker searches without permission of the occupant, illustrate the point. Such practices, sometimes deemed necessary, that shape the nature of school climate, sometimes called the hidden curriculum, are inappropriate in schools preparing democracy's citizens. With regular experiences of this sort, student-citizens can easily conclude that if such authoritarian behavior is acceptable for adults, it is acceptable for them as well. Schools where professionals act in oppressive and arbitrary ways are failing to fulfill their mission to prepare the next generation for participating in democratic self-governance.

Unlike totalitarian societies, democracies are limited in the methods they can use to influence the views of their citizens. To the greatest extent possible, schools need to avoid manipulation and indoctrination. In an absolute sense this is impossible for schools to do. However, they can expand their practices in ways that are more open and more respectful of the freedom young citizens should have.

BUILDING A RATIONALE FOR A SIGNIFICANT ISSUE

Regarding both the formal and informal curriculum, educators also have a responsibility to develop a rationale for what they do. This rationale should identify the reasons why the teacher is involving young citizens in the curriculum she or he has planned. The document should be available to parents, the school board and the school administration. Knowingly or not, all of us who teach and try to shape young minds, base the selection of content, including intellectual processes, on values and those values should be stated explicitly in a rationale statement. However, if the school administration and its teachers confine curriculum content to that provided by textbooks, then they have accepted the values of publishers and textbook authors as authoritative and teachers and school administrator have defaulted on their professional responsibility as they allow others to make curriculum decisions for them. Allowing textbooks to control the content of the curriculum reduces teachers from professionals to technicians who have lost their professional minds and have reduced their class members to mindless learners who are limited to memorizing one version of historical events or any social phenomena. The Issues-Centered Decision Making presented here encourages the involvement of student-citizens in the selection of content to the greatest extent possible. It also emphasizes the tentativeness of knowledge and the need to young citizens to understand that historical events may be subject to multiple interpretations.

Mindless use of textbooks can and does have consequences. We must remember that publishers of textbooks are necessarily driven by the bottom line of profit. Their desire for public approval resides in the selection of content that in their view would please the public at large. The following illustration serves as an example: the amount of space given to peace in textbooks either in the form of peace organizations or diplomatic efforts is overwhelmed by the amount of space given to wars. In addition, the concept of social class seldom appears in textbooks despite the fact that in this and any other society social class is a significant force that influences the kind of life people lead (Anyon, 1980).

Decisions about the selection of content for the curriculum are also based on the perspectives of administrators and teachers. These perspectives reflect the opinions these professional educators have of the values held by the school's community. Too often, these perspectives result in the avoidance of topics or issues that are perceived as too controversial or too sensitive. Sex education, nuclear war and race relations illustrate issues that are often sidelined because the community is deemed too conservative. Furthermore, not involving young people in a study of matters that are locally controversial sends a strong message. Hot topics are not talked about. Such issues may involve AIDS, abortion or saving the environment versus permitting construction and development to expand. Yet, such issues impact these communities and are too often decided by a few people since most are either not informed or are willing to let others settle these matters for them. Whatever the issue that is avoided, young citizens will act on it with limited and distorted knowledge learned outside the school without the benefit of rational dialogue and without concern for the quality of evidence and reason that can be applied to the issue in the classroom.

Educators need to recognize that the selection of content and methodologies is an ideological issue. The questions that need to be asked are: Which ideology will govern selection decisions? What values are involved? Who benefits from the ideologies? (Cornbleth,1998). Can administrators and teachers be more explicit, more deliberate and more dedicated to a more democratic ideology? Can they enhance their professional integrity by developing educational goals that are more likely to result in more informed and concerned citizens? Such goals will help to define them as professionals, which is always a slippery slope for teachers. They must not allow themselves to become technicians who are guided by others who write and publish textbooks. Dedicated teachers will not let this happen.

When teachers and administrators write rationale statements they must do so in terms of democracy. Their content and methodologies must serve democratic principles. A decision to involve young people in a study of the Civil Rights Movement instead of a chronological and linear study of Theodore Roosevelt's administrations is an ideological choice. It values consideration of a persistent issue that negatively influences marginal people in preference to a descriptive study of historical figures and events. Of course, Teddy Roosevelt's administrations could involve student-citizens in probing alternative views of his terms in office and his interest in conservation and the environment as significant social issues although that is not the usual way that his administrations are treated. This choice between the study of civil rights and Theodore Roosevelt is value–laden. It recognizes that it is impossible to teach everything and therefore wise choices need to be made regarding what is most important for citizens. This choice can be justified in terms of strengthening understanding, analysis and decision making around civil rights which is a persistent issue faced by citizens and one that is critical for a democracy. Teachers and administrators who take pride in their professionalism must give careful thought to what is taught, how it is taught and provide thoughtful reasons for what they do.

We are left with the democratic paradox (Mills, 1995). Given the restrictions on a democratic system to avoid coercive, doctrinaire methods, how can this society or any other achieve sufficient consensus for stability and social order? The response to this thorny dilemma involves two lines of reasoning. The first suggests that we place our faith in democracy's values to be ones that are judged worthy and superior by its citizens, in particular for student-citizens. When its principles and practices are compared to more authoritarian systems, there is little question that democratic values, if practiced extensively, are superior in their concern for human beings. Even this democracy with all of its warts and bumps, reveals itself to be more humane, more respectful of its citizens and more ready to advance diversity and pluralism than many others. Rational minds will find it so. While such a conclusion is reasonable and rational, it is an act of faith: a faith in the ability of the people to govern and to do so reasonably and honestly.

The second line of reasoning lies in the values of communitarianism that cherish our connections with diverse peoples in this society and on this planet (Barber, 1998; Houser and Kuzmic, 2001). Respect for others and the need for a predictably civil society need to intertwine and permeate life in a democracy. A sense of community is a long standing tradition in this country and it still exists though some of that community spirit has been eroded by urbanization and high levels of mobility in terms of where we reside and where we work. Consensus and cooperation need to be actively negotiated among peoples in every generation. As social studies educators we need to promote reasoning and respect for community in all that we do.

In a democracy we must place faith in reason. It is the foundation of our democratic experiment. This faith in reason is consistent with the work done by the founders as they wrote the Declaration of Independence and the Constitution—documents that express a belief in the capacity of ordinary people to elect representatives and participate rationally in the process of self- governance. Furthermore, people who have developed the capacity to reason are more likely to serve as guardians of democratic ideals are and they are the least likely to be manipulated by emotional appeals. In effect, citizenship educators in this society have no logical alternative than to embrace democracy and reason in all that they do. Consensus and unity cannot and should not be imposed. Instead, consensus needs to be negotiated by people who have the capacity and willingness to reason together. Consequently, educators must avoid doctrinaire practices and promote the development of reasoning abilities that represent the very fiber of democratic citizenship

CONCLUSION

The paradox inherent in democratic education has been presented in this chapter (Mills, 1995). The tensions between freedom and security have been laid out. Both content and methods that distinguish the counter-socialization process from conventional socialization practices, such as learning characterized by lecture–memory–recitation and/or the use of textbooks have been presented. While conventional approaches can be replaced by counter–socializing learning experiences, typically they are used in ways to manipulate the values and attitudes of student-citizens to favor a predetermined view. They may be encouraged to accept knowledge claims unquestioningly and their only intellectual task may be to memorize the subject matter in order to pass a test.

Each of the learning experiences presented in this chapter have been based on a deep respect for the minds of young people and their capacity to reason independently. They are also based on teaching experience that affirms that questions expand the intellect of learners. Respect for each individual further requires that the minds of students not be manipulated. Student-citizens need to be explicitly aware of the approaches used by the teacher and the reasons for their use. Teachers need to explain why they use the content and methods that they do. To treat student-citizens as dependent subjects, rather than as thinking individuals deserving of respect, is to violate the premises of democracy and democratic education. Teachers must not treat student-citizens as bundles of stimulus–response connections, nor are they mindless robots. Democracy is distinguished by the high value it places on each individual. Democratic education must do no less.

NOTES

1. Paula Fiscus, a third grade teacher at Broadview Elementary School in Bloomington, Indiana created open-ended dilemmas (stories) for her third grade class on a daily basis. These classroom activities were not tied to social studies explicitly but the questions asked by the teacher were consistent with the decision making aspect of the Issues-Centered Decision Making Curriculum.

2. This sample learning experience of discrepant information that contrasted two documents regarding Commodore Perry's encounter with Japan was designed by James M. Becker and Linda Wojtan at the Social Studies Development Center at Indiana University in Bloomington, Indiana. The production of this material was a follow-up to the U.S. Japan Textbook Study, funded by the Japanese–American Friendship Commission.

3. The first grade teacher involved in this situation was Jan Williamson, now an elementary principal in the Monroe County Community School Corporation in Bloomington, Indiana.

CHAPTER 4

THE SOCIAL SCIENCES
AND THE HUMANITIES
IN CITIZENSHIP EDUCATION

Contributions and Limitations

"Art education like aesthetic education can create domains where they are new possibilities of vision and awareness. Art educators can help feed into an expanded life of meaning, as we move through our own moments of being, our own shocks of awareness."

—Maxine Greene, 1978, p. 196.

The goal of social studies to foster a stronger democracy is not complete when either citizenship or social studies education is defined as merely the teaching of the social sciences. Educators, including some social studies educators, sometimes speak of the social sciences and citizenship education as if they are synonyms. They are not. Furthermore, the literature seldom makes clear how very differently the humanities and the social sciences relate to citizenship education and how the two might relate usefully to each other (Houser, 2005). In the absence of clarity on this point, the humanities are often seen as a supplementary source of knowledge, a role for which they are not well suited. Or, they may be construed to be an alternative approach to citizenship education based on emotional or ideological persuasion rather than the presentation of well-grounded facts derived from the social sciences. When the humanities are used for purposes of emotional or ideological persuasion in citizenship education, they

Democratic Education for Social Studies, pages 101–119
Copyright © 2007 by Information Age Publishing
All rights of reproduction in any form reserved.

serve a doctrinaire purpose, which is entirely inappropriate for a democratic curriculum. To be most effective, citizenship education should draw on both the social sciences and the humanities as equal partners. Subject matter can also be drawn from the personal experiences of young citizens or the teacher or from other fields of study where a particular specialization is useful for understanding the issue being studied. Importantly, the humanities and the social sciences serve as a *means* for understanding. They are not ends or goals for a democratic curriculum. The overarching goal of this curriculum, as presented in the first three chapters, is effective democratic citizenship. However, the humanities and the social sciences are symbiotic partners, the first focused on values, feelings, insights and perspectives; the second focused on empirical findings, making equally important contributions to the understandings and decisions that citizens must learn to make in an intelligent and responsible way (Atkinson, 1937). To illustrate, we can study about major events throughout history by reading historical accounts that represent serious historical scholarship such as those of Carter G. Woodson, Barbara Ward, Bruce Catton or Richard Hofstader. However, we gain a completely different perspective about the Vietnam War if we read Neil Sheehan (1988) *A Bright and Shining Lie* that reveals new data and new insights on the war. Citizenship educators do not have to choose between these diverse sources of knowledge and insights; they can and should use both to enlarge the perspective of student-citizens regarding the issues that they study. (Arnold, 1967; Selwyn, 1995).

Moreover, since this curriculum is responsive to diversity at home as well as in the global community, the humanities play a very special role in deepening the understanding of all citizens. Creating an understanding of the issues regarding diversity and pluralism that are evident in the United States as well as across the planet is simply incomplete if student-citizens are limited to only the historic and geographic facts that relate to those issues. They are even more restricted if their readings are textbook-dependent. However, if they also read novels by such authors as Maya Angelou, Alice Walker, Harriet Beecher Stowe, James Baldwin, Lillian Hellman, Paula Gunn Allen, Toni Morrison and Nadine Gordimer, their sensitivities are much more likely to be touched and their awareness and recognition for diversity, its interesting and attractive features as well as its substantial challenges, are likely to heighten. The same is the case for indigenous music that represents and communicates culture in very poignant ways (Cheselka, 1981). Art of many kinds (sculpture, photography, graphics, as well as oil and watercolor paintings) is still another medium that can add depth and meaning to understanding of other cultures. The powerful works of Diego Rivera that depict the plight of laborers in Mexico, the tragic portrayal of the plight of slaves in the United States by Thomas Hart Benton, the sculptures of Alexander Calder, the delicate art works seen in

Japanese scrolls as well as paintings—all of these and so many more tell stories that provide insights much more powerful than words. We live in a global age in which our contacts with other peoples, cultures and nations keep increasing in frequency, volume and importance. Americans take jobs in other nations, we do business abroad, we buy many foreign products, we sell goods to other nations, we even export jobs elsewhere to places where wages are cheaper (a very controversial practice), we join groups with international connections and we travel and connect (email) to many more places than U.S. citizens have usually traveled to before. Even in the United States, the intensification of contact with the diverse cultures that characterize our own society is expanding rapidly. Not knowing about different and similar cultural beliefs and practices in cultures, different from their own, handicaps the personal futures of our young citizens as well the future quality of this democracy (Michener, 1991).

THE LIMITATIONS OF THE SOCIAL SCIENCES IN CITIZENSHIP EDUCATION

Since the goal of this curriculum is to heighten the quality of participation by democratic citizens, social studies is not adequately defined as merely the teaching of the social sciences and history. This definition is inadequate for a number of reasons. To begin with, the experiences and issues encountered by citizens are far broader and more complicated than the facts and generalizations that have been accumulated by one or even all of the social sciences taken together. This lack of correspondences between the holistic life experience of citizens and the specialized perspective of social scientists is exacerbated when each social science is studied separately, as they often are in secondary schools. Citizenship educators need to keep in mind that significant, social and controversial, issues preceded the existence of the social sciences across time. From the beginning of recorded time, human beings have been besieged by issues that threatened the quality of their lives they tried to solve:[1]

> Contemporary social studies owes at least as much allegiance to social issues for its founding as it does to the discipline of history. . . . Social studies, including ideas about its nature and purpose, emerged as humans tried to understand and cope with their problems (Nelson, 1996, pp. 14–15).

Human beings have been confronted continually across time with such problems and issues as insufficient food, inadequate shelter and matters of survival. Such issues and many others continue to confront citizens, albeit in different ways and democratic citizens along with their governments must continue to address them.

The social sciences, either separately or collectively, provide a valuable but incomplete perspective on any given controversial topic or issue. They are, in essence, the means by which scholars organize knowledge. While their scholarship may yield significant and interesting findings, they are not able to prescribe the resolution of public controversial issues. Resolution of controversial issues calls for wisdom and is necessarily based on values. Social scientists cannot lay claim to such qualities as wisdom any more than the ordinary citizen can. In this regard, they are equals. For instance, as we increase our geographic understanding of what is possible in designing a complex urban center, we find that the geographer, who may provide very useful information about land use, is ill prepared to deal with conflicts over diverse human preferences that may represent the most significant aspect of the matter. Decisions about needed zoning regulations or the appropriate location for a particular community will apply such information, but policy decisions in a democracy are made with attention to the prevailing values of citizens and policy makers, available evidence, and the concerns and preferences advanced by local citizens. Geography, by itself, is not able to direct these kinds of decisions. The disciplines provide knowledge and it is very important knowledge, but final decisions must involve the values and the preferences of citizens in a democracy and the social sciences *must not* be the only source relied upon for that wisdom.

Certainly, citizenship educators must not disregard scholarly knowledge even though, taken alone it is not sufficient. However, a burning question related to an issue may lie in alternative conceptions of what is aesthetically pleasing that applies to the selection of a sculpture or a piece of public art. Resolution in such cases depends on the aesthetic values held by those involved, their capacity to justify the use of those values and their powers of persuasion that will help them in the realm of political action needed to gain approval for a particular piece of sculpture. Alternatively, the burning question may concern what is considered beautiful and a poet or an artist is likely to have more to contribute to this decision than a geographer does.

The real life of citizens includes significant learning that is influenced by the circumstances of their home, their workplace as well as by their interactions with their friends, their religious affiliations, the media and the world of entertainment. All of these settings contribute to citizens' knowledge and taken together, they influence their attitudes profoundly. Lessons learned outside the context of life experience, as with a curriculum based solely on the social sciences, are likely to be sterile and unconvincing.

The exclusive study of the social sciences provides only a part of the intellectual challenge needed by a citizen in real life. Citizens must somehow integrate all of their knowledge and experience into workable solutions to complex controversial issues. They must develop the broadest possible base of knowledge to guide their decisions and action usually concern issues that cut across disciplinary boundaries, such as the persistent issue of pollution of the earth's environment. Often various experts, because of their narrow and specialized concerns, stand in opposition to each other.

Furthermore, citizenship education in a democracy not only requires a command of complex intellectual abilities (particularly verifying truth claims and decision making) that exceed those required by the study of any of the social sciences, but it also requires that citizens learn to engage in the political process and learn how to influence governmental policies. It is difficult to see how these abilities can be developed exclusively within a separate discipline or even, in all of the social sciences.

The life experiences of student-citizens are the result of significant learning shaped by family, their religious affiliation, their health, gender, race, social class as well as by interactions with peers, adults, the media and the world of entertainment. All of these sources, taken together, shape the nature of their knowledge and attitudes profoundly. To some extent, these forces may contradict democratic values. Certainly, it would be possible to design a citizenship education program built entirely around first hand experiences of youth. In any case, in a democratic citizenship education program, we ignore their lived experiences, at great peril, that may determine whether they are at all motivated to pursue the issues that citizens need to understand. Learning that ignores the life experiences of young people is not likely to be viewed as useful and is likely to be seen as unconvincing, irrelevant and even boring.

Certainly, teachers can draw on the life experiences of young people to design an effective program of citizenship education built solely around the firsthand experiences of youth. The important point here is that we too often ignore or make little effort to learn about the personal experiences of the student-citizens we meet in our classes. However, building on these experiences can be far more motivating and is likely to be studied far more vigorously by young citizens than topics determined by the textbook or the school curriculum guide (Van Sickle, 1996). Too often, we ask our classes to invest their time and energy in answering questions they never asked or ones that have no meaning to them. Adults are also bored if they are exposed to lectures or readings that seem to be remote in time and place. However, if we engage their interest by tapping in to what we know about them, they can learn to be more effective citizens if they study matters that touch their lives. A few examples that may hold appeal for some learners follow.

- What policy should this school have regarding student participation in its governance?

- What policy should apply to students who are found using or selling drugs?
- Do you feel that your right to privacy is ever violated? How? What can you do about it?
- Should the school provide childcare to young mothers who want to graduate?

These issues which are also more personal than broader citizen issues can be used to suggest issues, such as:

- Should citizens be directly involved in the decisions governments make? For example, should all citizens have an opportunity to decide if the United States should go to war or should we leave such decisions to our elected representatives in Congress?
- Given selected case studies of individuals who sell drugs, how should the community respond in terms of policies and practices that are applied to such individuals?
- Are the privacy rights of citizens ever violated? What about identity theft? What can be done about it?
- What kind of drug policy should our school or community have?

Teachers may feel that responding to student concerns reduce the curriculum to the trivial or that so doing restricts choosing broader issues that are more significant. The issues that student-citizens suggest should be seen as starting points that teachers along with the class can build on to have young citizens recognize that their immediate issues can often be tied to broader issues that concern citizens more widely and that these broader issues often involve changes in social practices and policies. The important point here is that personal interests should not be ignored. They hold the potential for strongly engaging young citizens and heightening their interest in public issues.

Using issues that are important to student-citizens permits the application of similar teaching procedures to those that are necessary when broader, teacher-selected controversial issues are studied. Student-citizens can draw on relevant studies from the social sciences and from relevant humanities such as literature, art, film, music, and photography as well as other specialties that apply to their particular interests and concerns. From such sources, in both the social sciences and the humanities, they can gather and evaluate data and perspectives, prioritize and analyze values, as well as make and defend justifiable decisions that address the issue. These decisions must be supported with reasons and/or evidence. Furthermore, if the issue chosen is of special interest to them, student-citizens are more likely to be willing to pursue social action in behalf of their cause. Such learning experiences can be especially powerful for young people and can contribute very significantly to their competence as citizens. Social action will be discussed in Chapter 7.

A DISCIPLINE OF CITIZENSHIP

The idea of a discipline of citizenship is not new. Furthermore, limiting citizenship education to the social sciences provides some, but only some, of the intellectual tools needed for quality decision making on the part of citizens. Often, because of their narrow and specialized concerns, different individuals and different special interest groups will stand in opposition to one another. Moreover, experts from varying specialties and people from different cultural groups view issues quite differently. To illustrate, economists may see the issue of pollution in terms of the trade-off between the cost of pollution abatement and higher prices for commodities or in terms of the effect on job opportunities, while geographers are more concerned with long-term effects on the earth's biosphere and sociologists with how people's way of living is altered or threatened. For citizens to somehow resolve or at least accommodate these conflicts requires an intellectual, disciplined way of thinking, referred to in this curriculum as the discipline of citizenship. This discipline is not only different in kind, but it is broader in scope than the discipline exercised in any one social science.[2] The discipline of the citizen involves making judgments about the many kinds of knowledge and data, from many perspectives or ideologies from a large variety of sources that are relevant to broad, problematic and controversial social issues. It also requires the making judgments about the credibility of conflicting sources of information, including alternative interpretations among the social science disciplines and most importantly, making judgments about the competing values that are at stake in a given situation. The discipline of the citizen also includes making judgments about practical matters such as what possible spinoffs there might be since sometimes surprise effects may result from any course of action as well as how the interests of individuals and groups will be affected and what is politically possible.

Citizenship education in a democracy requires not only the development of complex intellectual abilities but, it also requires that citizens know how to engage in the political process, including how to influence policy and practices in any setting, whether the workplace, social associations or in relationship to government units at any level. Social scientists acting as scholars cannot help us implement these goals. Moreover, they are aware of this limitation. It is beyond comprehension to see how the broad intellectual abilities that are needed by democratic citizens can be developed comprehensively within the separate disciplines, of any or even in all, of the social sciences taken together.

TEACHING THE SOCIAL SCIENCES

When a curriculum is devoted to the social sciences, a distortion usually occurs in the translation of these disciplines into teaching subjects that go by the same name as one of the disciplines—that is; we say that we teach history, sociology or economics and our school courses carry these titles as well. What we teach and how we teach these subjects is vastly different from the manner in which scholars, in these fields, conduct their research. The research goal of a discipline is the discovery, interpretation, reinterpretation if needed, and the ordering of new knowledge. On the other hand, the goal of teaching the subject emphasizes the transmission of information, presumably from those who have knowledge to those who do not. This notion is consistent with the criticism that Paulo Freire (2001) made when he coined the concept "banking education," where knowledge is seen as an entity to be deposited into the empty minds of learners. Any discipline as a scholarly research enterprise is conducted in the hypothetical scientific mode. It is open to new facts, new theories and new interpretations of knowledge. In contrast, school subjects, more often than not, are taught in an expository mode. The goal in such subjects is the possession of the correct answer, the achievement of which usually closes the matter to further scrutiny or investigation. The prevailing scholarly interest in a discipline is with exploring new avenues of thought. By contrast, conventionally taught school subjects are directed to mastering answers and conveying facts based on the authority of experts and authors who write textbooks. Such facts are usually presented as definitive and seemingly absolute. This approach to teaching does little to strengthen the capabilities needed by democratic citizens. Teaching any one of the social sciences is an attempt to encapsulate the knowledge held by that discipline. As a result, the various and alternative research findings of the disciplines are usually distilled into a single version of affairs which may represent the current consensus of scholars, but student-citizens, too often, are not given any explanation of why a particular point of view prevailed over others or they are not even told that alternative views exist. This preferred version is then presented as an accurate one to young citizens. Yet, in the world of scholarship, interpretations of research findings are always tentative and always open to revision on the basis of further and more recent research. Furthermore, seldom do teachers or textbook authors include the idea of the tentativeness of knowledge in their treatment of topics that they present for study. Instead, student-citizens are unknowingly prevented from scrutinizing the subject in authentically scholarly ways. Instead, they are asked to accept the current consensus, memorize it and demonstrate that they have memorized it on a test. Such teaching of the disciplines stands in direct opposition to the curriculum presented here and more importantly, it contradicts the openness and questioning that are essential to democratic education and for democracy's citizens.

Certainly, validity about so-called facts is not so easily achieved. The disciplines upon which these subject areas rest are all hotbeds of controversy. Not only are scholars not of one mind, but there are numerous respectable and scholarly explanations for almost any human phenomenon. Scholarly works are continually being rewritten as new facts and interpretations emerge. For example, even the members of the President's Board of Economic Advisors, all presumably conservative, free enterprise economists are hard pressed to agree on any set of economic causal relationships.

The conclusions of scholars are both open-ended and tentative, awaiting the onslaught of scholarly criticism. In sharp contrast to these scholarly principles, the school subject based on the discipline is usually taught as thought the facts were closed to questioning. Not only is this true in the study of history, but also in geography, sociology, psychology, and economics in schools where such course offerings are available. The subject is usually taught as a compendium of answers to be narrated to young citizens, to be accepted by them on the authority of the textbook as well as the teacher and usually to be returned as fixed answers on quizzes and examinations. Seldom are the assumptions, qualifiers and doubts of scholars shared with classes. Research has demonstrated time and time again that much that passes for fact in textbooks is not a fact at all. Oversimplified and misleading interpretations and, in some cases, overt propaganda are passed off as definitive fact. Such practices are anathema to the very conception of the social sciences as well as to the principles and practices of democratic education.

Far too many educators appear to be insensitive to these distinctions. In fact, many social scientists also ignore these distinctions in their role as teachers and behave as authorities who possess the definitive truth on the subject they teach. Yet, concurrently, as they engage in scholarly work, they behave as scientists, open to the scholarly challenge of their peers. For example, Frederick Paxson, (1936) both historian and teacher, who probably had more right than many scholars in his time to pose as an authority on the history of the U.S. West, freely admitted in his classes that he had more problems in interpreting Western History than he had certainties. In such a spirit, both teaching and research could be treated in a more congruent manner consistent with the canons of scholarship. Such an approach would offer the promise that young people would recognize that there are divergent perspectives on most matters and that few issues have been resolved definitively for all time.

In a similar vein, the drive to "cover all of the material," an unfortunate aspect of too many social studies programs, is also incompatible with the preparation of democratic citizens.

Such practice virtually eliminates the possibility for honest and vigorous scholarship that is absolutely essential to the deliberative and open-ended processes associated with reputable scholarship as well as with authentic democratic education.

There is still another important and unrecognized distinction in the intellectual outcome and the scholarly pursuit of a discipline and the teaching of a subject that has not been made explicit. The open-ended and serious study of a social science as a social science can be applied meaning-fully to the countersocialization of student-citizens. However, the effect of conventional teaching of a social science as a body of known and definitive facts is restricted to socialization which does not engage the critical capacities of young people. The pursuit of a discipline, as a discipline, teaches student-citizens to question conclusions and provides an opportunity to verify factual claims. It holds the potential to open the minds of young citizens to different points of view. It raises reasonable doubt about what is presumed to be fact. Certainly, the scientific approach of the disciplines is conducive to greater open-mindedness which is also an essential condition for becoming an effective democratic citizen.

In contrast, the teaching of subjects by way of textbooks and lectures supports the socialization of young citizens. In practice, it emphasizes accepting the facts that are presented as unmitigated truth based on the authority of the author. It presents little or no opportunity to question or doubt. The world is seen as less open to change, as a place more fixed and final than it actually is. Independent thought is discouraged and there is little or no opportunity to engage in the processes of dialogue and debate that are so very important to democratic citizenship. Social sciences are not always as objective as scholars in these fields suggest (Myrdal, 1944; Guba & Lincoln, 1985). The value judgments and factual assumptions, sometimes unknowingly held by scholars, color their works. History and the social sciences, as they are often taught in schools, are usually overly simplified and truncated versions of these disciplines and carry with them an extra burden of unexamined and possibly fallacious assumptions. The danger here is that the status quo is perceived definitively as the way things are and should be. Whether this is done implicitly or explicitly, such practices deny opportunities for young citizens to wrestle with alternative interpretations or to evaluate the evidence behind factual claims. This condition means that "these fields of study are do-nothing social sciences" that preserve the status quo,[3] according to Myrdal (1944). As a consequence, the severe injustices suffered by African Americans, Native Americans, Hispanics, women and people with disabilities among others, were long covered up in our history under a cloak of ungrounded facts, omissions based on bias and attitudes that unquestionably supported prejudiced views. Such biases were unmasked due to strong pressures by groups and organizations to make the discipline of history include conditions faced by powerless and marginal peoples visible, along with their demands to right these wrongs with persistent scholarship to further legitimize their portrayal to learners at all levels.

These kinds of oversimplified, unexamined versions of human affairs have held sway in the teaching of school subjects based on the disciplines for far too long. These subjects are almost never examined for their veracity or credibility. Textbooks and the talk of the teacher manipulate young people into thinking that they are getting the unvarnished truth and that the way things happened are the only ways they could have happened. Nothing could be better calculated to stifle inquiry and to produce acquiescent, passive and bored young citizens who feel there is little correspondence between social studies and the way the world really works.

Another basic limitation of the social sciences as the sole source of content for citizenship education is that these disciplines do not and cannot support the values and valuing processes required by the decision making process. The facts taken by themselves are never sufficient to address nagging and complex controversial issues. Rather, it is the values that citizen decision makers bring to the table that usually determine whatever action is taken to deal with any particular issue. However, if their values go unrecognized or if their values lack clarity or are in disarray, citizens are then rendered powerless in influencing responsible and thoughtful decisions in both personal and public domains. This limitation of scholars regarding values and valuing is a condition faced by all social science scholars who strive for objectivity. This limitation gives citizenship educators reason to emphasize the importance of making decisions having given serious consideration to the values on which they are based and the values they hope to fulfill.

However, in a democracy teachers at all levels need to acknowledge a limitation as well. We must not expect our young citizens to agree with the values we hold. We cannot do so and claim to be practicing democracy in the classroom. Pressuring young people into conforming to values we want them to hold, is denying democracy at its core. This limitation represents a tight line that we must walk if democracy is to be accepted with reason as to its merits and not by coercing or manipulating young minds as is the case in authoritarian systems.

The social sciences are good at ordering knowledge, but they ignore the values that are involved in the dynamics of a given issue. A stronger source for the study of values is found in the humanities including philosophy, the arts as well as music. While historians and even social scientists sometimes take on the role of philosophers, it is seldom explicitly recognized that they are doing so. Furthermore, social studies educators should appreciate that values are not as likely to be pursued by social scientists as are the canons of objectivity applied to the search for verifiable facts, generalizations and conclusions. The social sciences as a source of content are very useful, but have serious limitations when it comes to values and decision making.

The reasons given above serve as the foundation for the curriculum presented here. The humanities and the arts have an equally strong place in the content used in preparing democratic citizens as do the social sciences and history.

The Contributions of the Social Sciences to Citizenship Education

All of this is not to say that the social sciences are not useful to citizenship education. Quite the contrary, the social sciences, when appropriately used, are of fundamental importance to citizenship education. The key question here is: What are the appropriate uses of the social sciences in the preparation of democratic citizens?

Democratic citizens do not and should not make decisions in a factual vacuum. The more information they have at hand and the more reliable that information is, the better the chances for a sound, supportable decision. However, the social sciences are not the only source of information needed to advance the wisdom needed for decision making. Journalism and the media, literary works, the arts, philosophy, ethics and religion, along with firsthand and vicarious experiences of the individuals and groups actually involved in a decision are all invaluable to citizens as decision makers. The social sciences are the sources of knowledge that are most thoroughly thought out, systematically investigated, organized, summarized and criticized by scholars. They make a powerful contribution to the understanding of the human condition and to the controversial issues faced by citizens. A dominant ethic in the social sciences, as is the case with all other sciences, is to be concerned above all with the facts, a condition that sets the sciences apart from all other sources of content and information.

At this point, two caveats need to be addressed. First, a decision maker using a given social science or several social sciences as major sources of information should understand that the social sciences are not fixed bodies of information that are good for all times. Rather, they are continually changing as scholars unearth new evidence. The knowledge held by social scientists is merely the best approximation of what scholars believe to be true at a given time. Moreover, the information that represents the social sciences will almost certainly be different tomorrow than it is today. This understanding is deepened if student-citizens are engaged in scholarly criticism and investigation. This experience will permit them to recognize and appreciate how difficult verifiable facts are to come by and how tenuous and temporary is our hold on them. In other words, the social sciences are to be taken seriously, for they are the most systematic knowledge we have, but not too seriously, for they are subject to change and even contradiction and subjectivity. For instance, teachers and their classes should not be led into the trap of accepting as true a particular version of economic events that economists have long since abandoned as untenable. Absolutism has no place in the social studies or in the decisions that citizens make.

A second caveat is that the information derived from the social sciences achieves its social meaning as it is used for solving problems and making decision. Facts learned, only to be held in memory, are most resistant to being retained and are quickly put out of mind. Learning them for no justifiable reason is next to useless, if not actually harmful and it certainly is a waste of time.

With these two caveats in mind, the citizen can use the social sciences to access reliable knowledge essential to decision making. Young citizens, in particular, need to learn how to seek out the facts that are relevant to a given set of questions and decisions that they have an interest in addressing. They must learn to respect facts that constitute a body of evidence and to reject claims to truth that are ungrounded. At the same time, they need to learn that to look at all facts with a critical eye when judging the reliability of truth claims is, without any question, more important than learning to memorize the facts themselves. To paraphrase Alfred North Whitehead (1929), the first question that citizens should ask of any set of facts is "Are they true?" The second question is: "What use can we make of them?" Careful thought about these two questions will give the citizen a sound foundation for high quality decision making.

If one can make the intellectual leap of assuming, as did Jerome Bruner (1965), that one learns to think systematically by engaging directly in the process, then the social sciences afford a most favorable opportunity to develop this intellectual ability. But, if this goal is to be realized, teaching in the social sciences must necessarily be organized around the problems of fact and interpretation that confront scholars in each of the social sciences. It is not enough, or even appropriate, merely to inform young people about the conclusions reached by scholars regarding matters of fact and matters of interpretation. Teaching in the expository mode, which is present in most social studies classrooms, is self-defeating if development of the capacity for grounded decision making is the goal. Instead, the hypothetical mode, which guides teachers to organize their classes around issues where claims to truth are contested and inquiry into controversial issues is conducted, is a much more productive and an inherently more interesting approach. It is difficult to conceive of how the memorization of textbook expositions leads in any useful way to developing these critical intellectual abilities that are so very central to democratic citizens.

The Contributions of the Humanities to Citizenship Education

As stated earlier, literature, art, music, drama, religion, photography, philosophy and journalism deserve recognition along with the social sciences as valuable resources for democratic citizenship education. The unique role of the humanities is to provide a rich arena for insightful exploration of the human experience. Scholars in the humanities seek to illuminate the meaning of life. Further, they are not limited by the canons of objectivity that guide the work of social scientists. Rather, they permit their subjectivity and their value judgments to freely influence their thinking. For example, John Steinbeck's *Grapes of Wrath* presents a poignant, wrenching account of the Great Depression as seen through the lives of people who were victimized by the economic crisis of that period. From this novel, one gains a more complex and holistic view of that era than can be seen through unemployment statistics of the period as garnered by social scientists. The point being illustrated and emphasized here is that both the humanities and the social sciences are essential to citizenship education. However, heretofore, the humanities have not played a significant role in citizenship education and their potential for providing future citizens with compelling insights into social issues in human terms has not been realized. Considered below are ways that the humanities can be usefully incorporated into a curriculum for democratic citizens.

Describing Human Events

A picture may be more telling than a thousand words. A fictional account in the hands of a skilled writer may paint a more vivid and more accurate picture than many pages of historical scholarship and documentation. Anyone who reads *All Quiet on the Western Front* will gain compelling insights into the human face of war. Such powerful novels allow us to gain insights into the human condition that cannot be realized in other ways. Other examples abound in all aspects of the humanities, the arts and music. Children may gain greater insight into feudalism from reading about and speculating about the meaning of a photograph or a clay model of a feudal castle, than from reading a textbook account of feudalism. Add to the photograph a model of the castle, a picture of a feudal knight in full armor as well as one of a peasant's cottage and you have rich material for explaining and understanding a way of life that is completely foreign to children today. In this context, some useful questions are: How did the people who lived in such buildings and who possessed such items make their living? What did they value most in life? Why did this way of life disappear? Are there any relics of this way of life around today? Would it be attractive to have lived at this time? Why? Notice that this line of questioning is not only issue-oriented in that there are no certain and definitive answers, but it is also thought-provoking. To many, this kind of learning is much more interesting. Further, the making of value judgments is an integral part of this questioning. Still further, the photograph or model can and should be tested against the facts obtainable from other sources to be verified.

Questions such as the following may also be raised: Is this an accurate or complete picture of feudalism? What may have been left out or what had been distorted in this representation? In like vein, historical facts such as those written about by Victor Hugo, Toni Morrison, Howard Fast, Alice Walker or Harriet Beecher Stowe, even when they are not fully accurate, can still be used as a basis for a lively discussion of what really happened in a given period of history and how that period might be best interpreted. How better to instigate a lively dialogue of what really happened in the French Revolution than by comparing the accounts in several historical works with Charles Dickens' *A Tale of Two Cities* or a journalist's account of a worker's strike. These alternative sources should be checked out against what historians have said about that event.

There are thousands of books, journalistic accounts, paintings, photographs and musical works that could be used for a deeper investigation of any episode in the human experience across time. The music from West Side Story and the lyrics played and distributed to a class can serve as a springboard to a discussion and study of gangs and violence. This music, a virtual classic, can tap student interests. The music and story taken together could raise questions such as, Why do gangs exist? What do they do? Why do their activities often become violent? What does becoming violent really mean? Do violence and terrorism have the same meaning? Are gangs like terrorists? What makes membership in gangs attractive to some people? What are the risks of gang membership? Is there anything that can be done to reduce gang violence? In this context, student-citizens could learn through their research and classroom dialogue that the search for what is accurate and certain is not as simple as merely memorizing the truth claims presented in textbooks.

Learning to be a citizen must move beyond simply knowing about events and people to deriving meaning about the significances of these events and ideas which requires serious and careful analysis and dialogue. It is the humanities and the arts that have the power to evoke emotional sensitivities and responses that permit the learner to identify with the times and the people involved, that trigger interest and that provide a more extensive and intensive picture than the social sciences by themselves ever can. It is here that the student-citizens can see and feel through the eyes of the painter, the novelist or the journalist.

Posing Value Questions

Memorization, however exhaustive, without concomitant understanding, is not only meaningless but it trivializes and even insults the events and people under study. It creates name recognition but does not add insight into the significance of the matter. The issues which citizens of a democracy need to address always involve value judgments as well as questions about claims for truth. For instance, it may be determined through scientific research that a certain percentage of the children in the United States suffer from a lack of sufficient nutrients to sustain a healthy life. Further, there may be data that supports a positive relationship between a child's level of nutrients and the poverty level of the child's parents. However, the question of what should be done about this condition is strongly related to values. Those who value self-reliance and independence of the individual or who believe in the classic theory of economic welfare as a law of nature may argue that nothing should be done. To them, undernourished children are simply losers in the struggle for existence. These children, in the minds of those who hold such values, should be allowed to sicken and die, in order to maintain the economic system which they believe is in the best interests of society in the long run, regardless of the human cost. In contrast to these values, those who believe in the democratic principle that everyone, including every young citizen, deserves an equal chance at the good life or those who believe that help should be provided to the poor and downtrodden may argue that society should subsidize the poor with sound nutrition at the expense of those who have grown rich.

At the point where contrasting positions and competing values clash, new facts may come into play. For instance, humanitarians may argue that the children of poverty sometimes do, despite their poverty, grow up to make substantial contributions to society as scientists, musicians, writers, artists and the like, while children of the rich sometimes grow up slothful and uncaring. In contrast, the classicist may cite facts to prove that such cases are the exception and that the recipients of welfare grow up to be dependent on handouts and are unable to escape their dependency. So the argument may go. Such contrasting and competing ideas and values are the stuff of the real world of citizens who must deal not only with the facts as best they can but also with their own values as best they can (Lockwood, 1990). Halberstam (1998) in his book, *The Children*, presents a serious and critical study that concludes that children are not highly valued in the United States. Such a study would be especially useful to sociology teachers or those who teach about world affairs and could engage in a study that compares the treatment of children in the U.S with the treatment children receive in other countries. Serious works of art, literature and musical lyrics can afford the clearest expression of values. Citizens need to explore these values in terms of the conditions they face in their own lives.

The discussion above leads to the salient point of this chapter. Without the humanities in citizenship education, young citizens are denied the opportunity to master the processes by which real life issues can be sensibly and intelligently understood and, perhaps, resolved. This process involves not only learning to identify the values that relate to the issue, but learning to sort out and arrange values in hierarchical order from the most important to the least. This process involves learning to validate values against facts and learning to make decisions among conflicting values, including values of greater and lesser good.

To illustrate, Myra MacPherson's (2002) *Long Time Passing*, when compared to a historical account, could focus attention on the important question of whether the war in Vietnam was morally justified, Frederick Douglas's (1995) *Narrative of the Life of Frederick Douglas*, despite inaccuracies, could be used to consider the moral issues surrounding slavery and the Civil War, as could Harriett Beecher Stowe's (1981) *Uncle Tom's Cabin*. These works provide such rich interplay of the factual and the judgmental that can help young citizens learn how to deal with the real issues of life. Therefore, social studies teachers who are also citizenship educators must accept the humanities as a full partner in civic education.

In a very creative and thoughtful way Garrett Hardin (1985), an ecologist, not a social scientist, has thought about the nature of reality in an alternative way that can contribute to more comprehensive understanding and more strongly grounded decisions. He posits three filters of reality that need the attention of decision makers in all settings: the literate filter, the numerate filter and the *ecolate* filter. For centuries, he explains, the individual who could read and write had a far richer intellectual life than those who could not and he emphasizes that important understandings take written form and need consideration as decisions are made (the literate factor). With the advent of science, the work of scientific scholars who focus primarily on empirical findings is functioning in a manner that Hardin labeled numeracy. Numbers, calculations, proportions and probability characterize their work. Both literacy and numeracy have their strengths and limitations. These two filters do not, in Hardin's mind, help us to comprehensively grasp the nature of reality. He introduces a third filter called the *ecolate* filter, a label used by ecologists which requires thinking that is broader and more varied ways than literacy and numeracy taken together. The *ecolate* filter that also has limitations, focuses on questions that cause the decision maker to think of long term effects. The search for understanding through these three filters, taken together, entails many and varied possibilities that might be helpful as educators prepare citizens to be democratic decision makers. The kind of framework that Hardin provides with his three filters can be very helpful to the decision making done by citizens who take their responsibility seriously. This kind of thinking is similar, though not identical, to that of the artist, the philosopher and the novelist who have moved beyond literacy and numeracy to examine reality more broadly as ecologists do. Importantly, Hardin points out that "caution and humility are the hallmarks of the *ecolate* attitude toward the world"—an attitude that is consistent with the tentativeness or uncertainty of knowledge and decision making. Hardin's thoughtful and creative work receives mention here to expand the concepts that citizenship educators can use as they guide young citizens who can learn to apply this framework to their decision making on either a personal or public level.

THE SOCIAL SCIENCES AND THE HUMANITIES IN THE SOCIALIZATION AND THE COUNTER-SOCIALIZATION OF YOUTH

It is possible for the social sciences to contribute to the countersocialization of youth that is so essential if democracy is to survive and flourish. This would occur most assuredly and without too much strain, for we would only have to teach the social sciences as they really are, as inquiry-oriented, open-ended disciplines and we would need to abandon straight expository textbook-based teaching as is now widely practiced. To the extent that textbooks are used at all for the purpose of gaining a grasp of human affairs, we would need to make a special effort to help student-citizens understand that a textbook really is a single, simplified version of affairs that often carries a subtle but penetrating and pervasive bias (Fitzgerald, 1980). Textbooks, our young citizens should realize, are versions of events that are simplified and often presented in a bland manner that is interpreted as boring and even distorted. We should deliberately help student-citizens to compare alternative versions of events and to look for and question the assumptions that underlie a particular presentation. In short, textbook presentations should be challenged and compared to other accounts. Student-citizens should develop the ability to engage in such serious criticism. Certainly, they should not be punished, either verbally or with failing grades, for quarreling with the textbook.

In a broader sense, the social sciences should be treated as they really are, with their virtues and their shortcomings overtly and explicitly considered. The problems of fact and interpretation confronting scholars should be honestly shared with student-citizens. Any study of a social science might well start with the issues and uncertainties that confront scholars. Thus, economics, the social science that makes the strongest case for being a "hard" science, would be revealed as a cacophony of scholarly economic problems rather than a unified set of theories that can provide final answers to all of the economic and social issues faced by human beings, this society and the global marketplace. From such experiences, young citizens learn to be observant inquirers better able to cope with the kind of changing, dynamic world in which democracy can flourish.

CONCLUSION

Some may object that this chapter has veered too far toward counter-socialization over socializing experiences. They may ask: What is the glue that holds a democratic society together? The position taken in this book rests its case on the belief that the strongest attachment to democracy is based on reasonableness and fairness. Once the maturing citizen sees democracy in this light, its very openness to contrasting and changing views becomes the tie that binds its people together. It is out of character with democracy to expect its citizens to be blindly loyal. Indeed it is out of keeping with democracy to impose itself by force or by doctrinaire persuasion.

The social sciences do provide a wealth of reasonably dependable information which, if understood as indicated above, is vastly superior to guessing about the facts. Interestingly, this body of information actually gains in usefulness if taken, as suggested, with a grain of salt. The humanities taken as a whole is a mixture of the bizarre, the unconventional, the controversial and the substantive. In the face of this array of diverse perspectives, student-citizens, who have learned to be intellectually honest and humble in the search for truth and who are not thrown into intellectual paralysis by the absence of absolute answers, have also grasped the essence of democratic citizenship. Persons with these kinds of predispositions and abilities are not likely to be easy prey to propagandists or to slick media presentations. Their commitment to democracy is more likely to be persistent because it is a reasoned commitment, a product of their own intellect, not a platitude without a rationale. This mindset is a necessary and vital trait of enlightened citizens of a democracy.

NOTES

1.   Jack Nelson has emphasized that human beings faced problems prior to the development of the social sciences. For a complete discussion see Nelson, J "The historical imperative for issues-centered education" in a volume edited by R.W. Evans and D. W. Saxe (1996) and published by the National Council for the Social Studies.

2.   For a thorough analysis of the complexity of a particular issue in a democratic society, see Longstreet (1977, 1982).

3.   See Myrdal, G. (1944) Volume 2, Appendix 2 for an exhaustive treatment of the of the effect of hidden valuation on the scientific study of history.

CHAPTER 5

DEMOCRATIC DECISION MAKING IN AN ISSUES-CENTERED CURRICULUM

If the quality of decision making is to be the primary concern of social studies instruction, we must take steps to upgrade the quality of intellectual activity in social studies classrooms.

—Shirley H. Engle (1960)

INTRODUCTION

Democracy envisions an open and dynamic society where individual citizens play a deciding role. In contrast to an autocracy, where all important decisions are made at the top and where most citizens, who are more appropriately called subjects in authoritarian systems, are expected merely to be compliant, the citizens of a democracy are ultimately responsible for creating the policies and actions implemented by their government. Democracy, to be effective, demands so very much more of its citizens. To be able to test truth claims, to generate reasons and to make decisions and justify them are abilities that support a stronger democracy and have the potential to expand social justice. This chapter addresses the intellectual processes involved in decision making.

*   *   *

Citizens in a democracy make a host of decisions that shape their own welfare as well as the welfare of others. In this particular democracy, which is a

Democratic Education for Social Studies, pages 121–144
Copyright © 2007 by Information Age Publishing
All rights of reproduction in any form reserved.

leading world power, some of those decisions impact the governments and peoples of differing cultures and other nations. Furthermore, some if not many, of those decisions will impact generations not yet born. One challenging example of new dimensions that impact the present and will be ever more demanding in the future is the challenge of democratizing globalism—a force that is likely to be persistent, controversial and challenging in the future. While globalization is often considered to be a significant economic dimension of international life, it is also cultural (the spread of music, fashion, social behavior) and has spread from nation to nation. It influences conditions confronting women, the poor across the planet, the spread of disease and provides instant communication accompanied by the power of television. We are able to know what is happening in the world immediately and this condition results in the need for faster decision making. For example, we have all heard tragic news about journalists who are taken hostage as they try to get a real picture of events, which requires getting all the information possible and making a decision very quickly about addressing these situations. Recent efforts by the United States government have tried to spread democracy to some of the former Soviet republics as well as to Iraq. However, those two examples illustrate vast differences in approach. In one case, we invaded with military force and in the other, consultants from the United States are invited to share their expertise with new governments in the process of reform. These conditions demand an educated citizenry who are competent intellectually, who can envision difficult issues in broad perspective and who can participate intelligently in the decision making process in behalf of the public good. In the future, supporting and caring about the everyday welfare of people elsewhere on the planet, whether they suffer from poverty or oppression or not, has become a matter of our self-interest.[1] A more civil and well-fed world community is the best guarantor of peace across the planet.

In the United States with increasing diversity among its 280 million people, immigration has become a major issue. The large number of illegal aliens that continue to enter the United States is of particular concern. There are many aspects to this situation but since we are a nation of immigrants, our treatment of immigrants must be respectful and humane. Many people still see the United States as a place where they can live better lives and for some, those advantages are worth the risks involved to come to this country illegally. Official estimates indicate that 11 million aliens are here, many with families who receive free services from public agencies. However, many of these aliens find jobs, bring their families, are law abiding and pay taxes as well. Large companies employ aliens at lower wages than they would have to pay American workers in order to expand their profits. This issue needs the support of informed citizens and Congressional representatives and senators as well as the administrative offices of the President. The answers to this issue are not simple particularly since many aliens have been here for many years. Moreover, the public does not seem to be sufficiently informed to form intelligent opinions and make this decision wisely.

INTELLECTUAL PROCESSES:
TWO LEVELS OF DECISION MAKING

For the purpose of creating a curriculum for democratic citizens, there are two levels of decision making that mandate attention by social studies curricula and teachers. First, student-citizens must be able to evaluate the accuracy and importance of information that they use as evidence to support the positions that they take regarding complex and often, controversial issues. Furthermore, they need to become aware of the biased prism through which they view ideas and values. Some biases characterize virtually all human beings. Among competing claims to truth which usually accompany controversy, young citizens, like their adult counterparts, must decide what to believe and what not to believe. They must learn to distinguish claims to truth that have validity from those that do not. In short, strong democratic citizens need to be skeptical. They need to raise questions about what they do not know or do not understand. Inescapably, they will always have to deal with some level of uncertainty in assessing the value of truth claims and they should learn to recognize that some tentativeness is always present. Therefore, virtually any idea and any decision is subject to revision if there is new evidence and/or new reasons that suggest revision.

As citizens consider issues at the local, national or global levels they need to be mindful of multiple perspectives—the views held by all actors who feel the influence of the issue and the consequence of its possible solutions. In any society, even a democratic one, power can and often does accumulate in the hands of the wealthy or others who through their use of power try to control social conditions that are important to them. To the extent this happens, the power of individuals and minorities becomes a mockery and democracy deteriorates. Furthermore, too often citizens assume a dichotomous we–they orientation with 'we' seen as right and 'they' seen as wrong. To illustrate, even the courts in this democracy have recently challenged policies and practices regarding affirmative action that provides more equitable educational and employment opportunities for minorities and women. The effect is reduced hope as well as less opportunity for minorities and their children to improve their lives in this society. Such decisions that disregard the value of equity and equality that are allegedly central to an authentic democracy minimize rather than strengthen democracy.

Paying serious attention to the concerns of all who hold a stake in any issue is not only a considerate stance to take, it is vital that our citizens understand its centrality to the lives of minority groups and women and to the vitality of democracy in this society. How we treat minorities and women in this society is a major test that represents the capacity of this democracy to address diversity. A significant insight for citizenship educators is provided by Allan Brandhorst (1992, 2004) who emphasizes that our personal identities, whether religious, economic socio-political and/or gender related can serve as barriers to open decision making where all sides of an issue deserve consideration. Student-citizens, like all adult citizens, hold such views consistent with their identities that can seriously limit the quality of democratic and open decision making. At a minimum, teachers can demonstrate or illustrate such limitations to help the next generation of citizens be aware of them and able to understand how they shape their thinking and particularly their values.

Secondly, decision making involves citizens in figuring out how to solve complex issues. Decision making is a complex process, which includes:

- How to define an issue
- How to gather data relevant to the issue
- How to test truth claims for their validity
- How to select and justify values that should guide their decisions
- How to strengthen public policies and practices that deserve support
- How to choose candidates for public office
- How to determine the political actions that they need to take to improve a given situation.

The performance of these tasks, each of which requires considerable intellectual prowess and self-discipline, is critical to becoming effective functioning citizens of a strong democracy. Clearly, the knowledge and abilities mentioned above require a wide range of intellectual abilities that transcend those included in any one or more disciplines or any fields of knowledge or areas of expertise.

In the interest of creating able citizens for a stronger democracy, they must be able to assess the effects and consequences of their decisions. Questions such as what will be the effects of this decision on the poor, on minorities, on women, on the handicapped, on those citizens who live alternative lifestyles and/or on the elderly are imperative. Without considering such questions, this democracy will not grow stronger and will not live up to democratic ideals or social justice values such as fairness, equity or equality. Proactive, thoughtful citizens who care enough to be informed, to decide and to act are vital to democratic public life and to the expansion of social justice. People who do not try to assume their civic responsibilities put greater responsibility on those people who do.

The overarching purpose of this Issues-Centered Decision Making Curriculum is to improve the quality of decision making by democracy's citizens as they respond to issues that require resolution. However, it is very important to recognize that the decision making process advanced here is applicable to virtually every domain of our lives and the lives of young citizens in our classes. Indeed, it is unrealistic to think that we can prepare people to apply this process in the public domain without their use of the same principles and processes in all aspects of their lives. The workplace, the family, friendship groups as well as social, neighborhood and voluntary organizations are all settings where democratic principles and practices, including democratic decision making, should be operative. This perspective returns us to the definition of citizenship provided by Lee Anderson (1990) in Chapter 2. Obviously, the school is not responsible for social interactions in these other settings. Nor can the school demand that student-citizens embrace the values of democracy and social justice. Nonetheless, citizenship educators have opportunities to affirm democratic values when they handle issues in the classroom. They can also enter these values by asking, What would be fair in this case? What would be more equitable? The greater the congruence of democratic principles and practices in all parts of our lives, the stronger our society and this democracy will be.

Benjamin Barber's (1998) work titled *A Place for Us* speaks to the need for a civil and strong democracy. Barber argues that between our public and our private realms are social spaces, often voluntary in nature, where democratic principles and practices need to prevail. He advances the desirability of creating a civil democratic society. In his words:

> Civil society is not an alternative to democratic government but rather, the free space in which democratic attitudes are cultivated and democratic behavior is conditioned. It is not a synonym for the private market but an antidote to commercial selfishness and market incivility. It treats democratic government as civil association's highest form of expression—the association of all associations: that is, common action in the name of liberty raised to its most general level. (p. 6)

His statement emphasizes the importance of civility to the development of democratic attitudes and values as well as the importance of democratic attitudes and values to civility as a guiding set of values for democratic dialogue. This principle makes the development of thoughtful decision making abilities crucial to the quality of our connections with others.

The first level of decision making, testing the validity of truth claims in this curriculum, contributes to the quality of decision making at the second level. Intelligently addressing public issues inescapably depends on the credibility of the data that supports the evidence. These two levels are inextricably linked with each one serving as significant goals for all social studies programs that take the mission of preparing citizens for democracy seriously.

Improvement in the quality of decision making at each of these two levels is best gained by directly participating in the process. The massive amounts of information that are passed on to student-citizens by way of the textbook and/or the teacher's lecture, without an opportunity to examine the validity of the supporting data and with little or no opportunity to apply the information in behalf of a position on an issue or to support political action regarding the improvement of some aspect of a given issue, does much to hinder the development of decision making abilities among our young citizens. Certainly, it does not help. Memorizing a host of facts, that are not applied to the real world in any meaningful way, but only to artificially constructed test situations, is likely to develop habits of disinterest in the content and a lack of awareness of the potential impact that the content may have on their lives. Indeed, we have a fair amount of evidence of the lack of interest young citizens have in their social studies classes (McGowan, Sutton & Smith 1990). The result is learning that is trite and easily forgotten. Such learning preempts the opportunity that exists to develop the necessary intellectual abilities needed by our successor generation.

Hilda Taba (1967) who, without question, contributed very substantial insights to our understanding of the development of thinking abilities in children, led us to recognize that thinking does not just happen as a by-product of learning content. Instead, thinking abilities develop as the result of actually engaging in the process. She also demonstrated that teachers can, by using thoughtful questions, develop stronger thinking abilities even in elementary school children. This learning principle is central to the curriculum that is advanced here. Education that emphasizes isolated facts is not useful. Speaking to the irrelevance of many school curricula, Alfred North Whitehead (1929) captured the essence of the matter:

> There is only one subject matter of education, and that is life and all of its manifestations. Instead of this single unity, we offer children geometry from which nothing follows, science from which nothing follows, history from which nothing follows. (p. 62)

If education is to become more effective, if more complex decision making among our citizenry is to be the result of the curriculum, then as Whitehead and Taba indicate, we must engage student-citizens in this process, not at some distant time, but here and now. The decision making process is vital to the strengths we would like our young citizens to acquire. If the subject matter we use in classrooms is to be both interesting and useful then the first question that student-citizens should be encouraged to ask of anything they read or hear is: Is the statement (truth claim) true? The second question to ask is: Is it useful and important information? Further, student-citizens need to learn to ask: What light does this statement cast on the issue or the policy I might propose? Or: How does it impact the action I should take to improve conditions that will help resolve this issue?

With only a little imagination, we can refocus the study of any of the social sciences or any other social studies content and even use sources such as textbooks and teacher lectures that lay claim to accurate information. By involving student-citizens in a re-examination and validation of key truth claims, we can create an authentic and realistic decision making situation. This is not an artificial exercise. The re-examination of truth claims is precisely what social scientists and thoughtful citizens continually do in the context of their respective responsibilities. Key truth claims held with tentativeness by social scientists are often controversial. Some scholars agree, while others do not. Frequently, social scientists have either disproved or have qualified truth claims found in textbooks. By teaching such findings as definitive without the opportunity to question them, we not only rob young citizens of their opportunity to expand their decision making capabilities, but we also destroy our own credibility as scholars and teachers by advancing inaccurate knowledge as if it were the unvarnished truth. Skepticism is essential not only for the scholar, but it is a mandate for the democratic citizen.

Student-citizens must be given the opportunity to develop the whole gamut of decision making capabilities that are so very crucial to the quality of democratic citizenship. It is reasonable to conclude that any piece of social studies content for which there is no connection to real life here and now, or in which no decision making opportunities can be provided, should be dropped from the curriculum.

Decision Making in the Testing of Truth Claims

The distinction between these two dimensions of decision making deserve elaboration. Testing the validation of truth claims is not unlike the scientific method. Scientists observe, collect and evaluate data and draw conclusions. In this process, concern for evidence and reason are paramount. Scientists strive to be objective, devoid of emotion about the outcomes of their studies. However, complete objectivity is elusive though scientists try to reduce the effect of their own biases and emotions. Social scientists who study human behavior experience additional difficulties that do not influence the physical sciences. They study human beings who may change their behavior from time to time on the basis of new experiences and among whom emotions might run high. This unpredictability produces ambiguity and may even invalidate their scholarly findings. Since human beings are very complex and are constantly changing as compared, for example, to Japanese beetles, knowledge about humans is often incomplete and uncertain. Student-citizens need to understand that there is a considerable potential for error in the conclusions drawn in social science research. They may be insightful but are tentative and subject to revision.

In the study of truth claims, how do we focus the attention of student-citizens into a decision making posture? Jerome Bruner (1965) has usefully pointed out that we do this by treating major truth claims as hypotheses that need to be tested by young citizens who should be helped to develop strategies for testing these truth claims against existing evidence. Or, continuing with Bruner's thought, we need to encourage student-citizens to suggest truth claims that are of interest to them. These truth claims need to be viewed as hypotheses whose validity needs to be affirmed with evidence. Treating truth claims as hypotheses stands in direct contrast to the frequent practice of treating truth claims as facts to be stored in memory. Converting truth claims to hypotheses has the net effect of placing the student-citizen, not the teacher, in the decision making position. As Bruner (1965) stated, "Emphasis on discovery...has precisely the effect on the learner of leading him to be a constructivist[2] to organize what he is encountering in a manner not only designed to discover regularities and relatedness, but also to avoid the kind of information drift that fails to keep account of the uses to which information might have been put." Herein lies the substantive challenge for social studies: our teaching practices must become more consistent with the Issues-Centered Decision Making processes suggested above.

Decision Making: Implications for Social and Controversial Issues

Decision making that applies to solving controversial social issues takes a different form than decision making limited to the validation of truth claims. This level of decision making needs to be guided by the following questions:

1. How can we make intelligent decisions and take thoughtful actions related to these issues?
2. What issues deserve attention?
3. What values should be pursued?
4. What public policies merit support?
5. What actions should be taken by individuals, relevant groups, and by public officials?

Certainly, facts play an important part in the intelligent resolution of controversial issues. The facts, which are truth claims supported by evidence and reason, surrounding the issue must be pursued at every stage of the process. This search for relevant and credible facts must be vigorous and relentless. No conclusions or decisions can be reached without them. However, citizens must also understand that decisions often must be made without all of the facts we would like to have. Indeed, some kind of action may need to be taken before the facts can be ascertained. Nor would having all of the facts, even if that were possible, necessarily resolve the issue because all alternative facts and solutions carry conflicting values in their wake. Furthermore, citizens must realize that every human being perceives a given situation differently and may bring unique and discrepant perspectives to the issue at hand. For example, the long and troubled relationship between the United States government and Native Americans was not void of facts. However, dramatically different perceptions and values prevented a meeting of the minds between these groups and tragically, those discrepant values often had violent manifestations. Values, of course, can and should be subjected to probing questions such as: Is this value consistent with other highly regarded values? What consequences will result from actions taken on the basis of this value (Hanvey, 1976).[3] Hanvey emphasizes that there are often 'surprise effects' after decisions are made that were not anticipated by decision makers. Moreover, it is possible that ultimate values will still come in conflict even within the same person.

What then is to be done with complex and controversial issues? How can they be studied rationally? John Dewey (1933) strongly supported the idea that problematic issues could be solved using the methods of science. He sought a relationship between rationality, which is a critical characteristic of a democratic citizen and the ordered objectivity of science. Dewey, it now seems apparent, overemphasized the scientific method and placed too much confidence in its principles and procedures. However, his analysis of a complete act of thought is still useful in ordering the study of a challenging controversial issue. A somewhat modified version of Dewey's framework follows:

Recognizing a predicament
Defining and stating the issue
Gathering and evaluating data that might constitute evidence
Hypothesizing alternative solutions
Predicting possible consequences
Deciding (and justifying) a preferred solution
Acting to implement the decision.

Dewey's prescription of how the thinking process could guide the study of issues is helpful, but it makes reaching the actual solution simpler than it really is. Decision making in the context of controversy involves more, much more, than following this recipe format. It involves values and value analysis. The hard part is making the well-grounded decision and acting upon it with justification. It is not unusual to find it necessary to make a decision before the facts are all in and sometimes actions must be taken immediately with little or no time for deep analysis. Moreover, people bring different values, different perspectives and different needs to the issue at hand. All of these deserve serious consideration by open, thoughtful and reasonable minds. Not only must a solution be worked out, preferably one that enhances the common good of society and/or the world community, but it must also be one that will accommodate some of the special needs and desires of specific individuals and groups that are affected by the issue. This process may not always include the greatest number of people and issues cannot always be solved on the basis of numerical strength. One of the weaknesses of democracies is that the majority can display a tyrannical posture and base their actions on values that maximize power and profit—values that are not democratic. There have been and will continue to be times when the circumstances of a minority group deserve priority regardless of their numbers. The examination of value commitments such as fairness, equity, freedom or other values will weigh heavily on the decision that people make. Student-citizens must learn to struggle with these value issues. Solutions that give consideration to these factors, transcend those that are strictly scientific.

Discussion and dialogue are the means for creating a workable response or appropriate policy. It is in the process of "talking it out" that young citizens need to make a serious effort to understand and accommodate how others view the issue. Thus, facts, values, perceptions and needs of the issue deserve thoughtful consideration. In the classroom, role-playing of under-represented points of view might serve as one useful approach to helping student-citizens learn to understand those with different points of view and thus facilitate a dialogue characterized by mutual understanding, if not agreement. Accommodation, reached in this way, may be the highest and most complex expression of democratic decision making.

Dialogue is the focus of Paulo Freire's (2001) view of learning.[4] Dialogue to Freire was much more than a teaching technique. Instead, he saw it as the basis for the most meaningful kind of knowing. He describes dialogue as a purposeful, goal oriented, and interactive form of communication where all parties involved seek greater understanding. When Freire combined dialogue as a way of knowing with raising the consciousness of peasants in South America about their oppression, he was imprisoned for the ideas he advocated. This event dramatically illustrates how authoritarian systems fear people who can think for themselves and who are competent in their ability to challenge the system and the oppression to which too many of them are subjected.

Another term important in Freire's framework is *banking education* which he characterized as follows:

(a) the teacher teaches and the students are taught

(b) the teacher knows everything and the students know nothing

(c) the teacher thinks and the students are thought about

(d) the teacher talks and the students listen meekly

(e) the teacher disciplines and the students are disciplined

(f) the teacher chooses and enforces his choice and the students comply

(g) the teacher acts and the students have the illusion of acting through the action of the teacher

(h) the teacher chooses program content and the students (who were not consulted) adapt to it

(i)   the teacher is the subject of the learning process while the students are mere objects.(p. 73)

Freire's characterization of banking education is all too evident in many present day classrooms.

Since the central message of this book is the improvement of the social studies curriculum to better prepare effective and democratic decision makers, citizenship educators need to explore how the democratic ideal impacts the decision making process. Democracy, a value in itself, also includes attention to other values that give democracy fuller meaning. These related values include respect for the individual, respect for the welfare of others and the common good, a belief in the value of free expression and dissent as well as equality or equity of opportunity for all citizens. The classic hypothesis tested by democracy resides in the process and values associated with self-governance. In effect, the central question for democracy and democratic education is: Does the citizenry have the competence, the knowledge, the values and abilities to make the decisions needed to create and sustain a stronger democratic society? The foundation for such values is usually learned by children early in life when they are not able to comprehend their full meaning. Stories and simple histories often provide the means by which children learn to identify with these values even though their understanding is very limited. Anyone who has observed five and six year olds saying the Pledge of Allegiance has caught a glimpse of their mindless way of reciting this patriotic ritual. At these ages, they like routines even if their meaning escapes them.

Sometimes, democratic values stand in opposition to each other. This tension is well illustrated in the context of civil rights where the values of freedom and equality can be at odds with one another. The owners of businesses may want the freedom to hire whomever they wish, while members of groups seeking more equitable conditions claim their rights using the value of equal opportunity. This issue is but one of many that requires careful thought and rethinking by each generation in order to maintain and expand the conditions that should exist for minorities, women and other marginal groups. Eric Foner (1998) emphasizes that every generation has to reconsider how the value of freedom is applied. Furthermore, each generation redefines the meaning of freedom as well as the full range of democratic values. By extension, if citizens are to make these decisions in an informed and wise manner, their education must provide the opportunity to develop such competencies. Enhancing these abilities is an imperative for the social studies curriculum.

The self-interest of citizens often finds itself in juxtaposition with thoughtful concern for the common good. It is natural for all of us want to fulfill our personal needs and desires. People who wish to sustain a democracy must recognize that obsession with one's self interest can be destructive to strengthening a democratic society. This contradiction represents a deep challenge to a democratic system. Can people, ordinary but educated people, not only recognize this contradiction in an intellectual sense, but also make decisions and act in ways that demonstrate that they have the capacity to limit their personal desires for the greater good of the society or the global community. In a society whose civic values are democratic, but whose economic values are capitalistic, these tensions surface regularly. Do I buy inexpensive clothes made by people in other nations who are exploited by profit seeking manufacturers? Do I buy a gas guzzling car that has a high status quotient when a smaller, more economical car would be preferable for environmental reasons? Should we, in order to consume fewer resources, have laws that place an upper limit on the cost of housing (this would restrict the freedom of a small, wealthy minority by preventing them from building multimillion dollar homes that exceed their needs)? Can we require that a percentage of their high level earnings be earmarked for charities that improve the quality of life of the very poor or contribute to improving the environment for all of us and for subsequent generations? No doubt, this proposal will sound like heresy to some, even as antiAmerican to others, so much so that it may never be given consideration in a public forum.

Using self-interest as a guide to decision making comes naturally to most human beings. However, participation in a democracy poses a challenge to this predisposition. This challenge is embedded in such questions as:

1. Regardless of personal gains, how do my decisions affect others?
2. Does my exercise of self-interest interfere with the welfare of my neighbors, my friends, my coworkers, my family, the welfare of less advantaged people in our society as well as other people on the planet?
3. In short, are there limits to freedom? What are they? Is it beneficial to remember the adage that my freedom ends where yours begins?
4. For what purposes should limiting freedom be acceptable?
5. Is the benefit of the common good an essential limitation of freedom?
6. Are there other limitations?
7. Does my chosen course of action decrease the extent to which this society can realize its democratic ideals?

These fundamental questions encourage all of us to look beyond self-interest and consider whether in the long run, our interest is better served by taking the concerns of, other peoples, other groups and larger communities into account. Furthermore, in a global age, our decisions are more likely to have an impact on people we do not know and generations we may never see. Yet the quality of their lives will have some bearing on the quality of ours. The need to nurture democratic conditions and examine the effects of our decisions on others requires that social studies programs lead student-citizens to examine questions in terms of the greater good. If citizens make decisions and take action solely on the basis of their immediate self-interest, democratic values would soon erode and become meaningless. While citizens need to be explicitly conscious of their own goals and interests, they must also be consistently concerned with the welfare of others and the preservation of democratic values. Otherwise, the system itself as well as the opportunity to participate in it will deteriorate. Furthermore, in the global context, this nation would deservedly be seen as self-centered and exploitative.

The temptation evident among some educators is to indoctrinate young people with the "right" values. Children may be told that they should value such ideals as justice, equality, responsibility, due process, freedom, diversity and the rule of law. Such values appear in children's stories and histories as facts to be taken for granted. In a democracy, such indoctrination of values ignores the fact that values themselves are problematic and often fraught with tensions when applied to specific cases. We say we believe in justice, but what justice means in a particular situation is not always easy to determine which explains why we have hung juries and people too confused to vote intelligently. If the value of equality is involved (only the poor go to jail, the rich get high priced lawyers) then the problem of what to value most may be very difficult to decide. Americans believe in freedom of speech and freedom of the press. Does this mean that newspaper reporters have the right to reveal secret war plans that they were told in confidence? We also believe that the public has a right to know. Does this mean that all governmental discussions and actions, including courtroom hearings and trials, should be conducted in full view of the public via television? The issues surrounding freedom in a democracy seem endless.

Indoctrination of values is an authoritarian rather than a democratic mode. In authoritarian settings, values are proclaimed, even when some values are inconsistent with one another and no questions or challenges are allowed. In contrast, democracy does not rest so much on fixed values as on the process of analyzing values and on their continual reappraisal. This condition leads to a stronger and more authentic commitment to thoughtfully selected values on the part of citizens and to a growing consistency in their reflective decisions based on values.

Alan Griffin (1942) succinctly summarized the place of value analysis in a democracy.

> The democratic refusal to espouse a hierarchy of preferred values is a positive insistence that values originate out of human experience, that standards arise through the common experience of peoples living and working and thinking and that authoritarianism is simply the arresting of the process through which values and standards are generated (p. 92).

The role of values in democratic decision making is profoundly complex. The capacity of citizens to handle the application of values to social controversy grows with experience. For citizenship educators in a democracy, this complexity must enter classroom dialogue to the greatest extent possible.

INTELLECTUAL IMPLICATIONS OF DEMOCRATIC DECISION MAKING

The compelling task faced by social studies programs and educators is to involve their student-citizens in the complexities of decision making. As stated earlier, this task embraces two levels of decision making. First, young citizens need to appraise the validity of truth claims and secondly, that they need to learn how to make intelligent and defensible decisions related to public policy and public action. The major components of each of these intellectual tasks are presented below. Although each component is described separately, they are actually intertwined and are not characterized by linearity.

Drawing Conclusions about the Validity of Truth Claims: Level 1

Testing the validity of claims made by politicians, journalists, government officials and citizens is a constant activity of concerned citizens since the ability to test truth claims is fundamental to independent and justifiable decision making. For educators, facilitating the testing of truth claims includes the processes described below.

Arousing Curiosity

A textbook passage might state: "Abraham Lincoln deserved to be known as the great emancipator. He freed the slaves." Or a student-citizen might say: "We shouldn't have to pay taxes to support welfare programs for the poor." Each of these statements contains truth claims that can be challenged and examined to be verified.

In order to stimulate curiosity about the merits of a particular claim, it is useful to introduce information or counterclaims that contradict the initial claim. Regarding Lincoln's stand on slavery, student-citizens with the help of librarians and teachers, can introduce a number of sources. On the one hand, is the claim that Lincoln was reluctant to free the slaves and that he did so only because it was necessary to save the Union. On the other hand, some believe, he really was the great emancipator who believed that slavery was morally wrong. Can both these claims be accurate? If so, how? If not, why? By introducing a counter claim, the teacher has increased the chances that student-citizens will be curious and challenged by the doubt raised by competing claims.[5]

Truth claims can be taken from the textbook, a statement made on a news or talk show, from newspapers and magazines or from a statement made by either a student-citizen or the teacher. The counterclaims (and there can be more than one) serve as alternative hypotheses. Since stimulating curiosity about truth claims is essential to involving students in the process of testing validity, it is important to underscore a condition well known to experienced teachers. Namely, not all students will find the question interesting or be naturally curious about knowing whether Lincoln deserved to be called the great emancipator. Making the question relevant to young citizens is basic to learning and calls for considerable creativity on the part of the teacher.

Using the Lincoln example, the following two possibilities may be useful. First, the teacher can create intellectual tension by dramatizing the issue. To achieve this, the teacher can probe the class in the following manner:

> What we are examining here is the reputation of a very important President. Was Lincoln really the Great Emancipator he is claimed to be? Or, was he more concerned with saving the Union at a time when it was threatened with the secession of the South?
>
> Was he both the President who saved the Union and a reluctant emancipator?
>
> Was he neither?
>
> What were his actual motives? Why, in a democracy, is it important to examine his motives?

In the examples above, the teacher attempted to create a tension-filled atmosphere. Furthermore, the teacher elicited perspectives of student-citizens about these questions. If the teacher has approached the topic with vigor and enthusiasm, student-citizens are more likely to respond in kind (Van Sickle, 1996).

Secondly, the teacher can personalize the issue. To relate the issue in a personal way to the class the teacher might proceed as follows:

> This question asks us to examine Lincoln's reputation. Is it appropriate to think of him as the Great Emancipator? All of us have reputations and we often think of others in terms of their reputations. Furthermore for Presidents, their legacy and how they are remembered are especially important. However, reputations are not always deserved. I remember a man who used to live in my neighborhood who was always called the "Old Crank." This man kept to himself and barely grunted when someone said hello to him. Actually, most of us were afraid of him. But, I will never forget the day when my brother was racing down the street on his bicycle and fell to the ground breaking his arm. No one was around except our neighbor, the "Old Crank," who drove him to a doctor to have his arm set. It didn't take us long to realize that he didn't deserve the reputation we had given him. Can you think of any people you have known who have reputations they do not deserve? Can you share those examples with us?"

After several examples, the teacher can bring the discussion back to Lincoln: "Is Lincoln's reputation deserved? How can we find out?"

Here the teacher has cast the issue in terms of the personal experiences of her class by asking them to share similar experiences in their lives. The matter of reputation is likely to interest adolescents and the previous discussion can relate that interest to Lincoln. These two examples do not exhaust the ways that motivation can be heightened. Each issue and each class will, of course, have to be met on their own terms and each teacher will need to be creative about finding ways to heighten the curiosity of each group of students. In order to heighten the interests of class members, this initial step is worth the serious thought of classroom teachers.

Supporting Truth Claims

Assuming that Lincoln deserves to be called the Great Emancipator, what evidence would we need to find to support this position? If Lincoln freed the slaves reluctantly, what evidence would we need to find to support this counter claim? Letters that Lincoln wrote, Lincoln biographies, his speeches, newspaper accounts and historical scholarship, whether in print or on the web, are all possible sources that can cast light on these questions. In each case, the class should be involved in identifying and searching out the evidence.

Collecting Evidence

Evidence can be found in many settings. Libraries, interviews with experts, films, videos, dvd's, the Internet, and scholarly journals are all examples. The journal, Social Education carries a column done by Fred Risinger that identifies very useful web sites for classroom use. In some cases, art and music can provide useful insights into an issue. Realistically, student-citizens will be limited to the evidence available to them. They will not have Lincoln's original letters or the newspapers of Lincoln's time, but they can gain access to historical works, to someone in the community who is a Lincoln buff or an historian whose specialty is the Civil War. They can and should analyze each of their sources in terms of their credibility. Which is the best source of evidence: a letter, a book, an interview with an historian or a journal article? Why? It will not be possible for student-citizens to exhaust all of the related evidence, but this condition that usually faces citizens. They have to make decisions without the benefit of all the evidence possible and young citizens need to learn that their conclusions are tentative and always subject to revision. Nonetheless, if young people are to learn to function as democratic citizens, they must be involved in identifying and appraising whether available evidence exists and is sufficient for them to draw conclusions or accept the information they examined.

Evaluating Evidence

Evaluating evidence is one of the more intellectually challenging aspects of testing a truth claim. For example, it might be possible to find several secondary school history textbooks that also claim that Lincoln was the Great Emancipator. However, student-citizens need to be aware that textbooks do not constitute a strong base of evidence to support this claim. Textbooks are, at best, tertiary sources that are three times removed from original evidence. Textbook authors and publishers often use secondary sources which are historical works written by scholars who have relied on primary sources such as personal letters, contemporary newspapers, government documents, and the like. Consequently, the information found in textbooks is remote from original sources and usually, is simplified for use at the secondary school level. Furthermore, textbooks will represent the bias of the author and/or the publisher, whether intentionally biased or not. Critical appraisal of all the evidence gathered, including material found in textbooks, is necessary if student-citizens are to learn how to reach thoughtful and defensible conclusions.

The following questions can guide the evaluation of evidence:

- Who wrote the account?
- What was the author's background and credentials? Was the author a firsthand observer, a scholar, or a journalist? How does this information affect the credibility of this evidence?
- If a close friend of Lincoln's wrote the account, is it more believable than one written by a historian many years later?
- Is the account biased? Please explain.
- Does the account support or deny the claim? What evidence supports your view?
- Is the account supported or contradicted by other sources?

Learning to detect bias is an especially important aspect of evaluating evidence. However, all authors bring their attitudes to the topic they are writing about. It is virtually impossible to be completely neutral. In some cases, the viewpoint(s) of the author will be very clear (e.g., Winston Churchill and his books on the Second World War). In others, the viewpoint(s) of the author need to be inferred. The use of emotional language, the emphasis given to some facts or the omissions of others (what they do not mention) provide clues to the author's bias. Importantly, the credibility of the evidence is directly influenced by the bias of the author. Citizens need to gain experience in detecting bias and in making judicious decisions about its effect on the credibility of the evidence being evaluated.

For instance, if a textbook passage states, "Abraham Lincoln is often called the Great Emancipator. He freed the slaves," this claim has little credibility unless it provides supporting evidence. Like all citizens, those who are student-citizens need to be able to identify whether such claims are supported or not and to recognize their considerable limitations. They need to be able to explore the bias on which any claim rests. Does the author use original sources? If the author cites support from another source, is that source credible? As young citizens learn to analyze the evidence critically, they can develop an understanding of how to build a strong case for the claims or arguments that they make.

In addition, seldom does any one source provide a definitive answer. If two or three soundly researched historical works present support for the conclusion that Lincoln really wanted to free the slaves, such evidence is stronger than if a secondary school textbook states that this as the definitive truth. Similarly, if Lincoln's personal papers support this conclusion; this evidence will be stronger than the opinions of authors who are devoted to preserving the most attractive image of Lincoln possible. As student-citizens evaluate evidence, they need to be encouraged to find several sources that corroborate their claim. One source, however strong it might be, is not sufficient to justify a given claim. Even though such a source represents a strong beginning, it will still need further substantiation.

Evaluating evidence is at the core of the search for truth and for making justifiable conclusions. Student-citizens need to recognize that their answers can never be totally definitive but that, like all citizens, they need to reach the most defensible conclusion possible on the basis of the evidence that is available to them. At the same time, they should be aware that if the evidence they have located is weak, they cannot reach any conclusion at all or recognize that it is extremely tentative unless and until they can locate stronger sources.

Another experience relating what is studied to the lives of student-citizens personalizes the issue. Sophie Haroutunian-Gordon (1991) of Northwestern University whose book, *Turning the Soul* describes a session she had with a class of inner city student-citizens using Shakespeare's *Romeo and Juliet* to tap issues in the personal lives of this class. She was able to have them identify with the issue that Romeo and Juliet faced. Some of them shared similar problems they had experienced in their personal relationships. At the same time, they found the dilemma of this classic work compelling. The transcript of her session with these young citizens is provided in her book and would be useful to both social studies and English teachers.

Drawing Conclusions

Is there enough evidence to support the truth claim? Or the counter-claim?
Does one or the other need to be modified?
Why?
How?

At this point, student-citizens need to pull together the evidence that they have been able to gather and evaluate it carefully. They must decide what conclusion is supportable on the basis of what they have found. They need to be encouraged to present their conclusion(s) with the strongest justification possible, knowing full well that they will be probed by their peers as well as their teacher. Classroom dialogue needs to be focused and rigorous. Both classmates and the teacher need to challenge the presenter with the same kinds of questions that were presented for evaluating evidence:

How do you know that is true?
Who wrote that? Is she or he qualified? How?
Did you find other sources that agreed?
Did you find some that disagreed?

Such questions should characterize the dialogue in the classroom where young citizens are engaged in serious and challenging thinking.

Making Decisions Related to Democratic Public Policy and Practices: Level 2

Learning to make decisions that are intelligent and justifiable is the essence of democratic citizenship. Without decision making abilities, citizens become much more susceptible to external manipulation. To that extent, democracies can deteriorate and drift into autocratic patterns. Consequently, student-citizens must have concentrated and intensive experience in wrestling with decisions that apply to social controversy in all of their complexity. Making such decisions includes the following dimensions.

Before the process of decision making can be set in motion, student-citizens must sense that a controversy or ambiguity regarding the best solution exists. Creating the need to resolve a sense of doubt or confusion is essential. The issues identified need to relate to their interests, roles and values. The issue of what is to be done with nuclear waste may be important to a young citizen whose parents are active members of the Sierra Club, while others may not be interested at all. Citizens may identify problems only in terms that influence them in their immediate context. For example, automobile workers might view the entry of foreign cars for sale in the United States as a threat to their employment. On the other hand, foreign auto dealers might find such cars financially lucrative if these cars are selling well. Soybean farmers, on the other hand, might recognize that the more other nations can sell to us, the more they are able to buy soybeans, grains and other products from us.

The challenge for citizens as decision makers is to perceive the problem in its broadest possible context so that its many faceted implications are apparent. Student-citizens need to make decisions by considering the welfare of all parties and not ones that are not solely limited to satisfying their own immediate desires or that of any single special interest group.

The issues selected for classroom dialogue must be connected to the interests of student-citizens. Otherwise, their involvement will not be sustained. Due to their limited life experiences, the interests of young citizens may be narrow and sometimes trivial. However, their interests are an important starting point and can be linked to the larger issues facing their community, their society and their world. For instance, such immediate concerns as drug and/or alcohol abuse can be linked to larger issues such as what should be the legal drinking age or what is the appropriate punishment for drunk drivers. Concerns regarding fairness are common not only at the secondary level but also at the elementary school level and can be tied to issues faced by minorities and issues of equity. Issues regarding local unemployment and inflation can be linked to national and global issues. To start the decision making process with the interests of young citizens does not limit the scope of the matters that can be considered. The challenge for social studies teachers is to expand the vision of their class so that the issues pursued for study require consideration of the broadest context possible.

Identifying and Defining the Issue

Determining what issue is addressed is a key consideration for any classroom, any group of young people and all citizens. Whatever the issue selected, the class needs to reach agreement on what the issue is. How the issue is defined will influence proposed solutions. Student-citizens, like adults, may see the issue differently and considerable dialogue may be needed to reach agreement on a definition. Regardless of the difficulty involved, identifying and defining the issue is part of the decision making process and broadly based interaction among class members should be encouraged. Young citizens should come to realize that it is possible to define a problem in a way that is beneficial to one point of view and should become able to recognize that strategy when politicians, the media or government officials use it.

Once the issue has been identified, the task of defining key terms in order to clarify the statement of the issue is vital. If the identified issue is, "What policy would keep people from littering?" the meaning of 'littering' must be defined. Does littering refer to depositing waste and leftovers on public property? Or private property? Or on both? Are there others aspects of littering that need to enter the definition? Before decisions are made, the class needs to reach agreement on the meaning of such key terms.

An important caution regarding the identification of the issue and the definition of its key terms is that individuals in the class should reach their own conclusions, albeit with the teacher acting as facilitator. The teacher must recognize that time and patience are prerequisites of a democratic class environment. Furthermore, if the teacher preempts the class by providing a succinctly stated issue and a clear definition of terms, young people will lose the opportunity to intellectually wrestle with these matters on their own.

Identifying Value Assumptions

Identifying the values that an individual or a group wishes to maximize in the context of making a decision is fundamental to actually making decisions. These values function as criteria for assessing both alternatives and consequences of solutions that are proposed regarding a particular issue. Being explicitly conscious of these values guides all the thinking that is done relative to a particular decision. These value assumptions will differ from individual to individual and it will probably be neither possible nor desirable to reach consensus on the value assumptions held by the group as a whole.

However, identifying assumptions is not limited to any one phase of the decision making process. If the class is exploring the issue of whether the community should restore the old library, some of the class may feel that preserving old buildings is a very valuable thing to do. Some may not. As the result of learning about the costs of restoration, some may begin to feel that the costs are too high not only for the present but also for the future. They will then be faced with resolving the tension between two values: the value of preserving the past and that of higher costs and perhaps, higher taxes. This tension is the foundation of learning. It provides an opportunity to analyze, to generate reasons and to locate and evaluate evidence. They must think about which of these values is most important and why. To what extent would they be willing to trade the value of preservation for lower costs and/or lower taxes? Like this example, most issues will cause ambivalence between two prized values: one that satisfies short term self-interest in the form of lower costs and/or lower taxes and another that satisfies long term goals that might have a lasting effect on beautifying the community not only for the present but for generations to come.

Since student-citizens will hold different views, any effort to force classroom consensus is not likely to be productive. Furthermore, in the context of democratic education, it is not desirable. Many student-citizens may feel pressured to comply with their peers or their teacher. Such compliance may have the effect of minimizing the level of their participation in classroom dialogue. It will also limit the quality and complexity of the thinking that they do.

Identifying Alternatives

Values, previous knowledge, experience and logic are all involved in the identification of possible alternatives. Furthermore, the more knowledge young citizens have about the issue, the more likely they are to identify thoughtful and well grounded alternatives. Before the class is asked to generate alternatives, they need information about the issue so that their alternatives are based on as broad an understanding as possible both about the nature of the issue and the peoples and/or groups who may be affected by the decision. Teachers must do everything they can to make sure that as many class members as possible participate in these intellectual processes. They also need to make sure that a full range of contrasting alternatives are generated in order to strengthen the basis of decision making and help identify related reading materials. Another important condition that accompanies the generation of alternatives is that listing them does not necessarily mean that they deserve commitment to them. Indeed, the teacher must guard against tendencies of young citizens that may represent a rush to judgment. Student-citizens need to be encouraged to suspend judgment until all alternatives and their consequences are considered and their base of information is as complete as possible. Otherwise, they may overlook a stronger and wiser alternative.

The sum total of alternatives needs to be as balanced as possible. If a class is in unanimous agreement on a particular alternative, only a single alternative will receive attention. In such cases, the teacher needs to present other alternatives or encourage student-citizens to think of other possibilities even if they do not support them initially. This process may strengthen their case since they will be familiar with what and how their opponents may think about the issue.

Predicting Consequences

After a sufficient number of alternatives have been presented, (at least three alternatives; two competing possibilities and a middle position) their consequences must be seriously considered. The evidence that can be gathered about the likelihood of consequences is very important and often hard to find. Both members of the class as well as the teacher should see that alternatives function as the basis for prediction. Once possible consequences have had the benefit of classroom dialogue, the basis for a stronger decision has been made.

Reaching Decisions

After generating as many alternatives as feasible and identifying their probable consequences, student-citizens need to prioritize the possibilities in terms of the values they are trying to realize. This aspect of the decision making process can be filled with tension since there is often no clear answer that fulfills all of the decision maker's hopes and goals. At this point it may be necessary for the teacher to ask whether the class is leaning toward satisfying their own self-interest or whether the decision serves a broader group of people. It is here that sensitivity toward others and the common good may be expressed. Certainly, the relationship between their values and the proposed decision need to be examined closely.

Justifying Decisions

In preparing people for democratic citizenship, it is crucial, absolutely crucial, that young citizens can defend their position as vigorously as possible. The intellectual tools for such a vigorous defense are evidence (which can include expert opinion if it is credible) and reason. In other words, what knowledge does the individual have that supports their decision and what reasons and/or evidence, including what high level values, can they offer to ground their decision in a persuasive and effective way? We must prepare our citizens to assess contrasting or competing views on the basis of how well they are grounded. If they are not thoroughly grounded, they should be rejected. The social studies classroom provides a setting where student-citizens can justify their decisions in written and oral form, where they can exchange and challenge each other's ideas, and revise their decisions if their arguments are found wanting. There are few other settings with this potential.

Tentativeness of Decision Making

Even when large amounts of information are available for decision making purposes, total knowledge is seldom available. Yet, the emergence of new information can alter the decisions that are made. For this reason, among others, there are no perfect or absolute decisions. Rather, citizens can only try to make the best possible decisions in the light of the information available and the values they hold. The need to cultivate an attitude that is open to new and conflicting ideas is a very important aspect of decision making in a democracy. Rigid views and fixed opinions contribute to an authoritarian posture that reduces or even eliminates the chances of further intellectual growth as well as the free exchange of ideas that are highly valued in a democracy. The right to change one's mind or to revise one's decision needs to be emphasized to all young citizens as they develop the intellectual strength necessary to function effectively as democratic citizens.

Taking Action

Optimally, after well grounded decisions have been made, student-citizens need to consider what action(s) they might take to advance their decisions. Such ideas may take a variety of forms (letters to the editor, a play to heighten the awareness of others in the school, an interview with local officials, posters for placement in local businesses, and the like). The best situation at this point would be to use a social action counselor who would help student-citizens with their preferred way of taking action. The social action counselor should be a teacher who is familiar with the community, its agencies and possibilities. It is also important that young citizens have a chance to debrief their social action experience to make meaning of what happened and evaluate it so improvements can be made.

CONCLUSION

In this chapter, two levels of decision making that are central to this curriculum have been presented and illustrated. The first of these levels was the testing of truth claims and the second was decision making as applied to solving or improving significant controversial issues. These intellectual processes are ones that are essential to raising the quality of thinking that democratic citizens bring to the issues of their times. Taken together, competence in these two processes should help student-citizens make better personal and public decisions. As educators we must do what we can to insure such learning outcomes.

NOTES

1. Self-interest can be defined in different ways. Often economic, financial or power terms are dominant. In this book, it is used to some extent to identify the self-interest of all peoples for a peaceful world. If a more peaceful world is our collective goal and we recognize that it is in our self-interest to create a non-violent climate across the Planet, then it is also in everyone's self-interest, including mine and yours, to reduce the number of people who live below poverty levels, to reduce oppression and to provide education and health care to the greatest number of people possible in our nation and across our Planet. Under such improved conditions, hostilities are somewhat less likely to break out and hatreds are somewhat less likely to exist. In this spirit, Dr. Charlotte Anderson, past President of the National.Council for the Social Studies introduced a new dimension in her conceptualization of global education. She is the only one, to my knowledge, who explicitly included the value of caring as fundamental to the curriculum framework she developed for the Association for Supervision and Curriculum Development (ASCD). This framework is exceptionally useful for those concerned with elementary grade levels. However, it has application for the middle and high school levels as well.

2. The literature on the constructivist theory of learning is substantial. It is also compatible with fostering intellectual processes that involves learners in creating their own view of reality.

3. Not only should citizens of a democracy understand that knowledge is tentative, but they should also be prepared to revise their views when confronted with new evidence or new reasoning. These abilities should increase the likelihood of a posture of humility, since none of us can be absolutely certain that our conclusions or recommendations are correct. Hanvey's work takes on special importance in this context, as it emphasizes that many activities we engage in may have surprise effects that we did not think of and never anticipated.

4. The conception of education that Freire's work represents is both theoretical also practical, as he applied his views of learning to oppressed peasants. See References.

5. The term, social action as used here, implies intervention based on well grounded decisions whose objective is to improve social conditions in some significant way.

CHAPTER 6

THE STATUS
OF SOCIAL STUDIES
PROGRAMS

As the social studies exist today in most schools, we somehow never get
to the present, or at best, we treat the present superficially. Important contemporary
and future problems are passed over in most schools, and young people graduate
from high schools not only knowing less than nothing about them, but having
no clear idea how to think about such problems.
—Engle and Ochoa, 1988, p. 115.

INTRODUCTION

This chapter, in the interest of providing readers with a relevant history of
alternative views of social studies curricula, describes seven different conceptions of social studies curricula. In this way, readers can consider their
preferences and values that provide the foundation for how we prepare
young citizens. Serious professionals should also become familiar with the
references. Young citizens everywhere are every nation's most precious possession. Given the rise of terrorism, the next few decades are likely to be
highly challenging. A great responsibility resides in the office of citizen in a
democracy to shape a system where its citizens must prove that self-governance can work even in a very diverse society, in a very complicated world
and in very troubling times.

*   *   *

Democratic Education for Social Studies, pages 145–185
Copyright © 2007 by Information Age Publishing
All rights of reproduction in any form reserved.

Despite many reform efforts in social studies advanced by educators as well as substantial federal contribution to create new social studies programs that are referred to as the New Social Studies,[1] social studies teaching and learning across this nation have not changed appreciably for well over a century. From many systematic classroom observations, it is fair to characterize social studies classrooms as knowledge-centered, textbook-dependent, often supplemented by teacher-lecture with regular tests that require memorization. There is little attention to public issues, to controversy or to matters such as social class, peace efforts in this nation's history, the labor movement or local tensions where environmentalists seeking to protect unused space are opposed to the actions taken by local developers who want to develop space for profit. Such concerns that represent the real world issues too often are deemed inappropriate or too controversial for young citizens to examine. The above quote by James Shaver sets a very appropriate tone for this chapter that aims to capture the essence of the status of social studies in our nation's schools. It is terribly significant that, despite school requirements that all student-citizens study United States History at the fifth grade, the eighth grade, the eleventh grade and many are required to take at least one course during their first two years of college, that all assessments indicate that young citizens who have earned passing grades in these several courses, know very little of our history and that they often find history boring and uninteresting. This seems to be true, even for those who choose to become teachers. They may resonate to the names of a few of the well-known figures such as Lincoln, Washington, Robert E. Lee and a few events such as the American Revolution and the Civil War. They may even remember a few dates such as 1776, 1860, 1914-18 and December 7, 1941. Their textbook-based instruction accompanied by teacher-lectures and followed by periodic tests across these courses failed to develop a depth of understanding or an ability to analyze or validate any claims their textbooks presented. Furthermore, very little factual knowledge seems to reside in their memory. Surely, we must agree that this system, no matter how well intentioned or long-lived, does not generate an appreciation of history for most young citizens and certainly does not develop the abilities needed for effective participation by citizens of a democracy. Young people appear to have memorized the necessary textbook information in the form of names of people, events and dates that were required to pass classroom tests. After that, much of what they memorized appears to have drained out of them. (I suspect, on occasion, we have all had this experience of fast-forgetting material we had memorized for test purposes).

One can only shudder to think of the time, energy and dollars spent for teachers, textbooks, building space and maintenance for this unproductive required curriculum across time. We must conclude that for most, if not all student-citizens, this approach does not work—it does not deliver in terms of its own goals nor does it enhance the knowledge and abilities young people need to contribute to a stronger democracy. Textbooks tell a story about the past that is definitive and certain. They do not suggest that any of the textbook's statements have a tentative quality and are subject to revision or reinterpretation, particularly if new scholarship on a given topic appears. Indeed, such traditional teaching practices probably contribute to attitudes such as "I don't like history!" or "I was never interested in politics!" that seem to prevail among many of our citizens who do not vote and many do not try to understand the issues that face their diverse society and their complex world. The greater the number of people who hold such attitudes, the weaker this democracy becomes and the less capable are the citizens of a democracy to engage in self-governance. This nation, an especially privileged nation with a commitment to democracy and to social justice, has not yet found ways to teach its young citizens to be competent citizens who are able and willing to address the public issues of their times. Alternative curriculum have been recommended across the years and are very evident in the social studies literature (Dewey, 1922, 1933, Rugg, 1921; Engle, 1960; Oliver and Shaver, 1966; Oliver and Newmann, 1967; Hunt & Metcalfe, 1955, 1968; Stanley & Nelson, 1986 among many others) and pertinent presentations are made with some frequency at professional meetings, but are seldom, very seldom, evident on a regular basis in our nation's classrooms.

Two scholars, one a British Canadian, Ruth Sandwell (2005) and the other English, David Hicks (2005) have reported on their comparison regarding the teaching of history in the United Kingdom and the United States. Their view of the teaching of history in classrooms in the United States is that it is a grand epic, a finished and indisputable story of people, events and dates that depicts an illustrious past that young people need to learn from their textbooks accompanied by supplementary teacher-lectures in order that young citizens pass periodic tests and pass the course. Strong differences exist in the United Kingdom where the law requires that history is taught as enquiry. Their curriculum involves young people examining primary documents and interpreting them. They draw their own historic conclusions based on the evidence available to them. The curriculum mandated in the United Kingdom appears to have considerable consistency with the principles of those offered by some reformers in the United States, including those who advocate Issues-Centered Decision Making curricula. The comparative studies of history teaching and history curricula by Sandwell and Hicks affirms the conclusion of this author and others regarding the disappointing status of social studies in the United States.

Why do these differences exist across nations that share a common language, whose populations are both culturally diverse and who both embrace democratic values? One compelling view is shared by Karen Riley (2005) who suggests that the reason for the persistence of the grand epic filled with "just the facts" may reside in a prevailing view among our citizens who sense the United States is a much younger and more diverse nation than the United Kingdom, one born in rebellion to secure freedom against British rule and one where teachers, parents and the general public expect the school to foster loyalty and patriotism to this relatively new nation among its young citizens. The challenges encountered by this new nation have been and are numerous and intense. It has been torn by a Civil War, received persistent waves of immigrants from a wide range of cultures, countries and who speak different languages, participated in two world wars and during the last century, also was engaged in the Cold War, the Vietnam War, Bosnia and a war in the Middle East. Concurrently, the United States has functioned as a leading world nation characterized by democracy and a capitalistic market economy accompanied by many public protests in behalf of multiple causes such as those giving support to civil rights, resistance to the Vietnam War, pro- and antiabortion, peace efforts, pro- and anti- gay rights, anti the Iraq War among others. Taken together, these events may serve to sustain the view that the public, school boards and some school personnel hold for studying history in a manner that breeds loyalty and patriotism. Therefore, to encourage young people to generate alternative and possibly conflicting views of the past is somewhat threatening and not seen as desirable by the public at large. Thus, the grand epic prevails, uncontested and unexamined in our textbooks, among our teachers and in our classrooms. However, in very established and much older nations such as the United Kingdom, where traditions run deep and where nationhood seems very secure, a more open approach consistent with the evidence-based and open-ended manner in which historians work is an acceptable way to teach national history. Riley's perspective seems to explain, at least in part, why curriculum reform efforts have not taken hold in the United States. Furthermore, our teachers are not comfortable with these reforms that require changes in the teacher's role to be that of facilitator rather than an authority on historical knowledge and a new set of classroom conditions and procedures that create more student–centered, issues-centered classrooms where evidence becomes the authority, not the teacher and controversy is the norm, not the exception. Neither have most of our teacher education programs in universities prepared teachers to teach young citizens in these alternative ways.

In Chapter 2 titled "The Citizen We Need in a Democracy," the qualities needed by citizens of a democracy as contrasted to subjects in an autocracy were briefly addressed. Democratic citizens do not simply have to develop an acceptable set of habits and behaviors. Rather, they need to have a strong commitment to democracy and the values of social justice that democracy entails. In addition, they must learn to exercise the abilities that represent higher level thinking and decision making that are at the heart of self-governance and the curriculum proposed here. They need to bring a broad base of knowledge along with depth of understanding as well as broad perspectives about the world they live in to their challenging roles as citizens. If student-citizens are able to acquire such knowledge and abilities, they will, as adults, become more effective and valuable democratic citizens. They will be able to expand and strengthen democratic practices and participate in efforts to expand social justice. Social studies educators must be mindful that we are not preparing citizen drones who have no interest or ability to participate in public life, but active participants who will demonstrate, a higher level of confidence that self-governance by the people can work and work well. As importantly, we must recognize that unless social studies programs are designed and delivered in a manner consistent with democracy or this goal will not be realized.

This chapter will examine the social studies curriculum as follows:

- The sources of confusion over the definition of social studies with attention to the deficiencies among the various configurations of social studies.
- Assessment of current practices in social studies programs including obstacles to reform of the social studies curriculum as well as a view of what needs to be done.

CONFUSION OVER THE DEFINITION OF SOCIAL STUDIES

Social studies is, at times, narrowly defined as the study of the social sciences and history which usually takes the form of the exposition of facts and generalizations about which social scientists are in reasonable agreement. However, social studies can also be defined more broadly as the critical study of the social sciences and history. This definition usually engages student-citizens directly in the intellectual process by which social scientists and historians verify truth. Finally, social studies may be defined even more broadly as the process of solving or ameliorating significant social issues which are often, controversial. In the latter case, the social sciences become instrumental in the learning process rather than serving as the goals of education.

From these three basic definitions, at least seven distinguishable configurations of social studies can be identified, each with a different conception of purpose and different projected outcomes, which, in some cases run counter to one another. Nor do all configurations serve the unique and distinctive goals of democracy equally well, if at all. They are presented here to help educators reflect on these alternative approaches. The author's bias that is dedicated to this Issues-Centered Decision Making Curriculum is evident in the following discussion. However, the presentation below identifies references for alternative views for readers who wish to explore this matter in greater depth.

In the following pages, each of these configurations of social studies will be presented and the potential of each for preparing citizens for a democracy will be examined.

Social Studies as the Social Sciences Simplified for Pedagogical Purposes

A definition of social studies given currency in the 1930s by Edgar B. Wesley (1937) that is still widely accepted in the field is that "the social studies are the social sciences adapted and simplified for pedagogical purposes." The careful reader will notice the use of the phrase, "the social studies are" which in Wesley's view refers to the separate scholarly disciplines that constitute the social sciences. In the proposed curriculum, "is" reflects social studies as an interdisciplinary subject because it draws on many disciplines to provide understanding of social issues. Whatever meaning Wesley may have intended for this definition, in practice it has been confined to an exposition of a relatively small number of facts from history and the separate social sciences and presented to young citizens as final truths to be committed to memory. Seldom is the opportunity to examine the validity of these claims provided to young citizens. Rather, it is usually expected that these truths be accepted as true by virtue of the authority of the textbook and/or the teacher. Frequently, there is no opportunity for student-citizens to know or question the scholarly assumptions that form the basis of truth claims. There is also little opportunity to question how the narrative might have been different if facts that were left out had instead been included. Finally, there is seldom an opportunity to compare and examine other versions of these claims to truth.

Three configurations of social studies that have emerged from Wesley's definition are presented below.

1. Social Studies as the Exposition of Truth Claims from History and the Separate Social Sciences

The most common configuration of social studies in this nation's classrooms is the exposition of facts and generalizations that scholars in the history and the various social sciences claim to be true at a given point in time. Historians tell us what happened and why. Economists tell us how economic phenomena are invariably related and so forth. These truth claims are filtered through, selected out and arranged by textbook authors and publishers for young citizens to accept as definitive truth. The result is that professional textbook authors, who are seldom scholars themselves, produce a vastly simplified version of events. These events are explicated to student-citizens by means of teacher lectures and by reading the textbook.

Subsequently, young citizens take tests on the content that was covered. They are expected to remember and presumably understand these selected facts that depict the past. The bottom line of such teaching and learning is that class members must be able to recall the content covered. Under this configuration, student-citizens are not encouraged to question the factual claims set forth nor are they invited to challenge authority. Teachers, scholars and textbook authors serve as the final arbiters of truth. Furthermore, young citizens are not encouraged to use the facts in thinking about any controversial issue. Certainly, we should not be surprised that student-citizens see little relevance in this kind of learning (McGowan, 1984).

A number of problems emerge with this configuration of social studies. First, it overlooks the fact that the social science disciplines which it seeks to explicate are, in themselves, hotbeds of dispute. Scholars in these fields are in continual and sometimes sharp disagreement over what the facts are and what they mean. On the basis of new research findings, scholars are continually revising their conception of what is true. In the field of economics, for instance, as contrasted with textbook versions of economics, there is almost total disarray. The very best scholars in the field are very hard pressed to explain, with any degree of certainty, the economic circumstances that the peoples of the world face today. There are many equally respectable theories that purport to explain current economic complexities. Since many of the so-called facts in the field of economics are so undependable, it is useless as well as dishonest to teach them to our student-citizens as if they were the whole truth. It is also somewhat of a misrepresentation to hold out the promise that the social sciences can be successfully simplified for pedagogical purposes. To simplify means to leave out part of the story. To illustrate, textbooks have often ignored the Native American side of the wars with the early colonists. This distortion is also the case for the American Revolution as seen by the United Empire Loyalists. Instead, the position of the American revolutionaries receives almost exclusive attention. Additionally, labor unions are seldom treated in depth, social class is seldom mentioned and wars get much more attention than efforts by organizations and individuals to build a momentum for a more peaceful world. This simplifying process contributes to the distortion of history and the social sciences, making them say something that they do not actually say.

Teachers must be mindful that these fields of study are not sciences at all if some knowledge is omitted and if the tentativeness of their conclusions is not made clear. Nor are they sciences if diverse or alternative views, events or peoples are withheld for whatever purpose. They are surely not sciences if the assumptions and qualifiers upon which their claims to truth are based are not laid bare. Simplified social science is only one short step removed from propaganda, however sincere the simplifiers are. Simplification defeats the possibility that student-citizens will receive a balanced, even though, a more tentative exposure to "the epic saga" perpetrated in textbooks.

A related concern evident in this configuration of social studies is that it teaches students-citizens advertently or inadvertently, to be unquestioning and accepting of authority, as befits autocracy, rather than to be the inquirers and skeptics that democracy requires. The weight of such teaching fosters conformity of beliefs by presenting what appear to the reader to be indisputable truths, in contrast to the intellectually skeptical orientation necessary for democratic public life. The fact that young citizens come to schools that have an authoritarian climate and a single view of our history—and a unrealistic view at that—means that this kind of curriculum does not foster stronger democratic citizens. Rather, the experiences they have tend to promote reliance of authority and would be fitting if were trying to encourage loyalty to an autocracy rather than informed and active citizenship in a democracy.

Still another problem with this expository configuration is that teaching and learning in this mode can very easily become very dull. Sadly, we have proof that it often does. Such teaching trivializes the study of the history and the social sciences. It burdens the mind with what Alfred North Whitehead (1929) called "inert ideas" that go nowhere. Social studies is boring to many student-citizens because it puts off indefinitely, usually forever, the opportunity to explore really significant questions, which are characterized by uncertainty and controversy and seldom have definite and final answers. Only in the open-ended exploration of such questions does excitement enter learning. Some of our strongest research makes it patently clear that young people enjoy classes where controversy is generated and different points of view are explored (Hahn, 1996). However, the focus of this expository configuration denies student-citizens the opportunity to develop their intellectual prowess to enable their more vigorous role in strengthening democracy.

2. Social Studies as Indoctrination

A variation of the expository teaching of social science facts and generalizations and one that rivals it in the frequency of school and classroom practice, is the use of social studies for purposes of propaganda. There are those who believe that the role of social studies curricula is to indoctrinate young citizens with certain understandings and points of view that are thought to be better than others or to be necessary to unify the nation and preserve establishment roles and values. Some individuals and groups in this society fear for its future unless their particular ideas of what is good and right are imposed on all. Based on such points of view, they would skew what is taught in history or economics to advance what they believe to be the common good.

For instance, only the strengths of capitalism are addressed, with no mention whatsoever of its problems and weaknesses. Similarly, the violence committed against people and property by the patriots of the American Revolution might be soft-pedaled, lest it suggest that disobedience to unpopular government action, as with anti–nuke protests, is an acceptable practice. Or the Vietnam War, which historians largely agree was a disastrous defeat for the United States, can be described merely as a tactical retreat or even a victory because such persons or groups believe that the United States can never be wrong and that this nation is always invincible. Ignoring our nation's shortcomings, and there are many, whatever they may be, is denying a comprehensive, balanced and honest education to young citizens who will need to view the issues of their time as ones that are debatable and raise questions to which they will need to supply justifiable responses. In a democratic setting, they must learn to be skeptical.

There are those, including many educators, who seemingly believe that tender minds should be told the facts, but only the facts that others identify for them. It is but one short, easily taken step from teaching unquestioned and unquestionable truth, as in the expositions of facts and generalizations accepted totally on the authority of the textbook, to teaching the truth, dressed up a bit or skewed to serve what some see as a patriotic responsibility or even self-interest. Such a fragile and deceitful truth is contradictory to the tenets of democracy.

Citizenship educators as well as citizens need to understand that any selection of 'so-called' facts has an ideological bias advertently or inadvertently. It is never neutral or completely objective. If, for example, student-citizens are not given an opportunity to study the war in Vietnam and instead, they study the decade of the '20s, this choice, like any choice, represents a value or set of values that are being applied to what young citizens learn or do not learn. However, it is possible for a teacher to make this choice inadvertently. The teacher could argue that time is running out and student-citizens in United States History need to know more about its past rather than more recent issues. However, the losers are future adult citizens and our democracy when citizens do not have a balanced picture of an issue as controversial as the War in Vietnam. All selections of content have an ideological base even if those making the selection are trying to be objective.

Textbook publishers, driven by the necessity to sell books are often self-appointed censors, who contribute to indoctrination by either omitting or watering down the coverage of any topic that may give rise to controversy. For instance, a study of ten social studies textbook series at the elementary level found these materials to be uniformly superficial in their treatment of important topics, arbitrary in their selection of topics and neglectful of topics deemed controversial (Elliott, Nagel & Woodward., 1985). These researchers found coverage of such topics as civil rights to be stylistic rather than substantive and the treatment of women and minorities as unrealistic. The question becomes, "What are the messages we want to send to our young citizens?"

There is also the possibility that the truth may be distorted unwittingly by teachers and others who may lack scholarly acumen and intellectual persistence. Scholars contribute to skewing the facts when they write out of ignorance or from ill-founded assumptions. For instance, it is now clear that historians, some of whom have been textbook writers, wrote in the post Civil War period with an anti-woman, anti-African American, anti-Native American and anti-labor union bias. This is a bias which only in the last few decades historians have tried to correct.[2] What were presented as fairly definitive facts about the Reconstruction period turned out not to be accurate facts at all. Historians also wrote mistakenly about African Americans because they did not know about their activities. In prior times African Americans were not studied. Seeing them only as slaves, these historians misinterpreted the potential of African Americans in circumstances other than slavery. Unwittingly or not, they wrote history with a decidedly establishment bias, which for years went unchallenged and was taken to be the hard truth. They even failed to note the participation of African Americans as soldiers in the Civil War when these men served but were placed aside in a separate organization from white male soldiers. Teaching history in an expository fashion, without questioning, contributes to the acceptance of such bias by student-citizens. This kind of teaching represents a very subtle, but pernicious form of indoctrination.

Still other problems exist with a configuration that intends to indoctrinate. Since small children have not reached the age of full rationality, they are unavoidably subject to indoctrination by parents, teachers and their peers. The inappropriateness of doctrinaire practices disappears once they mature, even as early for some young citizens as the upper elementary grades and certainly, by the time they are in middle school. At this level, they must learn to detect bias, to identify assumptions and to question authority. In a democracy, citizens should learn to think for themselves, to think analytically and to appraise the reasons and evidence that support their views and alternative views. To allow anyone, self-appointed or legally authorized, to decide what is safe for others to know or to think is a complete negation of democracy which is nothing if it is not to make decisions based on verifiable facts, wherever these facts may lead. Denial of the right to know is a significant step toward dictatorship and tyranny. Democracy prospers in the full light of day. We do not advance democracy by imitating the educational methods of dictators.

There is yet another problem with indoctrination. It robs young citizens of the opportunity to learn the skills of questioning and criticism so necessary for the development of the democratic citizen. Indoctrination dare not be conducted in any mode but the expository. As with the straight transmission of selected facts as indicated above, indoctrination is intolerant of questioning or hypothesizing. Student-citizens must not become believers who park their brains at the classroom door. In a very real sense, the exposition of a lie is not too different from the exposition of the facts, since any single truth is never the whole truth. Truths must be questioned and continually refined to achieve a more firmly grounded truth. This process is the hallmark of scholarship and is a set of intellectual abilities necessarily applicable to a fully functioning democratic citizen. Both a lie and a half-truth may be exposed by further questioning. In either case, the intellectual process is the same. Thus, whether we insist on a configuration of social studies that transmits mere facts or that transmits lies posing as the truth, young citizens do not have the opportunity to develop independent thinking skills and democracy is does not benefit from their intellectual contributions (Sandwell, 2005).

Despite their widespread use, it is impossible to see how either of these approaches contributes usefully to the preparation of democratic citizens. Each denies young people the right to know all of the facts that are known, as is their right in a democracy. They learn to be quite accepting of whatever they are told by their elders. One can hardly conceive of citizen characteristics that serve democracy less well.

3. Social Studies as the Study of Topics

The topical configuration of social studies is simply a variation of the exposition of facts and generalizations or of lies being passed off as facts. It is different only in that the subject matter being transmitted is broader in scope and cuts across the boundaries of disciplines or, at the elementary level, the subject matter is too simplistic to be treated as social science disciplines.

Originally, as Barth and Shermis (1979) have clearly pointed out, the study of a topic was often confused with the study of a social issue. For instance, the problems suggested for study in the 12th grade by the Committee on the Social Studies in 1916 were, in fact, topics, not issues or controversies. The purpose was not to involve young people in solving issues but to inform them about what were then defined as social problems. It was believed that the social sciences would eventually be able to resolve most social problems as soon as the facts were known. Yet, today, social scientists are far from certain about the power of science to solve society's issues. They recognize that social issues are very complex and often controversial in nature, involving moral, ethical and political questions as well as cultural, gender and racial concerns that science alone will not solve. Nonetheless, in many schools, social studies programs persist with a thoughtless curriculum rather than one that emphasizes multiple perspectives and scrutiny that lead to a vigorous decision making process. The proposed Issues-Centered Decision Making Curriculum provides such as opportunity for preparing young citizens to be adult citizens.

From this perspective, the differences between a topic and an issue are, in large measure, matters of the learning mode with which we approach the study. Is our purpose merely to inform student-citizens about the issue, along with its supposed solution or to involve them in the more knotty task of working out their own conclusions and possible solutions? The first is conducted in an expository mode, while the second is conducted in the more difficult and intellectually challenging hypothetical mode. The outcome of the first is information about the issue that can be held in memory for some limited period of time. The outcome of the second is a much less definitive sense of the whole problem, where efforts at resolution are always only approximations of a final and definite solution. In this approach, solutions are always tentative and temporary and they change as circumstances change. Uncertainty is a continuing characteristic of issues that our citizens face. Proposed solutions, more often than not, entail compromises between contending forces and diverse opinions. This is the real stuff of citizen problem solving. It is what democratic citizen must learn to do—a condition that is avoided by the topical approach. Surely, we can do better!

At elementary grade levels, common practice suggests that a topical approach is appropriate for children in their early years who are deemed too immature intellectually and socially for the introduction of uncertainty that hypothesizing entails. However, Maxine Dunfee (1970) and Dorothy Skeel (1996), both of whom had extensive experience in elementary schools, consistently pointed out that elementary aged children can and have responded to questions asked on an age appropriate basis. What is recycling and what can we do about it? is but one example. What is more, even first graders have written simple, short letters to the editor of their local newspaper encouraging adults to make greater use of the local recycling center—a small but, important example of social action. Disagreement occurs over the appropriate time to move into a higher level thinking and decision making mode. However, elementary grade teachers come to know their students very well and can sense when they are ready to be engaged in questions that do not have definitive answers. At that time, the learning mode switches from the expository to an active inquiry mode on the part of young children.

Moreover, in a recent study that tracked three of the strongest teachers in an elementary school, some evidence of decision making was in place (Ochoa-Becker, Morton, Autry, Johnstad & Merrill, 2001). As early as the third grade, children were observed thinking and talking about hypothetical dilemmas and giving reasons for their proposed solutions. As noted by Dorothy Skeel (1996), through questioning and carefully selected children's literature, there are a variety of ways that an Issues-Centered Decision Making Curriculum can be integrated at the elementary level. Commonly however, teachers rely on textbooks and mini–lectures to transmit subject matter to children and require that they commit that content to memory.

The foundations for higher level thinking and making decisions can begin in early grade levels as the work of Hilda Taba (1967) clearly demonstrated. Taba's questioning sequences for involving children in concept formation and for generalizing as well as those she created in the affective domain where young children examined feelings and values serve as powerful tools for heightening the intellectual levels of young children. Her research provides strong support for involving children at young ages in a great deal of intellectual activity. In any case, the burden on teachers of very young children to teach the truth as best they know it, is indeed an onerous responsibility. At the elementary school level, teachers must actively pursue the intellectual development of children, especially in the elementary grades.

In addition to the topical study of problems, the topical approach has been used by a number of curriculum reformers who insist that a study of social science disciplines needlessly divides the field and makes a proper understanding of the broad sweep of human events impossible to transmit. Notable among such reformers was Harold Rugg of Columbia University who attempted a discourse on human events in the United States that encompassed all of the disciplines (Rugg, 1921). Still another was Paul Hanna (1958), and his students at Stanford, who identified generalizations cutting across disciplines. Still another reformer was Lawrence Senesh at Purdue University, who wrote textbooks for the lower grades attempting to orchestrate all of the social sciences, ostensibly around an understanding of economics (Senesh, 1966). The overriding goal of these efforts was to unify or integrate the social sciences to make them more comprehensible for young people. All were attempts to explicate the facts to student-citizens as constructed by the author's perspective, which did nothing for encouraging a questioning posture on the part of young citizens. In addition, not only did the disciplines prove to be difficult, if not impossible, to orchestrate, but each discipline presented a contrasting, not a unifying view of social phenomena; young citizens were to accumulate the findings from the disciplines in memory without any opportunity to use these facts in a meaningful way. In any case, none of these efforts produced the kind of results that could justify the enthusiasm of their authors.

Another wider use of the topical approach comes about when someone decides that a particular area of concern is of such far-reaching importance that it deserves special treatment not accorded it in a curriculum devoted to the exposition of the disciplines. There exists a continuous flow of pamphlet materials published under the auspices of the National Council for the Social Studies as well as other professional organizations which provide information on a broad range of such topics. An important observation of these special topics in special publications is that, for the most part, they are strictly topical and provide information in an encyclopedic manner rather than emphasizing issues and encouraging student-citizens to take a questioning and skeptical orientation. Of course, in a few cases they may be used by creative teachers to encourage independent thinking and decision making, but they are seldom designed to achieve that end. This condition applies in too many social studies classrooms.

The Social Studies as the Critical Study of History and the Social Sciences

Attempts to reform the teaching of social studies have frequently taken the form of the critical study of the social sciences, in contrast to their exposition. Fundamentally, such reform involves a shift from the expository mode of teaching to the hypothetical. In this case, truth claims are treated as hypotheses for further study in precisely the same manner as they are treated by social scientists themselves. Student-citizens are expected to take on the role of fledgling social scientists. The purpose of this approach to social studies is to help young citizens become critical consumers of historical and social science scholarship as well as higher level thinkers in their own right. Such reform is consistent with the nature of the social sciences, since truth claims among social scientists are always tentative and open to further study. Factual claims are taken to be only approximations of the truth and are always subject to revision as new light is shed on them by further research. History is always being reinterpreted, sometimes dramatically so, as new facts come to light. Economists are always at each others' scholarly throats as there are always other respectable versions of claims to truth. In the world of science all claims to truth are subject to challenge.

Further, serious educational reformers are more concerned that young citizens develop, as fully as possible, their intellectual prowess and that they develop a habit of openness to new evidence rather than merely memorize unrelated and sometimes invalid factual trivia. To these reformers, the exposition and memorization of information is not a sufficient goal for social studies. They believe that it is far more important to advance knowledge based on reason and evidence and to develop the higher level thinking abilities upon which dependable knowledge rests. Their commitment is to putting student-citizens through challenging intellectual paces rather than merely telling them what scholars have previously learned. Two different conceptions have emerged from this orientation toward social studies:

1. Social Studies as the Critical Analysis of the Social Sciences

This configuration takes its inspiration from such scholars as Gunnar Myrdal (1944) who warned us in his classic work, *The Great American Dilemma,* of the misinformation and misconception of society that accrue to a simplistic and uncritical exposition of history, without knowledge of the assumptions and qualifiers known to historians and without consideration of other possible versions of historical phenomena. Alfred North Whitehead (1929) in his classic work titled, *The Aims of Education,* warned, not only about the uselessness, but he also emphasized the harm that can follow from education which fills the mind with "inert ideas" that is, with ideas that are merely received into the mind without being utilized, tested or thrown into fresh combinations. Whitehead wisely advised us that the first thing to do to any idea is to prove its truth and that the second is to prove its worth or usefulness. In social studies, the most illustrious proponent of this point of view was Alan Griffin (1942) of the Ohio State University, who focused on the teaching of United States history and particularly, on the validation of the beliefs of young citizens about matters of fact and matters of value (Engle, 1982). Griffin's student, Lawrence Metcalf of the University of Illinois extended this idea to cover the beliefs of young citizens regarding "closed areas" of society, which were questions so controversial that they were not freely discussed (Hunt & Metcalf, 1955, 1968).

The Indiana Experiments conducted at Indiana University under the guidance of Shirley Engle (1982) demonstrated that the use of the Whitehead (1929) formula: "Is it true and what can it be used for?" in studying textbook courses in world history, United States history and government was not only enthusiastically received by student-citizens, but it led to a stronger grasp of the subject matter and also to heightened thinking abilities. However, it proved to be very demanding of teachers, who were probably not prepared in this manner and perhaps, for this reason, it was not widely emulated in the schools (Massialas, 1963).

A simpler version of the "critical analysis of textbooks" configuration would consistently introduce an alternative version into the study of a textbook version of events. Such a practice rests on the knowledge that facts, at best, are hard to come by, even when sought after by careful scholars. It recognizes that young citizens are continually revising their beliefs about what the facts are and how they should be interpreted. Furthermore, there is more than one interpretation of any social phenomenon and social science scholarship is an open-ended process, resulting in tentative conclusions rather than unquestioned truth. This approach is therefore consistent with the nature of scholarship, in that it continually considers alternative versions of truth claims. Recent scholarly reinterpretations of significant events can be an excellent source of alternative versions to compare with textbook accounts. For example, recent research on Christopher Columbus as conducted by noted biographer Frederick J. Pohl (1986) among others, gives a very different account of Columbus than the one that was common in most United States history textbooks. Recent historic works suggest that Columbus was abusive to the Native People. Instead, all of us have read the sugar coated view presented in social studies textbooks.

One problem with the critical analysis approach is the greater amount of time needed to carry out the study. In place of the superficial coverage of large amounts of material, which the expository mode makes possible, the patient and deeper treatment of a relatively small number of controversial issues and topics is substituted. One must ask, however, whether the expository ground covering, which characterizes so many social studies programs, really achieves what we are after, which is a greater understanding of our social heritage and whether it provides the intellectual experiences needed for an active and vital democratic life?

A related problem is that many teachers have not been well prepared to guide their classes in an intense investigation. In addition, educators need a rich collection of resources to support this kind of study. The Internet provides much information that, though it must be evaluated critically, provides easy access to research related to significant issues. It is, of course, possible that over a period of time, a teacher, a social studies department chair or a school might accumulate files of necessary material which would present alternative views of events not commonly presented in textbooks.

In any case, the advantages of using a configuration of social studies that focuses on critical analysis are persuasive. The critical analysis configuration presents the social sciences as they really are, as scholarly, open-ended ways of studying social phenomena, not merely as compendia of badly skewed and outdated information. The social sciences represent live and viable tools for understanding the human condition and they have an overwhelming advantage of engaging in critical analysis over exposition in that they cultivate these tools of questioning and drawing defensible conclusions , both so very necessary for citizens of a democracy.

2. Social Studies as the Replication of Social Science Scholarship

The configuration of social studies just described places its emphasis on helping young citizens learn to be critical consumers of the social sciences. Another kindred version places its emphasis as nearly as possible on what a social scientist actually does. Jerome Bruner, who popularized the notion of "discovery" teaching and who taught his students in the hypothetical as contrasted with the expository mode, is the most widely known proponent of this view of teaching (Bruner, 1962). Bruner saw young people learning by actually doing social science and at the same time, mastering the structure of the discipline. There were, according to Bruner, two ways of proceeding: (a) by replicating selected works of social scientists from the raw data used by the social scientist or (b) by engaging young citizens in novel, previously unresearched studies of selected social phenomena.

In the first instance, young citizens would be given the raw data and then be guided to replicate the work of scholars as they organized and interpreted the data. Student-citizens would be encouraged to hypothesize about the meaning of the data, much like social scientists draw conclusions from their own research. Of course, they would compare their findings and interpretations to those made by the social scientists.

A variation of this configuration would have student-citizens engage in real and as yet unresearched, areas of social investigation. For instance, they could write some of their own history as part of their study of their school or their community or they could conduct sociological or economic surveys of their communities. Bruner's claim for such strategies was that they would transform learners from passive receivers of information to active learners better able to use information to solve a variety of issues. Seeing information as useful would heighten their intrinsic motivation for learning instead of being tied to grades or the approval of their parents and teachers. Information that was learned as it was used would be easier to remember and most importantly, student-citizens would learn to make defensible decisions. Bruner believed that the best way to learn how to problem solve was to actually experience the process (Bruner, 1962).

Although these heady claims to excellence have never been conclusively established, they furnished the impetus for the most extensive social studies reform movement ever undertaken in social studies education in the United States. The "New Social Studies" reform effort of the '60s and '70s enlisted the involvement of hundreds of social scientists as well as college and K–12 educators, most of whom had become thoroughly disenchanted with the tradition of textbook-driven expository teaching that seemed to have had a stranglehold on social studies programs in the nation's schools.

Sadly, it still does. Hundreds of curriculum projects were undertaken and a number were based on Bruner's ideas. Some excellent work was done in developing the project titled, Man, A Course of Study (MACOS), High School Geography Project and others as well. Despite the substantial financial support of the federal government for developing materials and educating teachers, these projects were not widely accepted. Teachers were not prepared to deal with materials that had no correct or final answers, nor to assume the role of a facilitator of learning rather than a source of knowledge. These materials reduced the direct control of their classes to which they were accustomed. Furthermore, traditional achievement tests based on the recall of isolated bits of information, no longer fit as measures of learning for the new curricula. Some parents and communities became upset because children were excited, and sometimes upset, about the controversial nature of the curriculum. In any case, hardly a trace of the New Social Studies remains today. Despite this condition, there are social studies educators who believe that some of these curricula were on the right track and would like to see a resurrection of some of those efforts.

Such a configuration of social studies would require resources, though many are now available on web sites on the Internet and would demand much more in pre-service and in-service professional development for teachers than any configuration discussed so far. One Social Studies Methods Course would not be sufficient. to prepare teachers to handle alternative curricula. Instead of textbooks, a far greater variety of materials would have to be available. Far more breadth and depth would have to characterize the preparation of teachers. As important is assistance with the new, less controlling and more facilitative role of the teacher that includes a more interactive and more equitable teacher–student relationship. This curriculum involves a new way of organizing classroom and out-of-classroom work, new ways to use source materials, more creative approaches to assessment along with strong academic work that would include both the content and the processes of the curriculum. These are challenging tasks for teachers and teacher educators who see intellectual development as the best, if not the only road to greater competence for democratic citizens. For them, these demands are worth the dedicated effort required.

Social Studies as the Examination of Significant Social and Controversial Issues

Still a third group of reformers would organize the social studies as fully as possible around the study of controversial social issues. Social studies, so conceived, is not to be confused with the expository configurations previously described in this chapter. Nor should the Issues-Centered Decision Making approach be confused with the involvement of student-citizens in the study of social science disciplines as proposed by Bruner (1962). The first of these reforms stops short of real world issues and settles for merely providing student-citizens with information offered as the uncontested truth; the second stops short of real world problem-solving by limiting study to the academic problems that social scientists face. In fact, social scientists when working as social scientists seldom concern themselves with the issues faced by citizens. The President's Board of Economic Advisors is of limited usefulness and is often ignored by policy makers because its members seem to understand only the economic factors in a problematic situation and are blind to other compelling alternative perspectives that may cast needed light on an issue. When tackling a knotty controversial issue, relevant and valid factual information must be drawn from the broadest possible base of knowledge and should not be confined to the comparatively narrow perspective offered by a single social science discipline. Seeking the broadest base of knowledge makes the search interdisciplinary and teachers would need to experience selected courses that were focused on public issues and where knowledge from whatever disciplines and other sources necessary to construct a comprehensive picture of the issue and to make justifiable decisions that would improve conditions surrounding the particular issue under study.

Those who see social studies as usefully organized around significant and sometimes, controversial social issues believe that a significant part, if not all, of social studies should directly attempt to involve young citizens in contributing to the resolution of public issues in all of their ramifications. Only in this way, they argue, can citizens learn to deal intelligently and responsibly with such issues. These reformers would criticize education on two counts: for its devotion to what can best be called background information, without guiding student-citizens to apply this information to anything useful and for avoiding the inevitable controversy and uncertainty which are intrinsic dimensions of Issues-Centered Decision Making Curriculum. Advocates of Issues-Centered curricula are also deeply concerned that important issues are seldom, if ever, treated in social studies classrooms. Today's social studies educators seem to shy away from issues where strong and acrimonious positions are in conflict. Abortion versus pro-life values, environment versus development, alternative lifestyles, pros and cons of going to war, global conditions, race, equality, poverty and welfare serve as examples of controversial areas that frequently are unexplored or they receive little mention in our nation's classrooms. Yet, the classroom represents one of the few settings where young citizens can rationally and thoughtfully learn about such controversies and begin to consider their resolution. It is classrooms where children should learn more about learning how to learn. While it is impossible to study all such issues, young citizens can tackle some of these issues and in so doing, learn how to come to grips with issues that they have not studied. Unfortunately, the adage that "there is an elephant in the middle of the room, but nobody is talking about it" certainly applies to far too many social studies classrooms that avoid content that is controversial. This avoidance of complexity and controversy does not expand the capacity of young citizens to address such issues with civility and competence and it further reduces the strength of our democracy because its citizens do not seriously think about, openly discuss or take a stand on these important issues that are highly debatable and emotionally charged. The more citizens play such a passive and inactive role and do not exercise their basic rights, the more a relatively few people will make decisions for them. A democracy does not really exist if citizens do not assume the power and responsibility that democratic principles not only permit, but encourage. We do not need citizens who mindlessly enjoy the freedoms we have, but do not feel any responsibility to make the system as strong as it can be.

Currently, the war in Iraq is an issue quite persistently in the news. This matter has a great deal of public presence, media attention and public concern. Therefore, it was surprising when a colleague recently interviewed fourteen secondary school students who were disappointed that their teachers would not talk about Iraq in class, even though these young citizens wanted to know much more about it. (Flinders, 2005). This is an educational tragedy. Some of these secondary students will soon be enlisting in the Armed Forces. This war started through their middle school years when they were not aware of its implications for them. Yet, their teachers will not talk about it! While the reasons for avoidance for teachers avoiding the issues surrounding Iraq are not known, I suggest that these teachers and their administrators want to avoid controversy or do not want have class discussions that may become overheated. Thus, ignorance prevails. Half a century ago, Hunt and Metcalf (1955, 1968) emphasized the necessity for attention to what they called "closed areas" such as prejudice, sex, religion, nationalism and social class. Closed areas were topics or issues not seen as proper for public conversation. These authors argued that many people hold unexamined beliefs and those beliefs that have not been rationally examined are, in effect, prejudices regardless of their being right or wrong. Importantly, they also pointed out that "closed areas" change from generation to generation. More recently, Evans, Avery and Pederson (2000) restated the arguments for dealing with what they called taboo issues and considered the causes that result in avoidance of these areas in the curriculum.

Despite the barriers to teaching about taboos which may reside in the community, in school boards and in classrooms, American educators must call for school boards, administrators and teachers not to avoid these issues. However, they should avoid the too frequent predisposition of teachers as well as administrators to engage in self-censorship because they assume the community will protest if such issues represent the content that is studied in social studies classrooms. The study of censorship, itself a controversial issue, is an issue that many young citizens find interesting for classroom study. Clearly, it is an important one.

Two possible configurations arise from this Issues-Centered Decision Making perspective and it is important to note that in both of them the social sciences and history are instrumental in leading to the goals of democratic citizenship although they do not serve as goals themselves. Both of these configurations emphasize that the overarching purpose of social studies programs is to prepare citizens who can think analytically, creatively and broadly about controversy and contribute decisions and actions that are thoughtfully, and responsibly made.

1. Social Studies as the Study of Significant Social and Controversial Issues

A stellar example of this configuration is found in the Public Issues Series, also known as the Harvard Social Studies Project developed by Donald W. Oliver and Fred Newmann (1967). In this series, significant aspects in United States history such as the American Revolution, the Railroad Era and the Rise of American Labor among others emphasize persistent issues of great concern then and now. These materials are published by the Social Science Education Consortium and available through the National Council for the Social Studies. See References. Importantly, they illustrate how the present and the past are connected. For example, the pamphlet on the American Revolution is taught around issues that retain both importance and relevance in today's world and raise such questions as, What is patriotism? Were Samuel Adams, Patrick Henry, Benjamin Franklin and Thomas Paine patriots or were they traitors? What is a patriot? What is a traitor? Do these concepts apply to any contemporary public figures? Under what circumstances should people refuse to obey their legally constituted government? Is violence ever justified in behalf of political goals? In the American Revolution who had the best reason to refuse to obey their government, the Committeemen at Lexington or African Americans at Pettus Bridge? What makes one reason better than another?

In the Public Issues Series, case studies are included in which actual people, past and present, have been confronted with these issues. Facts from history are actually used rather than memorized by young citizens in making decisions about these controversial questions. Student-citizens are guided to reach conclusions to the best of their ability in light of the facts and values they have at their disposal.

Scattered throughout this nation are individual social studies teachers who use such an approach, particularly in the study of United States history and to a lesser degree in economics, government and civics. Resourceful teachers who are bored and discouraged with expository textbook teaching are probably the most likely to make use of this configuration. Often, they do this without sufficient material or the level of administrative support necessary for optimum success. However, the Harvard Public Issues Series was among the bestsellers of the New Social Studies movement. A few of their publications have been updated, and published by the Social Science Education Consortium.

2. Social Studies as the Direct Study of Significant Social and Controversial Issues

It would seem obvious that the direct study of social controversy should serve not only as the central focus but also as the capstone course for the social studies program. However, the reality is that this configuration is little practiced in schools. In a study done by Alex Molnar (1983), teachers reported overwhelmingly that significant social issues such as nuclear disarmament, abortion and pollution should be studied in school but, just as overwhelmingly, they reported that such issues were not being studied. While teachers give lip service to the importance of controversy, there seem to be a range of obstacles that prevent the realization of a curriculum that is designed to prepare democratic citizens of high quality.

In the name of objectivity, social scientists have stayed away from public controversy. They leave these controversies to politicians and citizens. In a similar vein, social studies is hard pressed to prove that it has any real impact on citizen behavior. There is ample evidence, however, that speaks to the impotence of citizens who have completed social studies classes, but do not demonstrate any particular interest or competence in dealing with issues that plague their communities, their society or the complex world we all live in. It may be overly simplistic to claim that citizenship educators have been so preoccupied with teaching facts (the grand uncontested epic) that we have ignored focusing on significant and controversial social issues and have not taught young people to think analytically or creatively. Whatever the reasons, without the study of significant and complex controversial issues, the whole social studies enterprise loses its relevance and does not fulfill democratic goals. If effective democratic citizenship and a stronger democracy constitute our goals, then educators at all levels must give serious attention to such issues as the following values and issues: fairness, respect for others, (procedural values) as well as values related to substantive issues such as pollution, poverty, inequality and oppression that continue to diminish the quality of human lives across the planet as well as in the United States. Such issues must be a visible, central focus of social studies programs. An Issues-Centered Decision Making approach is the most pressing imperative facing social studies today.

ASSESSMENT OF CURRENT SOCIAL STUDIES PRACTICE

Social studies as practiced in the nation's schools reflects the framework titled "Social Studies as the Social Sciences (including History) simplified." The other frameworks are found infrequently, if at all. Moreover, social studies programs have dealt inadequately with values and have been ambiguous in their relationship to the Humanities. None of these practices has changed very much, since the term, social studies, appeared in 1916.[2] Yet, over the same period of time, there has been a persistent demand for reform in the field. Numerous social studies educators have called for reforms more consistent with democratic citizenship and using more intellectually challenging ways of learning that involve inquiry and reasoning over rote memorization of facts. Most of these advocates have recognized the central role of value analysis and of learning to resolve significant issues in the real world.

Often, a central debate regarding the curriculum is cast as history versus social studies. The reader should be aware that the configurations identified above do not follow that paradigm. Each of the configurations that have been described includes both history and the social sciences and the framework used is not based on the argument sometimes described as 'history versus social studies'. Instead, the descriptive framework of the configurations presented above was structured as follows: a) An expository curriculum that presents both history and the social sciences as established, not tentative, knowledge to be memorized by student-citizens. b) A history and social sciences curriculum that presents this knowledge as tentative and open to examination by student-citizens, and may involve them in replicating and validating the conclusions of scholars. Higher level thinking is important to this configuration. However, it does not deal with significant and controversial issues and decision making since social scientists do not and c) An Issues-Centered Decision Making Curriculum that uses history, the social sciences and other relevant sources of knowledge that illuminate the issue under study as means not goals. The overarching goal is not to memorize existing knowledge, but for student-citizens to validate it and use it as evidence for decision making purposes as is desirable and useful for effective citizens in a democracy.

Contemporary disputes over the relative worth of the study of history versus social studies often hinge on whether we assume curriculum should begin *with* academic subjects or as a search *through* them for material relevant to goals that may not inhere in the academic subjects themselves. All of the configurations above value and include the study of history. Although the study of history can result in perfectly acceptable instructional arrangements, whatever subject matter we embrace should first pass a Deweyan test of its relevance to "the direct interests of life."

Social studies reformers have included, prominently, John Dewey and others at Columbia University; Alan Griffin along with his students, Hunt and Metcalf and Martorella at the Ohio State University; B. O. Smith and students at the University of Illinois, William Stanley; Byron Massialas, Jim Shaver; Don. Oliver and Fred Newmann at Harvard as well as those who played a part in developing and applying the products of the New Social Studies movement of the 1960s and 1970s, much of which revolved around the work of Jerome Bruner. More recently, the works of such scholars as Charlotte Anderson, Lee Anderson, James Banks, Christine Bennett, Gloria Ladsen-Billings, John Cogan, Catherine Cornbleth, Ronald Evans, Geneva Gay, Carole Hahn, Diana Hess, Wilma Longstreet, Valerie Pang, Walter Parker, Jane Bernard Powers, Stephen Thornton among many others, have contributed to and expanded this reform tradition.

In one way or another, all of these reformers have urged that social studies should be an active, questioning exercise that provides a high level of intellectual activity and is consistent with democratic precepts and values of equity and fairness. For all of them, the intellectual activity that supported a thoughtful curriculum where young citizens pursued answers to questions of interest to them was of great importance. The primary function of education for democracy was to develop the capacity for thoughtful social criticism and the political competence needed to be an effective influence in their communities and in this society. Young citizens were to study the pros and cons of democracy and decide whether their commitment was with those values. Unfortunately, these principles need to be thoughtfully considered, and the opportunity to study them is not seen in many classrooms at both the school and college levels.

Instead, social studies programs as actually taught have followed the direction set forth by Edgar B. Wesley (1937) who defined the social studies as the social sciences simplified for pedagogical purposes. This orientation promoted the expository mode of teaching and instead of active learners; student-citizens become passive learners who were called upon to memorize the knowledge supplied by teachers and textbooks as sources of authority. This tradition remains in place despite the unprecedented issues and conflicts that constitute a major challenge for all who live on this planet. Wesley's way was easily accommodated by lecture and knowledge presented as if it was the whole truth. It seldom occasioned controversy.

Sadly, the deficiencies evident in citizen behavior in this society speak forcefully to the limitations of social studies as traditionally taught. We are coming close to becoming a nation of non-voters. Those who do not vote outnumber those who do. We seldom hear or participate in strong and vigorous conversations about public issues. Yet in a democracy, we should be able and willing to agree to disagree, to welcome and genuinely appreciate views discrepant from our own and be ready to understand and learn from them. Controversy may be and should be vigorously pursued but it should not result in animosity. People whose views oppose ours are intellectual opponents but not enemies. Not in a civil democracy where we must agree to disagree if we are to practice democracy with civility. More positively, it should result in intellectual challenge and broader and deeper understanding. This positive view of controversy is critical if we are to build a stronger and civil democracy and expand social justice.

Instead, our media in the form of television, newspapers and magazines appear to do our thinking for us. It seems clear that in order to hold the public's attention, they cannot confine their role to informing us by thoughtfully discussing public issues, but they must also entertain us. As a people, we know very little and do less in terms of international affairs—a domain of activity that continually becomes increasingly significant since it is not unusual for arms to be used and sold as well as troops to be deployed to global trouble spots such as Bosnia, Somalia, Haiti, Afghanistan and Iraq. Citizens of the United States have allowed a small number of people to control the direction of this nation's international policies and practices, while not many citizens can explain why we have sent military resources to one trouble spot or another. Furthermore and without question, the tragedy of 9/11 and the subsequent actions of the United States deserve much more thoughtful and active participation.

In some ways, the National Council for the Social Studies has helped to perpetuate an outdated curriculum tradition. Too many aspects of its annual meetings and its publications were characterized by a practical, how-to-do-it perspective. The Council, often in close alliance with textbook publishers and textbook authors, perpetuated an outdated model. Furthermore, the Council seemed to respond to global and societal change by responding to new variants in education such as consumer education, economic education and moral education as discrete points of focus without giving much thought to how the entirety of social studies was to be shaped and integrated. While it did create a set of curriculum standards, these standards do not give sufficient attention to higher level thinking, including decision making or to the very serious public issues (except for a token nod at the secondary level) whether they be historic-, contemporary- or future-oriented. Classroom research supports attention to issues and to providing opportunities for higher level thinking at younger ages in age-level appropriate form. The National Council for the Social Studies (1994) published a definition for social studies. It reads as follows:

Social studies is the integrated study of the social sciences and humanities to promote democratic civic competence. Within the school program, social studies provides coordinated, systematic study drawing upon such disciplines as anthropology, archeology, economics, geography, history, law, philosophy, political science, psychology, religion and sociology, as well as appropriate content from the humanities, mathematics, and natural sciences. The primary purpose of social studies is to help young people to develop the ability to make informed and reasoned decisions for the public good as citizens of a culturally diverse, democratic society in an interdependent world. (NCSS, 1994 p. vii)

Despite efforts by some members of the Council to include an emphasis on controversial issues central to the preparation of democratic citizens, this definition fails to emphasize public issues that are more likely to tap student interests and mentions them only at the secondary level. It gives insufficient attention to encouraging higher level thinking. This omission is difficult to understand. The Council published a set of curriculum standards that highlighted selected concepts from the social science disciplines and history as the knowledge base of the curriculum thus continuing the positivist, "just the facts" or just the right definition of social science concepts tradition that has existed in our classrooms for far too long. The presentation of these concepts was not far removed from the Wesleyan definition of social studies developed in 1937. A limited critique of these standards, written by this author (2001) appeared in Social Education highlighting the scant attention paid to public issues, to higher level thinking and to social action.[3] If I were rewriting that article today, I would highlight the importance of including social justice values. Hopefully, in the next revision of this curriculum statement, the definition of social studies will include public controversy and the standards will correspond more closely with the needs of democratic citizenship in the 21st century.

A spate of studies address the matter of classroom practice (Goodlad, 1984; Hahn, 1996; McGowan et. al., 1990; Ochoa-Becker, 2001). In addition, a well-known study of United States history textbooks by Frances Fitzgerald appeared in the *New Yorker* magazine in 1979. Textbook content, she found, had very little controversy and was modified to suit the political atmosphere of the times. These textbooks, produced by large corporate publishers, swayed back and forth politically to satisfy the passions of the day. During this period, a number of community-based critics became particularly vocal in the efforts to eliminate content that was undesirable from their perspective from these textbooks. Censorship of library and school materials became a virtual epidemic. The Kanawha County dispute that targeted the curriculum titled, Man, A Course of Study in the 1970s along with the far-flung efforts of the Gablers, self-appointed censors from Texas, who established a widespread network, censorship efforts haunted the field. Social studies educators must be especially mindful of the fact that textbooks are usually written from the point of view of the established and the powerful. One very significant textbook titled *A People's History of the United States* by Howard Zinn (2002) stands apart as an alternative view that reflects the perspective of ordinary and marginal peoples, but it is written to be used at the college level or with very able student-citizens. More recently, Zinn and Arnove (2004) have published original documents that were referenced in *A People's History of the United States—a highly useful reference for classes studying controversial issues.* This resource can be of enormous help to teachers who wish to present their classes with alternate views of United States history (See References).

Over time, textbooks gave little or no attention to marginal peoples such as African Americans, Native Americans, Asian Americans, Hispanics, the elderly, gays and lesbians, the disabled and women. In the same vein, little attention was given to the labor movement, environmentalists, anti–war movements and other social change efforts that challenged the status quo. In some ways, textbooks have had a fairy tale quality, devoid of controversy and problem identification or resolution, qualities which are central to a democracy. At best, such history is sterile and unexciting; at worst, it is a fraud.

Social studies is the school subject least liked by young people. Youth are not deeply interested in the past. Their lives are consumed with the here and now, with peers, with being accepted, dating, making friends and the like. When their classes require that young citizens read, memorize and take tests—there is little to be excited about. Student-citizens also report that they find the subject matter to be uninteresting. These views are probably derived from the incredible amount of trivia that they are required to remember, at least until test time. The comic strip "Shoe" demonstrates rare insight into the extent to which social studies is the memorization of trivia when Skylar's little friend inquires, "What is the name of the game when you try to answer a bunch of question for points?" Skylar responds, "Oh yeah, we play that in school. We call it American History." It also appears that social studies is the subject area where both young citizens and teachers demonstrate the highest level of ambivalence regarding its purpose.

Despite surveys of teacher attitudes that support the teaching of social issues, they are very infrequently taught (Molnar, 1983). As previously stated, reading the textbook and listening to a teacher's lecture are the dominant modes of instruction. These practices may be supplemented by other teacher-controlled activities such as watching films, using experts as guest speakers and filling in blanks in a commercially published workbook. There is very little focused and sustained classroom dialogue and when it occurs, it is teacher-dominated.

Classroom Practices for Assessment

This section will briefly describe classroom practices regarding assessment of learning achievements of young citizens. This aspect of teaching and learning has always been a challenge, particularly in social studies. The topics in social studies are broad and textbook information is too often trivial. Teachers create tests, usually ones that can be graded objectively in short answer, fill-in-the-blanks and/or multiple-choice formats. Such tests call for discrete answers that allow for consistent grading across all class members. An illusion of fairness is perpetuated in such tests—because each learner's success or failure on a given test is assessed in the same way for every members of the class. However, more importantly, fairness requires that any test must both adequately and accurately represent the aspect of the curriculum or subject matter that young citizens actually experienced prior to the test. Such tests necessarily draw on specific information such as names of significant people, dates and events that are mentioned in the textbook and/or represent information that has been emphasized in presentations the teacher has made or question and answer periods that the teacher conducted. Teachers try to create tests with a view to be fair regarding the breadth of coverage that the subject matter received in their classroom or in assignments that the class was given. However, this is not easy to do. Most importantly, teacher reliance on objective tests and their expectations of correctly memorized answers means many teachers are not engaging young citizens to demonstrate deeper understandings, higher level thinking and the political abilities needed by stronger democratic citizens. Instead, such tests measure whether student-citizens can remember, in the short run at least, what the textbook says or what has been stressed by the teacher in the classroom.

Less frequently, teachers create essay questions for assessment. Some of these essay tests call for memorization as well. "What were the causes of the Civil War?" is one example. This question exemplifies that student-citizens would need to draw on their memory of the knowledge presented by their textbook and their teacher. Much less frequently, essay tests that are open-ended are created which makes the taking of the test a learning experience of its own. What are ways in which the Civil War may have been avoided? Which of these ways would have worked best? Explain why. This open-ended question has no right answer and no class member is expected to answer it in the same way as others. Such essay questions are more subjectively assessed. Classes that have had previous experiences in writing such essays should have had an opportunity to create, with teacher guidance, the criteria by which their answers are judged.

Therefore, testing still stands as a challenge to any social studies curriculum and to teachers and their classes including the curriculum proposed here. No testing strategy will provide a perfect solution particularly when the overarching goal is assessing the extent to which young people have acquired the knowledge and abilities expected of strong democratic citizens. Assessment regarding this Issues-Centered Decision Making Curriculum will be discussed in Chapter 9.

Curriculum standards and mandatory testing have added a new responsibility for schools across this country. The enactment of the No Child Left Behind Act (NCLB) by Congress has made student-citizens increasingly test-conscious for all ages and all abilities, for teachers, for administrators and school districts. Requiring regular testing in math and reading (later social studies and science), this Act further diminished the importance of other subjects such as social studies, science, art and music. This condition is especially true at the elementary grade levels where teachers have the same youngsters for most of the school day. They are able to control the amount of time spent on particular subjects and because the mandatory tests assess only reading and math, the time devoted to those subject areas has expanded. Since the penalties associated with not demonstrating improved achievement can damage an administrator's, a teacher's and a school district's reputation, it is not surprising that the curricular emphasis is on those subjects that are subject to mandatory testing. Moreover, student-citizens at all grade levels now sense that those areas are the most important subjects as well.

In the last decade, most states have adopted social studies standards (AFT, 2001), but very few have actually developed and implemented tests that represent these standards. The National Council for the Social Studies (NCSS) has provided a set of standards based on concepts from the social science disciplines with a minimal amount of attention to significant and controversial public issues. These are used in some states. Some of the limitations evident in the NCSS standards are excessive dependence on the social science disciplines and not enough on significant and controversial social issues. Furthermore, insufficient attention is placed on developing intellectual abilities as well as not emphasizing the importance of real world involvement, service learning or social action, as ways for young citizens to be involved in improving aspects of their community or their society or the global setting as strong democratic citizens would do.

Some states use social studies standards developed by NCSS, others may use the National Standards for Civics and Government (2001) or the United States History Standards (1994; 2003) developed at UCLA or ones that have been developed by the states themselves. In addition, comprehensive work regarding testing in the subject areas of Civics, Economics, Geography and History have been done by the Council of Chief State School Officers that gives greater emphasis to higher order thinking skills. The implementation of new mandatory tests regularly administered in social studies classrooms looms ahead as another obstacle to an Issues-Centered Decision Making Curriculum.

Mandatory testing in social studies is a double-edged sword. If social studies is not tested, it is less likely to be taught. This observation is especially important in the elementary grades where teachers have more control over how young citizens spend their classroom time. One teacher expressed this point of view clearly, when she emphasized that she had to drop an integrated unit on dinosaurs that her classes both learned from and enjoyed, because she now had to give more time to preparing her class for the required reading and math tests. On the other hand, when social studies is tested, I would predict that most likely the test would include items that have specific answers requiring memorization. Such assessments are not useful for citizenship educators who want to see if their student-citizens are making progress regarding the abilities and perspectives needed by today's citizens in a democracy.

Increasingly, parents, the American Federation of Teachers and the National Education Association have expressed serious concerns regarding mandatory testing. Parents are expressing concern regarding the testing requirements included in the NCLB Act where decisions are made that schools need improvement and they may conclude that teachers are inadequate on the basis of one test. Parental concerns also relate to young people who require special education as well as youngsters from difficult backgrounds who are tested with the same expectations as those who start at a higher baseline. What the future holds is not clear. It seems reasonable to expect that parental concerns may lay the foundation for revision of this legislation. This action will only happen if teacher organizations as well as the public put a lot of political pressure on Congress to do so.

The kinds of classroom assessment tools described above prevail in many, if not most of our classrooms. The major weakness of current classroom testing is that it has little to do with the qualities we wish to see develop in the next generation of citizens. Missing from the above list are any long range studies that follow young citizens into adulthood to identify the kind of citizens they become so that the curriculum can be adjusted to better fit their needs. Assessment of the work of student-citizens emphasizes what can be remembered, sometimes even verbatim, from the text or information emphasized by the teacher.

Social Studies Programs: What are the results?

It is germane to ask: What outcomes follow from social studies as currently taught? Tragically, we do not know! We have never fully investigated what the systematic effects of social studies curricula are. Some basic questions whose answers could inform curriculum planners, administrators and teachers are:

What kind of citizens do our young citizens become?
Do they exhibit news-gathering habits after graduation?
Do they try to be well informed regarding public affairs?
Do they participate in public life on a regular basis? How?
Do they write letters to public officials, politicians and newspapers about public issues?
Do they attend public meetings?
Are they concerned with the public good or are they only motivated by self-interest?
Do they speak out on issues? Do they discuss important issues with others or with officials who can do something about them?
Do they agree or disagree with them in a civil manner?
Do they volunteer in their communities? How?
How much time is do they spend volunteering?

While such questions are asked, their answers are not easy to come by. Following high school graduates into adulthood is not an easy matter. Yet, the answers to such questions would be extremely useful in adjusting the curriculum and the learning process in order to prepare stronger citizens. While we do not have exact answers, informal observations that citizens do very little reading or discussion of public affairs seem quite believable. Seldom does one hear any major public issue discussed at dinners, at gatherings with friends, over the back fence or with children. From my vantage point, we are afraid to find out we do not agree. Instead of valuing debate, citizens shy away from it. Furthermore, active participation by citizens is at a minimum and seems to occur largely at times when property values of citizens are threatened or a zoning matter triggers concerns.[4] However, threats to national security can and have triggered higher levels of citizen participation (Thelen, 1996). In a study of citizen mail received by Senator Richard Luger of Indiana at the time of the Persian Gulf War, Thelen reported that the war activated a very high volume of correspondence with this Senator when compared to times when there was no such threat. .

Discerning scholars of citizenship education have observed, possibly with dismay, how ill-informed many U.S. citizens are about the most pressing issues of the day as revealed repeatedly by such indicators of public opinion as the Harris and Gallup Polls. The citizen in this democracy often appears to be a dupe or buffoon rather than a responsible student of public affairs. Such public evidence has led a serious, thoughtful, and active citizen such as Walter Cronkite, to conclude that the majority of our people are not adequately informed to intelligently exercise their franchise

(Cronkite1996). Cronkite, a celebrated newsman, places much of the blame on television and newspapers that report the news superficially without hard-nosed analysis and interpretation, much like the ways that are most often used in schools to prepare citizens in social studies. It appears that television and newspapers need to present the news to the public in brief form and in an entertaining style if they are to hold public attention. Many newspapers seem to have abandoned their time-honored tradition of reporting the news in depth.

However, the fault lies not solely with the media, but with citizens who accept and even demand the low quality of news that they are getting. To some extent, schools in general and social studies programs in particular must assume a large portion of the responsibility for having failed to meet the most significant goal for schools in this democracy, sharpening the interest, awareness and intellectual acuity of its citizens.

Recent reports based on the National Assessment of Educational Progress (NAEP) do not give social studies educators much comfort. Over time, the results have been disappointing. The Report on Civics in 1998 found that 31% of fourth graders were below what was labeled as the *basic* level of achievement; for eighth graders the percentage that fell below this *basic* level was 29% and for twelfth graders the percentage below this level was 35%. Only 21–22% of young citizens at each of these grade levels scored at *proficiency* levels. The white or Asian/Pacific Islanders did better at all grade levels than did African Americans and Hispanics. Furthermore, the knowledge component of these tests focused on questions related to a citizen's comprehension of democracy and the components that seek to expand the intellectual and political abilities (Patrick, 2000). The results raise more questions than are answered by NAEP. Whatever the standards applied, this national assessment has not served to validate social studies programs as a viable school experience.

The low intellectual level of public dialogue that characterizes the lead-up time of national, state and local elections serves as a significant indicator of what most citizens know as well as the level of their interest in public affairs. Politicians must raise millions of dollars from big money sources to whom they are beholden, in order to pay for television time and simplistic advertisements to try to sway public opinion because the public is overly responsive to television images and impressions. In turn, this situation permits the wealthy, particularly large corporations, through their contributions, to have undue influence on the conduct and outcomes of elections. Furthermore, thoughtful and capable candidates who discuss the issues facing us with considerable depth do not appear to be attractive to many citizens. Rather, citizens seem to be attracted to the television image, communication style and the kind of fashion statement candidates are making. Given this state of affairs, it is compelling to consider the possibility that the force feeding of unexamined truths and the emphasis on correct, but trivial, answers may have contributed to the quiescence of so many of our citizens. They appear to have become victims rather than agents for maintaining and strengthening this democracy. Whatever the reasons for the poor performance of our student-citizens, the social studies program is somewhat responsible.

Problems Facing Social Studies Programs

In this section, the obstacles facing social studies programs that emphasize an Issues-Centered Decision Making orientation are identified and described Heretofore, in this book, a number of barriers that make implementation difficult have been mentioned. These barriers show up in form of: expository and textbook teaching, far too much concern with coverage, censorship, lack of administrative support and inadequate teacher preparation at the pre-service level and lack of professional development at the in-service level. Along with the avoidance of values and valuing, which will receive considerable attention in the following discussion; these barriers need to be lifted through the determined and persistent efforts of those seeking to reform social studies/citizenship education.

Some of these obstacles, such as the persistent use of the expository mode of teaching in social studies classrooms represent the manner in which teachers themselves were taught and have been habituated to across time. Research tells us that teachers will lean on the expository models that they have repeatedly observed in their own education not only at the K–12 level but also in their college history and social science classes as well as the professional education courses they have taken in order to become teachers. Despite vigorous efforts by some educators to introduce alternative ways of teaching and learning, novice teachers quickly lay these aside, not only in their student teaching experience, but as first year teachers when they increasingly comply with the norms set by other teachers in the school. One can almost hear the advice of more seasoned teachers, "Forget about what they taught you at the university, this is the real world."

Present practice with its tradition of expository textbook teaching, more often than not results in coverage of topics big and small as treated in commercial textbooks. Coverage in most classrooms seems to be much more important to many teachers rather than depth. Frequently, teachers make the following kind of statement, "It's almost time for Spring break and I haven't finished the Civil War!" Social studies educators need to seriously examine the question of how important coverage is. In most of our nation's schools, young citizens study U.S. History three times (usually

Grades 5, 8 and 11) prior to high school graduation. Yet, test results on their knowledge of history are very disappointing. Young citizens do not seem to remember much history, despite the many assignments that teachers have asked them to do. If three years of 'covering' history has such very minimal results, we must identify other ways to treat subject matter that are more meaningful and useful to young people. Coverage of the textbook is not an adequate test of preparing citizens effectively. Obviously, the Issues-Centered Decision Making model advanced in this book is based on in-depth study of significant social and controversial issues that relate to the lives and interests of student-citizens and the world they live in. What is of paramount interest here is not the number of issues that are studied, but the expanded knowledge that relates to the issues studied as well as the intellectual processes by which they are studied. This wide range of intellectually and politically active experiences is more likely to engage the interests of young citizens because they can become more active than memorization assignments allow and because they begin to assume more adult like roles in identifying and recommending solutions. Once learned and applied, this process can be used repeatedly as student-citizens encounter new issues at the local, national, and/or global levels.

Expository teaching is reinforced by many department heads and administrators who also hold expository teaching solidly in their personal experience and in their frames of reference for teaching. At times, some administrators are so concerned with school discipline and order that the notion of noisy classrooms where vigorous discussions take place is very uncomfortable for them. These administrative roles create the political and social context and the school climate in which teachers teach and young citizens engage in learning. It is the administrators filling these roles who control awarding tenure to teachers, conduct their annual reviews and who, therefore, control what teachers do. Unfortunately, independence and autonomy are not professional characteristics that most social studies teachers enjoy. Compounding this condition is the fact that far too many administrators have a minimal awareness of alternative modes of teaching and of alternative curricula. The academic programs that prepare administrators typically do not emphasize knowledge about different curricula or school climate. Therefore, usually they do not encourage curriculum or teaching reform in their schools.

Those who prepare citizens also need to consider the matter of curriculum relevancy. It is important to ask:

"To whom is this curriculum relevant?"

"What bias does the curriculum have (and they all have a bias)?"

The position taken in the proposed curriculum is that curriculum needs to be relevant to the lives and interests of student-citizens. Additionally, the curriculum must honestly represent the real world with all of its promise and all of its problems. Such a curriculum is framed within an intellectual perspective where all knowledge is tentative and where knowledge, independent thinking as well as decision making are intrinsically valuable and necessary. However, following the interests of young citizens is not comfortable for some teachers who are accustomed to identifying, directing and controlling classroom events. Teachers will need time and practice to handle the proposed curriculum with ease and function more like facilitators than authorities.

Among the deficiencies in many social studies classrooms is lack of attention to pluralism, race, prejudice, discrimination and hate activities that have been well documented. (Southern Poverty Law Center, 2005). This lack of attention occurs despite the extensive work done by a substantial number of vigorous multicultural educators (James Banks, Christine Bennett, Gloria Ladson Billings, Carlos Cortez, Geneva Gay and Valerie Pang among many others) who have provided extensive insights regarding both theoretical and practical dimensions for teaching and learning about equality, tolerance and acceptance of diversity. The resistance to incorporating multicultural perspectives speaks to a deep, though poorly understood form of latent prejudice and racism among those who control public education (Banks, 1991). In this regard, the National Council for the Social Studies provided some strong support under the leadership of James Banks (1991b) whose work led to the creation of the N.C.S.S. Curriculum Guidelines for Multicultural Education. (See References) This position statement provides schools and teachers with clear suggestions and direction to develop a curriculum that addresses diversity. The Southern Poverty Law Center (2005) supplies educational materials for teachers and their classes that support teaching tolerance and respect for diversity. (See References) School libraries and social studies classrooms should have easy access to their publications and videos.[5]

Global education and the very challenging issues that the planet faces have not received appropriate curriculum implementation. Courses in international and global studies are not widespread and are usually electives, not required. Furthermore, world history classes, which come the closest to carrying content that address global issues that cross international borders, often do not involve student-citizens in studying such issues and making justifiable decisions about them. Yet, such issues should deserve serious concern from democratic citizens. The spread of contagious diseases across national boundaries, the global economy which effects every one of us regardless of where we live on the planet, poverty across national boundaries, world hunger, the proliferation of nuclear power and certainly, terrorism are a few of the transnational issues that should have the attention of educators at all levels. Social studies educators must understand that global education is *not* the promotion of globalism. Knowing the relationships among other nations in other part of the world can be especially helpful when considering the foreign policy of the United States. The goal of global education is to have young citizens comprehend how the world works along with knowing more about the dynamics of complex issues that face it and to consider what might be done to improve the challenging conditions surrounding these issues that affect the well-being of the entire planet.

The time frame of interest to most school-aged young citizens is the present and their fairly immediate future. For them, the past seems less important unless it is their personal past or unless the past helps them think about the here and now. Yet typically, social studies curricula emphasize history, whether it is United States or world history. The present and the future, but also the past, are characterized by change and controversy which need to be intelligently addressed if the people who live in this democracy as well as the planet are to move toward a more secure and comfortable quality of life. Historical knowledge does enlighten contemporary and future issues and the past needs to be drawn upon for comparative and comprehensive understanding. However, such knowledge is not comprehensively packaged in textbooks. History is not taught in this manner. In practice, young citizens are seldom focused on contemporary and controversial issues in schools. Instead, educators need to see the past, present and future as interactive. Terrorism, for example, an issue that has touched the United States and other parts of the world deeply in recent years, has a past that casts a long term perspective on contemporary terrorist events and these events can shape the meaning citizens give to its history as well as its present-day manifestations. Furthermore, citizens must consider its future. How citizens view the future, (whether terrorism will intensify or not) and how they think it should be dealt with, can influence how they understand both its past and present.

Social studies classes must have access to more timely materials such as journals, newspapers, thoughtful media presentations and the Internet, all of which can identify truth claims to be investigated and to be vigorously scrutinized for their veracity. Such issues confront even the most enthusiastic teacher with the need to identify and access relevant materials which is a task that can be simplified by a school librarian and the Internet .Useful web sites are identified in Social Education that focus on social issues for classroom use (Risinger, 2005). Additionally, searches conducted by students-citizens as they study particular issues should be collected by teachers for later use.

Values and Valuing

Teaching values and value analysis serves as still another problem. Many social studies curricula avoid thoughtful examination of values. This is not to say that teachers and textbooks do not promote values. Without a doubt, they do. In fact, even if they try not to, they cannot avoid communicating values in a variety of ways, formally and informally. Any teacher, advertently or inadvertently, communicates procedural values such as punctuality, meeting deadlines, not talking while someone else is talking, neatness and the like. Furthermore, the textbook communicates substantive values— some of which are obvious and some of which are subtle and virtually hidden. The simplification of knowledge that characterizes textbooks means that some knowledge, often because of hidden assumptions, is avoided. A strong example is found in the omission of concerns of assembly line workers for better working conditions that may not be mentioned at all.

The very act of selecting content for the textbook is guided by the values important to the author and the publisher as they reflect on the nature of public values. Leaving out the points of view of some historical actors related to an event and including others is another textbook practice that is value-based and distorts the accuracy of the statements made. To the extent that significant points of view are deliberately omitted is the extent to which the process of censorship is at play.

Teachers continually struggle with whether they should enter their own values into classroom discussions. Since some do not want to be faulted for being doctrinaire, they never take a stand that is clear to their classes. While teachers must not use the classroom as a bully pulpit, they can serve as models who share their experience in making decisions that come from a critical intellectual orientation and are grounded in evidence, reason and values. At the same time, they must assure student-citizens that their compliance with the values of the teacher is not expected. Instead, teachers must insist that their student-citizens take stands that they can justify on their own. Certainly, student-citizens should not feel any coercion to hold a particular point of view, but they should think carefully about the values that are important to them and be able to explain why they find those values important.

A serious shortcoming in most of the curriculum configurations described above is their ambivalence or outright neglect of the key role values play in resolving or improving the conditions surrounding significant social and controversial issues. The three expository categories either behave as though values do not exist at all or they teach values that are tucked away covertly in the text or the teacher's lecture as unrecognized assumptions never to be questioned. They are transmitted as fixed beliefs and accepted on the basis of authority or faith. It is seldom recognized that the values we hold, recognized or not, explain why we collect certain facts and ignore others and also explain why we make the interpretations that we do. The facts we select to use in all probability reflect our values. Facts often become important to us when they support our views. As important, it is seldom recognized that controversial issues arise not because all the facts are not known, but because the parties to the conflict bring different, competing values to the situation. Underlying expository approaches are substantive as well as procedural values, though they are seldom made explicit to young citizens.

The social studies categories above were based on the critical study of the social science disciplines, while immensely respected as intellectual exercises, are victims of their total orientation to the scientific process. They are dominated by the philosophical posture of positivism and the idea of scientific probability that finds only ideas supported by evidence, usually quantifiable, to be true.

Values, which cannot be quantified, get virtually no conscious consideration. Facts may play a role in selecting values. For instance, facts may be tested against various courses of action to see if a particular course is likely to lead to the value desired. Conversely, a given value may be tested to see if it leads to a desired course of action. However, this kind of factuality is seldom associated with the scientific pursuit of the facts of a discipline which is usually supposed to be value-free. Thus, the critical study of the disciplines does not help to clarify the nature of valuing nor does it teach how citizens can go about solving issues and improving social conditions since the kind of changes or recommendations that citizens make are necessarily value-based. The examination of recommendation for the values that stand behind them is central to addressing public issues comprehensively.

Even the categories that focus on significant controversial issues can shortchange values and valuing by treating controversial issues as if they were totally amenable to the facts. We may teach about cosmic waste, for example, by presenting all the facts we know, but without mention of the salient issue which lies in the conflict among beliefs of academic freedom, regarding how cosmic waste should be dealt with, the values embedded in free enterprise and the belief in the rights of all of the people to be protected from dangerous substances that are found in water, air and soil. Teachers can ask student-citizens to think about the following questions:. Which is the greater value? Which is better? To which should we accede or is some compromise necessary? These are questions that should engage the learning and the thinking of young citizens.

The proponents of the study of significant and controversial issues usually present the cleanest front regarding values as compared with all alternative configurations, in recognizing the central role of values in solving or improving conditions related to controversial issues. The Harvard Group of Oliver, Shaver and Newmann, who have been prominently associated with this conception of social studies, also developed materials that clearly placed conflicts over values in the forefront of how social studies should be taught (Oliver and Shaver, 1966; Oliver and Newmann, 1967).

In stark contrast to the neglect of values in most of the conceptions of social studies, the real world of public affairs is constantly dominated by value considerations. The early years of the 21st century saw a major economic debate that resulted in a tax cut that benefited the wealthy. The conflicting values that drive some economists, are seen clearly in the tax cut decision that passed the Senate 50-50 necessitating a tiebreaking vote by the Vice President serving as President of the Senate. On the one hand, we had economists from one camp supporting the idea that tax cuts will stimulate the economy while others expressed the view that it is a foolhardy move to cut taxes at a time when the national deficit is larger than ever and the nation's current expenses are especially high. Neither of these positions can be documented in ways that would fully prove the point. Warren Buffet, the stock market guru, has stated that given his salary level, a tax cut will yield a high dollar amount for him, but for his secretary who makes much less money, it would yield almost nothing. This comment represents a struggle between values that help the rich make bigger investments as opposed to having the average or below average wage earner make little or no gain at all. The gap between the rich and the poor is indeed widening.

It should be clear from this example that value issues are not as neatly resolved as factual issues. It is far easier to answer what the facts are than it is to answer the question of what are the values we should subscribe to in a given instance. Despite this difficulty, a social studies program that neglects value problems stops far short of teaching student-citizens how to think intelligently about the real world. We must dissuade ourselves of the belief that facts alone can solve significant social issues. Facts are useful as they are marshaled as evidence in the conflict between contending values. The persistent goal of social studies should be to raise the level of thinking regarding values in a conscious effort to be knowledgeable, rational, logical and consistent in the examination and ordering of values.

Values are never fixed entities whose definition or meaning persists across time and place. The meaning given, even to such a central value as freedom, depends on the circumstances. The exact circumstances of its meaning in one case, does not mean that it applies with the same meaning in another case. Democratic citizenship educators must abandon the idea that values can be taught, in the abstract, as fixed entities such as is emphasized by those who support character education. Such efforts result only in the mouthing of empty words rather than authentic commitment. Even when one is deeply committed to a value, it is intelligently and morally respectable to have some doubt about its justification in new situations.

Value examination and value utilization have an emergent methodology and are quite as much an intellectual discipline as the scientific search for facts that occupies the social sciences and history. It behooves the professional who is really concerned with democratic citizenship education to be quite as familiar with this discipline as with others. Sadly, social studies professionals, if we may judge by how and what they teach, show little awareness of this literature. Indeed, the social studies configurations that demonstrate the greatest degree of naiveté regarding values are the ones most often practiced in schools.

Included in the literature that should be familiar to the social studies professional are basic works on facts and valuations by John Dewey, particularly his *How We Think* (1933), and works by Gunnar Myrdal, particularly the first three appendices of Volume 2 of *An American Dilemma (1944)*. These are not current works; they are classics that still serve the social studies well. A number of social studies professionals have made a useful contribution to the literature on values and valuing in teaching social studies. Possibly the most comprehensive was the work done by Oliver and Shaver, *Teaching Public Issues in the High School* (1966), which was followed by the development of classroom materials by Oliver and Newmann, *The Public Issues Series* (1967), which demonstrates the classroom application of this approach. The work of Alan Griffin's (1942) students, Maurice P. Hunt and Lawrence E. Metcalf, *Teaching High School Social Studies* (1955, 1968) and Peter Martorella (1985) illustrated a somewhat different approach toward the same overall objectives. These works, and to some extent all work in the field concerned with these same goals, have been dependent on the basic thinking of the Columbia Associates, (Benne, Axtelle, Smith, & Raup 1943), who produced *The Improvement of Practical Intelligence*.

CONCLUSION

The configurations of social studies presented in this chapter in order to give serious citizenship educators as full a range of views as possible so that they may resolve the issue of what social studies should be as intelligently as possible. It is clear that the position taken here is that the preparation of strong democratic citizens is the goal and having that goal means we must prepare young people to play out their individuality in a manner that strengthens democracy. That position is best served by the critical study of the social sciences and the critical study of socially significant controversial issues.

This survey of configurations of social studies in this chapter is done in a manner that is virtually identical with what might happen in an Issues-Centered Decision Making classroom. The obstacles that are identified do not exhaust the problems that create resistance to curriculum reform in the nation's schools. However, we cannot deny that the minimal functioning of citizens poses a major threat to democracy, to its diversity, to its concern for social justice and the quality of life of all human beings on the planet. Professional commitment and dedication must reside at the heart of the matter. Hope rests among those social studies educators at both the school and college levels who care very much about the future of democracy as well as growth in the potential of young people who will serve as its citizens. Chapter 10 and 11 present conditions that are important to implementing such programs. School administrators and teaching personnel at school and college levels can and must do better. To a great extent, the strengthening of democracy and democratic education depends on them.

NOTES

1. The projects associated with the New Social Studies failed to reform the social studies curriculum for a number of reasons. However, selected projects deserve to be updated. Most importantly, they need to be reviewed by experienced teachers who are willing to integrate them into their curriculum. Especially valuable is Man, A Course of Study prepared for the fifth grade. It focused on three questions. What makes man [people] human? How did [he] they get that way? How can [he] they be made more so? These persistent questions with elegant and very interesting learning materials are still relevant and meaningful. The Social Science Education Consortium has published revisions of selected pamphlets in the Public Issues Series developed by the Harvard Social Studies Project. These materials are now available through the National Council for the Social Studies, 8555 Sixteenth Street, Suite 500, Silver Spring, Maryland 20910. (800) 683-0812. Web site: www.ncss.org They can be used with the middle and secondary levels.

2. In 1916, the United States Bureau of Education issued *The Social Studies in Secondary Education. A Six Year Program*. This report was result of three years of effort by the Committee of Social Studies of the Reorganization of Secondary Education of the National Education Association. The committee was chaired by Thomas Jesse Jones. (I found it interesting that in the Preface there was a brief reference to a "boy voting" and wondered briefly why girls were not mentioned. Then I realized that the year was 1916 and only boys voted. Then, I wondered how the rest of the document may have ignored the invisible roles of women at that time).

3. An article written by this author titled, A Limited Critique of the N.C.S.S. Curriculum Standards. (See References).

4. David Thelen (1996) a historian conducted an enlightening study titled *Becoming a Citizen in an Age of Television* that describes the high volume of correspondence from ordinary citizens to Sentaor Richard Luger (R) at the time of the Persian Gulf War. These letters display abilities needed by citizens to communicate with politicians, government officials, business people and the like. This work is an important read for social studies educators at all levels. It emphasizes that citizens do try to effect issues that are significant to them even though many do not vote.

5. The Southern Poverty Law Center has a number of strong publications for classroom use that focus on tolerance and prejudice reduction. Address: Box AA 548, Montgomery, Alabama 10548. Web site: www.SPLCenter.org.

PART II

A CURRICULUM FOR DEMOCRATIC CITIZENSHIP EDUCATION

CHAPTER 7

THE FRAMEWORK
OF THE CURRICULUM

The addiction to coverage is destructive.

—Fred Newmann, Phi Delta Kappan, (January, 1988 p. 346)

INTRODUCTION

The curriculum presented here for citizens of a democracy moves away from the conventional social studies programs as described in the previous chapter toward more open-ended and issue-centered decision making treatments of social studies. In short, movement away from presenting young people with the unqualified exposition of facts, taken to be definitive truths, whether from the social sciences or elsewhere, is encouraged. At the same time, the position taken in this book also encourages that young citizens give consideration to issues from the disciplines as well as public issues manifested locally, domestically and globally.

As presented here, the reformed curriculum embraces the issues that democracy has faced historically as well as those that apply today as well as the future. These kinds of issues serve as the appropriate locus for a disciplined study of democracy. Actually struggling with issues is the appropriate learning mode for nurturing citizens who will come to appreciate democracy on their own terms and who will develop the capacity to address the demanding issues that face democracy's citizens at all levels—from local to global. Importantly, democracy is not a way of life that is transmitted in unthinking ways. Instead, democracy is learned as it is questioned,

Democratic Education for Social Studies, pages 189–213
Copyright © 2007 by Information Age Publishing
All rights of reproduction in any form reserved.

thought about, criticized and as improvements in its practices are achieved and made evident.

The key to a curriculum that prepares citizens of a pluralistic democracy in a global age is its capacity to encourage young people to think and to make considered and justifiable decisions that they can act upon thoughtfully. Its content is never merely remembered without being thought about and used. The curriculum being proposed requires a more probing treatment of issues, ideas, values and materials, covering fewer topics than usual, though delving deeper into each and ultimately leading to defensible and reasoned conclusions.

The goal of this curriculum as well as the commitment of its author is to strengthen the abilities of citizens to make justifiable democratic decisions. This is the ultimate goal of social studies, a goal consonant with both Dewey (1933) and Bruner (1965) who argued that the only way to learn how to solve problems is to engage in problem solving. The following guidelines are suggested below to give direction to social studies curriculum development.

Goal

1. The curriculum should be highly selective of a comparatively small number of episodes and related issues, each of which will be studied in great depth. Covering a large number of topics superficially would be abandoned.[1]

2. The issues to be selected should be those of interest to student-citizens and with the greatest potential for encouraging thinking and confronting controversy as applied to disputes about competing facts, alternative historical interpretations or about alternative solutions to controversial issues. To the greatest extent possible, the curriculum should focus on such issues.

3. Student-citizens should continually be asked to make judgments about such matters as: What are the most defensible facts? How should these facts be interpreted? What should be done about a particular issue? Or, if the problem is historical, What should have been done differently? Why? Teachers should ask student-citizens to make value judgments as to whether decisions made about the past, present or future are desirable and most importantly, they must provide the reasons and evidence why this decision is desirable. The study of such issues needs to be open-ended, addressed in the hypothetical mode (Engle, 1986; Longstreet, 1977) and without pressure for closure on the correct answer.[2]

4. The social science disciplines including history and geography will not be treated as end products or goals. Nor are they summaries of definitive knowledge that are accepted without questioning and then memorized, but rather these fields of study should be treated as

sources of insights and information to be examined for their application to understanding and solving the issues at hand.

5. Since value questions of good and bad or of right and wrong are intrinsic to controversial issues and since ways of thinking about values are likely to be found in the humanities rather than the social sciences, selections from literature, art, music, religion, philosophy and journalism would be used along side and treated as importantly as selections from the social sciences and history in the thoughtful study of any issue. For example, historians have a lot to say about slavery, but so do authors like Harriet Beecher Stowe, William Lloyd Garrison and Stephen Crane, artists such as Thomas Benton and musicians such as Stephen Foster and his poignant "Old Black Joe."

6. The curriculum should use relatively large quantities of data (much more than could possibly be held in memory) from a wide range of sources (far more than could possibly be encompassed in a single textbook) to study in depth a relatively small number of issues (Newmann, 1988; Wiggins, 1989). The firsthand experience of student-citizens and teachers should be accepted and respected as one of the important sources of information for both identifying and studying any question or issue.

From these guidelines, a number of implications follow. The organization of the curriculum into units around a smaller number of highly relevant issues suggests the virtual abandonment or severe modification of survey-like courses, such as those dealing with United States history that student-citizens encounter two or three times in their school programs and that usually cover the same ground quite superficially. It also suggests that similar work needs to be done in geography and the social sciences. These fields of study frequently require memorization of the abstract ideas which provide a framework for the field and typically ignore the issues within the discipline or the relationship of the discipline to the issues of society. If survey courses are to exist at all, they need to pursue controversial issues in depth, which would require both major revisions in how time is distributed as well as substantial changes in the approach to teaching and learning in such courses.

Furthermore, the study of the social sciences, history and geography need to be represented with an attitude of tentativeness. Even economists, who often appear to be very certain of their conclusions, have difficulty agreeing on the meaning of economic events. Issues that young citizens encounter in their own studies and investigations are also worthy sources of issues for class consideration. The attitude of tentativeness also applies to actual issues evident in this society or across the planet. Of course, the study of issues identified from the investigation will cross disciplinary lines as questions and relevant data are pursued wherever they may lead.

The focus on issues entails greater flexibility in the selection and sequencing of study. To accommodate new and emerging issues and let go of issues that have been resolved will require continuous course revision. However, never are we likely to face a paucity of issues. Using chronology or the abstract frameworks of various fields of study, which are the usual bases for organizing curricula and courses, are not the most productive ways of handling sequencing of social studies courses or programs when stronger citizens are the goal. An alternative might be to follow the perceived immediate utility of the issue. To search in United States history or World history for persistent controversies is likely to be a more effective way to undertake historical study rather than being tied to chronology as an immovable framework for social studies courses. While building chronology or providing a time-based overview may be desirable at times, the sequence of the curriculum does not need to depend on the linearity of time. Creating or calling attention to timelines can be helpful as needed.

To illustrate the point made above, must student-citizens wait to study the pressing and devastating issues surrounding terrorism until we reach its temporal place in history, when it is treated quite superficially, in courses that merely survey historical events? Today, the public reacts emotionally to terrorism, yet they give little recognition to its historical persistence. Terrorism has been applied for what were thought to be honorable purposes such as the Crusades, the Civil War in the United States and in World War II (often referred to as the last good war). Terrorism takes different forms and uses in destructive ways such as the attack on the World Trade Center in New York City on 9/11, the bombing of Hiroshima and Nagasaki during World War II and the annihilation of Jewish people in the deadly concentration camps created by the Third Reich. It is used by oppressors to keep the oppressed in check as well as by religious fanatics to destroy their enemies. Would not, the study of these issues in a deep and thoughtful way be better dealt with now, when it is of great concern to our citizens rather than waiting until the right chronological moment arrives in either United States or World history? If teachers responded to its currency and adjusted their curriculum accordingly, they would take advantage of the relevant teachable moment and provide a setting where student-citizens could consider the matter rationally in a thoughtful classroom.

Another implication of the guidelines suggested above is the inappropriateness of student assessments that only measure whether the test-taker has memorized isolated bits of information. More appropriately, assessment would deal with the degree to which issues have been understood, the ability to generate useful interpretations as well as mastery of the intellectual processes, that is verifying truth claims and decision making needed in the resolution of significant and controversial issues. That is what citizenship education for a democracy is about.

The ideas advanced here are not altogether new. Reform movements in social studies from the time of John Dewey (1933) to the present have used them. Dewey supported the idea that, in a democracy, learning is more than a passive receiving of knowledge or truth but instead, it is the involvement of young citizens in solving problems in the real world. Alan Griffin (1942), an unrecognized giant in the social studies field, created a fresh rationale for teaching history. He saw the teaching of history not as a matter of requiring young citizens to store up the facts of history, but as the opportunity to lead young people to test their beliefs, both about what historical facts are and what these facts mean. What to believe and why were the persistent problems with which Griffin, not unlike Socrates, continually confronted young citizens (Engle, 1982).

The reform movement of the late 1950s to the 1970s, culminating in the "New Social Studies," included the work of Hunt and Metcalf (1955, 1968), both of whom were Griffin's students as was Peter Martorella (1985), as well as the works of Fenton (1967), Oliver and Shaver (1966) and the numerous projects spawned from the ideas of Jerome Bruner (1962). Each of these efforts were attempts to turn social studies away from mindless exposition and the memorization of facts to a deeper and more thoughtful study of issues, including such intellectual challenges as determining what the facts really are and what conclusions can be drawn from them. These issues may be taken from the disciplines or from issues of historic or contemporary public policy. Such study should lead to fresh perspectives and fresh conclusions that are solidly grounded.

In many of these reform efforts, the hypothetical mode was to be substituted by teachers for the expository mode of teaching. Most of these reform efforts afforded student-citizens the opportunity to become thinkers and decision makers and afforded teachers the opportunity to demonstrate that they really understood their subject and could relate it to the study of issues faced by society and the planet. Moreover, they would demonstrate that they knew the limits and shortcoming of their disciplines. The error made by the social studies profession was that so quickly decided that these reform projects were unworkable, rather than putting forth the effort to refine and improve them.

These reformers, many of whom followed John Dewey, were on the right track. The mission of this book to push once again at the frontier of transforming social studies into something more meaningful and useful in preparing citizens to become the effective in promoting what this democracy needs if it is to grow stronger in achieving its ideals for all citizens.

In some respects, the proposed curriculum is a modest change from the traditional curriculum. For instance, heavy reliance will continue to be placed on United States history, world history, geography and economics, but they will be taught in a special and different way. These subjects will be less concerned with memorization. Instead, they will focus on issues of the past, present and future. Young citizens will be encouraged to think deeply about and to reach justifiable decisions that may reduce or eliminate the issues faced by their generation. Furthermore, the usual content of these subjects needs to be broadened or combined with content from other disciplines and fields of study to accomplish the broad purpose of being fully relevant to the issues faced by citizens. Despite such alterations, the curriculum can still be recognized as good history and good geography or possibly, as better history and better geography.

The major influence in determining the curriculum to meet the educational needs of citizens will be drawn from the guidelines provided in Chapter 2, The Citizen We Need in a Pluralistic Democracy in a Global Age. Consistent with these guidelines the following curriculum strands receive emphasis.

Environmental Studies
Institutional Studies
Studies in Diversity
Significant Social and Controversial Issues
Decision Making
Internships in Citizenship
Electives (such as Sociology, Economics, Anthropology or timely topics such as the Palestine-Israeli conflict, cloning, or AIDS)
A Democratic School Environment

ENVIRONMENTAL STUDIES

Environmental studies is the in-depth study of issues that surround human use and abuse of the natural features that surround them. This study should focus on the issues that arise out of this earth–human relationship. Teachers should organize this study around important issues, which are subject to revision from time to time so that the curriculum reflects current realities and concerns. For example, at this writing the tensions between the actions of the President of the United States related to the matter of climate change (global warning) are at issue. At local levels, tensions between developers and environmentalists are both persistent and widespread. There are, of course, other issues of equal weight such as: What should we do relative to nuclear waste or industrial toxic waste? What is the nature of citizen response about the rapidly growing shortage of drinkable water on a world basis? What do we do about the destruction of the rain forests that are so essential to our ultimate survival on the earth? What do we do about the growing shortage of viable agricultural soils and the related shortages of food that confront many of the world's people? What can we do about the extinction of many plant and animal forms and the loss of genetic materials useful to science in the continuing development of the world's resources? Or, to cite a more exotic issue—one that might be of interest even to third graders—what can be done about the whales?

This list could be extended many times over. These questions will change or be modified as partial or complete solutions may be found. At times, solving some issues creates novel issues. Or, as Robert Hanvey (1976) has said, "We can't do just one thing." Changes resulting from the advancements we make usually have consequences, some of which, according to Hanvey are "surprise effects" and not all issues can solved scientifically.

If we alter the earth's organic composition, its ecology, its climate, we change our understanding of how the earth relates to the universe. In any case, these are the kinds of issues that environmental studies must entail. The goal in such study, is that young citizens will not only come to understand the many ramifications of these issues but that they will come to appreciate their complexity and enlist themselves in doing something sensible about them.

Obviously, geography can play a significant part in furnishing the information and materials about the issues listed above. This chapter does not recommend the teaching of geography for its own sake, but instead it supports the use of geographic information in thinking about significant issues. Memorizing the products of nations, a frequent task in geography classes, is of little use and young citizens quickly forget such information unless it is applied to the resolution of issues. Such lists of products are likely to be outdated quickly and are found easily if such information is needed. What is important is that student-citizens know how to find such information when needed. Practice in using the library, major reference books and use of the Internet are of great importance.

Sequencing content in social studies often has an arbitrary nature. Long characterized by the expanding environment guideline originated by Charles Murray (1964) and later refined by Paul Hanna (1958), which is the approach used in most schools and in textbooks (Le Richie & Cowan, 1992) has been challenged on several counts. When educators consider sequencing the study of controversial issues, there are few justifiable criteria to guide a curricular pattern. Should we teach about the environment in the third grade and again in the ninth? The answer is not clear. Obviously, the treatment of the subject will respond to the young citizens taught at each grade level. However, some issues are more complex, more controversial or more relevant to young citizens. To illustrate, what to do about the whales is not really a simple problem. It is a more complicated issue and one that expands to encompass the ecological crisis of the entire universe.

Identifying the scope of the issue and considering its complexity are two dimensions that need examination when planning the sequence of the curriculum.

In the process of assigning issues to particular grade levels, we should studiously avoid the fiction that children cannot deal with issues until they have a vast background of memorized knowledge of geography or any other subject. Such knowledge, because it is superficially learned and has no immediate use, does not stay in the minds of young citizen (or adults for that matter) and as a result, student-citizens are not in a better position to address issues than they ever were. We have only wasted time, effort and intellectual resources, which even young children have in great abundance.

To the extent that geography is likely to play a strong role in Environmental Studies, the issues involved will probably draw on geology and possibly paleontology, as well as biology, ecology and anthropology. The point is that the information needed should be vigorously sought regardless of the discipline where it resides. Much of the most readily available information on the environment appears in such periodicals as *National Geographic*, an Earth Justice publication titled, *In Brief* and major national newspapers. Highly informative articles have also appeared in *Time, Newsweek* and *American Prospect, The Atlantic Monthly* and the *Smithsonian*. Not to be ignored are the publications of World Watch Institute in Washington, D.C. directed by Lester Brown; it provides in-depth treatments of a host of global issues on a regular basis.[3] Teachers should examine these texts for the novel manner in which the subject matter is treated and a substantial file of relevant articles could be assembled without much difficulty. A number of important and popular books, both fiction and non-fiction, must not be overlooked. They are written by authors such as David Attenborough, Kenneth and Elise Boulding, Rachel Carson, Garrett Hardin, John Hersey, John Naisbett and Barbara Ward. Their works are both readable and informative. In addition, scholarly articles that appear in research journals would challenge strong students.

INSTITUTIONAL STUDIES

Institutional Studies are concerned with the origins as well as the present and future circumstances of the broad range of arrangements created to facilitate the functioning of societies. Such study includes the issues faced by institutions as they developed, the issues they face currently and the issues they are likely to face in the future. To study institutions is to move beyond a superficial understanding of society exhibited by many citizens and to achieve instead a deeper understanding as well as to consider ideas that may improve them. The purpose is to involve young citizens in the meaningful defense and improvement of institutions so that they serve the people of this society in democratic ways.

The following guidelines should enhance the study of institutions:

1. Institutions that express and protect the fundamental freedoms of democracy, the rights and beliefs which underlie all institutional arrangements

2. Economic institutions from banks and credit unions to the Federal Reserve System to such globally oriented agencies as the World Bank

3. Political institutions include political parties and their practices, political organizations (governmental and non-governmental) as well as the political lives of the public

4. Institutions that define our relationships with other peoples of the world

5. Institutions that are identified with the private sector, such as the family, marriage religious groups and organizations, non-governmental organizations and social groups of all kinds and their practices. For all institutions public or private, teachers must give attention to equity and equality issues that affect less powerful citizens and groups wherever they may be.

The study of the social institutions would focus on the hard questions that confront contemporary and future institutional development in light of democratic aspirations. The reference to hard questions implies questions that have no certain or immediately obvious answers. However, they raise issues that demand answers, even if tentatively. They may even be issues that have captured the attention of the active public. In any event, they are significant and controversial and provide excellent illustrations of issues that can be addressed by young citizens.

For instance, in the case of fundamental rights and beliefs, this content would relate easily to the Revolutionary and Constitutional Periods that would contribute much useful information. The following questions would give sharp focus to the study: What does it mean to be free? What does it mean to have freedom of one's person or freedom of one's home? What would our lives be like if these freedoms did not exist? What does it mean to have freedom of the press, or freedom of speech or freedom of religion? Which of these freedoms is the most basic and important? Why do you think so? What limits need to be placed on these freedoms? Are they justifiable? Who has the right to limit one's freedom? For which of these freedoms, if any, would you be willing to lay down your life? Why is that (these) freedoms especially valuable to you? Should a person's idea of what it means to be free change from time to time? Are all citizens of the United States equally free? Are the poor as free as wealthy citizens? Are minority groups as free as the majority? Are uneducated people as free as the educated? Can you identify ways our freedoms are not fulfilled? What is the meaning of the term, "land of the free"? What do people really mean when they say that they will defend the freedom for which many have fought and died? How can the conflict between religious freedom and compulsory school prayer be resolved? How can the conflict between the press and censorship in behalf of national security? What about the tension between property rights and the right of citizens to be protected from toxic wastes and the conflict over whether it is constitutional to establish racial quotas for purposes of college admission or employment?

In the case of economic institutions where the study of the post-Revolutionary War would make important contributions, the following questions would be useful: What are the most fundamental economic institutions? Which of the following have, in your view, most influenced the development of these institutions: the hard work of individuals who wanted to improve their economic lot, a great deal of open land and rich natural resources, the help of federal government in building railroads, air transport, usable waterways or building national interstate highways, dams, rural electrification and canals, foreign investors; immigration; huge markets around the globe, government regulation of business and trade, wars and/or avoidance of international involvement or free public education? If all of these factors contribute, what is their order of importance? What reasons and/or evidence would you give to support your answer? What role should the federal government play in supporting the economy? Why do you think so? What should the role of the federal government be in the struggle between organized labor and employers and the struggle of minority groups and women for equal economic opportunity? How can we best address the economic issues we face today such as the very high levels of poverty and homeless people? What can we do to reduce the growing gap between rich and poor? What should we do about the imbalance of males and females in top management positions? What about the social censure that still applies to gays and lesbians? The same question applies to minority groups as well. How can the economic opportunities of teenage mothers be expanded? Or the virtual elimination of family farms, many of which have been purchased by commercial food processing companies? In a global age, we must also be concerned with multinational corporations that employ many people and in some cases become more influential than nations. What should we do to preserve public parks at both the national, state and local levels?

Turning to political institutions: What should we do, as citizens of a democracy where it still costs millions of dollars for a Congressman or Senator to run for office and be elected? Citizens must be mindful that much of this money comes from those who expect to receive favors from government in return such as corporations, lobbyists and very wealthy donors? What needs to be done about conditions that allow moneyed sources to buy power and push poorer people into powerless positions? What should citizens do about our legislative system where highly paid lobbyists play a very influential role in determining legislation that favors special interest groups?

Each of these questions has significance. They are real issues that need to be understood, not memorized. Citizens must analyze and try to solve or improve conditions that affect them and other people on the Planet. If citizens abrogate this responsibility, other people will decide for them and all of us will get the government we deserve.

Obviously, these questions fit the study of United States history. Some may fit World History, Economics and/or Civics. Some may say that the curriculum being advanced here is not really new, that Institutional Studies is just another name for the study of United States history. A change in title is not being suggested here, but an issues orientation should guide the content of the course.

The study of the American Revolution or any other historical period in U.S. history, takes on an entirely different meaning when focused on the resolution of significant public issues. A strong example of the connection between historical periods and the issues citizens face is found in one of the Oliver and Newmann (1967) Public Issues Series where young citizens are asked, "Who has the best grounds for refusing to obey their legally constituted government, the Minute Men at Concord or African Americans at Pettus Bridge?" This question, which is not unlike many issues we face today, requires a much more serious and meaningful study of history than is ordinarily the case when the teaching of United States history is treated in a survey fashion that highlights chronology and does little or nothing for heightening the quality of democratic citizenship. Especially important is the intellectually challenging process that is entailed by raising such issues for young citizens of a democracy.

If United States history is to be used to explore questions such as those posed above, rather than just merely to be remembered, it will need to be a different kind of history. Such history must be taught in a way that both expands and deepens the study. It would have to expose problems of interpretation and verification that actually confront historians. It would need to guide young citizens to examine alternative interpretation of history. In short, it would need to enable students to think about the history of this democracy and to think about its issues in light of that history. Its purpose would be to enlist young citizens, here and now, and not at a distant future time, to work to preserve the democratic institutions they have inherited and to do this with the fullest possible understanding of the origins and issues faced by those institutions.

Obviously, such treatment of history could not be of the ordinary textbook variety. Textbook versions of events are ordinarily, with very few exceptions, too narrow in scope, too shallow in their treatment of topics, too parsimonious in providing detail and too occupied with merely chronicling a selected set of events that are to be confined to memory. It is not this memory of events and people that the thoughtful and active democratic citizen needs, but a much deeper and more involved grasp of the meaning of democratic institutions useful to the challenges of effective citizenship.

If textbooks are to be used at all, they should include generous references and excerpts of historians writing as historians rather than confine themselves to the words of textbook writers who are usually not historians. Historians who range widely over events, as do William McNeill and Leften Stavrianos[4] would have to be included as well as historians whose works go very deeply into historical events such as Barbara Tuchman and Bruce Catton. Frequently, excerpts of the works of such historians appear in respected periodicals or newspapers such as the Atlantic Monthly, Harper's, the New York Times or the Washington Post. Not to be overlooked are biographical and autobiographical accounts, diaries and copies of original documents. Of particular interest to the study of history is the work of Howard Zinn (2002), *A People's History of the United States, 1492–present* that provides alternative perspectives that emphasize the challenges facing a wide range of marginal people who also created this nation's past.

The purpose of such study is much more to make factual and moral judgments about events rather than to merely remember them. As Henry Steele Commager (1966) argued so brilliantly in his essay "Should Historians Make Moral Judgments?" history is not so much to be remembered as to be judged. Quite aside from the argument that has raged among historians since history was first written by Herodotus, Livy and Plutarch as to whether historians should pass judgment on the events they record, the usefulness of historical writing to the citizen comes from efforts to pass moral judgments on the events of history. Zinn's work, mentioned above, is a particularly strong example. As Carl Becker once argued, "Every man is his own historian" (1936), or as Commager (1966) put it, "The assumption behind the expectation that the historian should make our moral judgment for us is that the reader has no mind of his own, no moral standard, no capacity to exercise judgment.... Are those mature enough to read serious history really so obtuse that they cannot draw conclusions from the facts that are submitted to them?"

Since the making of moral judgment is the most basic of all of the functions of democratic citizens, student-citizens should be continually involved in making judgments about events and/or historical figures rather than merely remembering their names and specific facts about them. Such questions as the following would be helpful:

Was the violence and terror perpetrated against the Loyalists in the American Revolution justified in the cause of freedom?

Was the forced relocation of Native Americans from lands they had occupied for centuries right or wrong?

Were there better ways to deal with conflict between the Native Peoples and the settlers?

Were John Brown and his followers at Harper's Ferry justified in their effort to free the slaves?

Were the oppressive measures taken to keep workers from organizing and striking at Haymarket Square right or wrong?

How might the conflict between workers and their employers have been more fairly settled?

Were people who were out of work during the Depression deserving of help from the government? Why?

Using any of these questions should involve future citizens in grounding their answers in reason and evidence.

Not to be ignored in the study of institutions is the contribution of significant literature, art, music and journalism. Literary and artistic works are more likely than historians to capture the broad meaning of events and to emphasize the moral issues embedded in them. The authors of such works are particularly concerned with interpreting and evaluating human events. Through more subjective vantage points, their works are able to address dilemmas that human beings face in relation to historical and institutional studies that rely on a more data-based scientific approach. Educators must keep in mind that these two approaches complement rather than compete with one another to provide more complete and more complex images of the issues involved. The writings of Thomas Paine, James Madison, Thomas Jefferson as well as authors such as John Steinbeck, Barbara Kingsolver, Harriett Beecher Stowe and Azar Nafisi can serve this purpose well.

Such significant works are likely to have a moral focus. The author and the artist are likely to take sides, make judgments about what needs changing in the ways individuals and society behave and the values they embrace. For young citizens, these works provide models of how moral judgments are made. Thus, they serve as excellent resources for citizenship education and need to be seen by social studies educators as an integral part of the content that they teach. They are not merely frills added to embroider or enliven social studies classes. Some may feel that student-citizens should only read novels in literature classes. Learning should not be restricted on the basis of arbitrary divisions of subject matter. Literature is a strong element of the humanities. It should not be ignored when it adds to the relevance of what is studied.

For instance, how more succinctly to begin the study of human slavery than by reading Harriett Beecher Stowe's *Uncle Tom's Cabin* or Stephen Crane's *Red Badge of Courage*? Or, if a more scholarly work of history is preferred, Bruce Catton's *A Stillness at Appomattox* is well-written and informative? How better to be introduced to the crises of economic and political institutions and to the Great Depression than by reading John Steinbeck's *Grapes of Wrath*?

Literature, art, music and journalism are extremely rich sources of moral commentary regarding our social institutions. From the likes of James Fennimore Cooper and Thomas Paine in colonial times to such contemporary writers as James Baldwin, Gore Vidal, Langston Hughes, Lillian Hellman, Philip Roth and Alice Walker among so many others, there exists a rich supply of fictional sources than can bring depth and interest to the subject matter under study. These women and men of letters have much to say about the morality and immorality of institutions.

Obviously, a well-stocked library has an inestimable value for the in-depth study of institutions. If such a library does not exist in the school, it would be a first order of business to begin building one. The serious study of persistent and contemporary institutions and the issues they face requires it.

STUDIES IN DIVERISTY

Studies in diversity involve the study of differing cultures, of why people of different regions, historical backgrounds, nationalities, religions, ethnic groups, life styles, gender and handicapping conditions experience life differently. They exist in somewhat different cultures from each other and are too often perceived as entities who stand apart from the dominant culture. Especially important is the examination of how we can live usefully in a world of differing cultures; of how despite differences, diverse peoples share profound human similarities and of how we can turn differences into assets for improving the quality of life for all peoples both within this nation and across the planet. Without such understandings, the quality and survival of this nation and this democracy are at a serious level of risk (Baldi et al.; 2001, 2006). Furthermore, diverse peoples bring a wide range of distinctive insights and perspectives to public affairs. The dialogue is richer and perhaps more challenging if they are present. Our democracy is stronger and more in line with its principles when there is concern with equitable conditions for the many diverse peoples that populate this nation and this Planet. The following questions are illustrative of those that can be used in the context of cultural studies:

> Why do people of different cultures, of different religions, of different historical backgrounds, gender and the like grow up differently, behaving and believing in different ways? Why do these differences create tensions with

other people? Why do some people feel threatened by those who appear to be different? Or, by people who hold different views? How can these tensions be minimized? Do you know of any people whose beliefs and ways of behaving are so different from your own that you have trouble accepting them? In what ways? What can people do to minimize these negative feelings?

Human beings share many similarities with one another regardless of their culture. Can you identify any of those similarities? How can these similarities be used to reduce tensions between diverse groups? What is universal about cultures? Of all of the different cultural groups, which ones are the most difficult for you to accept? Why? If a cultural group reveals beliefs and behavior that are definitely opposed to your own, how should you behave toward them? If they are not citizens of the United States, should that make a difference in what you might say or do? How important are cultural tensions in the world today? Why do you think so? What order of importance would you give to the following issues: the threat of nuclear war, religious differences, pollution of the world's environment, world hunger, restrictions on the free exchange of goods? What are the reasons for your rankings? What can we do in this society to resolve cultural tensions?

It is likely that world history and U.S. history will be the major sources of information for answering such questions. However, it should be equally obvious that the study of world history or U.S. history from a textbook for the sole purpose of remembering the chronology of events will not be adequate. The history that is used for such study must present a more sweeping view of the world, more as it has been treated by Arnold Toynbee, Will Durant, William McNeill or Barbara Ward. Student-citizens would need to be encouraged to read history not to memorize it but, rather to use it to throw light on important questions or even to enjoy it. History should be read as suggested by the English historian, Christopher Hill, (1983) who said, "Any serious history deals with questions.... The narrative can be rearranged but the true originality of the historian lies in identifying questions that seem new to us.... This would help to explain why history has to be rewritten in every generation."

Obvious too, is the usefulness of materials from anthropology and sociology to buttress the understanding of cultural differences that are derived from history. Optimally, the historical study of cultural differences could pause at some point to study in depth, as an anthropologist would study cultures, a few selected cultures for a clearer idea of how cultures develop and change.

To support such study a strong library connection would be a necessity. Such a library would include scholarly books and articles of particular cultures, but they must always include serious popular periodicals and even newspaper articles that relate to cultural groups and the issues they face.

For instance, excerpts from the book, *The Unwanted: European Refugees in the Twentieth Century* by Michael R. Maurrus (1985) could put in stark relief the issues of ordinary people who face misunderstanding of cultural differences. Maurrus accents the terrible waste that results from such misunderstanding and prejudice. Still another is *Farewell to Manzanar* by Jeanne Wakatsuki Houston and James D. Houston (1973), which portrays the angst of a Japanese-American family who, even though they were United States citizens, were relocated to internment camps for security purposes during World War II. These books would serve as excellent starting points for challenging classes to think about the reasons for difficulties faced by people who are defined as different and to launch a meaningful exploration of the issues faced and the potential promise of differing world cultures. A directory of web sites dealing with culture needs to be assembled for use by teachers and student-citizens in connection with different issues that are studied.

The same argument applies for including materials from the Humanities in any serious study of cultures, as was advanced earlier for the study of institutions. For example, British society and its issues are afforded by such writers as George Bernard Shaw, the Brontè Sisters, Aldous Huxley and George Orwell. Equally useful commentaries about different societies are provided by Victor Hugo, Emile Zola and Nadine Gordimer. Powerful accounts of traditional Russian society in the 19th and 20th century are afforded by Fyodor Dostoevsky, Leo Tolstoy, Anton Checkov and more recently by Alexander Solzhenitsyn and Boris Pasternak. Other useful works come from the Japanese Kawabata and Yukio Mishima, from the Senegalese, Leopold Senghor's *Prose and Poetry* and from South American poets Jorge Luis Borges and Pablo Neruda.

SIGNIFICIANT SOCIAL AND CONTROVERSIAL ISSUES

From grades three through grade twelve, a controversial issue should be studied in as much depth as possible at least once each year. The purpose for studying controversial issues is four fold. The first reason is to give young citizens an understanding of major compelling issues such as the worldwide environmental crises, the threat of nuclear war, food shortage on a global scale and widespread poverty. The AIDS epidemic and the easy spread of communicable diseases are also issues of major significance. The Carter Center at Emory University in Atlanta, Georgia and the Clinton Foundation are major sources of information on AIDS. Such study should help young citizens understand the issues at stake, the relationships among such issues and to provide them with the opportunity to think, make decisions as well as to act upon them. Decisions and actions help young people see the world in mature ways that engages them in a manner befitting young adult citizens.

A second reason for examining issues is to give young citizens experience dealing with issues in much the same way as intelligent citizens do. As they leave high school they will have acquired the necessary abilities to make a quality contribution to their roles as democratic citizens. They will not only be informed about some issues but they will also have had some experience in working out solutions.

A third, closely related reason for studying a major issue each year, rather than waiting to the end of the social studies program, is that such study will emphasize the relevance of other work under progress in social studies classes. Young citizens will be able to understand why they are studying environmental, institutional and cultural issues. Hopefully, they will approach these strands in the curriculum with a greater sense of purpose. Such study will serve as the glue that binds all parts of the social studies program together. It will no longer be quite as necessary to claim limply that the study of these subjects will help them in the future as adults.

A fourth reason is that the study of real world issues, when combined with developing thoughtful solutions and trying to resolve them, is a way of treating young citizens as adults to the greatest extent possible. As teenagers address their issues of identity, which are often accompanied by some degree of rebellion, their growth and development can be facilitated by involving them in adult activities. Moreover, there are many instances of student-citizens at all grade levels effectively making changes in their schools, their communities as well as at broader levels. Letters to the editor have been written by first graders, third graders have participated in efforts to save the whales, middle school students have campaigned for political candidates and high school students have submitted reports on relevant issues to officials in public office. Participating in such activities triggers a sense of efficacy and student-citizens would have reason to conclude that it is possible to make a difference. Herein lies the major contribution that social studies programs can make to strengthen democracy and expand policies and practices related to social justice by empowering individual citizens.

The point of view presented in this book is based on the very strong belief that gaining the capacity to deal effectively with improving significant social and controversial issues by high quality citizens is the goal of citizenship education. It is also based on the work of Jerome Bruner (1965) that problem-solving abilities are best learned by engaging in problem-solving and consequently, the conclusion is drawn that problem-solving, in all its varieties, should be salient throughout the curriculum. These concerns of society as well as across the planet are the core around which the curriculum must coalesce. Knowing about these concerns and trying to solve them should be constantly fed by the rest of the school curriculum. They are not matters to be left to some far distant future.

To meet, insofar as possible, all of these purposes, major social issue should be studied for an extended period (at least three to four weeks), in as much depth as can be mustered, at one time during each academic year in each social studies classroom at each grade level in every school in the district. Great strength would accrue to such an effort if all classes in all subjects engaged in such study at the same time with the principal serving as the leader of the study. Obviously, if other departments in the school joined in, this effort would be enriched substantially. Importantly, science, the language arts, the fine arts and the music department could make significant contributions. Not to be ignored is the involvement of parents, community officials and the public as well. Adults with particular expertise, public libraries, local government agencies, media services along with public interest groups can serve as very rich resources to enhance the study of controversial issues.

The study in depth of a major controversial issue each year should provide young citizens with the sobering experience of studying something in school about which the whole community as well as their teachers are genuinely concerned. It is very likely that such an experience would set a tone for more thoughtful engagement by young citizens in all of their academic work, both within social studies and in other academic areas.

DECISION MAKING

The explosion of knowledge and the parallel explosion of technology have contributed in a challenging manner to how frequently the means of communication, together with an unsettling of values in today's world, have placed huge demands on citizens to be well informed and to know what values should be applied. Paradoxical as it may seem, it is actually more difficult today to know what is true than it was 50 years ago. The shear quantity of knowledge is much greater today, while in the past, the values at stake seemed to have greater clarity and there were not as many choices to make. The mushrooming of the means of communication technologies via computers and the Internet has opened tremendous opportunities to become better informed, yet simultaneously, it has created tremendous possibilities of having our thoughts manipulated by charlatans, politicians, religious fanatics and those interests who try to control what we think by shaping our opinions through the media. Thus persons such as Rupert Murdoch[5] who own and control widespread visual and print media have an inordinate influence over what citizens hear and how it is interpreted. These technological developments also threaten our privacy and computer hacks even threaten our capacity to communicate without our messages being distorted, discovered or destroyed.

The viewpoints of the poor or those who are at ideological odds with the establishment are heard less often. Corporate advertising on television and the slick popular magazines place limits on the nature of what is presented. Likewise, in the face of the unprecedented rate of change, traditional values are being called into question. The Civil Rights Movement in the 1960s is a case in point. At that time, what was seen as equitable treatment of minorities and women became very controversial matters. Values that had been held quite innocently were now seriously challenged and were in conflict. The issue of religious freedom and the proposition that there should be prayer in schools serves as an example. The number of such conflicts between values has multiplied many times in recent years. Citizens, frequently pulled one way and then another, are often confused about what to believe and what to hold more valuable. Under these conditions, it is far easier to fall victim to the overly simple answer and to the smooth talk of the unscrupulous.

In light of these conditions there is a need to help young citizens, whose opinions should be well-informed, well-reasoned and well-grounded to wade through the maze of information and conflicting value claims that are thrust upon them, to help them sort out the wheat from the chaff. The purpose of the school and of social studies is not to tell them what to think, but rather to help them to develop the understandings and the abilities to decide for themselves, what is or is not credible.

Four groups of questions would guide the study of the issues that reside in decision making. The first group is *epistemological* and the following questions can characterize this dimension of decision making.

- What is knowledge? What does it mean to say that we know?
- What is evidence? How do we know if it is reliable?
- What is truth?
- What are different ways of knowing? (by evidence, by logic, by reason, by intuition, by faith, by common sense etc.)?
- Which way of knowing is the most dependable? Why?
- How can one determine the dependability of claims to knowledge or of a scholar in a given field of study, a witness to an event, an expert in some line of endeavor, a textbook account, a proponent of a religious doctrine, a politician, a news report, an editorial and so on? What is dependable evidence in each case?

The second dimension is labeled *learning how to learn* where young citizens learn to access information of all kinds—in libraries with careful attention how to use card catalogs, indexes, references, almanacs, encyclopedias, digests and the like as well as being able to handle the computer, particularly the Internet as a source of data, electronic mail and chat rooms adeptly. Student-citizens should be familiar with these sources and able to access information from them. Schools and classrooms should have an adequate supply of computers so that young citizens can access them conveniently. There is no excuse for any young citizen to graduate from school without these abilities well in hand (Diem, 2006; Geima, 1997).

The third dimension is *communications*, which would center on the following questions:

- What are the purposes of the media? To inform? To present alternative views? To interpret, analyze or persuade? Since commercial television is paid for by advertisers, are representatives of the media restricted to support their points of view?
- How can we judge the dependability of what we read, or hear or are told by, radio, television, textbooks or in political speeches? How can one detect distortion or misrepresentation of the truth?
- In a political campaign, how does one decide what to believe? Some political posters, slogans and messages distort and exaggerate what they communicate.

The fourth dimension, *values* would raise such questions as:

- What do I value most? Do I have good reasons for what I value most?
- How can I know that my values are good values? Do they lead to desirable consequences?
- Can I arrange my values from most important to least important?
- What do I do when two of my values are in conflict? How do I decide if compromise is appropriate in a given situation?
- Can I determine the values of others even if those values are not made explicit?

A useful commentary on the kinds of values we hold was provided by Hunt and Metcalf (1968): a) They discussed values that are tied to higher values that are exemplified by values that respect human differences because they give rise to a stronger level of human dignity. b) They also discussed values that can be justified by their consequences such as valuing peace (over war) because it results in the saving of human lives or equality (over property rights) since equality results in respecting all individuals to the point that they have the same privileges as the dominant class. c) Hunt and Metcalf also included matters of taste in their discussion of values. These are exemplified by a statement such as: "I have never seen anything as beautiful as this painting." Values surrounding the concept of beauty (aesthetic values) can be disagreed with but not disputed. Beauty, after all, is in the eye of the beholder. Thus, social and political values can be justified in two important ways: by their logical relationship to higher values as well as by the consequences to which they may lead. Consequences are predictions or results that are hoped for—that we would like to see result from decisions that are made and actions that are taken. However, decisions are not certainties. Instead, they have different levels of probabilities that we can estimate but not precisely specify.

Questions like these need examination from time to time in many subject areas—in science and certainly, the language arts as well as in social studies. Teaching directed toward asking such meaningful questions could hardly be conducted without awareness on the part of teachers and student-citizens of the nature of dependable knowledge and of the nature of evidence or proof. Memorization which is contradictory to the proposed curriculum, tends to sweep such teaching under the rug. Student-citizens are supposed to remember predetermined and correct answers and are supposed to believe what they are told.

Even in a curriculum that emphasizes questioning and thoughtful responses by young citizens, there is a strong need to study the nature of knowing and analyzing values in depth, if young people are to cope with today's world of instant communication and a rapidly expanding and changing knowledge base as well as a complex and challenging world. Young citizens, more than ever, need to learn that because claims are made in books, in the news media or on the Internet does not bestow these claims with a mantle of accuracy. They are claims, not certainties, to being the truth.

Studies have indicated that children spend as much time watching television as they spend in school. Without a doubt, television and the computer serve as strong forces for learning and entertaining. They are forces that can range from being profoundly positive to profoundly negative in their consequences. Student-citizens must know that what they see and hear may result in their becoming critical consumers of the media but, they can also become patsies by accepting what they are served as the truth. They will need help with this problem but they also need help in becoming more critical textbook readers and discerning citizens.

The best of all possible worlds in this connection is for the social studies program in coordination with the rest of the school curriculum, to be equally interested in developing more higher level thinking, listening, reading and viewing abilities, to provide a jointly sponsored course in knowing, communicating and valuing to be offered midway through the middle school grades.

INTERNSHIP IN CITIZENSHIP

A one-year, one-day a week internship in a civic enterprise, an agency or organization, public or private, would serve as a natural progression from meaningful experience in thinking about and making decisions about controversial issues to taking action to resolve them. The internship is a transition from neophyte to adult citizenship.[6] Through the internship, young citizens upon graduation would have already been involved in what might well be as their continuing interest as adult citizens. Useful volunteer work, without pay, though required for graduation in a service, political, civic organization or with other interest groups can make a very strong impact on young citizens. Internships should be supervised by a teacher or by a facilitator, preferably a teacher who would arrange and supervise these internships. Regular seminar meetings to review community experiences that young citizens have had should be a necessary aspect of an internship dimension of the curriculum. Furthermore, some internships will be less successful than others and student-citizens need to understand why this was the case.

ELECTIVES

I like this idea and it is doable.

Electives can provide opportunities for student-citizens to study in depth the methods by which social scientists and historians arrive at dependable knowledge about human affairs. In this context, it would be interesting to compare the work of conventional historians with reform historians. The latter is well exemplified by the work of Howard Zinn (2002) in his compelling work, *A People's History of the United States, 1492–present,* as well as the works of other minority historians. Elective courses usually focus on economics, sociology or psychology where the nature of the discipline would be studied, along with its implicit and explicit assumptions and its methods of investigation. The findings of these disciplines (and there could be other disciplines or issues that might justify other electives) would not be the main emphasis but importantly, the findings would serve as the springboard for analyzing how the discipline functions. Student-citizens should engage in some laboratory practice by writing a short historical account, conducting a simple sociological study, studying a group of people such as an anthropologist would or reporting on a local controversy in journalistic style. All student-citizens would be encouraged to take electives, but they would not be required.

A DEMOCRATIC SCHOOL ENVIRONMENT

The position taken in this book is that not only does the overt curriculum of the school have to change to ensure higher quality citizenship but, the covert curriculum which involves all other experiences that young citizens have in the school setting, must change as well. More specifically, the climate in both the school and the classroom needs to reflect democratic principles in action. The school needs to function democratically, guided by values of fairness, equality and freedom. The case for democracy is lost if young citizens perceive the school as dictatorial and punitive. School rules, like society's laws, should be fair and reasonable and made with participation by student-citizens and teachers wherever possible.

In a fascinating study by Linda McNeil (1986), she found that in schools where the school administration was more democratic, social studies department chairs operated more democratically. She also found that the opposite was true. Where the school administration was autocratic, social studies department chairs also behaved more autocratically. School governance should never be arbitrary or coercive. The schools, their administrators and their teachers should never underestimate the ability and willingness of young people to participate in their own governance.

Democracy is also exemplified by the respect shown for intellectual honesty. Democratic teaching must demonstrate full respect for the canons of scholarship. Furthermore, full respect must also be given to the intelligence of student-citizens to think independently. Pressure tactics, being less than candid, talking down to student-citizens and/or using the classroom to propagandize are all teaching practices completely out of character with democracy and must never be employed to coerce the minds and behavior of young citizens. Teachers must exhibit in their own behavior a deep commitment to democracy as well as the qualities of intelligence and reason that characterize effective democratic citizens.

CONCLUSION

This chapter presents and explains the key dimensions of the proposed curriculum. This author and Professor Engle both recognized that a shift to this curriculum was a tall order. The change in the teacher's role as well as in the role of student-citizens is a very substantial one. However, serious change is necessary. Awareness of school funding that supports conventional teaching practices that have not been successful for the most part, can only lead to the conclusion that, across the years, tax dollars were poorly spent. However, a modicum of change can be started without implementing all of the key dimensions of this curriculum concurrently. In particular, the recommendation of a three or four week period spent by the entire school giving attention to a significant and controversial issue faced by the community could serve as a giant step forward. Obviously, the preparation of teachers for the implementation of this entire curriculum needs to be an on-going task. Neither are democratic school and classroom climates arranged over night. They need implementation that is both gradual and thoughtful. However, with dedicated administrators and teachers, there is no reason why each school year cannot bring about important changes without upsetting the current curriculum. Schools need to consider the key dimensions of this curriculum carefully and prioritize the manner in which they would like to proceed. Matters of implementation are discussed more fully in Chapters 10 and 11. The shift to democratic education requires substantial change in the roles of teachers as well as student-citizens. The shift can be gradual, but it is essential if democratic education is to meet its obligation to raise the quality of citizen participation. This curriculum framework should serve as the scope for an Issues-Centered Decision Making Curriculum. Educators should carefully review it when making changes in behalf of democratic education and designing a curriculum for student-citizens as well as new and experienced teachers.

NOTES

1. Support for the in-depth study of a few topics over the necessarily superficial coverage of many topics is provided by the following authors: Whitehead (1929, pp. 1–2), who warned of the uselessness, and above all, the harmful effects of "inert ideas, that is, ideas that are received into the mind without being utilized or tested or thrown into fresh combinations"; Myrdal (1944, pp. 1052–1053), who observed that to narrate history straight without stopping to consider the assumptions, implied or explicit, and the qualifiers chosen by the historians and without considering other scholarly versions of the events being described is tantamount to indoctrination; Richard Brown, an historian at the Newberry Library and Director of the Amherst Project, who established a number of units in which he demonstrated the feasibility of studying a few significant issues by what he called "postholing," which entailed studying these issues in depth as an alternative to the survey course in United States history; Fred Newmann (1996) who recognized the replacement of coverage of in-depth study as a primary need in the field; and many of the projects in the New Social Studies movement were based on the principle of an in depth study of a relatively small number of topics.

2. The argument for the use of the hypothetical mode over the expository in the study of social content was most succinctly presented by Jerome Bruner (1965, pp. 81–96). This idea was responsible for spawning the "New Social Studies" movement.

3. The address for World Watch Institute is 1776 Massachusetts Ave., Washington, DC 20036-1904. E-mail: www.pub@worldwatch.org. Their publications are especially useful for teacher background. In particular, their annual *State of the World* publication brings issues up-to-date and their *World Watch Papers* focus on a wide range of specific cross-national issues. A very important resource for school libraries.

4. Professors William McNeil and Lefton Stavrianos have authored history books with a global view and placed national history in the context of world-wide developments, trends, and events. These books are out of date but world history teachers would profit by examining copies to see how the authors have contexted national history in the global setting.

5. Rupert Murdoch is the owner of the News Corporation, Ltd., which includes among other things, the Fox Network, 20th Century Fox, The NY Post, The Times in London, BskyB (satellite TV in Britain), Star TV (in Asia). Ted Turner, the founder of CNN and Murdoch are competitors who own large segments of the media.

6. The research on service learning and social action is far from definitive. See Rahima C. Wade and David W. Saxe (1996) "Community Service Learning in the Social Studies: Historical Roots, Empirical Evidence, Critical Issues" in *Theory and Research in Social Education.* Despite the lack of clear cut research direction, these authors concluded that service learning is likely to contribute to the future involvement of young citizens in the social and political life of the community. They also suggest directions for future research.

CHAPTER 8

DEMOCRATIC TEACHING PRACTICES

. . . discussion is worth the effort, understanding and democracy depends on it.

—Walter Parker, 2001

INTRODUCTION

This chapter provides guidance for teachers who wish to function in the democratic tradition. This process is fundamental to implementing an Issues-Centered Decision Making Curriculum. It highlights aspects of democratic teaching that will not be too complicated. It gives attention to questioning, listening and the responses teachers use to nurture classroom dialogue. It also details information regarding useful resources for the library and classroom that both beginning and experienced teachers will find helpful.

*   *   *

An Issues-Centered Decision Making classroom requires democratic teaching practices to the greatest extent possible. This curriculum requires an open classroom climate and teaching procedures that embrace substantive knowledge about significant problematic conditions, controversial issues and higher level thinking focused on drawing conclusions, decision making and identifying values. It is extended by service learning or social action. Certainly, the teacher's ability to sustain dialogue

Democratic Education for Social Studies, pages 215–242

in the classroom by facilitating student-to-teacher as well as student-to-student interaction is fundamental to the goals of this, or any other democratic curriculum. These are challenging and demanding teaching responsibilities. For many, if not most teachers, these new learnings and responsibilities require letting go of conventional teaching practices that they have observed in their own schooling on a regular basis and in the case of experienced teachers who have taught for a number of years, such teaching practices have become habits that worked for them. Habits are always hard to break. However, a gradual letting go is possible. Nonetheless, letting go of teaching habits is not sufficient. At the same time, teachers must take on new practices that are necessary if this curriculum is to be implemented authentically and successfully. At first, teachers may find a facilitative role uncomfortable and the responses of student-citizens may be unpredictable but when the need is evident, most professionals who see the need for constructive change, can make adjustments and adjust their practices on a gradual basis.

Student-citizens have habits and expectations too. A gradual change will be more acceptable to them as well. Experience suggests that a facilitative role, asking questions instead of lecturing, engaging student-citizens in dialogue instead of expecting correct textbook answers, makes teaching as well as learning more exciting and more meaningful. These new teaching practices can contribute to the heightened confidence of young citizens as well as facilitating a higher quality of understanding and intellectual activity that they can bring to strengthening this democracy.

We need democratic classrooms that emphasize controversial issues and decision making as well as ones that stimulate a broad range of higher level intellectual processes. These classrooms must be settings where the thinking process is constantly nourished and where issues, ideas and values, however controversial, can be freely examined. The social studies classroom may well be the only setting where an open dialogue about significant issues can be rational and vigorous in ways that best prepare our young people for participation in a democratic society.

Democratic teaching requires teachers who are deeply committed to democratic principles and who see the development of informed, thoughtful and democratic decision makers as their most significant responsibility. A democratic decision making curriculum also implies respect for the idea that the intellectual process can best be stimulated in an open classroom environment. In an open setting, the exchange of ideas and maintenance of a sustained dialogue in a civil manner, however controversial, contributes to intellectual acuity. Such a setting is one where evidence, reason and values are seen as fundamental to decision making and is related to the improvement of a complex, pluralistic and democratic society that has a leadership role in the global setting. Only when teachers hold firm convictions about these educational values are their classroom goals and practices likely to genuinely represent the goals of this or any other democratic curriculum.

In a democratic classroom, the teacher's role is to stimulate thinking, encourage the expression of ideas with careful and continuous attention to the careful use of evidence and reason. Teachers need to provide opportunities for student-citizens to engage in a search for knowledge regarding controversial issues that always have multiple perspectives and they need to guide young citizens in the evaluation of their findings and the examination of their values. As importantly, teachers must promote rigorous and democratic dialogue where class members listen to each other and present competing ideas. Certainly, the teacher needs to be informed about the issues under discussion. However, the teacher does not serve as the major authority regarding knowledge about conditions and issues that are under study. This facilitative, but goal–oriented role, contrasts sharply with the more authoritarian role that more often than not characterizes teaching in today's social studies classrooms. Moreover, covering content so that it may be memorized, limiting questions to those that call for specified predetermined answers in a lecture–recitation–memorization mode applied to covering the and emphasizing trivial facts without exploring significant ideas are practices not compatible with the democratic classroom or with this proposed curriculum. Neither the teacher nor the textbook should serve as the ultimate source of authority regarding the credibility and validity of knowledge. In democratic classrooms, authority resides exclusively in evidence, reason and democratic values. The teacher assumes the role of a facilitator who stimulates classroom dialogue and provides opportunities for student-citizens to become able and informed decision makers.

Democratic decision making calls for a new and alternative teaching role that creates conditions where serious intellectual activity can take place. The shift away from a conventional and authoritarian teaching role is a substantial one. While this shift represents a challenging transition in how social studies teachers perform and in what they do as teachers and as citizens, it is needed if democracy is to be authentically and seriously nourished in the schools.

TEACHING AN ISSUES-CENTERED DECISION MAKING CURRICULUM

Citizenship educators need to create an open classroom climate and sustain stimulation of intellectual abilities that include higher level thinking and decision making. To the greatest extent possible, the democratic classroom must be open—open to all ideas, to all information and open to the examination of all values that apply to the particular issue under study. However, important ideas and information must be subject to continuous scrutiny by the members of the class and the teacher. Teachers and student-citizens, thinking and working together, should create criteria they use to validate knowledge related to the study of issues.

Knowledge

In this curriculum, evidence and reason are essential to support the validity and credibility of knowledge. Evidence may come in the form of experts who share their expertise, if their expertise is grounded in reason, evidence, observations and collected data that student-citizens can find in a wide range of sources—by interviewing people and using both the library and the Internet. Reasons may suggest values that are more likely to occur, possible predictions of what may happen (consequences) or motives that are desirable. On occasion, arguments on the basis of faith or providence may be entered as evidence by student-citizens with strong religious backgrounds. However, for student-citizens who do not hold similar religious views, faith or providence will not serve as evidence. Nor can the public school classroom be the arena for religious disputes. As teachers are well aware, to do so violates the underlying democratic principle of separation of church and state addressed in the First Amendment of the Bill of Rights.

The classroom teacher has the central responsibility for setting the norms that govern classroom dialogue that combines the subject matter (knowledge) related to significant social conditions or controversial issues faced by citizens as well as the intellectual processes that emphasize higher level thinking, value analysis and decision making that characterize this curriculum. The teacher needs to guide student-citizens to recognize that the quality and validity of authority can vary. Authority can be found in evidence, logic, reason, bona fide expertise or faith and providence although these several sources of authority may not be equal in quality. The norms of classroom dialogue should be set with the input from class members. Teachers who respond enthusiastically to their concerns will provide young citizens with authentic experience in an especially significant dimension of the democratic process that prepares them to be stronger citizens of a democracy.

Democratic Classroom Climate

To the greatest extent possible, the classroom must function in democratic ways. The norms of the classroom must permit the participants to communicate candidly and easily in a civil, supportive, yet stimulating manner. Since decision making calls for the testing of ideas, student-citizens who share their ideas openly must be treated with respect and encouragement. They must not be the victims of ridicule, sarcasm or worst of all, ignored. However, immature or limited the contribution of a young citizen might be, it should be listened to carefully, given serious consideration and used constructively if at all possible. Weak contributions must be respected and strengthened as well since the student-citizen who shared the idea is trying to contribute to the dialogue. Such efforts must be rewarded in an open classroom. However, the teacher needs to probe the responses of each student-citizen in order for that individual and the class to deepen their understanding of the point that the individual was trying to make. With any group of citizens, young or older, their contributions will vary in quality. To sustain classroom dialogue, all comments made by student-citizens must be encouraged and probed; weaker comments need elaboration by the teacher, if needed.

The democratic teacher has the responsibility for setting the norms for classroom dialogue with the class. Through their words and actions, teachers need to emphasize that the classroom is a place where significant questions and ideas are pursued, where all views are worthy of examination, where each individual has worth, where listening to others is a vital part civil dialogue and where the test of an idea resides in the strength of the reasons and evidence that support it. Teachers who create a climate guided by these values will provide student-citizens with direct experience in an authentically democratic process. Creating such an environment takes creativity and patience and there are no recipes. It makes common sense, however to proceed gradually.

Democratic teaching requires a setting that is open to all ideas and is purposeful. In this setting, both student-citizens and teachers pose and examine questions and issues. No compulsion for the class to reach consensus should exist. There are times, however, where consensus takes place because every member of the class agrees and unanimity is evident among all class members. Regardless of the unanimity, it is necessary that alternative solutions are open for class consideration and that each of these solutions is examined and evaluated. In every case, it is desirable for the class not to jump to conclusions (Beck, 2005).

Democratic classrooms should be settings where student-citizens feel free to say, "I don't agree. Abortion is wrong!" or "I know that AIDS is an epidemic. Can we hear from someone who has AIDS to learn more about it? This last student idea poses a challenge for the teacher. There will be times when young citizens are impulsive. Suggestions by student-citizens that violate the privacy of others will occur in an open classroom. In this case, the teacher needs to explain why such an invitation would violate an individual's privacy. The class needs to think of other ways that they can get the information they want. The point here is that members of the class are able to suggest issues and express strong opinions freely. Obviously, it is desirable for a majority of the class to agree with an idea that is proposed for study by the entire class. As always, minority views about issues to be studied deserve respect and consideration at a later time.

Bridges (1979) provides further insight into the nature of openness as related to discussion. He suggests that a discussion must be open in the following ways:

*hard to
bring
abou*

The matter is open to discussion.
The discussants are open-minded.
The discussion is open to all arguments.
The discussion is open to any person.
The time limit is open (This is not usually the case in classrooms,
although class discussions occasionally go on for several class meetings).

The learning outcomes are open, not predictable or specified. The purposes and practices of the discussion are out in the open, not covert. Teachers should explain to student-citizens why discussion of these matters is important for understanding and all of us learn when we really listen to the views of others and express our own. The discussion is open-ended, not required to come to a single conclusion. Bridges leads us to a deeper understanding of open discussion and provides educators with helpful guidelines that can foster an open exchange of ideas.

The following discussion identifies and explains aspects of teaching and learning that contribute to an open classroom climate.

Listening

Listening to the ideas of others is fundamental to serious and productive dialogue. Adults, when discussing issues, often do not listen. Instead, when they speak they want to make their point rather than pursue or address the ideas or viewpoints made by others. However, not listening reduces the quality of the dialogue because we all learn less about what others think. Furthermore, what often occurs is that the dialogue goes off in different tangents and the dialogue strays from its original concern.

It is especially important that the comments made by student-citizens who may see themselves as marginal or may be so viewed by their class mates, be accepted, explored and rewarded whenever their contribution warrants such positive recognition. This guideline especially applies to minorities, females, the handicapped or student-citizens who may not be popular or as respected as other young citizens in the class. While student-citizens are speaking, teachers sometimes become more concerned with what they are going to say next or with student-citizens who may be losing interest or class members who are making a rush to judgment instead of waiting for a complete analysis of an issue. If class members feel that their ideas do not receive serious consideration or that their teacher or their peers do not listen, they will not likely listen to others, to the teacher or to participate again. Neither are they likely to make further contributions to classroom dialogues. Most importantly, student-citizens are not likely to remain interested in the dialogue at all. If they are affirmed, they are more apt to continue to make contributions and that is the setting where learning takes place. While listening is a necessary part of what teachers do, it must also serve as a norm for the behavior of young citizens as well.

Restating the Ideas of Student-Citizens

One way to increase the chances that student-citizens will feel that their contributions are recognized is to paraphrase or summarize what they have said. Teachers can give recognition to comments made by student-citizens by saying: "As I understand it, this is what you said…" Such statements should be worded carefully to capture what the individual said. This exchange is followed by asking the class to respond to what was said. As a follow up, a teacher may say, "I think I have the idea. Is this what you mean?" or "Marie has said she thinks that a candidate who has already served in a public office has had more experience and therefore, she believes this candidate holds an important advantage over candidates who do not have such experience. What do the rest of you think of that idea?" Is that a reason to vote for that candidate?" Restatement and recognition affirm the student-citizen's contribution and helps to sustain interest and involvement. These practices are likely to result in future participation.

Teachers need to guard against any tendency to evaluate comments made by student-citizens too quickly. They, like their student-citizens, must not rush to judgment. Rather, every attempt should be made to understand clearly what has been said before making any kind of evaluation statements. If the teacher verbalizes any evaluation, that evaluation should be as positive as possible. (e.g., "I know you gave serious thought to your ideas and we should take a closer look at them" or "Can you tell us how you came up with that idea?" Negative or sarcastic comments are likely to reduce class participation since such remarks make any contribution made by others open to the risk of negative statements made by the teacher. Student-citizens become more reluctant to contribute. If class participation has shown signs of vitality and the class elicits energy and interest, it may be productive for the teacher to insert a competing point of view if one. However, teachers need to respond to their class members sensitively. Presenting a competing view without full consideration of the idea of a shy class member, could result in that individual's withdrawal. Before entering competing views, teacher should be as sure as possible that the individual who last spoke is able to handle a challenging opinion. If the young citizen is shy and needs more encouragement, the teacher should add to the comments made and have the class respond to the reconstructed contribution. With enough experience in classroom dialogue, both teachers and student-citizens should gradually become comfortable examining competing ideas. Certainly, that is the purpose of democratic dialogue.

Teachers who are just beginning to assume the role of facilitator would be wise to pair up with another teacher. They should be able to observe each other's classes and comment on the quality of classroom dialogue and the climate of the classroom. We all can improve with feedback and a friendly colleague is a useful source of constructive criticism. It is also useful to video tape classroom interaction for teacher feedback but also for analysis by the class to examine how well they are discussing the issue at hand.

Restating the ideas of student-citizens represents a significant way to encourage more broadly based class participation. This point has been underscored in a number of research studies including Torney, Oppenheim, & Farnen (1975). This study compared students from ten countries and concluded that a classroom climate where expression of ideas by members of the class is encouraged is the most significant factor related to positive classroom outcomes. Citizenship educators should consider this research seriously as it provides strong indication of worthwhile teacher practices related to open and democratic classrooms.

Presenting Competing Ideas

Classroom dialogue is an inherently strained and tense setting. On the one hand, the classroom should be comfortable and supportive but on the other hand, it should be intellectually challenging and open to competing views in the context of controversial issues. Research findings reported and summarized by Hahn (1996) affirm that the use of controversial content contributes to positive attitudes by young citizens regarding citizen duty, political participation and political efficacy as well as political trust and social integration. The study of controversial issues is central to education for democratic citizenship as set forth in this democratic curriculum. Ehman's research summary underscores the importance of controversy as facilitating a broad range of positive attitudes that are essential to effective citizen participation in a democracy.

Teachers need to recognize that it takes considerable courage, competence and maturity for young citizens to respond effectively when they are subjected to harsh criticism by their classmates or from the teacher. The effect of such teacher behavior is likely to be alienation with many young citizens. What the teacher may choose to do is present a contrasting view in a somewhat detached way with statements like: "I understand your point of view and the reasons why you support this view, but some people hold a different position. For example,

"Or alternatively…"; "There is a different point of view that goes like this…"; "Can you think about it and let us know what you think of it to-morrow?" It is important that young citizens not feel rushed because careful thinking takes time. Teachers should avoid confronting their class members impatiently or creating a tempo that calls for rapid response. The decision making process loses its dynamism unless competing views are given full consideration. Teachers will need to challenge ideas that are poorly supported or illogical, but not because the views expressed do not agree with theirs.

Understanding the School's Community

On occasion, it may be necessary for the class to have a dialogue concerning the views of people in their own community on a particular issue or to interview members of their community (Burke-Hengen & Gillespie, 1995). In a dominantly Catholic community, strong emotions and opinions may prevail regarding the matter of abortion; in a Hispanic community, the same may be true regarding a proposed policy that English become the official language or in a community with a military installation, raising concerns about wars or police actions may be especially sensitive. Student-citizens need to become aware that adult citizens often display emotional, rather than intellectual reasons and their attachment to values can be arbitrarily strong. They should also recognize that empirical evidence and thoughtful reasons offer stronger support than emotions. However, emotional reasons cannot be discarded. Importantly, this does not mean that such issues that carry a high level of emotion should be avoided. However, it does mean that these issues must be handled very seriously and thoroughly and sometimes, it is appropriate to obtain parental permission to deal with such issues in the classroom.

Humor

Humor plays an important role in easing the flow of classroom dialogue. While humor must not degenerate to the level of ridicule or sarcasm, it can focus on news events, foibles made by the teacher, public figures and even take the form of gentle teasing. It can be infused into classroom dialogue with cartoons (though not all political cartoons are amusing) that appear in newspapers or books and Compact Discs (CDs) that carry the performance of humorists such as Bill Maher (2004), Al Franken (2003) or Joel Pett (1982). The power of humor is that it both relaxes and stimulates the climate of the classroom. Each teacher will have her or his style of introducing humor, but its importance lies in the appropriate support and atmosphere it provides to sustain the dialogue in a friendly and civil manner.

Walking Our Talk

As all teachers know, the perceptions that young citizens have of their teachers influences the quality of their learning and their attitudes toward the subject. The question here is: What qualities of the teacher foster a thoughtful and democratic classroom? Fundamentally, the teacher has to exhibit those qualities entailed by the democratic decision making process. While openness and acceptance of comments made by young citizens are essential teacher practices, they are not sufficient. Teachers must enjoy controversy and the exchange of competing ideas. If teachers demonstrate their personal enthusiasm for the ideas that are contributed by their class members, it is far more likely that their student-citizens will as well. Moreover, it would be especially appropriate if teachers would share the process they followed personally to understand a controversial issue and the challenges of making decisions that would improve conditions surrounding the issue. Sharing a change of opinion and explaining why you changed it is one way to let your class know that you admit to changing your mind. For example, "I used to think anyone who wanted to could pull themselves out of poverty, by doing well in school, getting part time jobs and having friends who were trying to do the same thing. But, when I was in college I spent a summer working on a playground in a broken down urban neighborhood. That experience really changed my mind. Many of those children and their parent(s) lived in such difficult situations that there was no reason to hope that life could get better. In order to improve their lives, social agencies, religious organizations and schools would have to actively intervene."

Teachers also need to create conditions of fairness, equity and civility. Our society needs its citizens to live by these values. As much attention must be given to shy and reticent student-citizens as to those who are assertive and confident, to the less popular as well as the more popular, to females as well as males and to minority members of the class as well as the majority. Partiality or favoritism has no place in the democratic classroom.

Furthermore, teachers need to realize that the decision making process provides very few single answers or ones that are absolutely correct. However, some decisions are stronger that others. Very seldom, if ever, do any of us have one hundred percent certainty about decisions we make. The teacher's role with this curriculum is to stimulate thinking rather than to serve as a major authority on the correctness of subject matter. An authoritarian posture, especially one that engenders fear or high levels of anxiety rather than trust and respect, violates all of the premises of democratic decision making. A trusting relationship with young citizens is an essential component of a democratic curriculum. Teachers also need to be willing to share their own doubts and ambiguities with their classes to demonstrate that perplexity and uncertainty are aspects of democratic citizenship. These feelings are an integral part of democratic decision making and concerned citizens face issues that are controversial for which there are no single right answers.

Are teachers themselves, concerned, thoughtful and active citizen? Is the teacher genuinely concerned with public issues? Does the teacher get involved in social causes in her or his community? Is the teacher registered to vote? Does the teacher actually vote? Does the teacher regularly read the local newspaper, a national newspaper (the *New York Times*, the *Wall Street Journal*, the *Christian Science Monitor* or the *Washington Post*) as well as the local paper and news magazines that represent alternative points of view. Teachers will be much more effective if they serve as models of involved citizenship. If class members know that their teachers are active in community groups, political parties or participate in social cause organizations, the teacher's credibility is considerably enhanced. We must "walk our talk"! Teachers need to serve as models of political values for their student-citizens who may emulate them or otherwise, see through them in ways that reduce their credibility, if they are not active citizens themselves. In short, democratic teaching places high demands on teachers to behave as they want young citizens to behave.

An Issues-Centered Decision Making Curriculum requires that teachers persistently stimulate thinking during the course of classroom dialogue that is focused on significant problematic conditions and controversial issues. Stimulation can take the form of probing questions, presenting alternative and competing ideas and opinions, calling for the use of evidence and reason, clarifying consequences, fostering participation to improve conditions regarding the issue under study and facilitating class evaluation of the quality of the dialogue.

In the discussion that follows, essential aspects of teaching that are consistent with democratic decision making are highlighted. This curriculum does not lend itself to a set of prescribed, linear steps that a teacher should emulate, nor is there a single recipe or set of standard lessons that can be used. Described below are those unique aspects of teaching that facilitates this curriculum and distinguishes it from more conventional and more direct ways of teaching.

Creating an Open Forum to Identify Issues for Class Study

One purpose of an open forum in the classroom is to uncover the interests and concerns of class members that they are interested in studying further. In an open forum the class should be encouraged to talk about their future plans and the social issues that are of high interest to them. To start an open forum, teachers might distribute a list of several major issues that might be of interest to their particular young citizens. The list may suggest personal, community, societal or global issues. Further, they need to ask young citizens how they feel these issues might relate to their lives both now and in the future and how they would they rank these issues in importance. The ensuing discussion in an open forum would center on their explanations of which specific issues are important to them and why.

In a similar vein, classroom surveys could provide, in written form, background information about members of the class, where they have worked, lived and traveled, their favorite ways to spend their time—television programs, their habits and hobbies, their goals, their experiences (work, travel and extra curricular activities) and their plans and concerns about the future. If you could change one aspect of your life, what would it be? This question can yield insights into the perspectives that young citizens have. Teachers may wish to share their own responses to such surveys with the class.

Seminars

In a thoughtful and important piece of work, Parker and Hess (2001) present a typology related to open classroom organization that is both insightful and useful. Educators who are serious about democratic classrooms should read their article with care since it is one of the few that represent a vigorous effort to identify aspects of discussion based on classroom experience.

Seminars according to Parker and Hess (2001) have as their purpose the development, exposition and explorations of meanings related to the issue of concern. Here, student-citizens are encouraged to make meaning of information, of editorials and of materials they have uncovered in their research around an issue being studied by the entire class. The aim of seminars is to expand understanding of the issue at hand. Seminars have the potential to stimulate serious deliberation of an issue but seminars are not designed to lead to social action—a tendency that should be delayed in a seminar for a later time when the understanding of the issue has been expanded. However, there may be challenging conditions or events that need action now—such as help to hurricane, earthquake or tornado victims or relief from other issues that need immediate attention—such as action to be sure vaccines are available for debilitating and threatening disease. In the classroom, seminars are guided by a panel discussion led by class members who have done research on an issue and subsequently make a presentation to the class. Panel members would respond to each other's presentations followed by a question and answer period that involves the entire class.

Deliberation

Deliberation, as explained by Parker and Hess (2001), constitutes a plan of action that resolves or improves conditions related to a real issue. If successful, class members will reach a decision about what needs to be done to improve conditions surrounding the issue of interest. Some issues that classes will study are too massive to consider complete and permanent resolution by young citizens. However, there may be actions they can be taken to improve selected conditions related to complex issues (a clean water supply in their locality) in a small setting such as their school or community or in a minimal time period. During deliberation, values and their examination should play a dominant role since decisions and the nature of social action cannot be made without them. This process must not require consensus since each student-citizen has the right to his or her decision. Seeking total class agreement is not consistent with democratic education because citizens, especially democratic citizens, are not expected to agree. Instead, they should be encouraged to do the opposite, to disagree, but to do so responsibly by grounding their disagreement in evidence and reason—a condition that is both permissible and desirable in an Issues-Centered Decision Making Curriculum.

Identifying or Defining the Issue

While the teaching process for this curriculum is not linear, an early task for the teacher and the class is to specify and define the issue they wish to pursue. Specific issues selected for classroom study need to be related to the concerns of the class. While some issues may flow out of class members' school experiences (e.g., Why can't a special student lounge be established? or Why can't we have a day off for a class picnic?). Such issues are narrow in scope and are not likely to expand the perspective of young citizens regarding significant domestic, national or global issues. At the same time, these issues even though narrow, can provide important learning opportunities. Student-citizens can generate reasons both for and against any proposal; they can interview student-citizens in other classes, they can identify relevant values, generate alternatives, predict the consequences of those alternatives in order to make and justify decisions. The class might even decide to take action such as presenting a report to the principal, meeting with the principal, reporting to a student council meeting to garner support or presenting their report to at a faculty meeting or the Parent Teachers Association. If the class wanted to take action, it would provide an opportunity for student-citizens to consider alternative political strategies and their consequences, the mindset of their audience and not only would they make strategic decisions but they would implement them. To whom and how to make their presentation would be discussed carefully to increase the chances of bringing about their desired change Teacher support and guidance is very important here. It might be helpful for the teacher to inform the target audience(s) the class wants to influence what the class has done and that the use of political strategies is a learning experience in social change for the class.

While school–based issues of this immediate sort can have educational value, it is important to involve young citizens in issues that apply more broadly and involve significant subject matter of concern to democratic citizens. The student lounge matter can be connected to a community issue such as banning smoking in all public places. The issue requesting a day off for a class picnic could be linked to a broader question of what holidays should be recognized with a day off by the school district or by the state legislature or Congress. Teachers who are just beginning to move in the direction of this curriculum may wish to provide their classes with a set of broad, significant and controversial issues that are either historical, current or future-oriented which student-citizens can discuss and make a thoughtful selection of what they would like to study. Examples of issues in different historic periods follow.

"In the 1970s, should legislatures of the 50 states have approved the Equal Rights Amendment (ERA)? Should this Amendment be activated today?"

An example of another contemporary issue with future consequences is "Given that our national government has the highest deficit it has ever had, should citizens encourage the government to cut federal taxes"?

An example of a future-oriented issue is "Should the United States reverse its stance on the Global Warming Treaty that was not supported in 2001 by the United States in Kyoto, Japan?"

Historic, contemporary and future–oriented issues often overlap. Past and present comparisons and contemporary and future–oriented issues are of special interest. Comparison is a powerful intellectual tool widely used, to make the past relevant to the present and contemporary events useful to a comparison of speculations regarding future-oriented issues that usually trigger creativity. Other interesting comparisons: the League of Nations compared to the United Nations, the Vietnam War and the War in Iraq or the original Scopes Trial compared to the recent New Scopes Trial.

With issues that are broad in scope, teachers may guide the process of identifying the specific issue by presenting alternative views of a particular issue. Two or more contrasting editorials or two or more cartoons that present different viewpoints on a particular issue can serve as starting points to initiate the process of defining an issue. Every set of student-citizens will respond to different stimuli. Poignant selections from television, documentaries or videos can serve the same purpose. The use of contrasting points of view is advocated and illustrated by Massialas, Sprague, & Hurst (1975). Documents, photographs, charts, graphs or teacher-created materials can all serve as interesting springboards in the form of handouts or visuals to initiate the study of any issue. Comparing two points of view, two or more historical events can be very productive. Comparison of the American Revolution and the French and/or Russian Revolution; the culture of our society with the culture of Egypt or any other culture; comparing women's rights in China, Sweden and the United States provides an opportunity to gain more comprehensive understanding than when a single nation, culture or event is studied. Magazine articles, editorials, music (especially the lyrics of protest songs), conflicting quotations, primary documents and newspaper clippings are used as starters. Graphs that highlight the increase or decrease in population in their state, nation or country of interest can be used to highlight controversy. Why are some nations increasing in population while others are not? These springboards can all lead to serious investigation of significant issues.

Even though all class members may view the same materials, they are likely to interpret them differently. After student-citizens identify the issue they prefer to study from these springboards, they should justify why the class should study that particular issue. In this context, teachers should have the class recognize that people define issues in different ways and that their reasons for selecting what they did is likely to reflect their personal biases and values. This condition, of course, is also true of adult citizens, teachers and scholars.

Primary Sources

Primary sources are both interesting and important materials for both teaching and learning. They can bring history or contemporary issues closer to life for young citizens. Primary sources contain clues to history whether they are in the form of photographs, letters, dairies or artifacts that have been kept in families, libraries or museum archives. Many families have them. An old bill of sale, citizenship papers, old photographs of grandparents and great grandparents, old newspapers and old letters can be found quite easily. They offer clues about the lives of people of that time or what is said in a document may provide clues regarding when it was written if it is not dated in addition to analyzing the content of the document. These clues can serve as springboards for student-citizens to interpret and make meaning of a particular period of history. They can serve as springboards to the study of an historic issue. A newspaper from 1945 could trigger the question "Should the U.S. have dropped the atomic bomb on Hiroshima and Nagasaki?" Primary documents can provide evidence for hypotheses that the class wants to test. Teachers can make Primary Sources especially interesting if they share documents from their own families and give their class members a glimpse of their family lives (Peracocco, 2003). Of particular interest to teachers who want to expand their use of these materials is the issue of *Social Education* dated November/December, 2003 in which the dominant theme expressed in a number of articles was Primary Sources and their classroom use. This particular issue is full of useful suggestions for classroom use and also identifies ways to access primary sources on the computer.

Definition of Terms

Defining important terms is the intellectual task that follows identification of the issue. However, the need for clear definitions may occur at any time during the study of an issue. Definitions are essential to reduce ambiguity and increase the chances that all student-citizens share a common framework and a common set of meanings for discussing the issue. An issue such as, "What can be done to reduce poverty in our community?" forces the need for definition regarding what is meant by "reduce" and what is meant by "poverty." The definition of poverty cannot be easily answered by student-citizens themselves. Rather, a more authoritative or expert source should be consulted. Though a dictionary can be helpful, in this case, the term, poverty may be best defined by the United States Census Bureau or its meaning could be enriched in sociological references. A small committee of class members can be charged with the responsibility of identifying existing definitions to be considered by the rest of the class.

Another example regarding definitions can be found in the issue related to the internment of Japanese-Americans in World War II. The specific question might be: Were Japanese-Americans who were required to live in internment camps unfairly treated during World War II? After presenting the class with alternative views regarding the treatment of Japanese–Americans, teachers need to challenge the class to think about the meaning of the term "unfairly" In this situation what does" unfairly" mean? Does it mean that this punishment (people were forced to leave their homes and move to internment camps) was administered for security purposes during World War II, though it was not deserved by people who were United States citizens? Or does it mean that in comparison with other groups of United States citizens whose original nations were at war with the United States in World War II (Germans or Italians), Japanese–Americans were mistreated? The teacher needs to involve the entire class in wrestling with the definition of the term, "unfairly" before the issue is explored fully. The same meanings should be used by all student-citizens involved in researching the issue.

Probing Questions

Earlier, the decision making process was described in Chapter 5. Additionally, several categories of probing questions designed to stimulate the level of intellectual exchange are presented in Chapter 3. Definitional

questions, evidential questions, policy questions, value questions and speculative questions are intended to cause student-citizens to heighten their
level of thinking above recall and memory. They must have the opportunity to apply these kinds of questions to the issue they are studying even
though there may be no single right answer However, depending on the
strength of the justification (evidence and reason) some answers will be
stronger than others.

To illustrate, if a class is studying censorship of school and library materials, the following questions might be pursued:

- What does censorship mean? (A definitional question)
- What proof do we have that censorship exists in our society? (An evidential question)
- Should citizen interest groups be allowed to determine that libraries
  remove certain books? Why? (A policy question)
- Which is more important: intellectual freedom for all citizens or preserving the dignity of certain groups of people? Why? (A value question) Example: Should the children's book, Little Black Sambo be
  taken off library shelves because it depicts African Americans as cari-
  catures? (These questions are both value and policy question)
- What might have happened if the First Amendment to the U.S. Constitution that provides for freedom of speech and freedom of religion, had not been included in the Bill of Rights? (A speculative
  question)
- During the Iraq War, libraries and librarians were required by the
  United States government to report the names of people who
  checked out certain books that might be of interest to terrorists? Is
  this request a valid one? Should librarians comply with this request?
  (A value question)

All of these questions have dynamic, vigorous potential. Small groups
may select from the above and class members may add their own. The
answers to these questions have consequences for other people, and they
influence the credibility and quality of this democracy. None can be easily
answered. However, all require careful and serious thought and the
answers to each of them have a tentative quality. Furthermore, since these
are real question faced by citizens everywhere, the class may wish to present
a report of their findings to the local newspapers, to the administration of
the local public library, to the school board or to their legislators, congressional representatives and senators. Such presentations can be made orally
to these target populations accompanied by a distribution of their report.
The class will learn a great deal about how officials respond to input from
the public. Even, if the worst happens and they are ignored, they can think
about altering their strategy and trying again.

In spite of the desirability of probing questions, research indicates that most of the questions teachers ask are ones that ask student-citizens to recall facts and many other questions are procedural (e.g., "Take out your math books" or "Follow along in your books while the first section in Chapter 2 is read"). Needless to say, these kinds of questions do not create an intellectual atmosphere. Probing questions must become the stock-in-trade of teachers who prepare young citizens. Teachers must keep the frequency of recall and procedural questions at a minimum in democratic classrooms. Asking probing questions permeates aspects of the intellectual process that characterizes this curriculum and needs to become a part of every teacher's repertoire. Without the persistent use of probing questions which are fundamental to solid decision making, the intellectual development of young citizens is ignored and the quality of the next generation of democratic citizens is not developed.

Identifying Values

Student-citizens and teachers need to decide what values will serve as criteria for the decisions made by student-citizens in the case of the issue being studied? In the case of whether or not the old library should be saved, should the decision be made on the basis of cost (adding to the amount of money for people who pay taxes) or should it be made on the basis of creating more equitable conditions that would make the library more accessible by the broader community (a better location and a new facility)? Furthermore, should it be made on the basis of what best preserves our freedoms? Which values are most important? Why?

The possibilities will vary with every issue. If the issue is focused on the conditions that create pollution, salient values may be related to the costs of additional materials and labor for both industries and taxpayers as well as concern for protecting the health of citizens and the preservation of the quality of life in the community. If the issue is whether the old library is preserved, this issue can be compared to the pollution issue, do the values that need attention change or are there different priorities when addressing different issues? In other words, as the context changes, is the ranking of values altered? Prior to considering alternatives and consequences, student-citizens need to identify applicable values that they would like to enhance when making their decisions. However, educators must recognize that these values may change as the issue receives further examination. Furthermore, all student-citizens will not agree on all the values that should guide the decisions that are made. This divergence of ideas should be the basis for classroom dialogue and there is no need to reach agreement but, all class members should understand as fully possible the different reasons that resulted in the identification of different values and different decisions about the library's future compared with the issue on pollution.

Identifying Alternatives and Predicting Consequences

Knowledge plays a significant role in identifying alternatives and generating consequences. Student-citizens must engage in an intensive search for reason and evidence that will provide them with ideas about alternatives and consequences. They must examine their findings in terms of the evidence and the reasons that support them. At this stage, it is often useful to organize the class in small groups rather than engage in total class discussion. More young citizens are likely to participate in smaller group settings where shyer students will not feel as threatened. Organizing the class in small groups is likely to broaden the participation to a greater number of student-citizens. In order to generate alternatives and consequences, class members will have to gather information from a large quantity and a variety of sources that present different points of view. While the teacher may provide a few contrasting or competing sources, student-citizens will need to gather additional information. Conventional library sources will, of course, be helpful but, experts can be interviewed who might be able to make presentations to the entire class where the class as a whole has a chance to ask their questions. They can browse the Internet, suggest an appropriate video/DVD or field trip. After collecting data that leads to an identification of alternatives and consequences, these results are then shared so that the broadest range of possibilities can be examined by each group. At this point, the teacher's responsibility is to look over the alternatives to make certain that the alternatives are not skewed in one direction. There needs to be at least one alternative that is likely and desirable, one that is not likely or desirable and at least one that has some advantages and some disadvantages and may require compromise. The teacher needs to insure that a full range of alternative view is considered. If the alternatives are one-sided, a prepared teacher should present competing ideas that are not included, regarding the issue under study, pointing out to the class that their alternatives emphasized one side and needed to be balanced in order for a solid decision (one that recognized several sides of the issue) to be made.

Alternatives that provide options for decision making, play a role similar to hypotheses in a scientific or scholarly investigation. The implications of an alternative and the consequences to which it leads must be supported with as much evidence and /or reason as possible. The following statement is an illustration: "If the old library is torn down, the residential neighborhood surrounding it will deteriorate." This prediction regarding deterioration of a residential neighborhood requires evidence to be useful. Otherwise it is just a guess. Evidence is especially critical in the justification of selected alternatives as well as their consequences and student-citizens should be encouraged to do the deepest of searches in order to find strong evidence, evaluate it and use it. In this case, a small group of students could talk to an expert, such as a City Planner who might be able to share expertise as well as sources they could examine. Such questions as the following can guide the evaluation of evidence:

- Where did you get your information? From an expert, a scholar, a person who is experienced with the issue, from books or magazines, the teacher or the Internet?
- Is the source credible? Why do your think so?
- Are there contradictory sources? Are they credible? Why?
- Are there other sources that agree with the source you used? Are they credible? Why? Are there competing sources? Which case is the strongest? Why? How important is this issue and how many opinions do you need to provide strong support for your conclusion, decision or recommendation? Are there more pressing issues for the community?
- Is the author biased? How? Can you provide examples? Is the author so biased that the information presented may not be believable?
- How did your source reach this conclusion? Are you satisfied with the views expressed in the source? Why?

From time to time, teachers may find it useful to play devil's advocate, albeit in a supportive and constructive way, to see if the evidence presented can withstand the challenge of reasoning or counter-evidence. Moreover, throughout the process of identifying alternatives and consequences for a given issue, teachers must caution their classes not to reach their decisions too early. Like adult citizens, young citizens must learn that rushing to judgment can lead to the wrong decision! Rather, they need to analyze all the possibilities with as open a mind as possible.

Examining consequences also involves establishing a logical relationship with the values one hopes to realize as well as the available alternatives and consequences. Student-citizens must examine consequences carefully to see if they are likely lead to their preferred values. For example, if the neighborhood around the old library deteriorates and becomes less attractive or more susceptible to crime, these conditions will erode the quality of life for residents and small businesses in the area. The chances of neighborhood deterioration actually happening requires reasons and/or evidence which might include an identification of what has happened to neighborhoods with other projects in their own or in other communities before conclusions can be reached about the neighborhood's likely demise or before any justifiable decisions can be made. Both alternatives and consequences should represent realistic alternatives and consequences and even unlikely ones if someone has suggested them as well as ones that fall in between the extremes or on a continuum, alternatives and consequences would appear as presented in Table 8.1.

**Table 8.1.   The Minimum Range of Alternatives
and Consequences for Making Decisions**

1. Refurbish the old library (Likely/Desirable)

2. Refurbish but encourage renewal of the area around the library. (In-between)

3. Build a new library (Unlikely/Undesirable)

The above alternatives represent one set of possibilities. They are a bare minimum that the teacher may have in mind in case the class does not identify a full range of alternatives that represent likely points of view. Similarly, a full range of consequences should be identified.

As student-citizens assess the alternatives and consequences, they should be engaged in research wherever they may find it. The teacher must be prepared to fill out the full range of alternatives and consequences if student-citizens do not think of a full range of options.

Reaching and Justifying a Decision

After teachers and student-citizens carefully assess an issue they identify relevant values, alternatives and consequences, reaching a logical and justifiable decision can become even more difficult. The need for more knowledge as well as the need to clarify the values, alternatives and their consequences is virtually identical to the perplexities that citizens face. At this point, student-citizens need to rank order their alternatives and consequences and justify their decisions by identifying the strongest possible reasons and the best evidence available to support them. In addition, they need to provide reasons and evidence for rejecting the remaining alternatives. They also need to establish a reasonable relationship between the values they prefer and the final decision. The dialogue that follows will be as vigorous and challenging as the discussion leader, usually the teacher. It should facilitate the presentation of decisions made by various groups as well as their justification to their classmates. The teacher and classmates should feel free to probe and challenge each presentation. It is perfectly acceptable and perhaps even more productive if small groups of student-citizens work together rather than a single individual working alone. The teacher can ask if the decisions of student-citizens link to values, particularly ones that represent the common good. However, there should be no emphasis on creating consensus on a single decision. Student-citizens have the right to reach their own conclusions and make their own decisions as well as challenge each other's arguments. If the decisions are made in groups, there may be dissenting views. Neither classroom consensus nor compliance with the teacher's views is a necessary or desirable outcome but, class member decisions (recommendations) should be supported by evidence and/or reason.

While the above discussion of teaching is pertinent to the proposed curriculum, Appendix I provides examples of gradual implementation of this curriculum by a classroom teacher. It is hoped that this guide gives all social studies educators a picture of strategies that they can use on a gradual basis without trying to implement all aspects of the curriculum at one time.

Resources

Teaching and learning about historic, contemporary or future-oriented conditions and controversy demands a broad, thoughtfully selected set of resources. These resources supply the knowledge base that contributes to deep understanding of difficult social conditions and controversial issues, provide for higher level thinking (analysis, synthesis and evaluation) and making justifiable decisions (recommendations) about public issues. Newspapers, popular and scholarly journals, books and the Internet are very useful and provide needed information in one form or another: Data and well-reasoned opinions that are thoughtfully presented are fundamental to casting light and providing insights and evidence that help the teacher and the student-citizen draw conclusions and make decisions about the issue being studied. Although it would be wonderful if all school libraries were fully equipped and computers were both available and accessible to each student, it is possible to teach this curriculum with a packet of reading materials that teachers compile around the issue that was chosen for study. For that matter, until computers entered our lives, that is what teachers did. A few informative articles from popular or scholarly journals, a few pieces that carry diverse opinion that suggest recommendations and/or strategies to solve and address these issues are also necessary, along with pertinent videos, artifacts and a directory of web sites.

Newspapers, Popular News Magazines and Scholarly Journals.   At the middle and high school levels, the school library should subscribe to at least two national newspapers such as *The New York Times, The Wall Street Journal, USA Today, The Los Angeles Times, The Atlanta Constitution* and the like). Popular news magazines such as *Newsweek* and *Time* should be available. At the high school level a few journals such as the *Foreign Affairs Quarterly, American Prospect, The Economist* (an excellent British publication that presents alternative views on issues), *The American Monthly* published by the Hudson Institute in Indianapolis and, the *Atlantic Monthly* are desirable as well. A journal of particular interest is *World Press Review*, published by the Stanley Foundation, which presents views from other nations as they apply to significant issues and often reveal the views of other nations toward the United States. Understanding of multiple perspectives is enhanced by this journal and there is no other like it. In selecting publications every effort should be made to represent contrasting points of view so that young citizens have access to a variety of opinions. Making a balance of opinions available whether through editorials, publications or websites is both professionally sound and useful to young citizens pursuing knowledge of significant social conditions and controversial issues.

The resources described below will provide educators at all levels with materials that support this Issues-Centered Decision Making Curriculum. All of them were affirmed by educators with recent or current classroom experience. It is not intended to be exhaustive of all available and useful materials. However, especially for teachers who are just beginning to implement this curriculum for preparing stronger democratic citizens, these materials provide structure and procedures that will help them in their initial efforts. At the same time, for more experienced teachers, these source and materials can be very useful as well.

The American Forum.   *The American Forum* has been the foremost organization supporting international and global studies. It has held conferences for educators and developed publications (some of which are free to download) that are very useful for educators, classrooms and libraries. Some examples are:

> *An Attainable Global Perspective* by R. Hanvey (for all global educators)
> *The United Nations: Come Along with Me* by Nane Annan (Elementary)
> *The United Nations at 50: A Teaching and Learning Guide* (Two Versions: one for elementary level and the other for secondary)
> *Who are the Turks?* A CD-ROM manual for Teachers
> *Who are the Turks?: A Manual for Teachers* by Justin and Carolyn McCarthy (Secondary)
> *The Democratic Processes: Promises and Challenges* by L. Arkin and D. Bragaw (Secondary)
> *Families of the World* (Multicultural/Middle and Secondary levels)
> *Multicultural Education: A Global Approach* by Donald Bragaw and Scott Thompson (Secondary).

All of these and more are materials developed by the American Forum and are of high quality. Educators at all levels will find them useful for their professional development and for their student-citizens at different gradel levels. They are available from:

American Forum for Global Education
120 Wall Street, Suite 2600
New York, N. Y. 10005
Tel.: (213) 624-1300
E-mail:info@globaled.org
Website: www:globaled.org

Choices.   *Choices* is a program that focuses on both historic and contemporary/future-oriented issues. The units are carefully developed and provide both solid background information and alternative solutions (*Choices*) that include the rationale for each choice Their materials include such titles as:

> *The Cuban Missile Crisis: Considering its Place in Cold War History*
> *Freedom in our Lifetime: South Africa's Struggle*
> *U.S. Immigration Policy in an Unsettled World*
> *Global Environmental Problems: Implications for U.S. Policy*
> *Confronting Genocide: Never Again?*
> *A Forgotten History: The Slave Trade and Slavery in New England*
> *Shifting Sands: Balancing U.S. Interests in the Middle East*

Materials for both students and teacher resource books are available. These materials have a global orientation and are rich in detail. This program is based at:

Watson Institute for International Studies
Brown University
Box 1948
Providence, Rhode Island 02912
Website: www.CHOICES.edu

Using materials created by CHOICES is an excellent way for teachers to start to work with an Issues-Centered Decision Making Curriculum. These materials provide a model that teachers can use when developing new units on other issues. *Choices* supports both an Issues-Centered Curriculum with a global orientation and gives attention to pluralism and diversity.

Constitutional Rights Foundation (CRF).   The materials developed by this organization can be useful in Grades 3–12. At the elementary level they provide material titled People v. A. Wolf, based on the story of The Three Little Pigs that provides the basis for a Mini Mock Trial. At the middle school level, they have a series of mock trials and materials that emphasize the principles in the Constitution and the Bill of Rights. The secondary level includes both History and Government/Civics materials that include service learning suggestions, *Active Citizenship Today*. Their materials consistently emphasize higher level thinking including decision making. Issues such as criminal justice, the media and violence provide the themes of several publications.

Constitutional Rights Foundation
601 South Kingsley Drive
Los Angeles, Ca 90005
Tel.: (213) 487 5590
Website: www.crf.usa.org

National Council for the Social Studies (NCSS).   *National Council for the Social Studies* publishes the journal, *Social Education,* which all citizenship educators should be able to access. It serves the citizenship education purpose well. Recently, specific issues have focused on Primary Sources, the Environment, Technology and other public issues. In addition, NCSS has an extensive publications program that includes materials for elementary, middle school and secondary levels. For the Middle School Level they have publications titled, *Middle Level Learning* and for the Elementary Level, *Social Studies and the Young Learner.*

The following publications are of special use for this curriculum:

Social Studies and the World for all grades
A Link to the Past for all grades
Teaching Social Studies to ESL Students
Linking Literature with Life for all ages—an identification of literature that supports social studies goals.
Children's Literature in Social Studies. Hundreds of annotated and useful books are presented for all levels
Arts and Humanities for Social Studies for all levels with tested lesson plans
Homespun: Teaching Local History: Grades 6–12 with tested lesson plans
American History on the Screen: A Teacher's Resource Book on Film and Radio
Service Learning and t he Middle School Curriculum but useful for the secondary level but useful at the secondary as well.

Of particular interest is an excellent publication that can be used to guide teachers as they work with this curriculum is:

Evans, R. W. and Saxe, D.W. (1996). *Handbook on teaching social issues.* Washington, DC: National Council for the Social Studies. Bulletin 93. 403 pp.

This reference is especially suited to professional development efforts.

Materials identified above are available through:

NCSS Publications
P.O. Box 2067
Waldorf, Maryland 20602-2067
Fax: (301) 843-0159
Telephone: (800) 683-0812
Website: www.ncss.org

National Issues Forum (NAL).   *National Issues Forum* is a non-partisan forum for the thoughtful discussion of public issues. These forums can be organized by local organizations including middle and secondary schools around such issues as environment, civil rights, children, health, social security and others. Teacher guides are available. NAL has a strong interest in preparing teachers to be non-partisan moderators at the secondary level. The Forum can be contacted at:

National Issues Forum
100 Commons Road
Dayton, OH 45459-2777
Tel: (800) 433-7834
Website: www.nifi.org

Social Science Education Consortium (SSEC). *Social Science Education Consortium* associated with the National Council for the Social Studies, has updated selected pamphlets from the *Public Issues Series* that integrate issues faced by citizens in historical contexts using Primary Sources, cooperative learning, probing questions and comparing the issue in its historical context with similar contemporary issues. Titles are: *The American Revolution, The Cold War, Immigration, The New Deal., The Progressive Era, The Railroad Era, Religious Freedom* and *The Rise of Organized Labor.* These compelling materials can be used at either the middle school or secondary level. They were originally developed at Harvard by Fred Newmann, Donald Oliver and James P. Shaver. Teachers and student-citizens of United States History at either the middle or secondary levels would benefit from using these materials.

National Council for the Social Studies/SSEC Publications
P.O. Box 2067
Waldorf, Maryland 20602-2067
Tel.: (800) 638-0812
Fax: (301) 843-0159
General NCSS Phone: 301 588-1800.

Southern Poverty Law Canter (SPLC). *Southern Poverty Law Canter* is a dynamic organization that emphasizes legal as well as educational efforts to promote civil rights. It publishes a very useful journal, *Teaching Tolerance* that is very helpful to educators concerned with an emphasis on diversity and multicultural education. at all levels. A recent issue focused on such topics as bullying, immigrants, the Holocaust and service learning. School libraries should subscribe.

Southern Poverty Law Center
Editorial Office
400 Washington, Avenue
Montgomery, AL 36104
Tel.: (334) 956-8200
Website: www.teaching tolerance.org

A Reflective Teaching Instrument .   A *Reflective Teaching Instrument* found at the back of this book as Appendix II contains a checklist for teaching procedures that support this kind of curriculum. It was adapted from the work of E. Jadallah (1985). This instrument can be very useful to teachers as they examine their own teaching practices to see what correspondence they find between their teaching practices and the principles of an Issues-Centered Decision Making Curriculum. Many other sources are available. Those identified above would be helpful to teacher(s) starting to implement this curriculum. Teachers as well as young citizens can identify other sources that can support a democratic curriculum.

CONCLUSION

The essence of the teaching process, so strongly supportive of the curriculum advanced here, has best been captured by Alan Griffin (1942):

> The reflective examination of any proposition tends to develop skill in the use of the [reflective] method. The reflective examination of a belief to which one is committed tends to develop a reliance on reflection as a method of securing truth. But if we are headed in the direction of enabling the student at some time to choose his [or her] way of life, to make his [or her] decisions as between democracy and one or another of the available competing authoritarianisms, we need to act positively in terms of that purpose. For this reason, it is necessary to include, in addition to what has been said, three additional principles:
>
> > So far as possible, any belief under examination should be placed in clear opposition to other beliefs in the culture which are or appear to be inconsistent with it.
> >
> > So far as possible, students should be brought to see conflicts among their beliefs as exemplifying familiar controversial issues.
> >
> > So far as possible, subject matter drawn from those areas which are most sharply controversial within our culture should be deliberately preferred over equally evidential but relatively less highly charged subject matter. (pp. 193–194)

The repeated phrase "so far as possible" that Griffin uses in the above passage emphasizes that each procedure is problematic, in that it may incur the opposition of concerned community groups, parents or administrators. We have, in this democracy, reached the point where refusal to make the distinction between democracy and authoritarianism clear is dangerous as is ignoring such debilitating and challenging issues as poverty, racism and the continuing issues this democracy faces regarding equity, freedom and fairness. Even at some risk, we must seize the limited chance we still have to build a world fit for free men and women.

This chapter has identified and described a range of teaching practices and procedures as well as selected resources that can help educators at all levels move forward with a curriculum that enables young citizens to become stronger citizens. All of us want the next generation to receive an education that is stronger than the one we received. We want them to better understand democratic principles and be willing to apply them to social justice issues. Furthermore, their desire to improve the human condition and the resolution of controversial issues is vital to create a stronger democracy and to our worth as teachers. Our professional work must involve particular attention to diversity and pluralism as well as global issues that defy national boundaries and these conditions affect the quality of lives not only in this democracy but elsewhere on the planet. The richest dimension of this curriculum is reading and analyzing pertinent information in order to think through the alternatives and consequences of decisions that need to be justified. Democratic teaching does not come naturally. It is not easy. For most of us, it takes persistence, trial and error, patience and determination. However, over time, the satisfactions are enormous!

CHAPTER 9

ASSESSMENT FOR AN ISSUES-CENTERED DECISION MAKING CURRICULUM

Given today's concern for accountability and the national focus on education, making our case for the meaningful and appropriate use of tests will not be easy. But, we should not sit quietly by while teachers, students, and classrooms become pawns in political battles.

—Susan A. Adler, NCSS President
NCSS President's Message
The Social Studies Professional, 2003

INTRODUCTION

In this chapter, ways to evaluate classroom teaching and learning that are consistent with the goals of the proposed curriculum are identified. Evaluation can tell us a great deal about what our student-citizens have learned, what they have not learned and what they need to know. The perspectives about the relationship between this curriculum and the processes associated with assessment are included. When contrasted with more conventional curriculum goals, this relationship is especially important and challenging because learning that results from the study of historic, contemporary and/or future-oriented issues vary from one individual to the next and they are usually at a broader level than the specific facts drawn from a study where everyone must learn exactly the same specific information.

Democratic Education for Social Studies, pages 243–266
Copyright © 2007 by Information Age Publishing
All rights of reproduction in any form reserved.

Educators need to understand that the major goals of this curriculum include knowledge and higher level thinking abilities that support reasoned and evidence-based decision making. The knowledge component goes beyond knowing about the issue under study. Student-citizens need to consider the implications of the issue for diverse groups including minority groups and women as well as relationship of the issue for the global community. Higher level thinking emphasizes interpretation, analysis, creativity, reasoning, decision making and values. Collectively in this curriculum, these higher level thinking abilities (higher than memorization and obvious interpretation) are referred to as *intellectual processes.*

Additionally, service learning or social action experiences may be involved as the curriculum is implemented. At the outset, assessment of knowledge and understandings as well as intellectual processes will be the main concern for both teachers and student-citizens. In this case, weekly tests on chapters or even periodic tests that focus on textbook knowledge or specific knowledge from a lecture given by the teacher will not be appropriate. What each individual learns about a particular issue will be different. We should not expect their understandings to be identical. Certainly, we know that knowledge and reasoning are inextricably intertwined and separating them is seldom feasible. Therefore, the judgments that are made by either teachers or student-citizens will be subjective. Using assessment in geometry as a contrasting example to this curriculum, it should be clear that the understandings and abilities from this curriculum differ sharply from the kind of assessment required on geometry exams where it is clear that theorems and their applications need to be learned and practiced and these are sufficiently specific to permit objective assessment. In assessing this broader curriculum, assessment will inevitably involve subjectivity with teachers and student-citizens (when they are involved in rating the work of fellow class members. Both teachers and student-citizens must demonstrate as high a level of concern for fairness as possible. Moreover, in settings where it is possible to provide community participation opportunities in the form of service learning or social action, these citizen experiences are unique, not standardized and therefore call for assessment that is more individualized. Different agencies will involve young citizens in different tasks that are not predictable at the outset of their experience. However, the criteria should be set in advance to the extent that is possible. Input from the agency where the internship takes place is useful and desirable. Criteria may need to undergo change while the internship is in process and more is learned about the agency' needs. When this curriculum is in its beginning stages, these community experiences are not likely to be available because the priority focus for teachers will be the formal curriculum. It takes time, effort and political ability to make the case to the school board to approve the service learning and social action dimensions of this curriculum. It may be even more demanding to persuade them that a teacher who would serve as a Seminar Leader and Community Counselor is needed. These experiences take time and effort to arrange and supervise and preferably will be in the hands of a community counselor. However, assessment of these real life experiences is discussed later in the chapter.

The assessment for this curriculum has to be carefully developed. In this curriculum, student-citizens have a major role in deciding what issues are studied, therefore developing evaluation techniques and criteria in advance is not very useful. or desirable. Another concern is that knowledge and higher level thinking, reasoning and decision making cannot be separated from the knowledge gained by student-citizens when they accessed knowledge about the issue under study. We cannot isolate or separate knowledge from thinking and reasoning, nor should we. However, as assessments take place, teachers and student-citizens need to keep in mind that the overarching goal of this curriculum is not the mere acquisition of knowledge. Instead, it involves the application and analysis of knowledge in service of broad understanding of significant or controversial issues in ways that lead to thoughtful and substantiated decision making.

The following examples should illustrate the point. Let us suppose that a class has studied the treatment of Chinese immigrants during the building of the transcontinental railroad and were guided by the question of whether Chinese laborers were exploited at that time. Which of the following facts would merit inclusion on a conventional test?

- By the year 1860, approximately 35,000 Chinese immigrants had entered the U.S.
- Chinese laborers worked for the Central Pacific Railroad. To cut through the Sierra Nevadas, they had build tunnels through solid granite.
- The railroad builders needed cheap labor to make a profit.

Many additional "facts" could be added to this list. However, from the standpoint of an Issues-Centered Decision Making Curriculum, the answer is that not one of these "facts," nor all three of them taken together, is essential. In this kind of curriculum, the question that needs to be questioned is not whether pre-specified facts can be recalled, but how effectively student-citizens can appraise the worth of facts and relate them to decisions that need to be made regarding the issue at hand. Included here is the extent to which student-citizens recognize the role that values play in selecting facts and conversely, the role that facts play in influencing values. For this kind of assessment true-false or recall questions that assess whether so-called facts have been memorized will not suffice. ⎯⎯⎯⎯⎯

Suppose, on the other hand, the class is asked to respond to the following tasks, which include both subject matter as well as intellectual processes:

How to assess/ Need to be clear about expectations

- Some people argue that Chinese immigrants were exploited by railroad builders in ways not befitting a democracy. Do you agree? Draw upon our study of this issue and provide relevant evidence and reasoning to support your position.
- Now that you have defended your position state the opposing position and summon all the relevant evidence you can to support it.

Still another strong example of assessment is the work of Dr. Mark Previte,[1] who gave the following take home exam to his class for a final examination. It included two choices: Options A and B.

Presenting the Problem

It is a warm sunlit morning as you drive to work at the White House and reflect on your accomplishments as an advisor to the President during the past two years. Since this President has been in office, he has had nothing but praise in describing your hard work, initiative and creative thinking in solving the issues that have come to pass during the third year of his administration. As you enter you are asked to report to the Oval Office as soon as possible.

Option A

You enter the Oval Office and you find the President and one other presidential aide being briefed. The President appears to be quite concerned about something. The presidential election is only seven months away. The new president will be requiring an up-to-date analysis on problems that he/she will confront in the next four years. You have been given the challenging task of composing a position paper outlining the decision making process in relation to this problem in the hope of giving the president the information he/she needs to make an informed decision.

You must remember that the decision you are asking him/her to make will impact the lives of many people in the future not only in the United States but in the global setting as well. Events are happening at an accelerated pace and the President wants the paper completed and on his desk in three weeks.

Option B

The President has asked you to go back into history and find a decision that was made by a previous president that he/she could use today to help solve an issue that he faces presently. The past decision can be domestic (within the boundaries of the U.S. or international). Regardless of which questions you choose to answer your paper must contain the following information:

1. State and explain the primary issue that must be solved. Complete this step in paragraph form. (6–8 sentences). You should also include the goals that the President would want to achieve.

2. Insert a glossary of the important terms and phrases used in this paper in order to minimize any misunderstandings.

3. Identify and explain five secondary problems/issues that you can see in this situation. Write a paragraph (minimum 60 words) for every secondary problem that you encounter.

4. List and explain the values of at least ten groups/individuals involved in the situation that would be important for the President to know. Which individuals/groups will be influenced by this decision? What are their values, interests, vantage points in this situation?

5. Identify a minimum of six possible alternatives or solutions and their positive and negative consequences. You must use you imagination and create as many choices as possible. The more choices, the better. The following two questions are relevant to predicting consequences: a) What effects will follow from each alternative and what effect will each have on all the groups and individuals involved? and b) Will the alternative support or oppose the possibility of achieving your goals? Make sure that you explain the consequences from the following points of view: geographic, economic, historical, and legal.

6. Select the best alternative available. Be able to defend your decision with the best possible reasons, factual information, and evidence available. Rank the alternatives in their order of importance and write a minimum one page response.

7. A bibliography (10 sources minimum) will be compiled so as to determine the accuracy and reliability of your information. At least five articles should come from historical sources such as American Heritage, The History Channel, The History Net, or any other historical magazines or web sites. *Be sure all sources are credible.*

8. An appendix should be attached at the end of your paper. It should contain any maps, charts tables, documents, photographs, and/or diagrams relative to your position paper.

Let's consider at this point, the criteria that might be used by the teacher to grade the answers to these questions: The following criteria would represent the goals of this curriculum in terms of knowledge, including knowledge of significant issues, of diversity and of the issues facing the global community.

Criteria #1

Is the knowledge presented sufficiently comprehensive to serve as a strong base for making decisions?
Does it address issues facing diverse peoples?
Does it identify issues in the global setting? Which ones? Why?

Recall that earlier in this book, emphasis was placed on the strong role of subjectivity that applies to assessment as well. This is the place where teachers must ask themselves "Am I being fair in assessing the knowledge reported in each of these papers?" Does it address diversity or issues facing people who represent less powerful groups or issues facing the Planet that need to be solved or minimized, collectively? This exam is not a small task. Since these questions served as a take home exam, student-citizens had access to the school library and to computers for a three week period. If the knowledge reported is not sufficient, the teacher should make that kind of comment and reduce the grade in accordance with whatever grading system she/he is using.

These examples involve the interrelationship between knowledge, intellectual processes (higher level thinking), values and decision making) which are integral dimensions of addressing complex and/or controversial issues in a democracy. It is reasonable to expect that different student-citizens will use different facts to support their respective positions and while their facts may not necessarily be accurate, several of them may submit strong responses without relying on the same facts. To call for a single set of facts is to ignore conditions faced by even our most informed citizens who neither have all the facts at their command nor do they use the same facts as other people to arrive at decisions. To require knowledge of the same set of facts from the entire class is to contradict the way even the most informed citizens function. More importantly, requiring such uniformity, achieved through memorization and rote learning, denies the intellectual rigor entailed by this curriculum.

If such a curriculum is implemented appropriately, young people will play a significant role in shaping the nature of classroom content and discourse. Certainly, teachers will influence the general parameters of what is studied. Teachers may specify the topics to be studied in a general way (Westward Expansion, Checks and Balances, the Great Depression and so forth) and may also identify the intellectual processes that will be emphasized; but the specific way the content is structured, the questions that will be explored and the manner in which these questions will be investigated should be negotiated in classroom discussions where student-citizens are active participants in the deliberations. Therefore, while assessment procedures must be guided by the overall goals of the curriculum, at the same time assessment cannot be determined solely by the teacher in advance of instruction. The questions raised by class members and the nature of classroom dialogue must be represented as well. Consequently the strategies used to assess learning outcomes need to reflect the over-arching goals of the curriculum as well as the classroom events that transpired while the unit was studied.

In effect, both teachers and young citizens need to be reminded of the goals that guide this curriculum. Stated simply, the goal of such a curriculum is to foster thoughtful, informed, and active citizens who can make decisions in a democratic context that recognizes the tension between self-interest and the common good. This goal includes attention to pluralism as well as to problematic issues in the global setting.

This curriculum also embraces the tension that exists between two distinct, and sometimes competing, educational goals. One of these goals has as its aim the fulfillment of the individual and the development of personal autonomy and independence to the greatest extent possible. The other goal is cast in terms of contributing to a democratic society and participating as a knowledgeable and thoughtful decision maker. The proposed curriculum speaks to both of these goals. The discussion of socialization and countersocialization presented in Chapter 3 explored this matter more fully. In its emphasis on the development of intellectual abilities, this curriculum seeks to expand the power of all individuals to think for themselves, to form their own values, to make their own decisions, to have the ability to defend them and to act on their own convictions.

Simultaneously, it strives to strengthen civic responsibility, a commitment to the social good, and democratic values. This tension between empowering the individual and strengthening societal commitments is openly and explicitly recognized in this curriculum. Consequently, the process of determining assessment strategies also reflects this tension. On the one hand, we want to find out if young people can play an active meaningful role in making effective decisions regarding the issues they choose to study. On the other hand, can they demonstrate certain intellectual and political abilities needed by democratic citizens? Any assessment for the proposed curriculum will need to respond to both of these goals.

IMPLICATIONS FOR ASSESSMENT

The complexity and scope of the goals of the proposed curriculum, the involvement of young people in the process of learning and the presence of the tension between individual fulfillment and the social good have implications for the process of assessing student learning. Three of these implications follow.

1. Beyond Testing For Memory

This Issues-Centered Decision Making Curriculum combines the ideas related to social issues (which serves as its subject matter) with an intellectual and values dimension to develop higher level thinking and decision making abilities (which are all intellectual processes). Far too often, educators have relied exclusively on paper and pencil tests that focus on a limited context and factual information to assess student learning. These conventional assessment strategies typically require test taking that emphasize the memorization of dates, events and people. Questions such as the following are commonplace on class tests given to students-citizens:

- Which side fired the first shot in the Civil War?
- What happened at the Battle of Saratoga?
- What was the year of the Stock Market Crash?

These questions represent trivial learning of little significance to the lives of citizens. There is little reason to remember the answers to the above questions unless they provide help in understanding an issue of the past, present or future. Such limited knowledge does little to empower citizens to address complex and controversial public issues. Nor does it help the individual become a better citizen. Furthermore, with the use of the Internet, the answers to such questions are just minutes away. The questions listed above do not tap higher level intellectual abilities. The major point here is that memorization of this kind of information is of little use and that assessment needs to include alternative strategies in order to assess higher level thinking abilities and the understanding of complex or controversial social issues adequately.

2. Issues-Centered Decision Making Curriculum

Assessing knowledge that student-citizens have gathered and applied, the extent of their reasoned respect for democracy and their intellectual and political abilities are all entailed by this curriculum. Assessing progress of student-citizens with respect to these several components is a central responsibility of teachers. However, the assessment procedures used may be explored with members of the class and even influenced by members of the class. In the last analysis, teachers must insure that the components are effectively represented in the assessment strategy.

3. A Collaboration Between Student-Citizens and Teachers

Since this curriculum calls for teacher-student negotiations regarding the selection of content and learning experiences, it would be a contradiction to impose assessment techniques that are externally determined without also permitting class members to participate as fully as possible in the

determination of assessment strategies. As assessment procedures are
negotiated, both student-citizens and teachers will address the tension that
exists in a curriculum that seeks to serve the individual and society, one
that fosters individuality and independence, while at the same time
strengths social cohesiveness and concern for the common good.

Each of these implications challenges conventional assessment practices. Furthermore, these implications call for an alternative orientation to
assessment as well as changes in the roles of both student-citizens and
teachers. Nonetheless, the goals of this curriculum will be negated unless
the process of assessment is as consistent as possible with the democratic
principles that are the foundation of this curriculum. The content and procedures used for any kind of assessment communicate to teachers and
young citizens alike what is valued, what pays off and what one needs to do
to be successful in a particular setting. An assessment process that is externally determined, by either teachers and/or commercial test publishers,
one that emphasizes memorization of factual information, or one that is
designed on an *a priori* basis without the involvement of the class communicates a message that is contradictory to the participatory values embedded
in this curriculum. In effect, the message is that what is important is
remembering those facts that teachers or commercial test publishers deem
desirable, that the teacher is still the sole external authority whose standards are the only ones that count and that the intellectual dialogue that
takes place in the classroom is not significant. These conditions blatantly
contradict the democratic values of this curriculum.

Teacher-student collaboration is just as important in the process of
assessment as it is in the planning and implementing of the curriculum.
However, we also recognize that teacher-student negotiations are subject to
limitations. For example, student-citizens are not free to decide whether
assessment will take place or not. For that matter, neither are teachers.
They are classroom realities that neither can avoid. What is always evident
is that teachers must determine a letter grade for each member of her/his
classes. In addition, neither class members nor teachers can responsibly
suggest spurious or frivolous kinds of assessment. Collaborative discussions
need to be entered into in a serious and responsible manner by both teachers and student-citizens. These limitations do not diminish the value of collaborative assessment. Rather, they help to define the context in which
collective agreements can be reached. By participating in the shaping of
the assessment process, student-citizens are given greater control over what
happens to them and have the opportunity to exercise greater responsibility with respect to their own learning. Conversely, if teachers impose assessment procedures unilaterally, they deny the opportunity for shared
responsibility and foster an authoritarian rather than a democratic relationship with students. Procedures that teachers insist upon make it clear

to young citizens that compliance with authority is still the order of the day. Further, such practices create a climate in which democratic problem-solving becomes as arbitrary and authoritarian as practices that might be found in more rigid political systems.

ASSESSING THE PROGRESS OF STUDENT-CITIZENS

In this case we are concerned with goals related to (1) knowledge and intellectual abilities, (2) commitment to democracy, (3) political participation abilities, and (4) attitudes of young citizens toward public issues and citizen participation.

Knowledge and Intellectual Abilities

In this curriculum student-citizens should be able to differentiate relevant from irrelevant knowledge, demonstrate their ability to place facts in a meaningful context and assess the validity of factual claims. Knowledge must address issues in the following areas: environmental studies, institutional studies, studies in diversity, social issues including problematic developments in the global setting and values. Such knowledge can come from history and the social science disciplines as well as any other field of study that contributes to the understanding of the issue that is under study. This could include such fields as law, medicine, art, music, literature and even the hard sciences. As long as the knowledge is credible, can be validated and casts light on the issue of interest, it can come from virtually anywhere.

Student-citizens should be able to make effective use of reason and evidence to support their decisions about significant and/or controversial issues. If the issue is controversial, student-citizens should be able to explain the various opinions about the decision of their preference and their grounding for it. Like older citizens, they need to be identify and understand multiple perspectives that differ from their own preferences.

The abilities that follow are ones that should be evident in an assessment of what young citizens have learned. The abilities listed below combine both substantive knowledge as well as intellectual processes which include higher level thinking, decision making and values.

1. Being able to size up an issue and identify the central conflict or the main issue including the underlying values that are at stake.
2. Being able to select information that is relevant to the issue and to relate it logically to proposed solutions.

3. Being able to judge the reliability of various sources of information, including both firsthand experience, reasoning and research-based information.

4. Being able to see an issue in its broadest possible context including the value considerations involved. Such questions as the following try to broaden the context of the issue that is being pursued:
   - How would European nations, which we have viewed as allies, view the United States if we continue to ignore efforts such as the Kyoto treaty? What about Japan, Australia and New Zealand?.
   - Most of you are growing up in a country that is seen as an advanced democracy. Some Americans are sure it is the best place in the world to live. Your task is to compare it to democracies in other nations such as Canada, Sweden, Norway and Australia. Can you prove that we are the best? What criteria would you use for comparison purposes?. Especially useful reference is a United Nations Publications, *Human Development 2000* which compares countries on several criteria and *The Economist;* a British Publication titled *Pocket: The World in Figures.* See References.

5. Being able to create a scenario of likely consequences regarding any proposed solution to an issue. This could take the form of a written statement or a photo essay combined with an oral presentation. Whatever the product it should include as many possible consequences that could follow whether they support the decision or not. One result that might occur is an understanding of the risks involved in a given solution along with a thoughtful discussion about whether the risks are worth taking.

6. Being able to make reasoned judgments where the evidence is conflicting or where there is conflict between desired values. Since knowledge cannot be separated from intellectual processes, the goals identified above represent the essence of the proposed curriculum. In classrooms, particular topics or issues will be selected for study. Westward Expansion, the U.S. Congress, or the Cultures of the Middle East might be explored. Or issues such as World Hunger, Environmental Pollution, or the Expansion of Human Rights might be pursued. Once a topic or issue has been determined, the class and their teacher will identify the central questions that they wish to pursue. For purposes of illustration, let us assume that a class studying Westward Expansion has agreed to explore these three questions:

   (a) Were Chinese immigrants, who provided the manual labor for building the Transcontinental Railroad, exploited?

   (b) What could have been done to improve this situation?

(c) Could the tensions between Native Americans and the U.S. Government have been minimized during the last half of the nineteenth century? How might that have been done?

Young people will need to turn to several sources to find evidence about whether exploitation of Chinese immigrants did indeed take place. They will appraise these sources in terms of validity and examine them from several points of view. They will report on their findings in class, discuss them and reach their own decisions about the best answer to the question. Most importantly, they should be able to defend their decisions in a manner that demonstrates their full use of reason and evidence.

ASSESSMENT STRATEGIES

To design appropriate assessment strategies, we face the challenge of representing the dynamic intellectual processes as well as the substantive knowledge that student-citizens have gained in this unit of study. The following assessment strategies are suggested.

Projects

Projects can take the form of (a) a written essay or paper, (b) an oral presentation, (c) a debate, (d) a photographic essay, (e) a slide-tape presentation (f) a dramatization, (g) a documentary, or (h) a plan for social action. Other ideas for student projects can be generated by both student-citizens and teachers. Such projects are a particularly useful means of appraising progress because they involve both knowledge and intellectual skills. Most importantly, these projects should involve students in the exploration of serious questions and their search for answers should involve the critical examination of multiple sources. These are not projects where a student-citizen merely turns to an encyclopedia or some other single source. Rather, the project must demonstrate an active search for truth, harnessing and evaluating evidence from a variety of sources in the presentation of defensible decisions.

Let us suppose that for the purposes of assessment several class members debate the issue, "Resolved that Chinese immigrants were exploited in the building of the Transcontinental Railroad." The use of a debate format permits individuals to demonstrate that they can draw upon relevant knowledge, evaluate their sources and information and defend a position in a way that is supported by reason and evidence. In the context of the debate they will encounter challenges to their position and have an opportunity to demonstrate their capacity to respond to these competing ideas.

Furthermore, the debate format, combined with the criteria for evaluating student performance, can be determined through the combined efforts of teacher and students.

Both the students and the teacher should be involved in appraising student projects. The teacher need not, and should not, be the sole authority in determining the worth of the project. After a project is presented, both the teacher and the students can evaluate the project using criteria such as those in Figure 9.1. In addition to rating the project, they can use the space provided to explain their ratings and make suggestions for improvement. In the interests of the entire class, the evaluation done by s should be completed anonymously. This assessment activity can culminate in a class dialogue in which students are encouraged to examine their strengths and weaknesses. An elected committee from the class might contribute to this process.

While this assessment strategy is more complex than administering a teacher-made test, it holds the potential for contributing much more to the learning process. In other words, it serves to increase awareness of the abilities involved in being a reflective citizen. Furthermore, it involves young people in a peer review process. It honors their individuality, while at the same time expanding their perspectives about the nature of serious thinking. Finally, it removes the teacher from the role of an ultimate authority to whose standards all must comply and gives class members, whose work is being assessed, a broader base of feedback that will necessarily be more

---

Does this project do very well (W), adequately (A), or poorly (P) in representing their understanding of the issues related to Chinese railroad workers?

Does the project:
- Reveal that the student-citizen took a stand with respect to the appropriate treatment of Chinese railroad workers?
- Present in detail the reasons and/or evidence needed to defend the position(s) taken?
- Demonstrate understanding of alternative positions and supporting rationales and/or evidence
- Demonstrate understanding of the consequences and supporting rationales and/or evidence.
- Demonstrate in the discussion on alternatives and consequences what values are involved as well as the possible risks associated with these alternatives.
- Indicate that those responsible for the project are able and willing to consider opposing views.
- Indicate that the developers recognize their own biases.

Figure 9.1.   Criteria: Student Project

comprehensive than that provided by a single source. In effect, the assessment process is another way of learning to be analytical and decision-making. The quality of classroom dialogue represents the grist of teaching and learning in this curriculum. Whether student-citizens contribute ideas, raise thoughtful questions, give reasons and use evidence to support their ideas can be observed in day-to-day classroom discourse. There is no need to wait for the scheduling of a major test. Over time, it is in the context of classroom participation that class members reveal the strength of their intellectual abilities. Classroom dialogue is so salient to the goals of this curriculum that every effort needs to be made to appraise its quality.

Classroom dialogue can be appraised by the teacher, by a selected student-citizen acting as observer, by a teacher colleague, or by a small committee of class members who are elected by the class. Class observation permits student-citizens to become more acutely aware of the factors that contribute to a valuable intellectual dialogue. At periodic intervals, the teacher may interrupt classroom dialogue and involve the class in an appraisal of how well they are performing. Are we supporting our ideas with evidence? Are we listening to each other? Are we on topic or off on a tangent? Such questions as these involve the class in an examination of their ability to participate in intellectual discussions. Another teacher (a colleague invited to visit class) can help the teacher diagnose the strengths and weaknesses of class discussions. In addition, by listening analytically to responses by student-citizens, another teacher can infer the intellectual abilities of the individual class members. Another teacher can provide a fresh perspective that classroom participants might otherwise ignore. Therefore, using all of these evaluators is likely to be more beneficial than using any one of them.

The criteria for evaluating classroom dialogue are similar to those for evaluating a student project. While these criteria need to be agreed to by both the teacher and the class, the following questions should provide a starting point for appraising class discussions:

- What proportion of students participate in class discussions?
- Do those who do not participate appear to be intellectually engaged?
- Do student-citizens listen to each other?
- Do they ask clarifying questions?
- Do they challenge each other's points of view?
- Do they probe for clear definitions and explanations?
- Do they support their ideas with evidence and/or reason?
- Do they appear to be relatively free of teacher domination?
- Does the dialogue remain focused on the major questions?
- Can students relate the question under study to other situations?

In appraising classroom dialogue, we are especially interested in the growth of young people's intellectual ability and the quality of their participation over time. Consequently, appraising classroom dialogue periodically is desirable. A reasonable schedule would provide for such appraisal may be conducted once a month or once every six weeks. A videotape recorder could serve the useful purpose of permitting both teachers and the class to carefully assess a particular classroom discussion. Furthermore, a videotape would allow a closer analysis of each person's participation over time and provide external feedback to the class as well as the teacher about the collective performance of the class.

OPEN-ENDED ESSAY QUESTIONS

Paper and pencil tests, whether commercially developed or teacher-made are likely to represent limited learning outcomes. Such tests most often emphasize factual information or stipulated definitions that do not represent the broader goals of a curriculum. However, some paper and pencil exercises can be useful.

Open-ended essay questions may be used to assess broader goals. Such questions permit divergent responses and can provide evidence about the ability of student-citizens to function at higher intellectual levels. Earlier in this chapter, open-ended essay questions developed and used by Dr. Mark Previte was presented. That essay was a take home exam and therefore it was possible for student-citizens to have access to key sources that they identified earlier—both library and Internet resources. Some would quickly criticize that this kind of exam is too easy. However, the other way to look at it is that citizens have access to these kinds of resources (though not enough of them are actually used). Nonetheless if we graduate stronger and more capable citizens, they may want to be better informed and therefore would make use of these resources. Some examples of open-ended essay questions follow:

- Do you agree with the following statement: Racism and discriminatory attitudes towards people of color was a major factor in the conditions faced by the Chinese immigrants? Explain the reasons for your conclusion.
- Suppose that you were a member of Congress in 1881. A bill has been proposed to ban further Chinese immigration. How would you have voted? Defend your position with reasons and evidence. Identify the values that are guiding your response and explain why those values are important to you.

- "If an effort were made today to ban any particular group of people (let's call them Hupsters) from immigrating to the U.S., would you support it? Defend your answer. What are other responses that might be made? What would be the consequences of each point of view for the people of the United States, for the reputation of the United States and for the Hupsters, the people who would like to immigrate to this country. Please discuss the values that would be involved in each case and explain the importance of those values. (The name of the group is hypothetical so that issues such as race, health, education levels or civic responsibility would not enter your answer). Simply stated the question is: Should we ban the Hupsters from immigrating to the United States? Why?

Each of these questions allows students to reveal their understanding of the issue and to demonstrate their thinking abilities. Obviously, the responses to these questions will take different forms and will challenge the subjectivity of the teacher to evaluate the answers as fairly as possible.

In a manner similar to the procedures suggested for student projects, the teacher along with the class can determine both the pool of questions and the criteria for evaluating the answers. The following are suggested criteria that might help student-citizens think about criteria as the basis for a rating their answers.

1. Does it demonstrate the understanding of knowledge relevant to the issue? Does the answer address diversity? Does it respond to issues of global concern?
2. Does it reflect the individual's position on the issue?
3. Does it present reasons for the position taken?
4. Does it present evidence to support the position taken?
5. Does it reflect awareness of competing sources of evidence?
6. Does it reflect awareness of the values inherent in the positions advocated?

The kinds of test questions suggested here are consistent with the goals of an Issues-Centered Decision Making Curriculum. Further, both the design and evaluation of such questions can be done by both class members and the teacher and can reflect both of their perspectives as well as provide experience with the process of compromise. Even the process of appraisal can involve students. On selected occasions, class members can exchange papers and rate each other's work. Subsequently, a rating by the teacher can take place. Again, student-citizens can benefit from a broader base of input and the teacher need not serve as the sole authority.

Each of these assessment strategies represents both objective and subjective elements. The criteria for appraisal, which are openly and collectively arrived at, make the standards clear to everyone. This condition reflects the objective dimension of assessment. However, the process of applying the criteria and making a judgment is much more subjective. All raters are guided by the same criteria but they will bring different perspectives and different levels of sophistication to the task. Some educators might argue that this process is too subjective to meet the canons of evaluation. However, from the vantage point of this curriculum, the strategies suggested here are comparable to the way many citizen judgments are made. Furthermore, the appraisal of abstract ideas and higher level intellectual abilities does not lend itself to objectivity. While it is possible to construct appropriate multiple-choice tests, it is not feasible or practical for student-citizens and teachers to collectively design such instruments. The tension between objectivity and subjectivity that is inherent in our suggested strategies parallels the manner in which ideas are judged by responsible citizens in any public setting.

A Reasoned Commitment to Democracy

This goal represents a value, both in terms of content and process. Values are inherently difficult to assess. Direct questions that probe student-citizens for their opinions are not likely to be productive since the respondent is likely to know what answers are expected. However, careful observation of the behavior of student-citizens particularly during class discussions offers a more useful way to determine whether student-citizens reveal values that are consistent with democratic principles and whether they hold their values in a reasoned way.

Questions such as the following can be helpful to the observations made by the teacher:

1. Does the student's behavior demonstrate respect for all of his or her fellow students? This behavior may take the form of listening to others, acknowledging competing views or asking clarifying questions of other class members.

2. Do the arguments advanced by the student-citizen demonstrate a respect for democratic values such as treating each individual with dignity even those who disagree, equality of opportunity, minority rights and freedom of expression, religion, and the press?

3. Using reason and evidence, can the student support the values that he or she holds?

4. Does the student seriously consider competing points of view?

Each of these questions calls for careful judgment. The teacher needs to carefully examine evidence derived from what student-citizens do and say prior to drawing conclusions about their values. To a considerable extent, the judgment made will have a subjective quality. While subjectivity can never be entirely removed from human judgment, teachers need to make every effort to make these judgments equitably (fairly) for each member of the class. Importantly, judgments about the values held by a student-citizen have no place in the grade that is assigned by the teacher. To use these judgments about the individual's commitment to democracy or grading purposes would negate an important premise of an Issues-Centered Decision Making Curriculum that encourages young people to reach their own conclusions about value judgments. Rather, the observations suggested above provide feedback to both student-citizens and the teacher about whether class members are demonstrating a reasoned commitment to democratic values. This feedback can become the basis for student interviews conducted by teachers where these observations are examined and discussed on a one-to-one basis.[2]

Political and Social Abilities

Political ability as well as the ability to work in groups represent important dimensions of this curriculum.. In terms of political abilities, some of the citizen action competencies identified by Newmann, Bertoccie, and Landsness (1977) are very helpful.[3] These competencies evaluate the ability of citizens to communicate effectively, interpret data, describe the political-legal decision-making process, justify personal stands on controversial public issues, apply principles of justice and work cooperatively. These abilities substantially overlap with those of our earlier discussion related to assessment of knowledge and intellectual processes. However, the ability to work in groups is also included in this curriculum and they will be discussed subsequently.

Political skills will receive particular attention in the Internship component of the curriculum. Teacher and peer evaluations of written and oral reports, such as those described earlier, continue to represent the basic form of assessment. However, student logs, in which each student-citizen is asked to describe and reflect on community-based experiences, represent another important assessment tool. Here, students are asked to share and interpret their experiences. The log kept by students is a way to make meaning of the internship. At the same time, it is a vehicle for teachers to examine what students report about what they learned and how they interpret what they learn. Teachers can also raise questions in these logs that can give the individual food for thought. Discussions in the Internship Seminar, which would be led by the Community Counselor under ideal conditions, also offer similar opportunities. While assessment has value in finding out what student-citizens think they are learning, feedback and other interpretations of what occurred are helpful but letter grades are not appropriate. They would have little meaning and would not lend themselves to justification. How would a teacher explain why an individual got a B instead of an A? The teacher would not be present in the Internship experience. Using Pass/Fail instead of letter grade appears to be more sensible.

The assessment of group skills is often overlooked, although group settings provide the context for making many public decisions. Indeed, the effectiveness of citizens is related to their ability to function effectively as members of groups. Appraisal of student progress should give attention to this important aspect of citizen behavior.

Guided observations by students, the classroom teacher and an external observer are the most useful approaches for assessing student growth with respect to group skills. The following questions suggest possible points of focus for observing groups as they work in the classroom. However, to the greatest extent possible, the guidelines for such observations need to be developed collaboratively by the class and the teacher:.

- *Extent of Participation:* Who participates? Who does not? Do a majority of students participate in group discussions? Do some dominate while others remain passive? Who dominates? Who remains passive? Who makes thoughtful contribution? Does anyone display thoughtless contributions?
- *Quality of Participation:* Is the exchange of ideas in groups entered into enthusiastically, reluctantly, or not at all? Are the contributions of student-citizens relevant or tangential?
- *Listening:* Do student-citizens listen to each other? Do they seek clarification of ideas presented by other members of the group? Do their comments build on the contributions of others, rather than only showing interest in their own ideas? Do they demonstrate interest in the perspectives taken by others? Do they show a willingness to consider all ideas including unconventional ones?
- *Communication Skills:* Do class members present their ideas clearly? Do they illustrate their ideas with relevant and clarifying examples? Do they give explanations for their ideas? Do they defend the positions they take with evidence and/or reason?
- *Autonomy:* Do student-citizens demonstrate independent thinking? Can they independently appraise ideas in the face of group pressures for agreement? Do they demonstrate a capacity to defend a reasonable position independently of group pressure or criticism? Do group members challenge each other's ideas?

While group abilities can be conceptualized in many ways, the questions presented above serve as a starting point. The information obtained by careful observation can foster growth in group communication if student-citizens are provided with feedback. This kind of assessment provides teachers with a deeper awareness of how their students-citizens are functioning in groups and it is desirable that they provide the class with feedback. On the basis of such knowledge, classroom environments can be strengthened so that they more effectively respond to the goals of a democratic curriculum.

Attitudes Toward Civic Education

Whatever the subject matter of the curriculum may be, educators are usually concerned with the attitudes that their student-citizens develop toward that subject. Teachers of reading hope that their students will not only learn to read, but that they will enjoy reading and develop a habit of reading throughout their lifetimes. Similarly, educators concerned with preparing citizens who can understand, analyze and make decisions about social issues hope that their student-citizens will want to continue to learn more about these matters and that they will apply their intellectual abilities in their personal as well as their public lives. Such attitudes represent an inescapable by-product of authentic learning. But whatever subject is taught, we can be sure that each individual will develop attitudes toward that subject, the topics that they studied and the classroom experiences they had.

In this curriculum, we are particularly interested in whether students express interest in:

- Knowing about social issues? About how issues impinge on minority groups and women? About how the issue under study relates to the global community?
- Participating in social issues discussions?
- Clarifying their ideas about an issue?
- Defending their ideas in a public forum?

Too often, assessment strategies do not include plans for assessing attitudes toward the subject matter. Yet teachers can benefit from knowing more about the kinds of attitudes their class members hold.. Regardless of how well class members are meeting the explicit goals of the curriculum, if their learning does not generate a positive attitude toward being an informed citizen or if they find the teaching uninteresting or tedious, little has been accomplished.

Three approaches to assessment may be useful here. Careful teacher observation of student interactions and behaviors, interviews with student-citizens and student surveys all can provide helpful indicators about student attitudes.

Whether students participate in classroom discussions or projects enthusiastically, half-heartedly or not at all probably provides the strongest clue about the attitudes they hold. Over time, what student-citizens say and do (or for that matter, do not do) provides insights to perceptive teachers about how members of the class feel about their subject. Observation of classes can be strengthened by asking a colleague to serve as an impartial observer of student interaction. This procedure can yield perspectives the classroom teacher may not have considered. Such observations may focus on the following kinds of questions:

- Do students seem to be involved?
- Do they appear interested?
- Do most of them participate in class discussions?
- Do they ask probing questions?
- Do they give detailed explanations?
- Do they initiate ideas or topics for the class to consider?
- Do they share relevant experiences of their own with the class?
- Do students reveal that they have energetically searched for information through newspaper clippings and additional readings?
- Do they ask about additional readings?
- Do they express interest in attending related events in the school or community? Watching relevant television programs?
- Do they discuss social issues with their friends and parents?
- Do they engage in community activities outside the school setting?

These questions are only illustrative. The main purpose of this suggested list of questions is to examine the degree of interest expressed by members of the class.

Interviews with Student-Citizens

One-on-one discussions with the teacher can free students to discuss feelings they may not express in the presence of their peers. They may be more honest and may offer more constructive suggestions in an interview setting. Interviewing students, even though they may feel awkward) also demonstrates that teachers are genuinely interested in their classes as individuals. Such interviews will be more effective if the teachers and student-citizens have developed relationships that are open, intellectually honest, and supportive. Further, if the teacher takes the suggestions given by student-citizens seriously and responds to them in overt ways in the classroom, members of the class will recognize that the interview settings is a meaningful one that deserves to be taken seriously.

Surveys of Student-Citizens are still another way to appraise attitudes toward the subject. Teachers can develop a set of appropriate questions (similar to those identified under Student Observations above) and ask students to respond to them anonymously in writing. Surveys will not reveal as much detail as interviews, nor will it be as possible to assess the intensity of the responses. Nonetheless, a periodic student survey can yield useful information about student perspectives.

Implementing any of these approaches communicates to student-citizens that teachers care about what is being learned and are willing to provide an opportunity for student expression that is all too often ignored. Further, student feedback can directly benefit teachers to the extent that students make useful suggestions for improving the quality of their classrooms and they, in turn, provide feedback to the individuals in their classes.

CONCLUSION

This chapter has treated four components of appraising learning consistent with decision making: (a) knowledge and intellectual goals, (b) student commitment to democracy, (c) group and political skills, and (d) attitudes toward public issues and citizen participation. For assessment to be comprehensive and to provide useful feedback to teachers and students, each of these four components needs to be represented in the assessment of learning with respect to the goals of a problem-solving curriculum.

Furthermore, in addition to the assessment strategies that are described in this chapter, the use of follow-up studies that survey or interview students after they have graduated are strongly recommended. This strategy can provide strong indications about the impact that the curriculum has made on their lives as citizens and provide useful information that identifies the strengths and weaknesses of such a program. Such questions as the following might be asked of graduates:

- Do you keep up with community and national issues?
- Are you active in community affairs?
- Do you subscribe to news magazines?
- Are you registered to vote?
- Did you vote in the last election?
- Have you followed the discussion related to contemporary issues?
- Do you belong to any civic groups?

These questions represent a starting point. We wish to emphasize that follow-up studies should try to establish the extent to which graduates of the program are informed, responsible, and active citizens.

Clearly, the assessment strategies identified in this chapter are not exhaustive. However, they are all consistent with the principles of reflective decision making. First, they represent both the content and the intellectual processes involved in decision making and de-emphasize memorization of specific information. Secondly, they respond to specific classroom activities that students have experienced and are not determined prior to instruction. Thirdly, they are collectively negotiated by the teacher and the class, so that the teacher is not the sole authority.

The assessment strategies suggested in this chapter depart markedly from conventional practice. Nonetheless, these strategies represent our best response to appraising progress made by student-citizens in a curriculum that fosters higher level understandings and intellectual skills. At a time when accessibility to computers can increase the ease of scoring more objective, multiple-choice tests, it may seem arrogant and even old-fashioned to suggest the use of assessment strategies that are more subjective and less amenable to computer efficiency. However, in our view, the goals of the proposed curriculum offer substantial hope for enhancing citizen competence in a democracy. The learning tasks involved are complex, conflict-laden and sometimes abstract. This curriculum, I strongly believe, can produce more knowledgeable, more thoughtful and more committed citizens. It follows that the appraisal of citizen learning cannot be cast in simple, concrete terms. Like the curriculum itself, its assessment is demanding and challenging. Most importantly, the assessment process must mirror curriculum goals. To maintain conventional assessment practices with a curriculum that challenges the reach of student-citizens and teachers is not only to contradict but to negate the potential embedded in democratic education.

NOTES

1. Dr. Mark Previte, who was a department chair and an experienced teacher at Northern Cambria High School, North Cambria, Pennsylvania shared this example of an exam he had used with his class. The reader will notice the parallel to the Issues-Centered Decision Making Curriculum. His exam is open-ended; an unlimited array of answers is possible; knowledge and higher level thinking are integrated it calls for evidence and requires the application of relevant knowledge and values to the decision(s) that are made. This exam involves holistic issues, rather than specific information that can be graded more objectively. Criteria for evaluating these responses are necessary to maximize uniformity of judgment. However, subjectivity cannot be avoided—a condition that characterizes most decisions we make.

Dr. Previte has since joined the faculty of the University of Pittsburgh at Johnstown. I have made a few small changes in my presentation of his exam which is an excellent example of assessing the goals of this curriculum.

2. This curriculum's goals for stronger citizens for a stronger democracy involves educators who are willing to walk a line between the principles of democracy to which they expose their classes and about which they seek understanding but, these very same principles require that they not demand agreement or commitment by young citizens. Such demands contradict and violate freedom of thought and freedom of expression that are essential to democracy. Other curricula that claim their goal is better citizenship do not emphasize this fine line with the possible consequences that educators do not make this distinction. Therefore, although the classroom may create a democratic climate, student-citizens must recognize that this kind of class-room is a choice from other kinds of classroom organization. Importantly, democratic principles require that teachers not use the classroom as their bully pulpit and that democratic educators must not indoctrinate. Further-more, many young citizens will recognize the contradiction and respond in ways that are not authentic, although they may please the teacher.

3. For those who wish to pursue community social action experiences, the publication by Newmann, Bertolucci and Landess (1977) offers guidelines and examples that can be very useful to teachers and department chairs. Despite its date, the presentation is highly relevant.

CHAPTER 10

IMPLEMENTATION AT SCHOOL AND CLASSROOM LEVELS

We have expected a great deal of our schools and our teachers and have often been disappointed. The answer is not to lower our educational expectations, however, but to state them clearly so that the conditions necessary to their attainment become more clear.

—John Goodlad, 1990

INTRODUCTION

The last two chapters of this book are both concerned with implementation. Chapter 10 focuses on (1) a curriculum plan at the school level as well as (2) creating plans by a social studies department or by a single teacher or by several teachers for their classrooms. The suggestions made here are under the control of schools, administrators and teachers. Chapter 11 deals with broader conditions needed to support this curriculum more comprehensively—academic freedom policies, democratic school and classroom climate and teacher education programs that would make implementation of this curriculum stronger if they were in place.

Democratic Education for Social Studies, pages 267–286
Copyright © 2007 by Information Age Publishing
All rights of reproduction in any form reserved.

CONVETIONAL SCHOOL SUBJECTS
AND THE STUDY OF ISSUES

In the original version of this book, Engle and I debated the efficacy of alternative approaches for the implementing an overall plan for this curriculum. We were tempted to reject entirely the conventional memory-lecture-recite curriculum with its heavy dependence on textbooks and encourage schools to start from scratch with selected content tailored to focus on important controversial issues. We rejected this idea for a number of reasons. First, each of the disciplines upon which social studies relies is a field of inquiry separate and different from that of other disciplines. Moreover, since each has its own set of questions to ask and its own way of conceptualizing and looking at data. Disciplines are somewhat resistant to amalgamation. In studying significant social conditions and controversial issues that fall primarily in the area of one discipline, more understanding results from the simple process of comparing findings in one discipline with findings in another field. The interdependency of geographers and historians is a case in point. The frequent clash of views evident by writers of fiction and biography as well as those of historians and economists are others. In working with complex issues it is very important to understand why it is that people, even different scholars, hold different views of events and ideas and how and why these views vary. Secondly, our views were chastened by the experience of the "New Social Studies" which was so promising when examined on paper, but was summarily rejected by teachers despite the great promise those innovative curricula held for transforming social studies from a meandering, thoughtless memory process to one that was engaging and thought-provoking. Teachers rejected those curricula despite the gargantuan resources, both human and monetary, invested in their development. Many teachers found it too drastic a break with their customary behavior. They could not find themselves nor could they find the subjects they were used to teaching in the "New Social Studies." The new programs required them to change what they taught and how they taught it. Importantly, teachers who had always taught in the expository mode were very uncomfortable with the open-ended questioning that the "New Social Studies" required. Furthermore, teachers had not been directly involved in the creation of the new materials and therefore did not feel any ownership in them. Many teachers felt they were set adrift in unfamiliar territory.[1]

This proposed curriculum would encourage teachers at all levels to be more open in questioning that engages higher level thinking as well as responding with interest to the diverse answers that young citizens are likely to suggest. However, these curriculum goals are ones that are achievable in the more conventional framework of the existing social studies curriculum.

For example, the issues to be dealt with identified in the initial three strands of our curriculum, environmental issues, institutional issues and issues in diversity bear some resemblance to the conventional curriculum of geography, United States history, world history and sociology that outlines a number of curriculum strands.(See Chapter 7). These strands provide a context for identifying related issues for the curriculum. By using these regular school subjects somewhat differently than they are taught traditionally, the objectives held out for the first three strands of the proposed curriculum can be realized. Taught differently, we concluded that these regular social studies subjects would lead to a far greater understanding than that ordinarily achieved by rote learning of textbook material. If a class decided to study pollution, young citizens would search out the causes and the effects of various kinds of pollution, the extent of pollution and the procedures that might help to minimize or eliminate it. They may even have thought about what actions had to occur to improve our environment by talking with or sharing their reports with public officials or agencies that were concerned with pollution as well. While studying about institutions, they may have learned how some corporations mistreat not only the environment but their personnel or how some corporations influence the kinds of laws that are passed (or not passed) with the substantial amounts of money they make available to candidates for public office. Some corporations contribute to both political parties to insure the support of each of them regardless who wins the election. In choosing conventional school subjects as the setting for examining problematic human conditions and controversial issues, the idea that the scope and sequence of subjects or topics to be covered is of paramount importance is an erroneous priority. The case for scope and sequence rests on the doubtful assumption that if all the topics deemed important receive attention, however superficially, that teachers have met the goals of the curriculum. Instead of that set of faulty ideas, teachers need to treat a few issues in substantial depth, while highlighting other topics to the degree necessary. If the teacher knows that some topics, events, or changes require a chronological perspective, either the teacher or a group in the class could put one together for examination by the entire class. Looked at in this way, the subject matter to be covered and the order in which it is to be covered is of less importance than is the in-depth treatment of selected social conditions or issues that need the thoughtful focus by strong and knowledgeable democratic citizens. This condition does not eliminate the necessity for making choices regarding issues or controversies selected for study, but at least the pressure to cover everything is off the table and educators are free to pursue deeper understanding of the subject matter that young citizens study.

The subject matter of social studies at each grade level has changed little over the years. Periodic efforts to change the scope and sequence of the curriculum have been little more than tinkering with the details of the traditional or conventional curriculum. Therefore, sidestepping or ignoring the issues related to defining scope and sequence is a stance that educators can justify. Instead, the conventional curriculum with its courses in geography, United States history, world history, government and in the early grades the study of the expanding environments, affords a sufficient framework for the in-depth study of significant social conditions and controversial issues. This curriculum can come alive in the existing curriculum framework found in schools at this time. This approach to implementation means that there is no need to reject the existing curriculum and teachers, departments and administrators can focus their efforts on implementing different teaching and learning procedures in the classroom with student-citizens (Daley, 1991). To this end, a pair of teachers can take some initial steps on a gradual basis. See Appendix I for further suggestions regarding gradual steps toward implementation for one, a few, or a department of teachers in one school. The order of priorities for gradual implementation should be considered and decided by teachers who wish to change the teaching and learning that takes place. Administrators in combination with an elected faculty committee could concurrently develop a plan to make the school's climate democratic. School educators need to consider/decide what would best serve the arrangements that already exist in the school setting. The preceding description of gradual implementation is but one example. There is no linear formula. Especially helpful to teachers is Appendix II, A Reflective Teaching Observation Instrument which is a checklist that gives teachers feedback on their teaching style. This checklist also provides suggestions for teaching practices that are consistent with an Issues-Centered Decision Making Curriculum.

This discussion on implementation intends to support teachers as they change their teaching practices and at the same time create a fresh learning environment for young citizens. This shift by teachers from an expository treatment of whatever subject matter they teach to one that draws attention *to* the issues embedded in the content of a discipline or in public issues that are historic, contemporary or future-oriented. Teachers and their classes will need to identify the issues and controversies, both problems of fact which are referred to here as 'truth claims' and problems of decision making, embedded in the subject matter that they are teaching. To illustrate, if the class is starting a study of the American Revolution, some important issues might be:

- Is revolution, which involves violence, ever justifiable? Why?
- What was the stance of the United Empire Loyalists at the time of the Revolution? Were they justified? Why? If you had lived at that time, how would you have felt about the Loyalists? Why?
- Could this Revolution have been prevented? If not, why? If so, how?

For that matter, scholars of the hard sciences such as physics, chemistry or biology, think of their disciplines not so much as compendia of settled knowledge as repositories of unanswered questions. Scholars see their discipline as not only a body of knowledge, but even more importantly, as a systematic way of thinking about and studying problems. The scholars in these disciplines, see much more importance in finding answers to unresolved cases where as yet unrecognized problems guides their research, than in recording and transmitting the little that is believed to be true. In this vein it is, of course, impossible to think of disciplines as ever being complete or final. Instead, they are always open to new knowledge, new findings and as such, always tentative about any conclusions or solutions that are drawn. It is therefore, an error to think of any discipline as merely knowledge transmitted to others. Geography and history, for example, if looked at in this tentative and unsettled way, are each a cacophony of unanswered or partially answered questions and issues. Recently, even the long standing view that Columbus discovered America that all school children learned for years has been reinterpreted. We have seen heated disputes among historians as to who discovered America, when and why (Zinn, 2002). Alternate views of Presidents John Kennedy, Lyndon Johnson and Bill Clinton have been published recently. Many more examples are available to illustrate the tentativeness that characterize every field of study and this tentativeness should make all of us realize that our conclusions, as well as scholarly conclusions, should never be viewed as certainties that will never be challenged. Even in personal decisions are we never completely sure that we have bought the right car, purchased the right gift or resolved problems between friends as well as possible? If we are honest with ourselves, we know that certainty eludes us and we come to understand that the more important the decision, the more careful we must be. Might it not be better to get young citizens right into the middle of controversies about what these Presidents were really like, than to pass off a few doubtful facts as the truth? It would certainly be more honest! Would not student-citizens, even those in intermediate grades, learn vastly more about the discovery by talking about some aspects of the controversy than by memorizing a few doubtful and questionable facts? There continues to be a very important debate raging over the meaning of the First Amendment to the Constitution of the United States, an issue central to the quality of this democracy. Might it not be more effective as a way of learning about the Bill of Rights to engage student-citizens directly in this debate? It would certainly be more interesting.

It is of course impossible to study all issues in the depth necessary to support serious thought and decision making. Selecting a few of the most significant, most manageable and most interesting issues to young citizens will be necessary. In different communities, different issues may be of compelling interest and seen as especially controversial. The endangered environment in some communities is challenged by developers who provide employment to citizens of the community; unemployment is a pressing issue in others when large business contract their work to other nations in order to pay lower wages; and building new highways to expand the economy that threaten the nature of neighborhoods whose paths they cross are all examples that may be seen as very controversial in communities where they impinge on the quality of human lives. These unresolved issues provide the opportunity to study, discuss and debate them and try to do something about them. In such classrooms that young citizens become stronger intellectually, informed decision makers and the kind of citizens we need for a stronger democracy. Furthermore, in the context of such issues they can confront matters of fairness and equity.

In order to provide context and a sense of progression, subject matter not directly related to controversies may be briefly reviewed without stopping to commit anything to memory. The memorization of vast quantities of factual material without focus on an issue or a question worth answering is a colossal waste of educational time. Facts memorized in this way are almost impossible to remember and are frequently outdated before there is any occasion to use them. In contrast, facts learned in the context of trying to answer an important question or contribute to the resolution of an issue are almost impossible to forget because they have purpose and meaning. A further benefit of such learning is that any issue studied in depth will eventually relate quite naturally to many others, if not all issues since the whole universe is one universe. Study in depth of a few issues is a more effective and interesting way to order the whole universe of facts than is the superficial coverage and memorization of great numbers of facts. It is much more like the task of well informed citizens of a stronger democracy.

Educators at all levels concerned with strengthening the education of democratic citizens must look at the subjects they teach with a fresh perspective. To be effective citizen educators, they must honor the disciplines that underlie their subjects as serving as the important investigative tools that they really are. They must abandon the transmission of a dubious view of history as definitive and unchallenged to our young citizens. The broader perspective associated with an Issues-Centered Decision Making Curriculum is necessary to the preparation of citizens of a democracy who need to be able to think deeply and make up their own minds about the issues facing their community, this society or the planet at large. In advancing this challenge, teachers need to think more like the scholars in their own fields that they selected as their majors in college.

Turning to the remaining strands proposed in this curriculum such as significant social conditions and controversial issues, issues in decision making, internships, electives and a democratic school and classroom environment all require special arrangements, but none really interfere seriously with the existing scope and sequence of the curriculum. Each is of such central importance in the preparation of citizens for a democracy that the special arrangements necessary are well worth the effort if we wish to see young citizens support an ever more vigorous democracy. Attention to the latter five strands of the Framework presented in Chapter 7 will vastly improve the performance of student-citizens. Certainly, such changes are worth a sincere effort on the part of social studies educators at all levels

SUGGESTIONS FOR IMPLEMENTING STRANDS OF THIS ISSUES-CENTERED DECISION MAKING CURRICULUM

1. The In-depth Study of Significant Social Conditions and Controversial Issues

The in-depth study of a major issue by a school would entail setting aside of at least three or four weeks in each school year, during which all young citizens enrolled in social studies classes in a school at all grade levels, in lieu of their regular curriculum, would study in-depth, together with their teachers and to the extent possible, with their parents, one important social issue in the school community. If this special event in the school culminated in a set of recommendations regarding the issue studied for appropriate community agencies to consider and if arrangements for its publicity are made in the local community, student-citizens, teachers and the school district would be seen as accomplishing something worthwhile. Quite apart from the knowledge gained, this approach would give a tremendous boost to the idea that social studies is really about something real and worthwhile after all, that the content is useful and it represents subject matter about which adults, parents, principals and teachers in other subjects as well as social studies are all concerned. The boost to the morale of student-citizens and to teachers in the event of implementation of this approach would be beyond measuring.

2. Citizen Internships

The citizen internship requires that every young citizen pursue a role in the life of the community by actually working on an regular basis in some adult citizenship activity. It would replace no course presently taken in school. Such experiences could take the form of work in a social agency, an organization devoted to a particular cause, a government agency (the mayor's office for example), an active group of citizens concerned about an issue or engaged in a community project. Especially attractive are arrangements for student-citizens who would pursue a citizen action project about which they had made recommendations during a classroom study of an issue (Nader, 1999). Seminars should accompany these projects and activities where young citizens could reflect on and make meaning of their real world experiences. If these experiences were a regular part of their school program, young citizens would be much more likely to continue such activity as adult citizens after high school graduation. This investment by a school district is likely to have the very substantial payoff over time. Student-citizens are not likely to forget the nature of this kind of community experience.

The Seminar that accompanies community experiences is especially important to consider the value of the attempts to alter conditions in the community. Seminars not only present understandings of the subject matter but they call for higher level thinking abilities as well. Furthermore, not all projects will be successful; student-citizens may be disappointed and may need to reach a point where they understand that not all such efforts attain their goals. They need to learn from any mistakes that can be identified and think seriously about what could have been done to improve their results or perhaps, what can till still be done. Such problems as: Were sufficient numbers of people involved? Did the leadership think about possible resistance to the project ahead of time? Was the timing appropriate? What other strategies need consideration? They should leave the seminar with a stronger idea about how change takes place and with some confidence that they gained some understandings and abilities they can apply to the real world.

3. Electives

The electives would be different from the usual electives in two respects. First, the study would emphasize the nature of the discipline rather than its findings; that is, the study would inquire into the kinds of questions that scholars in the discipline ask themselves and it would inquire into the process used by scholars to investigate these questions. The main change over the conventional curriculum that would be needed here is that teachers would know their disciplines History, political science, economics, sociology, psychology sufficiently well to deal with them critically.

Student-citizens would engage directly in practical citizen experiences. The objective would be to learn how to use a discipline as scholars use it in the thoughtful study of a significant issue. This objective would replace the practice of using the tentative findings in a discipline to influence young people toward particular narrow points of view not justified by scholarly findings.

The study of economics, for example, would start by identifying some of the important questions or gray areas that economists are working on and about which they are frequently in disagreement. Young citizens could compare statements of leading economists regarding some event of current economic importance to each other and differences in opinion examined with efforts to explain and understand them. Student-citizens will quickly learn that there are about as many problems in the field of economics as answers and that there are a variety of ways of interpreting economic events depending on what one values most and how one is situated in life in terms of social class and access to power.

4. The Study of the Decision Making Process

The implementation of the proposed strand in Decision Making is a special case with very little precedent in schools and colleges except possibly courses in logic, ethics, linguistics, epistemology and semantics that are very rarely offered in high schools and are only seldom taken by future teachers. This strand is an effort to respond to the problem of knowing what to believe in a complex technological and pluralistic society in a global age. Citizens are overwhelmed with many messages, some of which are cleverly crafted to deceive rather than to inform. Television programming and the Madison Avenue advertising images that accompany it, threaten to destroy more enlightened educational efforts to encourage higher level thinking and decision making. While social studies teachers may correctly think of themselves as being on the front line in the effort to sort out the wheat from the chaff in this respect and to provide opportunities for serious thinking and reasonableness into the behavior of young citizens, the question of what values to hold clearly is a problem that calls for a solution to which the whole school should dedicate itself. The most talented teachers in the school should be enlisted and supported in developing courses and programs that face up to this value-centered issue.

5. Democratic School and Classroom Climate

The provision of a democratic environment in the school is taken for granted if the school is to have any part in developing democratic citizens. It is unlikely that a school run in an authoritarian manner can somehow inexplicably produce thinking, independent, self-directing democratic citizen. Furthermore, for a school to have its greatest impact with respect to developing democratic behavior, such behavior must be favorably exemplified in all aspects of the school: in the way the school is administered, in how young people are involved in the governance of the school and in the professional and participatory way administrators, teachers and staff relate to one another. Most important of all, is the way in which teaching and learning are conducted in all classes of the school. But, the social environment in the school and the classroom needs to be friendly, upbeat, and equitable and all personnel should participate in decision making. Is the intellect of student-citizens and their right to question and to know, highly respected by teachers? Is the content of what student-citizens learn connected to the real world or is it just a game set up so that the teachers and other adults will always win? A school that is genuinely serious about providing a democratic environment might set up a committee composed of democratically selected students, teachers, parents and administrators to study democracy in the life of the school, to prepare reports on democratic practices in the school and to make suggestions for its improvement. Appendix III presents a list of actions that may be taken to democratize a school is provided. It is a serious and provocative piece created by a colleague, Professor Tom Gregory from Indiana University, for work he did with a school in Colorado. It is not as a recipe but is offered with recognition that careful selection might be made from this list that is appropriate for a particular school setting.

IMPLEMENTATION OF THE CURRICULUM
AT THE GRADE AND COURSE LEVEL

The implementation of a curriculum for democratic citizenship at the grade, subject and unit levels is primarily a matter of selecting compelling social conditions and issues that target problematic social conditions and controversies, to be studied appropriately to that grade level and subject area. Subsequently, it is a matter, first, of planning how the knowledge afforded by that subject can be used to illuminate these social conditions or issues and secondly, of devising strategies for teaching and learning for achieving this end.

Usually, subjects taught in school have a curriculum defined by textbooks, which are usually organized so that young citizens remember facts and generalizations in the order that publishers use in explicating a subject. Such learning may bear little relationship to how young people, or adults for that matter, may use information in thinking about important public issues. In studying one issue in depth, it becomes necessary to skip around in the textbooks and to consult a broad range of other sources to get all of the information needed to think about the matter. The textbook may well suggest issues for further study; but, other resources that treat some aspect of the issue in detail will be needed without question. For instance, "rain forests," possibly mentioned in the geography textbook, in connection with the study of Brazil or in connection with the study of climates, might well suggest a broader problem such as 'the preservation of ecological balance on the earth'. In turn, this might lead to a more flexible and searching way to use the textbook as well as a need for additional sources to flesh out the study of the issue. In this case, articles from such sources as *National Geographic, Earth Justice and/or The Scientific American* would be useful.

To continue in this general vein, geography, whether it emphasizes world, regional, or national geography, would be brought to focus on three issues, as follows: (a) How can we make better use of the variations in weather over the earth? (b) How can we better protect the fragile ecosystem of the earth? (c) What can we do to reduce hunger among peoples of the earth? Each of these questions triggers a myriad of questions that the class can pursue as ways of investigating these questions which have the almost inevitable effect of freeing student-citizens from the need to memorize vast quantities of factual material in the unnatural order imposed by textbooks. It makes it possible, instead, to carry on an investigation naturally, as scholars and citizens do when investigating a real problem. It casts the student-citizen in the role of being, as Bruner put it, "the organizer of his [her] own thoughts," a way of thinking which he says "is far more powerful" than is merely memorizing something (Bruner, 1965). To further illustrate, the kinds of questions that are suggested in a study of the issue of how to protect the fragile ecosystem of the earth, the following questions may be helpful:

* What is an ecosystem?
* Why is the ecosystem important to us?
* Where on the earth is the ecosystem most under threat? Why?
* Is it possible to repair a threatened ecosystem? How?
* How are endangered species related to the threat to the ecosystem?
* Where on the earth is there the greatest threat to endangered species? Why is this so?
* Where on the earth are useful things being done to protect the ecosystem?
* Is it inevitable that some elements of the ecosystem will be destroyed while others survive or prosper?
* What should be done, if anything and by whom to restore the ecosystem?
* Who should be responsible for protecting the ecosystem?

Also suggested by such a line of questioning are different ways of investigating the issue. For instance, in the very beginning before we contribute to student burnout by memorizing geographic facts neatly classified into national, regional and world geographies as textbook writers persist in organizing them, a series of open-ended case studies might be initiated. Issues could include some of the following: Protecting rain forests in the Amazon and elsewhere entails the imminent danger to all fish species from ingesting plastic and other forms of waste; the threat of toxic waste to the groundwater supplies of the earth; the rapid depopulation of wild animals on the earth; the growing shortages of space for people to live on the earth; hunger and poverty on the earth; desertification; the world's wet-lands; the effect of pesticides on the ecological chain; the promise and problems of high-tech agriculture and many, many others.

There are literally thousands of well-researched articles in such maga-zines as the *National Geographic, Smithsonian, Harper's,* and the *Atlantic* as well as hundreds of books and scholarly articles to support the develop-ment of such case studies. As an alternative, or possibly a supplement to such case studies, classes could view and discuss documentary films such as "Continents Adrift" (American Educational Films) or videos and DVDs that attend to similar issues. Certainly, the Kyoto Treaty is a controversial matter and there ate strong views that support or reject United States refusal to sign the treaty. The Internet along with Google searches and a list of web sites on the Internet, identified by teachers or found by student-citizens would provide much more. People in the community who work in related areas such as biologists, environmentalists, conservationists, for-estry managers and scholars could share their expertise and perspectives with the class. For these experiences, the class should prepare a set of ques-tions that class visitors should address in their class presentation.

Such a series of studies would immediately immerse student-citizens into the very heart of geographic study. It would give every young citizen the feeling of being an important participant in an important study. It would place resources, including textbooks, in their proper place as materials to be selectively used rather than merely remembered for some later unknown use. It would place geographic study in the only context where geography becomes meaningful, as it serves as the context of the major and significant public issues that face the peoples and nations of the entire earth.

In a somewhat similar vein, social studies classes could focus on the study of United States history at upper grade levels on a series of the insti-tutional issues that have dominated various periods in our history. This kind of study may come as a welcome relief to student-citizens who are fre-quently required to repeat and refresh their memory of the same narration of our history usually three times over in their fifth, eighth and eleventh grade school experience, with little gain in either mastering the facts or understanding them. For example, the Revolutionary War period could be brought to focus on the broad problem of revolution. Such questions as the following could be explored:

- Did conditions in the colonies in the late 1700s really necessitate rev-olution?
- Were there steps the colonists could have taken before engaging in revolution?
- Are there other ways than revolution for bringing about social change in society?

- What are they? What are their strengths and weaknesses?
- Under what conditions, if any, should people disobey the law? Please defend your position?
- Is it equally right or wrong for governments to break the law than for individuals to break the law?

Under this kind of questioning, not only will the Revolution itself be thoroughly understood and possibly reinterpreted, but it raises similar questions that are of great importance in contemporary society. Connecting the past to the present makes the study more relevant to young citizens. Student-citizens will not only be refreshed regarding some historical facts and understandings, but they will be able to use them in thinking about real and important issues of their own day.

In like vein, teachers could focus on the period of discovery and settlement with particular emphasis on the treatment afforded to Native Americans and/or new immigrants to this country. Student-citizens could consider how the government should have responded to these minorities. The study might include successive waves of immigration and the controversy over immigrants) from Mexico or from other nations into the United States, or people who are detained and in some cases, tortured because they may hold information about the disaster of 9/11.

Young citizens could study the Civil War to try to decide whether the anti-slavery movement was primarily an economic or a moral issue. Going further, student-citizens might examine whether compromise could have resolved the slavery issue rather than rather than by war. If so, what would the nature of the compromise be?

The study of the Civil War in this way would bring into play the rich literature (*Uncle Tom's Cabin, Gone with the Wind* (only excerpts because this film consumes approximately four hours) or *Red Badge of Courage*, novels that are outside strictly historical treatments which relate to the Civil War and the anti-slavery movement. Similarly, the period after the Civil War, the "Age of Big Business," could focus on the questions of whether or not the government treated business, labor and labor unions justly or whether the public was treated freely during this period. The Haymarket Square Affair or books by the so-called Muckrakers could be studied as points of departure for an in-depth study of some institutional issues, many not fully resolved to this day, although others have emerged. The abuses of large corporations in the treatment of their employees are serious matters of concern. There are many other examples. Other periods in the history of the United States could be treated in similar ways.

In World history, teachers may identify the major issues of world history that confront the peoples of the world. For instance, it would seem unconscionable, in light of the world situation today, to neglect a comparative in-depth study of the principles of the Islamic and Western worlds and have student-citizens give serious consideration to how these contrasting cultures and religions can live peacefully on this planet.

The serious study of world history might well start right here.[2] Obviously, this kind of investigation is one that requires resources, books, magazine articles and use of the Internet as well as thoughtful interpretations of events by contemporary scholars, journalists and news analysts. These resources will far exceed the presentations possible in any textbook. It would require digging deeply into a very few important questions and leaving aside the rest, at least for the time being. While the textbook will probably be useful and could be consulted from time to time, teachers should encourage young citizens to read more broadly and to gather as much information as possible on the issue or topic to be used in thinking about the issues. Teachers should be ready to provide them with a few articles and web sites that present contrasting points of view to initiate the study.

We now turn to the challenge of the study of history at lower grade levels. At this stage, children are not sufficiently experienced to study major controversial issues of the kind illustrated above. However, if textbooks are used they should be rich in detail, as indeed some United States history textbooks are. The emphasis on remembering a few facts from history should be abandoned in favor of the sheer pleasure of hearing the story, as told by the historian, a biographer or a historical novelist, in all of its vivid detail. Young children will actually remember more and understand better, what they read or hear, if the teacher does not drill in facts, but gives emphasis to a full and detailed story, and uses that story to think about some important, or even just interesting, questions. Educators at all levels should be primed to ask probing questions about what young people read, and use selected literature, a powerful tool for young learners, to be followed by class discussion. Both remembering and understanding will be greatly facilitated if the story is frequently interrupted, to raise questions with a focus, not factual questions, but questions that have no definitive answers.[3] For example, about the period of exploration and settlement, teachers could ask: What do you think about the conditions faced by Native Americans before Columbus landed? What people in the age of exploration and settlement do you think got the best deal? Who, the worst? Why do you think so? Can you think of a better way that settlement of the Americas might have been carried out? Why do you think so?

A second way to introduce the problematic into the teaching of history at the fifth or sixth grade levels is to confront children with alternative versions of well-known factual episodes and then to help them solve the riddle. Examples of such questions include: Who was really the first to explore the North American continent? Would you agree that the industries started in the late 1800s did a great deal to benefit to the United States? What problems did they create? Strong cases are made on all sides of these and many other interesting questions that could be raised. In discussing these questions, even young children will begin to learn to question and not to take everything for granted. These are important attributes of democratic citizenship.

The Study of Selected Controversial Issues

It should be clear by now that a curriculum that focuses on the study of a few important controversial issues is highly preferred. It is also a more fitting curriculum for the preparation of citizens. Implementing such a curriculum involves merely highlighting or omitting entirely a large body of material that is not as essential for citizens to fully understand and address. This book is not the only source that takes this position. After making a comprehensive study of U.S. high schools, T. S. Sizer (1984) concluded tersely, "less is more." Otherwise stated, more about less is not only better, but is absolutely essential if our goal is to enable youngsters to gain substantive knowledge, expand their ability to think and decide in ways that support the challenges faced in this pluralistic democracy in a global age.

Fred M. Newmann (1990) in a study originally reported to the Board of Directors of the National Council for the Social Studies, cites the penchant of social studies educators to race through content as one of the most serious problems that confronts the field. "Racing through content," he says, "is useless. Students forget most of it in a few months." Newmann wisely says, "Students must spend sustained time in the comprehension and analyses of content to develop both knowledge and thinking skills...." The pressure to cover large amounts of material in a survey fashion must be resisted and instead a few topics should be studied in greater depth" (p. 243).

Issue(s) of whatever kind(s) are the logical point on which to focus study in depth. The curriculum presented by Engle and Ochoa in 1988, again by Ochoa-Becker in this publication and to some extent successfully employed by each with their classes, is not alone. A number of such models exist.[4] This proposed curriculum is distinguished in three respects. First, it employs in-depth study for most of, if not, the entire social studies curriculum; not just a portion of it. Second, it involves conventional social studies classes to serve as a primary vehicle for organizing such study. Third, the goal of any in-depth study would be the attempted solution, or at least clarification of an issue: as an issue of fact, an issue of interpretation, an issue of values, an issue of public policy or a combination of these. Higher level intellectual processes receive strong emphasis. Young citizens should not only be challenged to make decisions but to justify them as strongly as possible.

From the very first, the issue(s) and questions under study should be saturated with information. A wide range of sources should be considered; including textbooks, that may be read quickly for an overview, but not memorized. Journalistic accounts, biographies, diaries, web sites on the Internet, Google searches, official documents, primary documents, scholarly interpretations, popular articles and fiction, related to the issue, must be identified and analyzed by student-citizens and their teachers. There is no reason for emphasis on memorization. Serious scholars of events use large quantities of information but they do not waste time memorizing anything. Thoughtful citizens remember what is important because the issue or issues are important to them. As the study of a topic is focused on a particular issue, the search for information should be continued and even intensified. This search should precede, up to and even beyond, the moment that student-citizens make decisions or recommendations. As the issue is more clearly defined (for example, to focus the study of the Revolutionary War period on the issues of revolution), information gathering will become more research-like, honing in on answering the questions that are raised in studying that issue. For instance, was the revolution really necessary? Would we have been worse or better off today if it had never occurred? Was Martin Luther King's violation of the law justified when he was jailed in Birmingham, Alabama? Under what conditions is breaking the law justified? Are the guerrillas who fight against military dictators throughout the world today, like or unlike the patriots of the American Revolution? There is obviously no end to such investigations. The questions begin to suggest the information needed but questions are also generated by the information gathered. This is a program for dealing with quantities of facts, focused on answering real questions rather than on memorizing a few facts that by their very brevity are likely to be misleading, if not trivial.

Identifying the Issue

Student-citizens may be given the following issue: "Under what circumstances is a refusal to obey the law justified?" or "Was the American Revolution justified?" Later, under very skillful questioning, student-citizens should learn to identify issues in the content for themselves. The teacher may ask, for instance, such leading questions as: What do you see as the similarities and differences between the American Revolution, the Civil War and the Civil Rights Movement of the '60s? What do you see that was common to all of them? In what way was the situation in which a Minuteman found himself similar to or different from that of a soldier in the Confederate Army or a Civil Rights protester in the 1960s? Or, at a later stage, student-citizens should be able to respond intelligently to blunt inquiries: "What do you see as the most important issue posed by the American Revolution? What more would you like to know about it?" For instance, a member of the class may ask, "Were all American colonists patriots? Were there those in the colonies who were opposed to the Revolution? Who were they, how many were there and why did they oppose the Revolution? What part did radicals and rabble-rousers have in bringing the Revolution about? The teacher or some young citizen might raise the query: "Was the Revolution more a movement for independence or for democracy?" Approached in this way, an issue which was supposed to have narrowed study to a small field to be studied in-depth has been exploded, so to speak, into a large field which includes almost everything worth talking about. The responsibility then, is to narrow down the scope of the issue to one, or a few questions, that are manageable. It is good, however, to know that these questions are related to many others, possibly all the questions one could usefully raise about the United States.

Probing Questions

As student-citizens search for information, contrasting interpretations and points of view, their efforts call for the use of the probing questions that were explained in Chapter 5. How credible is this information? Are there deficiencies in any of the information I have gathered? Should I still use it? Why? Is there sufficient evidence and/or reason to support my decisions or recommendations? What alternatives have I rejected? Why? What values do I want my decision to support? Why? These are questions any teacher should use in her or his classroom. The regular use of such questions would represent a major step forward regarding the implementation of this curriculum.

Resolving the Issue

In a democracy where competing views should be evident, compromise often becomes a virtual necessity. Sometimes, compromise is impossible and people must agree to disagree. In no case, should the teacher insist that a single answer be agreed upon. To such questions as, "Was the American Revolution justified?" or "Under what circumstances, if any, should a people refuse to obey the law?" there are two or more sides, each with reasons that try to justify the answer given. Majority reports, minority reports and even multiple reports may be in order, even after student-citizens have discussed the controversy at length at every level of its study. Understanding the complexity of the issue is probably a better outcome than forcing agreement in order to have one final position. It is not only better, but necessary for student-citizens to debate alternative positions than to avoid debate and agree simply on one. Such outcomes are far more consistent with democracy and contribute to the richness of the classroom experience with diverse views—an inescapable quality of democratic life. Importantly, the decisions made by class members could take the form of a position paper they present or send to relevant public or private agencies at the community, state, or national levels. Some decisions may target international agencies such as the U.S. State Department or other Cabinet departments, the United Nations, the European Union, the World Bank or the International Monetary Fund among many others or relevant organizations in other nations. This procedure could result in social action for young citizens. Without a doubt such a study could generate considerable enthusiasm as young people try to influence the real world. They should realize they may not succeed and that strategy, timing, and knowing key people is very important. Teachers should encourage them to reconsider what they would do if they tried again.

Continuity and Variation

This Issues-Centered Decision Making Curriculum provides the opportunity for a wide variation, in content, while at the same time ensuring that there will be no serious void in the content covered. Since this curriculum is readily adaptable to the conventional curriculum framework, the disciplines thought to be relevant in the education of citizens will be used, thus insuring continuity in the curriculum. At the same time, the issues serving as the focus of study in any discipline at any time may vary widely, in order to take advantage of currency, relevance, interest and even manageability for teachers, student-citizens and their access to relevant resources. The in-depth study of any issue spreads out to touch other human concerns and quite naturally, will fill in voids in information that might exist. For instance, a meaningful understanding of contemporary institutions and their issues might quite reasonably follow from an in-depth study of the American Revolution or of the Constitutional period. However, such understanding could develop quite as well from the in-depth study of the growth of U.S. industry. In either case, the one would spread to encompass the other.

Teachers, administrators, school systems and teacher education programs might follow quite different implementation paths in accordance with their own unique capabilities and resources to the same approximate end. All of the professionals involved must direct the education of young citizens to have deep insight into how our institutions and their issues developed. This kind of overlapping in the midst of wide variation would bind together the whole curriculum and at the same time reflect the way in which scholars and intelligent citizens think about our history, a process which young citizen would come to emulate.

CONCLUSION

There is no single way to implement a curriculum of this kind. Gradual implementation, perhaps, one teacher, one class or one issue at a time, one aspect of building a democratic climate in the school and classroom, or two or three teachers and their classrooms at a time, may provide teachers and administrators with information about the strengths and weaknesses of what has been changed and a basis for improvement. Administrative support of faculty, at both the school and college levels and young citizens, is vital to the process. Also essential are some dedicated and enthusiastic teachers willing to release some control and willing to persist in providing student-citizens with classrooms where they can express ideas and learn how to defend them. Since many teachers are responsible for four or five classes on a daily basis, focusing on one class initially may be the most manageable approach rather than altering all classes at the same time. Above all, we must begin and we must persist. The quality of individual citizen participation is at stake. So is the strength of our democracy. (Resources and learning materials as well as a strong working relationship with the school librarian is treated in Chapter 8 on Teaching).

NOTES

1. An important result of the "New Social Studies" is that the developers of the materials generated a lot of intellectual excitement. However, classroom teachers who would be the ultimate users of these materials were not involved in the development of these new and different materials. In retrospect, there has been recognition that this lack of teacher involvement was one of the reasons that contributed to the rejection of these materials for classroom use. The new materials embraced different content and a different way of teaching. Workshops were held to prepare teachers to use the new materials. The most successful ones were those where the administration of the school and the teachers who would be using the materials were both in attendance and the administrators would support teachers who were trying to implement the new curricula for the first time. This may be an opportune time to mention that the curriculum presented in this book has been reviewed by teachers who have a high interest in improving the quality of democratic citizens.

2. Comparing Islamic and Western worlds would contribute to a wider understanding that our young citizens would have of the contemporary conflicts in the Middle East. This approach is consistent with "teaching history backwards," an approach that gained some popularity in the '60s.

3. Providing young citizens with learning experiences that result in a skeptical view of what they hear or read, supports the recognition that for any claim to truth their may be alternative descriptions and explanations.

4. The writings of John Dewey, the curricula developed by Fred Newmann, James P. Shaver, Don Oliver, Maurice Hunt, Lawrence Metcalfe, Charlotte Anderson, Lee Anderson, Jack Nelson, Stuart Palonsky, Byron Massialas among others have similar goals and provide similar, though not identical directions, for the preparation of citizens.

CHAPTER 11

CONDITIONS NEEDED
FOR AN ISSUES-CENTERED
DECISION MAKING
CURRICULUM

*A more robust democratic politics, I argue, would render the concerns
of a democratic education not less, but more important. Just as we need a more
democratic politics...so we need a more democratic education to further democratic
politics. If we value either, we must pursue both.*

—Amy Gutmann (1999, p. 18)

INTRODUCTION

The purpose of this chapter is to explore three conditions that would provide wider ranging support for the implementation of this curriculum in a
particular school environment. Readers should continually ask the following question as they read this chapter: Can school boards, administrators,
colleges, faculty at both the school district and college levels, all of whom
are necessary players in designing and implementing this curriculum, actually make the changes needed to implement a curriculum that would
enhance the quality of citizenship? Briefly, the question is whether the public schools and universities in this nation are able to create and sustain citizenship education programs that are democratic in nature. Can these key
actors energetically apply their verbal commitments to initiate and support

Democratic Education for Social Studies, pages 287–308
Copyright © 2007 by Information Age Publishing
All rights of reproduction in any form reserved.

a more democratic curriculum? Of course, they can—but they must begin (and begin soon!) to alter a curriculum that does not deliver, in terms of creating stronger and more effective citizens. Unless democratic changes are implemented, our democratic system is at risk. Too many of our citizens will become less and less able to preserve it. If we want to maintain and strengthen it, changes in the curriculum are imperative.

*   *   *

The more teachers and administrators find the following conditions present, the more able they will be to realize the goals of this democratic curriculum:

1. A democratic school and classroom climate
2. Protection of academic freedom
3. Professional preparation consistent with democratic principles for both novice and experienced teachers.

There are teachers and administrators who are sufficiently dedicated to creating school and classroom environments where a more democratic curriculum is sustained (Rossi & Pace, 1985; 1998). In some cases, such reforms are confined to a single classroom or a single school with no explicit support from colleagues or from the policies and practices of the school administration or the school board. The classrooms studied by Rossi and Pace (1985, 1988) as well as an in-depth study that focused on Mountain Open High School (Gregory & Sweeney, 1993), a small alternative high school with a highly personalized program in a large public school district, serve as examples of substantial change in behalf of more democratic education. Mountain Open High, an open enrollment school, whose population came from a wide range of socioeconomic backgrounds from across the entire school district, deserves the democratic prize. This high school, with its very democratic orientation, involved young citizens in designing their own curriculum from an array of specified options. Their selections had to help them meet a number of pre-established competencies among which they could make choices. The strong decisions that students, not their teachers, make is the significant feature here. To permit these decisions, the school, its principal, teachers and the school board had to believe in the capacity of students to do so. Their competencies included understandings, intellectual abilities, values and participation. This school illustrates the possibilities that exist for school and classroom reform in public school settings as do the open classrooms of individual teachers who decided to "go it alone" and try something different that was based on questions, not single-minded answers, that were of interest to the class, that let go of the textbook as well as the teacher as authorities and that turned young citizens loose to find some answers for themselves. Furthermore, their answers were right only if they had sufficient reasons and evidence to support them.

The professionals at Mountain Open High displayed a high level of energy and integrity that demonstrated strong trust in young citizens to develop their understanding of the "real world" and that gave them room to learn from their mistakes. Such reform is terribly challenging and it can be very frustrating. However, it is professionally satisfying and fulfilling of the school's primary mission. It involves decision making in pursuit of experiences that create the means for meeting the competencies prescribed by the curriculum. It avoids the usual simplistic view that the same content and learning experiences fits all young citizens.

Without a high level of commitment among administrators and teachers, it is certain that democratic education will not be strengthened. There are, and always will be, a few individual teachers and administrators who work to implement a more democratic curriculum. These educators serve as testimonials to professional integrity and to democratic education. The important work of such teachers and administrators is difficult under the best of circumstances. However, it would be considerably easier if supportive conditions such as those addressed in this chapter were in place. The following conditions will be examined:

- Protection of academic freedom
- Implementation of a democratic school and classroom climate
- Teacher education for both novice and experienced teachers

Many benefits can accrue from these conditions. Nothing stimulates and rewards teachers and student-citizens more than the experience they gain in a school and classroom environment where their views are taken seriously and where they are encouraged to contribute to decision making about real life issues. In addition, an emphasis on academic freedom will allow young citizens to examine materials and issues that are controversial as well as issues that are unresolved in this society and/or across the planet. They will deepen their understanding of these issues and strengthen their competence as democracy's citizens to respond to these serious problematic areas. If teacher education programs, at universities and professional development programs in school districts, are designed in keeping with the principles of democratic education, both novice and experienced teachers will be in a stronger positions to prepare the next generation of citizens for a stronger democracy. They can learn to apply more democratic teaching procedures. Any teacher who wants to teach more democratically can do that. However, if they work in teams of two or more, they can help each other to learn, provide feedback and think through problems together. Teachers can observe each other's classes and other teachers in action in a far less threatening manner than could be done by any administrator. In turn, they will gain deep satisfaction from the growth that young citizens display in their ability to handle the complexity and controversy that characterizes democratic public life.

SCHOOL AND CLASSROOM CLIMATE

Creating and working in a school and classroom that is open to the views of young citizens, where they feel free to speak out and challenge each other and even challenge their teachers, where shy class members begin to gain confidence and participate in small and later, large groups and where student-citizens learn how to defend and justify their views cannot help but enlarge the professional satisfaction that comes to teachers and administrators who provide young citizens such opportunities. Such satisfactions are not common in our social studies classes, but with encouragement and support teachers can learn to facilitate class discussions and reduce the amount of lecturing that is done. Most importantly, they can rather easily learn to ask questions that are intellectually challenging. None of the statements made here should be construed to mean that professionals in the school setting are not well-intentioned and responsible. They are. That responsibility involves not only concern for the safety of young citizens, but insuring that all young people are treated with respect, are listened to and are treated as worthwhile individuals.

Much has been written about democratic school and classroom climate. However, little has been done! Schools in the United States have hardly changed across time in the way they organize themselves, how administrators and teachers make and enforce rules and create hierarchical line relationships by which school personnel relate to one another. The pecking order is clear. The school board and administration is at the top and young citizens are at the bottom—an arrangement that certainly reveals more about authority than it does about democracy. In most classrooms, authoritarian practices are common and little recognition is afforded to democratic principles. The actions taken by administrators or teachers are neither responsive to nor facilitative of democratic learning to young citizens. They are more, much more, representative of order, security and authority than of democratic values such as equality, equity freedom, fairness and respect for diversity. Too often, there is no evidence of caring-not a smile, not a pat on the shoulder and not a positive word.

Despite their "tight ship" orientation, too many schools have become settings of increasing violence, including shootings and killings. A tragedy beyond words! We must seriously ask ourselves, does the emphasis on authority work? As professionals we must ask ourselves, does our strong emphasis on order, contribute to the rebelliousness and the hostility that feeds the violence that results in these school tragedies? Furthermore, for a variety of infractions, young people are suspended or expelled with African Americans disproportionately represented in these extreme school punishments.

Teachers, much like student-citizens, are given little decision making opportunity and are too often treated as technicians, rather than as educated professionals who can make thoughtful contributions to school and classroom decisions. Too often, teachers and student-citizens are expected to follow orders. And too often, without raising questions, they do. Another persistent question that professionals need to seriously consider is: To what extent, this authoritative climate contributes to teacher burnout? How long can teachers continue in environments where there is more fear than caring, more control than constructive openness.

There are, of course, explanations for school practices that lay aside democratic values in the name of order and security. Our society sends many, perhaps most, of its unsolved problems through the school house door. Young people who are influenced by drugs and alcohol, disrupted and even violent, home environments, issues of poverty, poor health, abuse and crime account for large numbers in many schools. Such conditions affect substantial percentages of school populations. Too many young citizens have few adults who are inspiring models to guide them to become caring, responsible and democratic adults. While these characteristics do not apply to each and every public school, or each and every student-citizen, many schools have to cope with similar conditions. High school populations are often quite large—too large—a condition that depersonalizes the interactions between principals, teachers and young citizens. Considerable evidence exists regarding the benefits of smaller school that are more caring and less bureaucratic. However, the personnel of many schools are often overwhelmed by security and control issues that they were not ever prepared to handle. Police, locked areas and locker searches contradict democratic values and practices. They send messages that say order is much more important than freedom, fairness and equality.

The solutions to these very challenging issues lie beyond the scope of this book. However, the ideas guiding this curriculum must be kept alive and educators at all levels (K–12 through college) must, to the greatest extent possible, create much more caring and supportive school and classroom environments where serious learning and serious thinking can take place. Recently, the Gates Foundation (Bill and Melinda Gates of Microsoft) have made substantial financial commitments to support a large number of small high schools or academies. Their goal is to improve public high schools and graduation rates by creating small, focused learning communities that help students achieve. This effort is a promising one that will hopefully minimize the bureaucracy of public schooling and pay serious attention to the growth of individuals whom public schools are trying to educate. The reader is strongly encouraged to read about the work of the Bill and Melinda Gates Foundation to improve American education. Actually they have embraced much wider goals but their view of what is needed in United States education is inspiring. The Gates Program is built on positive assumptions about young people and what they can accomplish. An informative Web site is: http://www.GatesFoundation.org/

In too many classes and schools, the physical décor is grim, walls need painting, plumbing needs repair and many school buildings are in need of substantial reconstruction (Kozol, 1992). Too often little attention is paid to displaying examples of diversity existing in most school populations or the classroom work of young citizens unless it comes only in the form of displaying athletic trophies won by the school across the years. The appearance of too many schools is neither warm nor welcoming. Surely, we can do better.

Moreover, school districts and school principals are often under a legal mandate that requires the testing of their young citizens on a regular basis. This mandate results in their exerting the influence of their offices to require teachers to emphasize curricula that respond to the subject areas that are emphasized on these tests. Neither social studies nor citizenship education are required, but in some places such tests are given. (Segall, 2003). In an increasing number of instances, test scores are printed in local newspapers and some principals and teachers are very concerned that their "heads might roll" or their reputations might be very negatively damaged if the test scores do not improve over the previous year's scores. Therefore, it is not surprising that principals admonish teachers to emphasize subject areas that are more likely to ensure high test scores. Consequently, less time is spent on class projects in social studies because more time has to be spent on reading and math. Therefore, teachers have less time to encourage creativity and independent thinking because subject areas that are tested must receive more attention and use up more class time. Tragically, these tests do not contribute to what educators need to know about the extent to which young people are learning to be stronger democratic citizens. Citizenship education, it seems, does not count!

Thirty by thirty foot classrooms with 35 desks lined up, sometimes nailed down, in straight rows, the teacher's desk and blackboards at the front of the room, perhaps a few maps and a textbook for each student constitutes the common appearance of many classrooms (Kozol, 1992). Many classrooms look just like they did one hundred or more years ago. Learning is supposed to take place in such settings that are hardly welcoming, that value order over creativity and where young citizens as well as their teachers are to be seen and not heard. The description above would not be out of line if we were describing schooling in a third world nation or schools in an authoritarian society. However, these are schools in the United States, a nation that prides itself as being an advanced world democracy where individuals are highly respected, children highly valued and where there is an appreciation for diversity and citizen participation. Sadly, these school environments seem to say we really do not care about the young—a perspective shared by David Halberstam (1998) in his book, *The Children*.

Nor do we appreciate diversity or the expansion of civic abilities that can grow out of opportunities to work in a wide range of social agencies in the community. This book advances a curriculum on behalf of a stronger democracy. At the same time, democratic curricula, such as the one proposed, cannot function with much promise in a closed atmosphere. School boards and school administrators must enact policies and practices that support the creation of school and classroom climates that exemplify democratic principles. This matter must be addressed seriously by all who work in the school setting including secretaries, maintenance and cafeteria workers. The school can benefit and more effectively implement a democratic curriculum if all of the adults who work in the school think of themselves as a team that collectively understands the mission of promoting a stronger democracy as a total school mission.

How the leadership in schools, including principals and department chairs, manifests itself through central administrators in the school setting is very significant to building a democratic school and classroom climate. In an insightful research report based on four detailed case studies, Linda McNeil (1986) found that schools could often be characterized as bureaucracies and that bureaucratic practices were justified by the argument that a smooth-running school promotes learning. She puts it well:

> But when the attention to "smooth-running" begins to control the educational practice in a school, teachers react in ways that *reduce* educational quality rather than enhance it. In fact, teachers tend to control their students in the same way that they are controlled by administrators. (p. 334)

Thus, whether the climate found in the school and classrooms is consistent with democratic principles lies heavily in the hands of school administrators who set the tone for school and classroom climate created by teachers. Their understandings and values regarding a democratic education are crucial to the realization of a democratic education that fulfills the mission of the public school.

The critical importance of a democratic climate receives strong support from research that tells us that young people may learn more from these subtle dimensions of schooling than from the formal curriculum (Ehman, 1980; Hahn, 1996). In order to provide a firm foundation for democratic education, school administrators in tandem with teachers, need to make decisions and take action that will create the atmosphere in which such a democratic curriculum can thrive. Consequently, school administrators and teachers need to be deeply committed and willing to apply their energy to creating a school setting that is as open, fair-minded and partici-pates in shared decision-making as much as possible.

Democratic school environments can take many forms. They call for substantial changes in the principles and practices that administrators apply to the ongoing operation of a school. Conventional administrative patterns that are hierarchical have been in place for so long that no one thinks of changing them in favor of policies and procedures that would open school environments to become spaces where open dialogue and controversy are valued, not feared, where teachers are not just permitted, but encouraged, to create open classroom climates and where they and their student-citizens are free to study and assess contrasting sides of signif-icant and controversial issues, in order to make decisions that they can defend intellectually and justify to others.

Once this level of dedication is evident among school administrators, it will pervade all that they do and will, in turn, encourage department heads and teachers to behave in similar ways. In effect, this change requires the creation of a new and different culture in the school setting. Such changes, though very demanding, are also essential if the conventional, textbook-memorization-recitation view of teaching is to be replaced by more enlight-ened pedagogy that delivers a more engaging, constructive and compelling education.

Democratically-oriented school administrators must be particularly con-cerned with activating democratic principles and practices such as: sharing decision making with student-citizens, staff, teachers, other administrators and other school employees as well as persuading the school board to affirm such arrangements. The following practices are worth serious con-sideration:

- Treating each individual with respect and care on a consistent basis.
- Engaging student councils and student courts in handling issues of school and classroom discipline in ways that are taken seriously. They must not serve as window dressing.
- Modeling behavior by teachers and administrators that is consistent with respect for pluralism, with diverse student-citizens and profes-sionals, They need to see to it that both the school and its curriculum visibly demonstrate attention to diversity, including gender as well as issues, influencing the entire global community.
- Encouraging faculty, staff, and student-citizen involvement to design democratic practices for school and classroom management.

- Encouraging both teachers and student-citizens to plan together to develop constructive conditions for teaching and learning and to generate criteria for assessment and evaluation policies, mutually.
- Providing resources that support investigation of multiple sources for understanding and taking a defensible position regarding controversial issues (both print and technological), facilitating relevant classroom speakers, as well as field trips.
- Communicating with and involving parents in the development of curriculum and school practices.
- Involving parents, school boards, teachers, and student-citizens in the design and implementation of academic freedom policies and procedures.
- Establishing the position of Community Counselor, who is a teacher who can guide and arrange social action and service learning experiences, handle seminars where young citizens give serious consideration to the meaning of their community experiences and analyze them for their effectiveness.

Many of these suggested democratic practices are implemented, to some extent, by teachers and administrators who genuinely respect young citizens and allow them to make important decisions, who activate student courts and student councils, who involve student-citizens in selecting issues for class study and who also make serious efforts to communicate with parents about school matters. Since in many schools, some of these procedures are already in place, making subsequent moves toward fulfilling democratic education should be seen as building on the existing foundation, instead of beginning anew.

Creating democratic schools and classrooms at the elementary level is as important as doing so at the middle and high school levels. Often, assumptions are made that these children are too young to comprehend democratic principles. Ann Angell's work (1991) comprehensively reviewed research that strongly affirmed the importance of democratic school and classroom climate at the elementary level. Angel wisely states:

> ...that democratic climates may be particularly influential in elementary classrooms is suggested by political socialization research which indicates that young citizens at the elementary level are constructing political concepts (Abraham, 1983; Connell, 1971; Moore, Lare and Wagner, 1985; Stevens, 1982). This research notes that young children express interest in the political world and they form long lasting political attitudes (Greenstein, 1965; Hess and Torney, 1967). Patterns of tolerance and dissent seem to be well developed as early as the fourth grade (Zellman and Sears, 1971). Feelings of political efficacy appear to advance as students advance through the elementary grades (Easton and Dennis, 1968; Glenn, 1972; Hess and Torney, 1967)

whereas initially high levels of political trust appear to decline among first, second and third graders and in the later elementary years, especially among young citizens of lower social economic status (Glenn, 1972). In addition, psychological research indicates that the elementary school years are a time of potentially rapid development in perspective taking ability (Selman, 1976). Taken together, these scholars suggest the elementary years represent a critical socialization period during which schooling experiences may influence the development of political and social attitudes (Angel, pp. 250–251).

While all possibilities for democratic administrative and teaching practices are not exhausted in this discussion, the administration of our schools must be conducted in a manner as consistent as possible with democratic principles. Since democracy in the United States is one of the more advanced democratic systems on the planet, one would think that democratic schools and democratic educational practices would have become the order of the day much earlier in this nation's history. Yet, very few schools consistently demonstrate democratic practices. Instead, bureaucracy and authority prevail.

The modeling of democratic practices by all adults in the school setting is an imperative in the preparation of democratic citizens. Ehman (1980), in a comprehensive review of political socialization research, concluded that young people in classrooms where they had opportunities to explore controversial issues were more likely to have a stronger sense of political efficacy. That conclusion must not be overlooked as administrators and teachers take initial steps toward implementing a democratic climate for an open curriculum. A strong sense of political efficacy means that young citizens believe they may have some success if they try to make improvements in democratic public life. We must expand that outcome. Our teachers must do everything they can to involve young citizens in thoughtful and active exploration of controversial issues.

How schools make rules and how student-citizens who break the rules are treated, serve as strong influences on the quality of school and classroom climate. Evidence exists that allows all of us to conclude that these practices have some impact on what young people learn about democracy. How school and classroom discipline is conducted also demonstrates the strength of commitment held by both administrators and teachers regarding democratic education. Far too often, school administrators make school rules arbitrarily without the input of teachers or young citizens and implement them arbitrarily without explanation. Only infrequently are there instances of student courts or student councils where student-citizens who are charged with breaking the rules are judged by their peers who are guided by values and the principles associated with due process, fairness, consistency and openness. There is no better place than the school for the young to learn about the application of democratic values as they participate directly in such learning experiences. It is here that our successor generation can learn through experience how democracy works. The school is the only agency that can provide this opportunity for a large proportion of young citizens in upper elementary, middle and secondary schools to gain experience in democracy throughout most of their school years.

Some educators will argue that in some schools there is such rampant disrespect of school rules that some schools constitute a war zone. Indeed, the presence of police, security mechanisms and unwarranted locker searches are much more suggestive practices in prisons, rather than schools. While none of us can explain how some schools became so very difficult, and even dangerous, it is clear that unless young people are treated with respect on a sustained basis and unless the school curriculum is related to their concerns to the extent possible, educators can hardly expect respect from young people in return. In short, we must walk our talk, if we are to encourage the quality of citizenship that maintains and strengthens democracy.

Skiba and Peterson (2003) have identified school programs that can help young people resolve conflict in civil ways.[1] These programs included the products developed by Educators for Social Responsibility,[2] a nonprofit organization that has produced a number of publications focused on conflict resolution about which teachers reported that their use resulted in less physical violence and increased cooperation in their classrooms. It was also found that such curricula raised self-esteem, improved classroom climate and led to a reduction in fighting. It was also noted that teachers listened more closely to what young people said. Schools need to use such programs and make sure that teachers are well prepared to use them. Recent tragedies in our schools, so mandate.

Teachers and administrators are regularly called upon to handle infringements on school rules or acts of anger and hostility from their student body. How these issues are handled contribute to the quality of the school in powerful ways. Many teachers and administrators, who represent the authority of the school to young citizens, see themselves as arbiters of these disputes. Others view these disputes as opportunities for young people to resolve their own issues and make decisions more independently and democratically. They ask each of the young people involved to share their view of the conflict and to recommend a fair solution. Thus, the responsibility falls on student-citizens to resolve the dispute. Rather than becoming dependent on adult authority, these young people have a chance to learn, to struggle with the issue and make decisions that they can justify and apply.

There can be little question that school personnel who take major steps toward expanding student-citizen involvement, that encourage competing points of view to be analyzed and discussed and that provide student-citizens with opportunities to take a position and defend it, will be much more likely to graduate young citizens who are better prepared to assume their citizenship responsibilities in public life.

ACADEMIC FREEDOM

The preferred academic content in this curriculum takes the form of historic, contemporary and future-oriented social issues that are often controversial and subject to higher level thinking abilities including an emphasis on decision making, values and community participation in the form of service learning or social action. Therefore, it requires the protection and practices of academic freedom as it applies to K–12 settings. Academic freedom has been cherished and fought for by scholars and students across the centuries. It has been essential to scholarship and scientists as they search for the truth as comprehensively as possible. In advanced democracies such as the United States, it is a logical correlate of the value of free expression guaranteed by the First Amendment to the Bill of Rights. Like all freedoms, academic freedom requires constant vigilance and protection. Moreover, like all freedoms, in a civil, democratic society, it is subject to limits. For example, we know we must not shout "fire" in a crowded theater because of the consequences when a crowd is frightened. Democracy's citizens also know that one person's freedom, when taken to extremes, may conflict or interfere with the freedom of others. However, all citizens must have the opportunity to know the truth as fully as it is provided in the resources that they research and analyze. Furthermore, no citizens, including teachers, have the right to forcefully impose their views on the privacy, space or the minds of others. They must not use the classroom as a bully pulpit.

In several earlier chapters, academic freedom and its importance have been mentioned. In this chapter, the intent is to provide more depth to this concept which is so central to democratic citizenship education. Since academic freedom is a necessary condition for this curriculum, some suggested principles and procedures are presented below. Educators, administrators, teachers and teacher educators have the responsibility to involve their classes in open dialogues regarding controversial issues where a wide range of ideas are welcome. These ideas can be examined for the degree of reason and/or evidence they may or may not contribute to the issue at hand. Unlike nondemocratic societies that directly inculcate the young with their preferred ideology, democracies, which are also ideological, are not free to inculcate democratic values in the same manner. The value of freedom in democracy necessarily contradicts the imposition of values. What we seek for our young citizens is that they accept democracy after thoughtful consideration of its merits and awareness of its deficiencies. There is no system that places higher values on the rights of individuals who also have responsibilities and limits. Freedom does not mean that individuals can do anything they want. Civility and social justice require otherwise. However, this curriculum is based on a deep commitment to democracy, which despite its frailties and its continuing struggle for improvement, is among the most attractive and compelling political systems the world has seen. The high value it holds regarding the rights of the individuals as well as the principle of self-governance by its citizens guides public policy through a republic made up of elected representatives.

In the United States, courts at state and federal levels have ruled on academic freedom cases from time to time. Many court decisions have affirmed intellectual freedom at the K–12 level. The cases of Sterzing, Keynes, and Tinker (a student) provide a few examples (Ochoa, 1979). These decisions have strengthened academic freedom practices in the schools. Other court decisions have ruled negatively. The famous Scopes Trial and the recent Scope-alike Trial both drew national attention, the Island Tree case and the case of Theresa Burnau in Warsaw, Indiana have ruled in favor of parents who want to shield their children and the children of others. These cases sometimes relied on the principle of local control of schools. Nonetheless, academic freedom has a historic tradition because of courageous teachers and courageous young citizens who have been willing to take their cases to court and withstand the financial, social and personal costs involved. It is important to be aware that not all court decisions have supported academic freedom principles.

In the early grades, we socialize the young. Most classrooms are equipped with the United States flag and the Pledge of Allegiance is a daily routine even when children are too young to understand it. In the democratic curriculum proposed here, creating a democratic school and classroom climate is strongly advocated in order that young citizens are both respected by and learn to relate to democratic principles. In a sense, in the school and classroom under these conditions, democratic principles and practices become important understandings. In other aspects of their lives, the family, the peer group and institutions, democratic values may or may not be as evident.

As their maturity permits, young citizens engaged with this curriculum will be guided by counter-socialization for the purpose of learning to analyze social conditions and controversial issues and critique the strengths and weaknesses of our political system as well as others. The preservation and strengthening of democratic practices requires citizens who have acquired the understandings, the reasoning abilities and the commitment to the improvement of democracy through the processes of socialization and counter-socialization. At higher levels of maturity, young citizens can begin to accept democratic values, not as blind truth, but based on their reasoning and the evidence that may exist, their recognition of democracy's strengths and weaknesses as well as the positive and negative aspects of capitalism. All of us, who believe deeply in democracy as the best hope for humanity, believe that the arguments in favor of democracy constitute a very compelling case and will be so perceived by young citizens. It is here that citizenship educators must have faith in the strength of democracy's values to prove themselves to each succeeding generation of citizens. In other chapters, it was stated that there is a fine line for teachers to walk between inculcation of democratic values and engaging young citizens in a thoughtful reasoning process. As educators, neither our motives or desires, nor our deep commitments to democracy allow us to intentionally manipulate the minds of student-citizens who must thoughtfully come to their own defensible conclusions in a democracy. Therefore, we will, as citizenship educators, encourage democratic values by using evidence and reason, but we must not deliberately inculcate young citizens to blindly accept them.

Existing organizations can be of considerable assistance when teachers find themselves in difficulty because of materials they use or activities they encourage. The National Education Association, the American Federation of Teachers, the American Civil Liberties Union, People for the American Way, the American Library Association, the National Council of Teachers of English and the National Council for the Social Studies can be considerable sources of support and are worth contacting for guidance if such challenges occur.

Two experienced teachers, whom I have interviewed, reported instances of parental complaints, but in both cases these teachers felt they had the support of their administrators both in their school and in the school district's central office as well as assistance from their teachers' organization (Ochoa, 1979). Very little research regarding academic freedom has been done on K–12 teachers. Therefore, it is impossible to estimate the extent to which supportive conditions are present in schools and classrooms. Terribly disappointing was one recent report (Flinders, 2005) where 14 secondary students reported that their teachers did not give any classroom attention to Iraq. Due to the long tradition of struggling for and maintaining academic freedom, schools have a history regarding this important concept. It is likely that faculty at all levels are familiar with the concept and function in ways that integrate its principles into the ongoing practices of the school and curriculum. Therefore, educators are not starting from scratch. Rather, they are building on a compelling legacy. However, the protection of academic freedom requires energy and commitment from the school board as well as from professional personnel, if a curriculum that prepares democracy's citizens to address significant and controversial issues is to be implemented effectively (ACLU, 1968).

Guidelines for Educators Regarding Academic Freedom

Academic freedom applies differently to the K–12 setting and the college level. At the K–12 level, it is constrained by the legal requirement that young citizens must attend school until they are at least sixteen and therefore, they are an involuntary audience. This condition contrasts sharply with college students who are more mature and who attend colleges and universities voluntarily. This situation calls for teachers and administrators at the K–12 level to apply the guidelines of age-appropriateness and relevance to course objectives, selection of materials and teaching procedures (Flinders, 2006). Some of these guidelines have been supported by court decisions. Many teachers take these principles into account when selecting subject matter as well as materials and/or methods to be used in their classrooms. It is such practices that educators need to deepen and expand to strengthen the tradition of academic freedom (see Doyle, 2004).

The following guidelines are suggested practices that relate to an Issues-Centered Decision Making Curriculum:

1. Prior to starting a unit that entails controversy, the teacher should develop a written rationale and description for the unit to inform the principal and to use if questions or complaints are raised (Shaver, 1992). This rationale should be shared with the principal so that he or she is informed and it will serve as a strong defense if needed for parents, the school board and/or the administration.

2. When teaching and learning about controversial issues is the focus of the curriculum, teachers must ensure that student-citizens have gathered and analyzed knowledge relative to the key questions they are studying. Classroom dialogues must not be reduced to sharing uninformed opinions.

3. During classroom dialogue regarding these issues and their solutions, the teacher must make sure the class carefully considers alternative points of view. If student-citizens do not present a full range of views, the teacher must be prepared to do so. This condition is essential for a comprehensive assessment of these alternative solutions and for a balanced treatment of the possibilities.

4. The teacher should inform parents prior to starting a controversial unit. If any parent objects, the teacher and administrator should be prepared with an alternate assignment for that youngster to be carried out in another classroom or the school library. It is far preferable to provide such alternatives, rather than deprive the entire class of learning about a controversial issue. Parents have the right to exclude their youngster from the unit under consideration, but they do not have the right to deprive all youngsters from studying a particular controversy.

5. The school board and school district should have written policies in place that affirm academic freedom and the teaching of controversy. This practice is essential for all schools in a democratic society. These

policies should result in procedures to be followed when complaints do arise. It is also wise for a school district to appoint an advisory board of citizens, parents, teachers, and students to review complaints when they occur.

6. Teachers need to guard against self-censorship and the tendency to play it safe as they select issues, materials and methods that address controversy. Only by reading such materials will student-citizens learn to detect bias and analyze the strength of the point of view being presented.

7. New, inexperienced teachers who have not yet established their footing are wise not to focus on highly controversial issues in the classroom. After they have acquired tenure combined with a solid professional reputation, they would be in a much stronger position to defend their professional decisions.

Two quotations comprise the conclusion for this discussion of academic freedom. One is taken from an unpublished paper presented by Professor Jack Nelson (2001) when he received the Academic Freedom Award from the National Council for the Social Studies. His insight as a scholar and teacher is valuable for all of us. In this paper, he widened our awareness:

> The de-professionalization of teaching that accompanies the curriculum standards movement has serious repercussions beyond the classroom. It leads to the concerns about the protection of academic freedom for both teachers and students and the threat the standards might pose to the essential purposes of education in a democracy. If not in the schools, where will students be able to examine controversial topics in a reasoned and thoughtful way? (pp. 1–4)

Nelson has it right. Where indeed? It is terribly clear that tests are standardizing the curriculum and placing teachers under tremendous pressure to teach to the test

The second quotation is from Justice William O. Douglas, who stated in a dissenting opinion: "Ultimately all the questions in this case are really boiled down to one—whether we as a people will try fearfully and futiley to preserve totalitarian methods, or whether in accordance with our tradition and our Constitution we will have the confidence and courage to be free?"

THE PREPARATION OF TEACHERS FOR AN ISSUES-CENTERED DECISION MAKING CURRICULUM

The preparation of teachers for this democratic curriculum is both critical and challenging. It is critical because the way teachers are taught strongly influences the way they will teach (Goodman. 1988) and the methods used by their previous teachers tend to fall in the memorize-recite-test mode. However, with commitment, knowledge, and abilities that foster democratic teaching and emphasize that serious attention be given to gender, diversity, and global perspectives, it is much more likely that the next generation will have the necessary competence that they and this democracy deserve. It is this goal that must be embraced by teacher preparation at colleges and universities, as well as professional development programs in schools and school districts.

Both the preparation of teachers at the university and the preparation of experienced teachers in professional development programs in school districts need to address the expanded abilities required by an Issues-Centered Decision Making Curriculum. Of course, the administration should facilitate the changes they need to make in teaching practices as much as possible. The preparation of undergraduate and graduate students as well as tenured and nontenured experienced teachers must be guided by the democratic practices required in this democratic curriculum. Some will be returning students who have interrupted their education for family reasons or change-of-career reasons. They will vary by background, gender, ethnicity and previous experiences. The greater maturity of these older students is a strength they bring to their roles as teachers. There are not many educators who are proficient in democratic teaching practices but they must all start somewhere to expand their teaching repertoire (Dumas, 1993).

Certainly, the small number of teachers who currently attempt to implement democratic curricula can be partially explained by the lack of emphasis on democratic education in their teacher preparation programs. Overall, most teachers carry conventional images of teaching (read the textbook and lecture notes, memorize and take tests on the covered materials) in their minds. Instead, they need a broader awareness of how to handle and implement an Issues-Centered Decision Making Curriculum. At both schools and colleges, preparing teachers in a manner consistent with democratic principles is challenging because it involves fostering, but *not* imposing, a commitment to democratic principles. Thus, faculty members at both the university and school district levels need to walk the very tight line between an open curriculum which allows future teachers to shape their own beliefs on the one hand and teaching procedures that represent democratic values on the other. This challenge is one that teacher education faculty share with faculty at the K–12 level. Moreover, commitment to democratic principles, while absolutely essential, is not sufficient to prepare teachers differently process involved in handling controversy. The success of such teacher education programs resides in the competence, the care and the commitment of teacher educators who are responsible for the preparation of teachers. They must be willing and able to advance democratic curricula. They too, may be starting from scratch. Unfortunately, most of them have not received this kind of preparation but if they are willing to experience some trial and error, the experience is likely to be a satisfying and exciting one. Moreover, the ability of teacher educators to create a model of an open classroom environment, where strong dialogue around complex and controversial issues can be learned first hand, is sorely needed. Cutting edge research conducted by Parker and Hess (2001) using *structured academic controversy* indicates that demonstrating the processes associated with classroom dialogue is not enough. These researchers concluded that prospective teachers might participate actively in model classroom demonstrations of classroom dialogue and even enjoy it, but participation alone did not expand their competence or improve their confidence in facilitating democratic dialogue in their classrooms. The Parker-Hess conclusion, that experience in dialogue is not sufficient for novice teachers to learn how to conduct dialogue about controversy, led them to recommend that explicit, direct instruction, which may involve lecture followed by practice, may be necessary to develop such abilities. When learning to be competent in a complex, intellectual, and socially interactive teaching style, direct instruction becomes an additional or alternative approach to understanding the elements of this style and can contribute to finding ways that teachers can actually perform more effectively. When we acquire the ability to swim, drive a car or use a computer, direct instruction of the procedures is useful. A point not to be ignored is that learning to handle controversy should be followed by sufficient practice so teachers feel quite confident to initiate the procedures associated with *structured academic controversy* in their classrooms.[3]

Despite gains across time in the education of a diversity of peoples in the United States, teaching practices continue to be very resistant to change not only at the K–12 level, but also at universities. The preparation of teachers came to require a bachelor's degree, which usually involves four or five years of college. However, the internal characteristics of these programs across this nation have solidified, if not atrophied. In the main, most, if not all, teacher education programs in social studies education have the following characteristics:

- Two years of general studies that include introductory courses in a range of disciplines where the teaching provided by college instruc-

tors (at large universities these instructors are often advanced graduate students) is largely in the lecture-memorize-test mode.

- An academic major in one of the social sciences that requires the
  equivalent of approximately 30 semester credit hours. This number
  may vary across states and institutions. These courses are usually
  taught in the lecture-memorize-test mode and most prospective
  teachers elect history as their major since that subject is most frequently taught in schools.

- Professional Education courses in educational foundations, social
  studies methods and evaluation, usually taught in the conventional
  mode, are required. In addition, some preliminary classroom experience and the required student teaching under the supervision of
  both a classroom teacher and a university supervisor are mandated
  experiences. During their student teaching experience and their
  beginning (pre-tenure) years of teaching, future and first year teachers are strongly influenced by the advice of experienced classroom
  teachers. Such socialization of beginning teachers becomes ever
  more prominent during their initial years of teaching as they adapt
  to their new working environments. (Goodman, 1988, pp. 23–51)

Many criticisms can and have been made of this pattern of teacher preparation. In this case, the criticisms discussed below, though not exhaustive,
are related to the principles of citizenship education in a democracy. First
of all, many, if not most teacher education programs do not provide experiences in democratic citizenship as a bona fide aspect of the preparation of
teachers who will be responsible for the education of young citizens. Little
attention is given to social justice—equity, fairness, diversity or to global
issues. Seldom are opportunities available for future teachers to work in
community or governmental agencies, to study controversial issues in an
interdisciplinary way or to make recommendations to public agencies or
political figures regarding what could be done to improve the situation
regarding an unsolved issue. Neither are they provided opportunities to act
on their public values and make recommendations as citizens may to fellow
citizens or public officials. Nor do they have a chance to observe and examine legislative, judicial or administrative agencies at work. Yet, we expect
these young people, often 20 and 21 years old when they accept their first
teaching position, to become citizenship educators without the benefit of
learning experiences that enhance their awareness and competence
regarding democratic practices and principles as applied to schooling and
education (Adler, 1991, 1993).

Secondly, the teaching methods that future teachers observe and their
experience as college students, too often in large and anonymous lecture
halls, are most often taught in the textbook/lecture-memorize-test mode,

which is a continuation of the teaching style that prevailed at the K–12 level. Most college professors or their teaching assistants emulate their former teachers. Furthermore, few courses engage their classes in addressing challenging and controversial issues and future teachers are infrequently involved in the intellectual dialogue in classes where the lecture/ textbook format dominates (Dumas, 1993). Therefore, schools and colleges of education are also culpable. Moreover, in one or two methods courses, teacher educators are expected to convert a college student to a social studies teacher which is quite a leap from their college student status. Of particular concern to the preparation of citizenship educators is fostering awareness of democratic principles including freedom, equality, fairness, pluralism in a global age (Adler, 1991, 1993).

The suggestions provided above provide a starting place for those who are dedicated to strengthening the programs that educate teachers for a democracy. The following discussion is limited to the kinds of changes that deserve consideration by those who are responsible for teacher education programs and those who teach both academic and professional courses. The latter goes beyond courses and extends to those who supervise classroom teaching experiences for future citizenship educators in a democracy.

The following characteristics are suggested for teacher preparation programs that aim at graduating strong citizenship educators for a democracy:

1. Each future social studies teacher should experience an internship in a social or governmental agency in their community.

2. Each future social studies teacher should take at least one, preferably two, interdisciplinary courses that are devoted to the study of controversial issues, some of which focus on equity, pluralism and diversity and many that are set in the context of global conditions and issues. In such classes, future teachers should be involved in an interdisciplinary analysis of such issues, where they can draw on a wide array of sources and where they make decisions and recommendations about how the issue at hand can be minimized or related conditions can be improved. In the final analysis, future citizenship educators should be able to defend their decisions with reason and evidence. Importantly, such courses should provide them with competence derived from direct experience with the tasks of democratic citizenship. Experienced teachers could be invited to audit these courses.

3. Future and experienced social studies teachers need to take methods courses that are devoted to preparing them to become effective facilitators of classroom dialogue focused on broadening their understanding of the issue under study, elicitors of student interest in the selection of issues to be studied and creators of an open and democratic classroom climate where any idea can be expressed and

where all conclusions, values, and decisions are open to challenge based on reason and evidence. Experienced teachers might find auditing these courses especially helpful,

4. Future and experienced social studies teachers must be knowledge-able regarding the concept of democracy including academic free-dom and its application in the school setting. In this regard, teacher educators as well as future teachers should be able to articulate a rationale that provides justification for the content, methods and materials that they use in their classes. This rationale statement should be completed prior to starting a study of a controversial topic and a copy given to the principal who should know what you plan to do and have an opportunity to make suggestions.

5. Given that controversy needs to be the focus of classroom dialogue, lack of attention to providing experience and building competence in conducting dialogue in teacher preparation programs clearly dis-advantage prospective teachers and reduces the quality of demo-cratic education. If we genuinely want to improve the experiences that young people have to prepare them to be stronger democratic citizens, we must find the time, energy and commitment to teach ourselves.

Much more can be said about improving teaching education programs to be more democratic to expand attention to equity and diversity in the form of multicultural education, including gender issues as well as issues facing all marginal people in addition to providing teachers with alterna-tive perspectives about global conditions and issues. Teachers who want to make changes in their teaching style will find Appendix I, Gradual Imple-mentation and II, A Reflective Teaching Instrument. especially helpful.

CONCLUSION

Putting an Issues-Centered Decision Making Curriculum in place is not an easy matter. While it can be done incrementally, it also makes sense to think of the comprehensive implementation period as guided by a five year plan. Working on matters such as school and classroom climate, academic freedom policies and the preparation of teachers takes time, patience and endurance. As importantly, change of this magnitude requires tolerance for experiencing setbacks. This curriculum is complex and requires a com-plex support system. Dedicated administrators and teachers are essential to its implementation. But, it is worth all of the effort and energy if we develop more confident, knowledgeable citizens who can take an informed and caring role as citizens who have had experiences that can guide their intellect and their actions in behalf of issues that need citizen attention. The quality of our young citizens and our democracy is at stake.

NOTES

1. Professor Russell Skiba, Indiana University-Bloomington has done considerable research on how schools maintain order and has identified curricula that may be helpful for teachers and students that help reduce conflict.

2. Structured Academic Controversy (SAC) is a specific format for teaching social issues used by Walter Parker and Diana Hess in their research on future teachers and how to teach them to handle controversy in their classrooms. By itself, class demonstration does not seem to help novice teachers to understand the techniques of discussion. When presented with model discussions, future teachers seem to become preoccupied with the content rather than the processes related to conducting a discussion. Parker and Hess suggest that direct instruction in the process of discussion may be necessary.

EPILOGUE

A fundamental goal of schools in this democratic nation is to educate young citizens in order that self-governance can flourish. In support of this goal, one that is essential for this democracy, the purpose of this book is to improve school curricula, particularly in social studies; to strengthen the quality of citizen participation. This Issues-Centered Decision Making Curriculum seeks to accomplish this goal by emphasizing knowledge of significant social and controversial issues as well as expanding the development of intellectual and political abilities needed by young citizens to address the challenges of the new century. It draws heavily on the teachings of John Dewey using student interests to study relevant issues, engaging student-citizens in seeking solutions to both personal and public issues in a reasoned and evidence-based way. It encourages, but does not mandate belief in democratic values associated with social justice—equality, equity, fairness and freedom.

Many educational reforms, past and present, do not address the matter of curriculum needed for effective citizenship in a democracy. Charter schools do not do so. Vouchers do not do so. The curriculum standards - testing and accountability movement does not do so. In fact, the use of standards and testing use up classroom time that might otherwise be used for citizenship education.

In the 1960s a host of creative social studies curriculum projects collectively labeled the "New Social Studies," heavily funded by the federal government, were developed and tried in selected schools, but they failed to replace the narrow textbook-bound curriculum that have become a habit in many social studies courses. In the first version of this book, published in 1988, Shirley Engle and I offered a broader and more democratic curriculum as an alternative to the persistent 'back-to-the basics' rhetoric of the '70s and '80s. School practices during this period reflected an increasingly lower priority for social studies. Fewer social studies offerings, fewer social

Democratic Education for Social Studies, pages 309–313
Copyright © 2007 by Information Age Publishing
All rights of reproduction in any form reserved.

studies credits required for graduation and a number of schools eliminated social studies curriculum coordinators. Some became general curriculum consultants. In any case, the social studies curriculum was not the focus of innovation. Instead, social studies was characterized by a predictable narrow curriculum based on the knowledge presented by the textbook and the teacher.

Citizens, of course, must be able to read, write and calculate (these were the basics as promoted in the '70s and '80s), but these abilities are not sufficient for effective citizenship in a democracy. Beyond proficiency in these basics, citizens must be able to address, with a high level of competence, the questions and issues that concern the welfare of all citizens in this pluralistic nation and on this troubled planet. Nothing less than our well-being, our democracy and our survival as human beings on this planet are at stake. This version of the original work proposes the same fundamental curriculum with some expanded features that are made explicit. Attention to multicultural education, global education and the values related to social justice are included. Every generation of citizens need to see a more democratic form of citizenship education as a basic element of the curriculum as well. This curriculum must not be construed as another fad or a temporary fix. Outstanding educatiors, scholars, journalists and citizens have written about it and talked about it across the last century. Examples are: Anderson. L., Anderson C., Bruner, Cornbleth, Cherryholmes, Cox, Dewey, Engle, Griffin, Hahn, Hess, Hunt and Metcalf, Johnson, Longstreet, Massialas, Nelson, Newmann, Oliver, Palonsky, Parker, Patrick, Rugg, Shaver, Stanley, Sweeney, Taba, Tucker and the list goes on. The principles in this curriculum are an imperative if the next generation and this democracy is to thrive in the 21st century.

No citizen is born with the necessary understandings and abilities necessary for an effective public life. Nor are they born knowing how to resolve issues and improve conditions that contribute to major problems. Some of our citizens are not able to see the long term, because they are so ensconced in the immediate issues of their lives. Some seem not to care or they find news reports boring. Some do not trust in their elected representatives. Schooling provides the paramount way that citizens can and must learn about the dynamic nature of this democracy. In this society, we need citizens who are responsive to the expanding diversity of this nation as well as to the complex challenges of diversity, interdependence and the significant issues of the global community.

The new version of this book appears at a time when young citizens and teachers find themselves deluged by a proliferation of curriculum standards and concomitant mandatory tests. In the '90s, virtually all subject areas including United States history, geography and civics developed curriculum standards, all funded by the federal government. Social studies was not included. However, the National Council for the Social Studies issued social studies curriculum standards for the Social Studies, which received no federal support. Federal dollars went to separate subjects not to an interdisciplinary field like social studies. Accountability, captured in the No Child Left Behind Act passed by Congress, has become a powerful, political imperative that has a substantial influence on the nature of curriculum in the first decade of the 21st century. These practices negate what thoughtful educators had in mind. The standards and tests threaten teachers. They also threaten administrators. Ringing in my ears as I write, are the words of an outstanding local teacher who had been told, "heads would roll if test scores do not improve." I was amazed to hear the quiver in her voice when she publicly shared her concern. When such a dedicated and competent teacher agonizes over mandated testing, a wakeup call for all educators is in order.

These tests for accountability mean that we do not consider varied home backgrounds or the diverse social conditions that young people experience. Regardess of abilities, interests, attitudes and the varied life experiences of young citizens, teachers must teach them in ways that the tests require.

Like all public servants, teachers must be accountable—but that accountability only makes sense if teachers are encouraged to involve their classes as seriously and competently as they can in expanding their understandings as well as their intellectual and social abilities. Not all young people are alike, not all learn in the same ways and not all, even want to learn. Using tests for accountability purposes means that our student-citizens are all alike, and their teachers simply need to drill them sufficiently until they can answer the questions correctly. Where is there a hint of regard for human differences and the creativity that many classrooms demonstrate? Where is there a hint of recognition of diverse populations (the handicapped, young people whose primary language is not English) who foil no matter how hard teachers engage them in drill and practice? Furthermore, the amount of money spent on creating standards, developing tests and the school time lost in preparing young citizens to pass these tests is enormous. The damage done to the creativity of teachers to devise curriculum suitable for their classes and to the work of capable, enthusiastic teachers is beyond measurement. Given the distortion to the curriculum because teacher allocate increased amounts of classroom time to drill and practice that relates to what is likely to be asked on the test, instead of a curriculum created by teachers makes the phrase that frequently circulates: "Every child is left behind" rings true to many ears.

By contrast, this Issues-Centered Decision Making Curriculum or any other democratic curriculum would involve young citizens in seeking answers to the following kinds of challenging questions: Was the war in Iraq justified? Should we have engaged in more extensive diplomatic efforts prior to the Iraq war? Should we have sent a larger military force? What is pre-emptive war? Was it justified in relationship to the War in Iraq? Teachers could ask similar questions in historical contexts such as the American Revolution, the Civil War, World War I, II or the Vietnam War. In fact, young citizens could learn a great deal by a comparison of these wars and the consideration of such questions as Why do wars start? Can wars be prevented? How? Were any efforts made to stop these wars? What can we learn from former wars that are now history, that would be useful to us in the future? Wrestling with such questions, engaging in related classroom dialogue, participating in projects that draw on the thinking and creativity of student-citizens to search for answers to such questions set in the past, present or future, is much more consistent with the demands of democratic citizenship than textbook-based instruction that requires the memorization of so-called facts, soon forgotten.

The ideas in this new curriculum are not easy to test. In fact, objective measures such as short-answer, fill in the blank or even multiple-choice items will not do. However, judgments can be made of papers that student-citizens write, oral presentations they make or ideas they contribute to classroom dialogues. We will have to accept that those judgments will be more subjective but the learnings will be more important. Asking young citizens to support their answers with reason and evidence is not only more challenging and interesting than memorizing the presentation in the textbooks, but it also builds the foundation for a heightened quality of democratic citizenship. Teachers can generate probing questions about any issues such as those related to Westward Expansion, the Spanish-American War or the Depression as well as for contemporary and future-oriented issues such as cloning, expanding stem-cell reseach, euthanasia and gay and lesbian marriage. Continuing tension over the dynamics between freedom and security in this democracy is one example of a persistent issue that has always been and probably always will be with us. More recently, issues such as the conducting stem cell research, abortion and cloning have grown out of medical, sociological and technological research and these issues will continue to be with us in the future. Such questions and the search for understanding in order to make grounded decisions are the intellectual grist of highly competent citizens of a strong democracy. We need more citizens who can approach the issues of their time with this intellectual vigor. Our citizens must have the ability to handle these intellectual challenges and the schools must be capable and responsible in realizing such goals. However, the present social studies curriculum evident in most schools, gives almost exclusive attention to historical topics and emphasizes memorization of textbook material. Young citizens, in the main do not find this curriculum interesting and little of it remains in their memory. By so doing, such curricula uses class time that teachers could use to expand the potential of young citizens to become capable of the self-governance that serves as the sine qua non of public life in a democracy.

This book is available at a time when social studies is being undermined by attacks as well as neglect. It is under attack from the standards and testing mandate legitimized by the No Child Left Behind Act (NCLB) that results in teachers, laying aside creative projects and using class time to teach all young citizens what is.likely to be on the tests. The same law, NCLB lessens the time for social studies (and other subjects) but it also ignores the social studies as a subject area to be tested. For far too long, schools have persisted in a textbook-recitiattion-testing mode of teaching that has dominated the social studies curriculum. These common teaching practices allowed textbook publishers and their authors, not the school district, nor its professional administrators or teachers to determine the content of the social studies curriculum. This practice has stripped teachers of their professional expertise, turning them into technicians who follow the curriculum represented by the textbook. The message of the current book is both an antidote and a refutation of this brazen attack.

This book is both an update and a revision. Originally published in 1988, it is long overdue. In 1995, Shirley Engle died and I developed some chronic health issues. These events delayed completion of this volume. This new version includes scholarship that is more recent and also represents some changes in this author's thinking. Whether Shirley Engle would have agreed with such changes is unknown, but he was not one to ignore new evidence or new reasoning out-of-hand. This volume gives stronger emphasis to social justice, to pluralism and global perspectives and to democratic school and classroom climate concept. Democratic citizenship is set in a universal context where each of us is primarily, a member of the human species with whom we share profound similarities. Concern for the welfare of others on this planet stems from this recognition.

The first edition, well received by our colleagues, to this day remains one of more frequently cited references in the field. I have tried to maintain as many of Shirley Engle's words as possible and have missed deeply the opportunity to interact with his intellect. As those who knew him are well aware, once he was persuaded intellectually, Shirley became robustly passionate about his views. Without question, his spirit permeates this work.

—Anna S. Ochoa-Becker

GRADUAL STEPS TOWARD IMPLEMENTATION

For Teachers and Administrators

No matter how long or how hard the journey, it begins with a single step.
—Old Chinese proverb

This traditional piece of wisdom may have been first used by those people who started to build the Great Wall of China. However, it applies to curriculum change as well.

This curriculum will mean that you and your student-citizens will think and act differently from some of the routines to which you have become accustomed. We all know that habits are hard to break. However, when the goal is worth it, most human beings change and take that first step if necessary. "To prepare strong citizens for a democracy is a stronger democracy" is indisputably a worthy goal for every social studies educator.

FOR TEACHERS

The following suggestions are provided for a single teacher, a pair of teachers or a department of social studies teachers:

Democratic Education for Social Studies, pages 315–320
Copyright © 2007 by Information Age Publishing

The First Task

Think about your present classes and the curriculum you provide for them.

What is your teaching like?
What do students do?
What do students expect in your class?
What do you expect of them?
What knowledge is emphasized?
What abilities are promoted?

For each teacher and each class the answers will be different. However, your answers will provide an understanding of where your "journey" is starting.

Then, assuming that you have read both this book and this Appendix, identify an aspect of this curriculum that would be the easiest for you to try and the most interesting for your students to experience. As you do this, you are identifying your *first teaching step.* (I make this point because I believe that all of us are encouraged when our attempts to do something a bit different go well and for continued change, some feeling of success is very important. Though, your first trial may not go perfectly, you will learn more from it if, from an overall perspective, it is received well by the young citizens in your class. Therefore, for your first try, do not pick the class (section) that has been the most challenging for you. Select that class (section) that has been most responsive and involved. Even limited success makes it easier to examine our strengths and weaknesses. Just as importantly, the class should experience your first step as positively as possible.

I want to emphasize that even the most courageous among you, must not try to implement the entire curriculum as a first step. One step at a time, allows you to try on a teaching style examine it and think through ways to improve it? I also want to suggest that working in pairs or with another teacher of your choice, is likely to be the most productive arrangement in implementing something new. You can think through what you will do together and arrange to sit in and observe each other's classes in order to provide feedback. I strongly suggest that you use Appendix II *The Reflective Teaching Observation Instrument* selecting those parts of it that apply to the change that represents the "startup" you have chosen. A fellow teacher is a much preferred source of feedback to a supervisor or administrator. If a teacher goes it alone, he or she will forego some of these advantages. However, some teachers prefer to work alone.

What part of this Issues-Centered Decision Making Curriculum would feel most comfortable to you and your students? In other words, where and when would you find your best chances of succeeding? This is the fundamental question for those interested in finding and trying their first step. Some possible responses are:

1. With the ongoing subject matter that the class is now studying, apply the probing questions that are presented in Chapter 5. The most important question may be "Do you think this statement, drawn from their textbook, is true?" This is an *evidence* question that is central to the understanding that just because something is in print does not mean it is true or that it represents the whole truth.

2. A Project that represents a change in the kind of assignments young citizens experience. If a teacher chooses to replace his or her usual way of evaluating student citizens with a Project (as described in Chapter 9), he or she will provide them with an opportunity to actually use the knowledge they have studied and their intellects to create a meaningful product that they can present to others. The teacher, preferably with class input, needs to decide the kinds of options available.

If the class has been studying the American Revolution, possible options may be:

(a) Creating a short skit that depicts the mixed feelings of the colonists, who were mostly British subjects, about participating in a revolution against their mother country where they still have relatives and friends. This would require a 4-5 student group.

(b) A debate that may have taken place between two colonists who felt the revolution had to happen and that the independence of the colonies was necessary if the colonists were to be able to control the quality of their lives without being exploited (taxed, required to feed and house British soldiers in their homes etc.). Another two student-citizens would take the side of the United Empire Loyalists who were planning to leave the colonies rather than fight against the British soldiers from their motherland.

(c) A discussion between Thomas Jefferson and Benjamin Franklin about the importance of independence for the colonies. This could involve two student-citizens discussing the possibility of the Bill of Rights and what it should address.

Obviously other examples could be generated. These examples should clarify how projects provide opportunities for more meaningful understanding of what is learned. They also integrate knowledge with intellectual processes and make some use of the knowledge learned rather than just memorizing it. These assignments can be an enjoyable learning experience. More than one group of students could choose any of the options available or suggest one of their own.

The first time this is done, the teacher could create a set of criteria that will be used to evaluate the projects. In future efforts, the class with guidance from the teacher, should participate in setting the criteria and eventually all class members can rate the projects presented to the class.

These latter steps of involving the class in the setting of criteria and rating their peers' presentations represent the beginning of altering class climate from one that is totally controlled by the teacher to one where there is a more shared (more democratic) control and decision making with the students.

Note: At the outset of such classroom changes, the teacher(s) involved should inform their department chair and/or their principal. This procedure is suggested not because what is presented here is controversial (it is not) but, those responsible for the school should know what is happening in their classrooms.

Subsequent steps in implementing this curriculum depend on how the teacher and students responded to the first steps. Some feedback from the class is in order. As the teacher and the class are ready, they may identify some issues that they are interested in that they would like to discuss more fully. Some class time where they can think about and suggest ideas is necessary after which they should have a day or two to think about it before each student identifies their preference and those preferences are submitted to the teacher.

FOR DEPARTMENT CHAIRS AND ADMINISTRATORS

Your support of your teachers as they take the initial steps to implement this curriculum in their classes is crucial. Moreover, this curriculum requires action on the part of the school administration as well. Otherwise, the climate in the school is likely to contradict the democratic emphasis that emphasizes democratic values in your social studies classrooms. Some of our strongest research supports the climate of the school as a significant dimension of the curriculum and the learning experiences of young citizens (Hahn, 1996).

It may be useful for you to lay out a possible 3-5 year plan with an elected committee of teachers with recognition that implementation may move more slowly or more quickly depending on your assessment of how each phase of your plan worked effectively.

The goal for administrators is to make the climate and the governance of the school as democratic as possible. This condition will provide young citizens opportunities to observe and participate in making the school more democratic.

First Steps

You may wish to start with limited changes depending on the on-going practices in your school. These changes might include volunteers to assist in the school office and library but, you may wish to work toward having an elected committee of students review school rules on an annual basis and possibly suggest changes that are reviewed by an elected faculty committee as well as the Student Council. This procedure would begin to make school governance a shared experience between professionals and the student body and the Student Council becomes more than the window-dressing it often is. This activity should result in recommended changes (policy) that receive serious consideration by the school's adult personnel. When changes may affect the cafeteria, maintenance staff and the like, these changes should be reviewed by them.

You may wish to draw up a 3–5 year plan in concert with an elected faculty committee and take the plan to the school district's school board for their information. This effort represents curriculum change at its best. It recommends the participation of the professional personnel of the school give consideration to more democratic school-wide practices that recapture the fundamental purpose of public schools to preserve self-governance. We all want the schools to prepare strong democratic citizens who will continue to improve social conditions that extend democratic values more fully in the interests of social justice and the common good. See Chapters 10 and 11 for an expansion of these ideas.

Giving teachers, school personnel and students the opportunity to provide input and make recommendations are at the foundation of a school that wants to claim it is democratic. Sharing power with all of these groups relies on trust that they can make responsible decisions. At the same time, all participants should recognize that they can make mistakes that they need to own up to and subject to vigorous analysis and revision. Such is the nature of democracy.

If educators implement this curriculum fully, it will result in a greater number of citizens who are informed, thoughtful and willing to participate in the improvement of this democracy. Such improvement includes attention to the quality of life for marginal peoples that requires more vigorous application of social justice values such as fairness, equity, equality, freedom and concern for the common good.

Note: Administrators and Department Chairs need to assume responsibility of informing the school board of the direction of curriculum change involved in this curriculum. In doing so, they need to obtain the approval of an academic freedom policy that supports the study of controversial issues. To do so, when no community controversy exists, is far preferable than trying to deal with an issue in progress.

A REFLECTIVE TEACHING OBSERVATION INSTRUMENT

Note: I have included this instrument to assist educators who implement this curriculum in the classroom. It was developed by Ed Jadallah (1985), as a doctoral student at The Ohio State University and who is now on the faculty at the University of Maine.

I encourage those beginning to implement this curriculum to review this instrument carefully. While it is consistent with the proposed curriculum, it has a few variations. This version of the instrument exemplifies the process of investigation for drawing conclusions about the validity of knowledge. The same process applies to decisions where values are central to the process and to the decision. With the approval of Professor Jadallah I have made a few adaptations to the Instrument.

Finally, if teachers have their class sessions videotaped or observed by another teacher, they can review their teaching as well as student responses with this instrument in hand.

This checklist is derived and adapted from Edward Jadallah, *The Development of a Reflective Teaching Instrument.* Columbus, Ohio: Ohio State University, 1985 (unpublished doctoral dissertation).

*   *   *

Democratic Education for Social Studies, pages 321–328
Copyright © 2007 by Information Age Publishing
321

THE TEACHING PROCESS

Identifying an Issue

To what extent does the teacher:

1. *Ask divergent questions to identify an issue?*

   The teacher asks questions that confront students with issue situations. Divergent questions allow for a variety of answers. The teacher does not seek a single "right" answer, only plausible and sometimes, best responses. The teacher may ask, for example, "How might the United States improve relations with France? What do you think might happen if the United States builds a wall on the U.S.–Mexican border to prevent the entry on illegal aliens? What effect will the war in Iraq have the relationships between other nations in the Mideast and the United States?

2. *Use materials to introduce conflicting data?*

   The teacher uses newspapers, books, magazines, pictures, recordings, autographs, or other means that guide students to identify or discover an issue. For example, the teacher may read aloud two conflicting editorials on the subject of the new drunk driving laws. The teacher may also show pictures that illustrate both impoverished and wealthy lifestyles within the same city.

3. *Ask probing questions that identify inconsistencies or contradictions in the beliefs, opinions or ideas of students?*

   The teacher, after listening to a student express a belief, asks a question focusing on other beliefs that may either be consistent with or contradictory to the first belief. For example, the teacher may hear students concur that "Any form of censorship is unconstitutional and it's the government's responsibility to protect our freedom of speech." The teacher then asks the students, "Do you feel it is all right to spend tax dollars to provide protection for the American Nazi Party to hold a rally in Skokie, Illinois?" Students who disagree with tax monies spent in this manner or who feel that Nazis should be allowed in America, are forced to re-evaluate the first belief. Thus, an issue is identified for class investigation.

4. *Ask students to state the issue or question in their own words?*

   The teacher, after initiating the problem situation asks probing questions to help students narrow the focus of the investigation. For example, the teacher might ask, "What do you see as the problem? Can you phrase this problem as a question? What are some of the specific questions that you think need to be answered in order to improve or solve this problem?"

5. *Ask students to define ambiguous or new terms to help make the problem clear and precise?*

The teacher asks questions about specific terms that may need to be defined and clarified so that the issue/question is clearly understood by all students. For example, if the issue/question to be investigated was; 'What effect has technology had on American lifestyles?", the meaning of "technology" and "lifestyles" may need to be precisely defined in the context of the investigation. The teacher could ask, "What kind of technology are we talking about? What do you mean by lifestyles? Are you referring to our present lifestyles, or those in the future or the past?"

Developing Hypotheses

To what extent does the teacher:

6. *Present students with a hypothesis to test?*

The teacher foregoes having students identify a problem and instead, gives them a predetermined hypothesis that they can test against evidence. For example, the teacher might read a quote from a book, newspaper, or magazine to support or refute with evidence.

7. *Ask divergent questions to solicit hypotheses?*

The teacher asks questions that require students to offer an opinion or hypothesis about possible solutions to an issue/question. Student responses are usually based on past learning or personal experiences. For example, the teacher may ask questions like: What are some possible causes of the Vietnam War? What effect may the present Iraq War have on other nations in the Mideast? Should the President of the United States meet with the President of North Korea?

8. *Present data and then ask questions to solicit hypotheses?*

The teacher presents newspapers, books, magazines, pictures, recordings, word lists, diaries or other data sources that can be used to generate hypotheses. The teacher then asks questions that require students to make inferences, projections, and classifications or to state relationships. This may be done on an individual basis or in small or large group sessions.

The questions asked by the teacher may be phrased in the following manner: What do these pictures indicate about life in China? Based on these newspaper clippings who do you think will win the Democratic Part's nomination? Why did Ben Franklin make this comment in his diary?

9. *Ask probing questions to help students identify sources that could be used to identify and locate could be used to generate hypotheses.*

   The teacher, after having students identify and clarify an issue/question asks them questions that will guide them to sources that relate to the issue/question? For example, a teacher may ask "Where could we find more information about the Native Americans? How could the Museum of History help us find out more about Native Americans? Can you think of what might identify useful websites or other resources that could provide information that would answer our issue/questions?

10. *Provide time for students to gather sources and formulate hypotheses?*

    The teacher, once students have identified reasonable and accessible sources, encourages students to locate these sources and investigate them for hypotheses related to the issue/question. For example, the teacher may allow students to gather information in a library or browse through materials that are already available in the classroom.

11. *Ask students to suggest possible evidence that might support or refute their hypotheses.*

    The teacher, once students have formulated clearly defined hypotheses, asks them to determine what kind of evidence they would expect to exist if their hypotheses were true and if their hypotheses were false. For example, the teacher may ask "What evidence would you need to find to help you prove the hypothesis that the most early settlers were farmers? What evidence would suggest that most early settlers were not farmers?"

12. *Ask probing questions to help students identify and locate supportive and non-supportive evidence?*

    The teacher, after having students identify supportive and non-supportive evidence, will ask questions that will guide them to sources that relate to the evidence they are looking for. For example, a teacher may ask, "Where could we find evidence about the occupations of early immigrants? What kind of books might we refer to? Can you think of any other sources or places that might tell us about the occupations of early immigrants? Can we identify some websites that would help?" (The teacher could distribute a list that could be helpful).

13. *Provide time for students to locate sources and gather evidence?*

    The teacher, once students have identified reasonable and accessible sources allows them to locate these sources and investigate them for evidence related to the hypotheses being tested. For example, the teacher may allow students to conduct a survey, interview people, gather information in a library, pull up websites and use materials that are already provided in the classroom.

14. *Present data and then ask questions that require students to test their hypotheses.*

The teacher presents data sources that can be used to generate evidence that supports and/or refutes the hypotheses. The teacher then asks questions that require students to identify supportive and non-supportive evidence, evaluate the validity of the evidence and its source, and state relationships between the evidence and the hypotheses. For example, the teacher may say, "Read this letter written by Benjamin Franklin. Can you find evidence that supports or refutes our hypothesis about slavery in Colonial America? Do you think the information contained in this letter is accurate? How can you be sure?

15. *Asking probing questions which lead students to evaluate the validity of the evidence they have collected.*

The teacher, once students have collected evidence to support or refute their hypotheses, may ask them to prove that the evidence collected is factual, not just opinions, biases or assumptions. For example, the teacher may ask, "What other sources have you found that supports this evidence? Have you compared this evidence with other sources? What did you find out? Is this evidence current? Who wrote it? When was it written and why? Is your evidence consistent?

16. *Ask questions that require students how to relate the evidence to the hypotheses being tested.*

The teacher will ask students how the evidence they have collected either supports or refutes the hypotheses being tested. For example, the teacher may ask, "What evidence did you find that provides support for the hypothesis that the early settlers were farmers? Why do you think that this evidence actually proves that they were farmers? What evidence did you find that might refute our hypotheses.

Developing Conclusions

To what extent does the teacher:

17. *Ask students questions that require students to state conclusions concerning the issue/question based upon the valid and invalid hypotheses they have tested?*

The teacher, after students have tested their hypotheses, will ask divergent and evaluative questions to guide students in developing conclusions. For example, the teacher may ask, "What hypotheses provided an accurate view of the negative effects technology has had on the lifestyles of people who live in the United States? What evidence do you have that supports this conclusion? What can we definitely state about the effects of technology?

Applying Conclusions to New Data

To what extent does the teacher:

18. *Present new data and ask students to find evidence that supports or refutes their conclusions?*

    The teacher introduces new data that is relevant to the initial issue/question but has not been used by students to develop their conclusions. The teacher will ask the students how the new data either supports or refutes their conclusion. For example, the teacher may introduce two medical journals and ask. "What evidence can you find that provides support for the conclusion that advanced technology has increased our life expectancy?"

CLASSROOM CLIMATE

Facilitating an Open Discussion

1. *Arrange chairs in seminar or small-group style?*

   The teachers ask students to arrange the chairs in a circle or semicircle so that communication between students and the teacher will be face-to-face, or the teacher has already done so.

2. *Direct student-to-student interaction?*

   The teacher asks students to comment on each other's opinions and ideas. For example, the teacher may say, "John said that Abraham Lincoln used the issue of slavery merely to further his political career. He, in John's opinion, was a political opportunist. How do the rest of you feel about this statement?

3. *Direct the discussion to many students, not just a few?*

   The teacher asks questions and solicits opinion from a wide variety of students to ensure that a few students do not monopolize the discussion.

4. *Talk briefly or stop so the she or he does not monopolize the discussion?*

The teacher makes most explanations, reviews and responses to student questions or comments brief and to the point. He or she deliberately pauses and provides time for students to respond and ask questions.

The teacher may directly solicit comments and questions from students or may pause for a while and give some nonverbal cue to students indicating they are invited to begin discussion.

5. *Allow time for students to reflect on the issue/question being discussed?*

The teacher deliberately pauses after important comments or questions to give allow students time to think. The teacher may say to students, "Let's stop and think about this for a while," or "This requires serious consideration. Let's think before we make any hasty judgments."

6. *Point out what is relevant and non-relevant in the discussion?*

The teacher deliberately draws the attention of students to those aspects of the discussion that are important and relevant and courteously draws attention from irrelevant discussion. The teacher may say, for example, "That is a very important observation. Let's pursue it further." In the case of an irrelevant comment, the teacher may say, "That is an interesting comment, but let's redirect our attention to the main topic."

Empathy and Acceptance

To what extent does the teacher:

7. *Give examples that relate to what the student is saying?*

The teacher describes or explains a similar instance related to what a student has just described or explained.

8. *Listen attentively and without interrupting while students express their ideas, opinions and questions?*

The teacher pays close attention to what students are saying and provides nonverbal cues such as nodding their head and maintaining eye contact to encourage continuation of expression.

9. *Provide students with corrective feedback in a non-threatening manner?*

The teacher uses data to help students discover that what they are saying may be wrong. Rather than presenting herself or himself as the authority on the subject, the teacher directs the student to data sources that contradict what the student is saying. The teacher then asks students to explain the contradiction. This procedure allows students to retain the integrity of changing their own minds and keeps the quest for knowledge in a spirit of reflective thinking.

10. *Make remarks which indicate that the student's comments are appreciated, accepted and subject to analysis?*

The teacher provides students with positive feedback when they participate in discussions and at the same time facilitates a critique of analysis of their comments. The teacher might say, for example, "Thanks for the interesting observation. You seem to have done a lot of reading on the subject. Let's examine how your ideas compare with others in the class or with experts in the field."

11. *Redirect the focus of the discussion when a student appears to be uncomfortable or self-conscious.*

The teacher, on observing a student's reaction to a question or comment, provides the student with an option not to answer the question at all or not offer a comment. The teacher may say, for example, "Think about it for a while and I'll get back to you," or the teacher may direct a question to the whole class, "What do the rest of you think about…?"

Establishing and Maintaining Rapport with Students

To what extent does the teacher:

12. *Make non-threatening humorous remarks when relevant?*

The teacher eases the tension of a discussion or relaxes students prior to a discussion with a humorous anecdote.

13. *Address students by their names and friendly mannerisms such as a smile, approving nods, pats on the back, and so forth?*

The teacher conveys to students through verbal and nonverbal signs that they are liked and that their participation in class is respected and appreciated.

Note: This check list covers the main aspects of reflection and emphasizes the use of *probing questions* as imperative to the entire process of reflective thought.

HOW DEMOCRATIC SHOULD A HIGH SCHOOL BE?

Please check the statements which you agree should be a high school practice. Please cross off those statements that you judge should not be a high school practice.

The purpose of these questions is to help clarify how democratic faculty and administrators want the school to be.

1. High school students, through their duly elected representatives meeting as a Student Council, should make decisions about student matters (for example. What activities the school will sanction and when and where they will occur.

2. High school students should have one or more seats on most school committees to insure that the student views on issues are considered before decisions are made.

3. A serious infraction of high school rules should be considered by a duly constituted panel of students who hear the case and decide on an appropriate punishment.

4. High school students, working with their permanent faculty advisors, should play the major role in determining the shape of their individual academic programs.

5. High school students should hold a majority on all school committees, except those dealing with budgetary and personnel matters.

Democratic Education for Social Studies, pages 329–330
Copyright © 2007 by Information Age Publishing
All rights of reproduction in any form reserved.

6. High school students should hold a strong voting majority on all school committees including those reviewing candidates for teaching positions.

7. A high school should have regularly scheduled (weekly?) all-school meetings, led by students, at which students and faculty can discuss matters of school-wide interest.

8. Students should have an equal voice with the faculty in defining the school's graduation requirements.

9. A high school should operate on a "consensus" model, with students and teachers having an equal say in deciding how the school should function. All decisions must conform to school board policy.

10. A high school should have a procedure that enables individual students (or teachers) to propose a "day of dialogue" on an issue—for example, the war on terrorism—that is of immediate concern. If the school community deems the proposal to have sufficient merit, a school day is set aside to discuss that issue.

11. If the outcome of the "day of dialogue" is a clearly stated position that is the consensus view of the school community, the high school should be able to advocate that view publicly, working collectively to make it a reality.

Note: This questionnaire was developed by Professor Tom Gregory, School of Education, Indiana University, Bloomington, Indiana. Its intended use was to have faculty and administrators clarify the extent to which they were willing to give up their authority to allow students influence in shaping the nature of school climate. It is an unpublished paper and is used with Professor Gregory's permission.

REFERENCES

Abraham Lincoln: A leader of honor. (2001). [Abraham Lincoln Website.] Retrieved February 13, 2002 from the World Wide Web: http://www.abrahamlincoln.cc/

Adler, S. A.(1991). The Education of Social Studies Teachers. In J.P. Shaver, (Ed.) *Handbook of* Research on Social Studies Teaching and Learning. New York: Macmillan. 210–221.

Adler, S.A. (1993). The social studies methods course instructor: Practitioner researcher. *The International Journal of Social Education, 7*(3), 39–47.

Adler, S. (2001). Education students to be effective participatory citizens. *The social studies Professional. (Newsletter).* National Council for the Social Studies. 3.

Adler, S. (2003). The president's message. *The Social Studies Professional (Newsletter).* Washington, DC: National Council for the Social Studies.2

Amedeo, J. (2002). *Civic knowledge and engagement: An IEA study of upper secondary students in sixteen countries.* Amsterdam: IEA.

American Library Association. (2004). *The most frequently challenged books of 2004.* ALA website: http://www.ala.org/ala/oif/bannedbooksweek/challengedbanned/challengedbanned.htm#mfcb. [Retrieved August 2004].

American Federation of Teachers (2004). *NCLB: Its problems, its promise.* http://www.aft.org/pubs-reports/index.htm

Anderson, C., Nickles, S.K., & Crawford, A.B. (1994). Global understandings: A framework for teaching and learning. Alexandria, VA: Association for Supervision and Curriculum Development.

Anderson, L. (1979). *Schooling and citizenship in a global age. An exploration of the meaning and significance of global education.* Bloomington, IN: Mid-America Program for Global Perspectives in Education. Social Studies Development Center.

Anderson, L. (1990). A rationale for global education. In Tye, K.A. (Ed.) *Global education: From thought to Action.* Alexandria, VA.: Association for Supervision and Curriculum Development, 13–34.

Angell, A. (1991). Democratic classrooms in elementary school classrooms: A review of theory and research. *Theory and Research in Social Education, 19*(3), 241–266.

Democratic Education for Social Studies, pages 331–346
Copyright © 2007 by Information Age Publishing
All rights of reproduction in any form reserved.

Anyon, J. (1980). Social class and the hidden curriculum of work. *Journal of Education, 162*(1), 67–92.

Apple, M.W. (1982). *Education and power.* Boston: Routledge & Kegan Paul.

Arnold, R.L. (1969). The goal:Educating for human becoming. In T.F. Powell (Ed.) *Humanities and the Social Studies,* Bulletin no. 44. Washington D.C: National Council for the Social Studies.

Atkinson, B. (Ed.). (1937). *Walden and other writings of Henry David Thoreau.* New York: The Modern Library.

Bahmueller, C.F., & Patrick, J.J. (1999). *Principles and practices of education for democratic citizenship: International perspectives and projects.* Bloomington, IN: ERIC Clearinghouse for Social Studies/Social Science Education. (ERIC Document Reproduction Service No. ED 434 866).

Baldi, S., Peri, M. Skidmore, D.,. Greenberg, E. (2001). *What democracy means to ninth graders: U.S. State results from the international IEA Civic Education Study.* (NCES 2001-096) U.S. Department of Education Statistics, Washington, DC: U.S. Government Printing Office.

Banks, J.A. (1991). Multicultural education: Its effects on students' racial and gender role attitudes. In Shaver, J.P. (Ed.), *Handbook of Research on Social Studies Teaching and Learning: A Project of the National Council for the Social Studies.* New York: MacMillan, 459–469.

Banks, J.A. (1991). *Multiethnic guidelines.* Washington DC: National Council for the Social Studies.

Banks, J.A. (2000). *Cultural diversity and education: Foundations, curriculum, and teaching.* New York: Allyn & Bacon.

Banks, J.A. & Banks, C.A.M. (1993). Social studies teacher education, ethnic diversity, and academic achievement. *The International Journal of Social Education, 7*(3), 24–38.

Banks, J.A. & Banks, C.A.M. (2005a). *A handbook of research on multicultural education* (second edition). San Francisco: Jossey-Bass.

Banks, J.A. (2005b). *Democracy and diversity: Principles and concepts for educating citizens in a global age.* Seattle, WA:The Center for Multicultural Education, University of Washington.

Barber, B.R. (1992). *An aristocracy of everyone.* New York: Times Books.

Barber, B.R. (1995). *Jihad vs. mcworld.* New York: Times Books.

Barber, B.R. (1998). *A place for us: How to make society civil and democracy strong.* New York: Hill and Wang.

Barth, J., & Shermis, S. (1979). Defining social problems. *Theory and Practice in Social Education, 7*(1), 1–19.

Barton, K.C. & Levstik, L.C. (2004). *Teaching history for the common good: Theory and research for teaching about the past.* Malway, NJ: Eribaum.

Bass, S.J. (2001). *Blessed are the peacemakers: Martin Luther King, Jr., eight white religious leaders, and the "Letter from Birmingham Jail."* Baton Rouge, La: Louisiana State University Press.

Beck, T. A. (2005). Tools of deliberation: Exploring the complexity of learning to lead elementary civics discussion. *Theory and Research in Social Education, 33*(1), 103–119.

Becker, C.L. (1936). *Everyman his own historian.* New York: F.S. Crofts & Co.

Becker, J. M. & Wojtan, N. (1983). *Parallel passages: A comparison of Japanese and U.S. textbooks.* Bloomington, IN: Social Studies Development Center, Indiana University.

Becker, J.M. (2002). International and global education: Ever the twain shall meet? *International Social Studies Forum, 26*(1), 51–59.

Belenky, M.F., Clinchy, B., Goldberger, N., & Tarule, J. (1997). *Women's ways of knowing: The development of self, voice, and mind* (10th anniversary ed.). New York: Basic Books.

Benne, K. D., Axtelle, G. E., Smith, B. O., & Raup, B. (1943). *The improvement of practical intelligence.* New York: Harper and Brothers.

Bennett, C. (2005) *Comprehensive Multicultural education: Theory and practice.* (5th ed.) Boston: Allyn and Bacon.

Berman, S., & LaFarge, P. (Eds.). (1993). *Promising practices in teaching social responsibility.* Albany, NY: State University of New York.

Berti, A. & Andriolo, A. (2001). Third graders' understanding of core political concepts (law, nation-state, and government) before and after teaching. *Genetic, Social and General Psychology Monographs, 127*(4), 346–377.

Bickmore, K. Elementary c about conflict resolution: Can children handle global politics? *Theory and Research in Social Education, 27*(1), 45–69.

Bloom, L.R. (1998). The politics of difference and multicultural feminism: Reconceptualizing education for democracy. *Theory and Research in Social Education, 26*(1), 30–49.

Brandhorst, A.R. (1992). Foreign policy issues: A high school application of the Engle and Ochoa reflective teaching model. *Social Studies, 83* (3). (pages needed)

Brandhorst, A.R. (2004). Identity-centered conflict, authority, and dogmatism: Challenges to the design of social studies curriculum. *Theory and Research in Social Education, 32*(1), 10–23.

Bridges, D. (1991). *The socio-psychological perspective.* Lanham: University Press of America, Inc.

Brown, L.R., Renner, M., & Halweil, B. (2000). *Vital signs 2000: The environmental trends that are shaping our future.* New York: W.W. Norton.

Bruner, J. (1962). *The process of education.* Cambridge, MA: Harvard University.

Bruner, J.S. (1965). *Man: A course of study.* Occasional Paper No. 3. Washington, DC: National Science Foundation. (Available from ERIC, Document #ED178390).

Bruner, J. (1965). *On knowing: Essays for the left hand.* New York: Atheneum.

Bruner, J.S. (1972). *Culture, politics & pedagogy.* In Ronald Shinn (Ed.), Culture & the school, New York: MacMillan. 42–53.

Burbules, N.C. (1993). *Dialogue in teaching.* New York: Teachers College Press.

Burke-Hengen, M., & Gillespie, T. (Eds.). (1995). *Building community: Social studies in the middle school years.* Portsmouth, N.H.: Heinemann.

Butts, R.F. (1989). *"What should the schools teach?"* Bloomington, IN: Phi Delta Kappa.

Center for Responsive Politics. (2006a). *2004 Presidential Election.* [Homepage of the Center for Responsive Politics]. Retrieved July 5, 2006 from the World Wide Web: http:// www.opensecrets.org/presidential/index.asp

Center for Responsive Politics. (2002). *2000 Presidential Race. Source of Funds.* [Homepage of the Center for Responsive Politics). Retrieved March 19, 2002 from: http://www.opensecrets.org/2000elect/source/AllCands.htm

Chapin, J.R. (2005). Voting and continuing volunteer participation of 1988 eighth grade social studies students 12 years later. *Theory and Research in Social Education.* 33 (2) 200–217.

Cherryholmes, C. (1999). *Reading pragmatism.* New York: Teachers College Press.

Cogan, J. & Kubow, P. (1997). *Multidimensional citizenship: Educational policy for the 21st century.* Tokyo: Sasakawa Peace Foundation.

Commager, H.S. (1966). Should the historian make moral judgment? *American Heritage,* 17, 26–27, 87–93.

Cornbleth, C. & Waugh, Dexter. (1995) *The Great Speckled Bird: Multicultural politics and education policy.* New York: St. Martin's Press.

Cornbleth, C. (1998). An American curriculum? *Teachers College Record,* 99(4), 622–646.

Cornbleth, C. (2001). Climates of constraints/restraints on teachers and teaching. In W.B. Stanley (Ed.). *Critical issues in social studies research for the 21st century.* Greenwich, CT: Information Age Publishing, 73–96.

Cronkite, W. (1996). *A Reporter's Life. New York: Random House.*

Daley J.K. (1991). The influence of administrators on the teaching of social studies. *Theory and Research in Social Education, 19*(3), 267–282.

Dewey, J. (1922). *Human nature and conduct: An introduction to social psychology.* New York: Modern Library

Dewey, J. (1933). *How we think.* Boston: D.C. Heath.

Dickens, C. (1859). *A tale of two cities.* Boston: Books, Inc.

Diem, R. (2006). A positive or negative force for democracy: The technology instructional paradise. *The International Journal of Social Education, 21*(1), 148–154.

Douglas, W. O. in Ochoa, A. (1979). N.C.S.S. Presidential Speech in Previte, M. A. & Sheehan, J. (Eds.). (2002). NCSS Presidential Speeches, Volume 2, p. 146. N.C.S.S., ERIC Clearinghouse for Social Studies. Bloomington, IN: Social Studies Development Center.

Douglass, F. (1995) *Narrative of the life of Frederick Douglass.* New York: Dover.

Doyle, R.P. (2004). *Banned books: Resource book.* American Library Association.

Dufour, J. (2005). Nobel Laureate Mohamed ElBaradei: Preventing nuclear proliferation peacefully. *Social Education, 70*(1), 14–18.

Dumas, W. (1993). Preparation of social studies teachers at major research universities. *The International Journal of Social Education, 7*(3), 59–65.

Dunfee, M.(1970). *Social studies for the real world.* Columbus, OH: Merrill.

Easton, D. & Easton, J. The child's acquisition of regime norms: Political efficacy. *The Political Science Review, 61,* 25–38.

Ehman, L. (1969). An analysis of the relationship of selected educational variables with the political socialization of high school students. *American Educational Research Journal,* 6(4), 559–580.

Ehman, L. (1977). Research on social studies curriculum and instruction: Values. In Hunkins. F.P. (Ed.), Review of research in social studies education,

1970–1975 Bulletin 49. Washington, DC: National Council for the Social Studies. 55–95.

Ehman, L. (1980).The American school in the political socialization process. *Review of Educational Research, 50,* 99–109.

Elliott, D.L., Nagel, K.C., & Woodward, A. (1985). Do textbooks belong in elementary schools? *Educational Leadership, 42*(7), 22–26.

Engle, S. (1960). Decision making: The heart of social studies instruction. *Social Education, 24*(7), 301–304, 306.

Engle, S.H. (1982, Fall). Alan Griffin (1907–1964). *Journal of Thought, 17,* 45–54.

Engle, S.H. (1986).Late night thoughts about the new social studies. *Social Education, 50*(1), 20–30.

Engle, S. H. & Ochoa, (1988). A. S. *Education for democratic citizenship: Decision making in the social studies.* New York and London: Teachers College Press.

Epstein, T. (2000). Adolescents' perspectives on racial diversity in U.S. history: Case studies from an urban classroom. *American Educational Research Journal, 37*(1), 185–214.

Evans, R. (2004). *The war on social studies: What should we teach the children?* New York: Teachers College Press.

Evans, R., Avery, P.G., & Pedersen, P. (2000). *Taboo topics: Cultural restraint on teaching social issues.* The Clearing House, *73*(5), 295–301.

Evans, R. W. & Saxe, D.W. (Eds.) (1996). *The handbook on teaching social issues.* Bulletin 93. Washington, DC: National Council for the Social Studies.

Federal Election Commission. (2006). *Voter registration and turnout 2004.* Homepage of the Federal Election Commission. Retrieved July 5, 2006 from: http://www.fec.gov/finance/disclosure/srssea.shtml

Fenton, E.F. (1967). *The new social studies.* New York: Holt, Rinehart & Winston.

Fitzgerald, Frances.(1980). *America Revised.* New York: A.A.Knopf.

Flinders, D.J. (December, 2006). Adolescents talk about the war in Iraq. *Phi Delta Kappan, 87*(4), 320–323.

Foner, E. (1998). *The story of American freedom.* New York: W.W. Norton.

Foreign Policy Association (1969) *Dangerous Parallels: A Simulation Game.* Chicago: Scott Foresman.

Frank, A. (1958). *Anne Frank: The diary of a young girl.* New York: Pocket Books.

Franken, A. (2003). *Lies and the lying liars who tell them: A fair and balanced look at the right.* New York: Penguin Group (USA) Inc.

Freire, P. (2001). *Pedagogy of the oppressed* (30th Anniversary Edition) (N.B. Ramos, Trans.). New York: Continuum. (Original work published 1970).

Friedman, T.L. (1999). *The Lexus and the olive tree: Understanding globalization.* New York: Farrar, Strauss, and Giroux.

Friedman, T.L. (2005). *The world is flat: A brief history of the twenty-first century.* New York: Farrar, Strauss, and Giroux.

Gardner, H. (1993). *Frames of mind: The theory of multiple intelligences* (10th anniversary ed.). New York: Basic Books.

Bill and Melinda Gates Foundation. Grantee Profile.Bill and Melinda Gates Foundation. www.gatesfoundation.org. [Retrieved June 12, 2005].

Gay, G. (2000). *Culturally responsive teaching: Theory, research and practice.* New York: Teachers College Press.

Gilligan, C. (1993). *In a different voice: Psychological theory and women's development.* Cambridge, MA: Harvard University.

Gilligan, C., McLean, J. & Sullivan, A. (1997). *Between voice and silence: Women and girls, race and relationship.* Boston: President and Fellows of Harvard College.

Giroux, H.A. (1992). *Border crossings: Cultural workers and the politics of education.* New York: Routledge.

Glenn, A.D. (1972). Elementary school children's attitudes toward politics. In B.G. Massiala (Ed.), *Political youth, political schools: National and international perspectives.* Englewood Cliffs, NJ: Prentice-Hall.

Glenn, A.D. (1990). Interactive video technology: Its status and future in the social sciences. *International Journal of Social Education, 5*(1), 74–84.

Glenn, A.D. (1997) Technology and the Continuing Education of Classroom Teachers. *Peabody Journal of Education, 72*(1), 122–128.

Gonzales, M.H., Riedel, E., Williamson, I., Avery, P., Sullivan, J., Bos, A. (2004). Variations of citizenship education: A content analysis of rights, obligations, and participation concepts in high school civics textbooks. *Theory and Research in Social Education, 32*(3), 301–325.

Goodlad, J.I. (1984). *A place called school. Prospects for the future.* New York: McGraw-Hill.

Goodlad, J.I. (1990). *Teachers for our nation's schools.* San Francisco: Jossey-Bass, Inc.

Goodman, J. (1988). Constructing a practical philosophy of teaching: A case study and critical analysis. *Teaching and Teaching Education: An International Journal of Research Studies, 4*(2), 23–41.

Goodman, J. & Adler, S. (1985). Becoming and elementary social studies teacher. *Theory and Research in Social Education, 13*(2), 1–24.

Gordimer, N. (1981). *July's people.* New York: Viking.

Gregory, T.B. & Smith, G.R.(1987). *High schools as communities: The small school reconsidered.* Bloomington, IN: Phi Delta Kappa.

Greene, M. (1978). *Landscapes of learning.* New York: Teachers College Press.

Greene, M. (2001). *Variations on a blue guitar: The Lincoln Center Institute lectures on aesthetic education.* New York: Teachers College Press.

Gregory, T. & Sweeney, M.E. (1993). Building a community by involving students in the governance of the school, in Tom Gregory and Gerald Smith (Eds.), *High Schools that work: Creating community.* New York: Routledge.

Griffin, A.F. (1942). *A philosophical approach to the subject matter preparation of teachers of history.* Unpublished dissertation, Ohio State University, Columbus, OH.

Guba, E., & Lincoln, Y. (1985). *Naturalistic inquiry.* Beverly Hills, CA: Sage.

Gutmann, Amy. (1999) *Democratic education.* Princeton NJ: Princeton University Press.

Halberstam, D. (1998). *The children.* New York: Random House.

Hahn, C.L. (1996). Research on issues-centered social studies. In R. W. Evans, & D.W. Saxe (Eds.), *Handbook on teaching social issues. NCSS Bulletin 93.* Washington, DC: National Council for the Social Studies, 25–41.

Hahn, C.L. (1998). *Becoming political: Comparative perspectives on citizenship education.* Albany, NY: State University of New York Press.

Hanna, P.R. (1958). Design for a national curriculum. *The Nation's Schools, 62,* 54–56.

Hanvey, R. (1976). *An attainable global perspective*. New York: The Center for Global Perspectives.

Hardin, G. (1985). *Filters against folly*. New York: Penguin Books USA Group.

Haroutunian-Gordon, S. (1991). *Turning the soul: Teaching through conversation in the high school*. Chicago: University of Chicago Press.

Harris, D. (1996). Assessing discussion of public issues. In R.W. Evans & D.W. Saxe (Eds.), *Handbook on teaching social issues. Bulletin 93*. Washington, DC: National Council for the Social Studies, 288–297.

Hartoonian, M.(1997). Education is about producing...not consuming. *Social Education, 61*(6), 365–366.

Hartoonian, M. (1997). *Guide to curriculum planning in social studies*. Madison: State Department of Public Instruction. (ERIC Document 440030).

Haste, H. & Torney-Purta, (1992) J. *The development of political understanding: A new perspective*. San Francisco, CA: Jossey-Bass.

Helwig, C. (1998). Children's conception of fair government and freedom of speech. *Child Development, 69*(2), 518–531.

Hess, D. (2005). Should intelligent design be taught in social studies courses? *Social Education, 70*(1), 8–13.

Hess, D. (2002) Discussing controversial issues in secondary social studies classrooms: Learning from skilled teachers. *Theory and Research in Social Education, 30*(1) 10–41.

Hess, R. D. (2006). *Political attitudes of children*. NJ: Transaction Publishing.

Hess, R. D. & Torney, J. (1967). *The development of political attitudes in children*. Chicago: Aldine Publishing.

Hibbings, I. & Theiss-Morse, E. (2002). *Stealth democracy: Americans' beliefs about how government should work*. New York: Cambridge University Press.

Hicks, D. (2005). Continuity and constraint: Case studies of becoming a teacher of history in England and the United States. *The International Journal of Social Education, 20*(1) 81–92.

Hill, C. (1983). History and culture. *The Random House Encyclopedia*. New York: Random House, 944–1431.

The History Place Presents Abraham Lincoln. (2001). [The History Place website.] Retrieved February 13, 2002 from: http://www.historyplace .com/lincoln/

Houser, N.O. (2005). Arts, aesthetics, and citizenship education: Democracy as experience in a postmodern world. *Theory and Research in Social Education, 33*(1), 45–72.

Houser, N., & Kuzmic, J.J. (2001). Ethical citizenship in a postmodern world. *Theory and Research in Social Education, 29*(3), 431–461.

Houston, J.W., & Houston, J.D. (1973). *Farewell to Manzanar; a true story of Japanese-American experience during and after the World War II internment*. Boston: Houghton Mifflin.

Howard, Tyrone C. (2004) "Does race really matter?" Secondary Student Constructions of Racial Dialogue in the Social Studies. *Theory and Research in Social Education, 32*(4), 464–502.

Hugo, V. (1960). *Les miserables*. (L.Wraxall, Trans.). New York: Heritage.

Hunt, I. (1964). *Across five Aprils*. Chicago: Follett.

Hunt, M.P., & Metcalf, L.E. (1955). *Teaching high school social studies.* New York: Harper & Brothers.

Hunt, M.P., & Metcalf, L.E. (1968). *Teaching high school social studies: problems in reflective thinking and social understanding* (2nd ed.). New York: Harper & Row.

Hutchins, R.M. (1982, March/April). The aims of a democratic society. *The Center Magazine, 15*(2), back cover.

Jackson, P. (1968). *Life in classrooms.* New York: Holt, Rinehart and Winston, Inc.

Jadallah, E. (1985). *The development of a reflective teaching instrument.* Unpublished doctoral dissertation, Ohio State University, Columbus, Ohio.

Jefferson, T. (1816). Letter to Charles Yancey. In For, P. L. (1899). *The writings of Thomas Jefferson, Vol. 10.* New York: G.P. Putnam and Sons.

Jennings, M.K. & Niemi, R. (1981). *Generations and politics.* Princeton, NJ: Princeton University Press.

Johnson, D. & Johnson, R.T. (1996). Conflict resolution and peer mediation programs in elementary and secondary schools: A review of the research. *Review of Educational Research, 66*(4), 459–506.

Keane, J. (1995). *Tom Paine: A political life.* Boston: Little Brown.

King, M.L. (1963). Letter from Birmingham Jail in Bass, S. Jonathan (Ed.) *Blessed are the* peacemakers: Martin Luther King, Jr., eight white religious leaders, and the "Letter from *Birmingham Jail*". Baton Rouge: Louisiana State University Press.

Klingman, W.K. (2001). *Abraham Lincoln and the road to emancipation, 1861–1865.* New York: Viking Penguin.

Kornbluh, M.L. (2000). *Why Americans stopped voting: the decline of participatory democracy and the emergence of American politics.* New York: New York University Press.

Korten, D.C. (2001). *When corporations rule the world.* San Francisco: Berrett-Koehler.

Kozol, J. (1992). *Savage inequalities: Children in America's schools.* New York: Harper-Perennial.

Kreidler, W.J. (1984). *Creative conflict resolution: More than 200 activities for keeping peace in the classroom.* Glenview, IL: Scott, Foresman.

Kreidler, W.J. (1991). *Teaching concepts of peace and conflict* (2nd ed.). Cambridge, MA: Educators for Social Responsibility.

Kreidler, W.J. (1997). *Conflict resolution in the middle school: A curriculum and teacher's guide.* Cambridge, MA: Educators for Social Responsibility.

Lawrence, J. & Lee, R.E. (1955). *Inherit the wind.* New York: Random House.

Leming, J.S. (1981). On the limits of rational moral education. *Theory and Research in Social Education, 9*(1), 7–34.

LeRichie, L.W. & Cowan, E. (1992). The political socialization of children in the expanding environments sequence. *Theory and Research in Social Education, 20*(2), 126–140.

Lesko, N. (1996). Past, present, and future conceptions of adolescents. *Journal of Educational Theory, 46*(4), 453–472.

Lesko, N. (2001). *Act your age! A cultural construction of adolescence.* New York: Routledge Palmer Press.

Lockwood, A. (1999). A place for ethical reasoning is social studies. *The Social Studies, 76*(6), 264–68.

Longstreet, W.S. (1977). Decision making: The new social studies. In *Decision making: The heart of social studies instruction revisited.* (Occasional Papers No. 1). Bloomington, IN: Indiana University, Social Studies Development Center.

Longstreet, W.S. (1982). Action research: A paradigm. *Educational Forum, 46,* 135–158.

MacPherson, M. (2002). *Long time passing: Vietnam and the haunted generation.* New York: Doubleday.

Maher, W. (2004). *Keep the statue of liberty closed: The new rules.* New York: New Millenium Press.

Markandaya, K. (1954). *Nectar in a sieve.* London: Putnam.

Marrus, M.R. (1985). *The unwanted: European refugees in the twentieth century.* New York: Oxford University.

Martorella, P.H. (1985). *Elementary social studies: Developing reflective, competent, and concerned citizens.* Boston: Little, Brown.

Massialas, B.G. (1996). Criteria for issues-centered content selection. In Evans,R. & Saxe, D. (Eds.) *The handbook on teaching social studies. Bulletin No. 93.* Washington, DC: National Council for the Social Studies, 44–50.

Massialis, B. G. (Ed). (1963). The Indiana experiments in inquiry: Social studies. *39*(3).Entire issue.

Massialas, B.G., Sprague, N.F., & Hurst, J.B. (1975). *Social issues: Coping in an age of crisis.* Englewood Cliffs: Prentice-Hall.

McGowan, T. (1984). Does methodology make a difference? A comparison of instructional practices of teachers and student attitudes toward social studies. *Theory and Research in Social Education. Research, 8*(1), 22–39.

McGowan, T.M., Sutton, A.M., & Smith, P.G. (1990). Instructional elements influencing elementary student attitudes toward social studies. *Theory and Research in Social Education, 81*(1), 37–52.

McNeil, L. (1986*). Contradictions of control: School structure and school knowledge.* New York: Routledge & Kegan Paul.

McNeil, L. (2000).). *Contradictions of school reform: Educational cost of standardized testing.* New York: Routledge & Kegan Paul.

McNeill, W.H. (1973). *The Ecumene: Story of humanity.* New York: Harper and Rowe Publishers.

McPherson, M. (1984). *Long Time Passing.* Garden City, NY: Doubleday.

Meltzer, M. (1996). *Tom Paine: Voice of revolution.* New York: Franklin Watts.

Merryfield, M. (1992). Preparing social studies teachers for the 21st century: Perspectives on program effectiveness from a study of six exemplary teacher education programs in global education. *Theory and Research in Social Education,* XX(1) 17–46.

Michener, J. A. (1991). Music and the social studies. In National Council for the Social Studies (Ed.), *James A. Michener on the Social Studies: His Writings in Publications of National Council for the Social Studies from 1938–1987.* Washington, DC: National Council for the Social Studies, Bulletin No. 85, 3–5.

Miles, M. (1971). *Annie and the old one.* Boston: Little, Brown.

Mills, R. (1995). The unrecognized role of paradox in social studies education. *Scholar and Educator, 18*(1), 54–61.

Molnar, A. (1983). Are the issues studied in school the important issues facing [hu]mankind? *Social Education, 47,* 305–307.

Moore, S.W., Lare, J.& Wagner,K.A. (1985). *The Child's Political World: a longitudinal perspective.* New York: Praeger.

Mosher, R., Kenny, R.A. Jr., & Gerard, A. (1994). *Preparing for citizenship: Teaching youth to live democratically.* Westport, CT: Praeger.

Murray, J.C. (1964). *Challenges to democracy: A tenth anniversary symposium of the Fund for the Republic.* New York: Praeger.

Myrdal, G. (1944). *An American dilemma* (Vols. 1–2). New York: Harper.

Nader, R. (1999). *A delicate balance: An essential introduction to American government: Ralph Nader's practicing democracy 1997: A guide to student action.* New York: St. Martin's Press.

National Council for Social Studies (1994). *Curriculum standards for the social studies: Expectations of excellence.* Silver Springs: National Council for the Social Studies.

National Center for History in Schools (1994). *National Standards for United States History: Exploring the American Experience.* Los Angeles: University of California Press.

National Standards for Civics and Government (2003). Calabasas, CA: Center for Civic Education.

Nelson, J. (1996). The Historical imperative for issues-centered education. In Evans, R.W. and & Saxe, D.W. (Eds.) *The handbook on teaching social studies. Bulletin 93.* Washington, DC: The National Council for the Social Studies. 14–24.

Nelson, J. (2001). *Academic freedom in times of stress.* National Council for the Social Studies. Academic Freedom Award Presentation. Washington, DC: Unpublished Paper.

Nelson, J. (2001). Defining social studies. In Stanley, W.B. (Ed.) *Critical issues in social studies research for the 21st century.* Greenwich, CT: Information Age Publishing, 15–38.

Nelson, M. (Ed.). (1994). *The social studies in secondary education: A reprint of the seminal 1916 report with annotations and commentaries.* Bloomington, IN: ERIC Clearinghouse for Social Studies/Social Science Education.

Neruda, P. (1990). *Selected odes of Pablo Neruda* (M.S. Peden, Trans.). Berkeley: University of California.

Newmann, E. S. (1986). Priorities for the future: Toward a common agenda. *Social Education. 50*(4) 240–250.

Newmann, F.M. (1990). A test of higher order thinking in social studies: Persuasive writing on constitutional issues using the National Assessment for Educational Progress. *Social Education, 54*(6), 369–373.

Newmann, F.M. (1991a). Promoting higher order thinking in social studies. Overview of a study of 16 high school departments. *Theory and Research in Social Education, 19*(4), 324–340.

Newmann, F.M. (1991b). Linking Restructuring to Authentic Student Achievement, *Phi Delta Kappan, 72*(6), 458–463.

Newmann, F.M. (1992). *Student engagement and achievement in American secondary schools.* New York: Teachers College Press.

Newmann, F.M. (1996). *Authentic Achievement: Restructuring schools for intellectual quality.* San Francisco: Jossey-Bass.

Newmann, F.M., Bertocci, A., & Landsness, R.M. (1977). *Skills in citizen action.* Madison: Citizen Participation Curriculum Project.

Newmann, F.M., & Oliver, D.W. (1970). *Clarifying public controversy: An approach to teaching social studies.* Boston: Little, Brown.

Niebuhr, R. (1971). Without consensus there is no consent. *The Center Magazine, 14*(4), 2–9.

Niemi, R.G., & Sanders, M.S. (2004). Assessing student performance in civics: The National Assessment for Educational Progress. 1998 civics assessment. *Theory and Research in Social Education, 32*(3), 326–348.

Niemi, R.G. (1990). *The relationship between secondary education and civic development.* New Haven:Yale University Press.

Noddings, N. (2002). *Educating moral people: A caring alternative to character education.* New York: Teachers College Press.

Noddings, N. (1992a). "Social studies and feminism." *Theory and Research in Social Education. 20*(3), 230–241.

Noddings, N. (1992b). *The challenge to care in schools: An alternative approach to education.* New York: Teachers College Press.

Ochoa, A.S. (1979). Censorship: Does anybody care? In Previte, M.A. & Sheehan, J.J. (Eds.) *The NCSS Presidential Addresses, 1970–2000.* National Council for the Social Studies and ERIC Clearinghouse for Social Studies/Social Science Education, Volume II., 133–146.

Ochoa, A.S. (1986). Academic freedom. Two teachers' views. Presented at N.C.S.S. annual conference, 1986.

Ochoa, A.S. (1990). *Academic freedom to teach and learn: Every teacher's issue. (Ed.)* Washington, D.C: National Education Association.

Ochoa-Becker, A.S. (1999). Decision making in middle school social studies: An imperative for youth and democracy. *Clearing House, 72*(6), 337–340.

Ochoa-Becker, A.S. (2001). A limited critique of the National Council for the Social studies curriculum standards. *Social Education, 65*(3), 165–168.

Ochoa-Becker, A.S., Morton, M.L., Autry, M.M., Johnstad, S., Merrill, D. (2001). A search for decision making in three elementary classrooms. *Theory and Research in Social Education, 29*(2), 261–289.

Oliver, D.W. & Newmann, F.M. (1967). *Public Issues Series* (Harvard Social Studies Project). Columbus, OH: Xerox Corporation.

Oliver, D.W., & Shaver, J.P. (1966). *Teaching public issues in the high school.* Boston: Houghton Mifflin.

Onosko, J.J. (1996). Exploring issues with students despite the barriers. *Social Education, 60*(1), 22–27.

Orwell, G. (1949). *Nineteen eighty-four.* New York: New American Library.

Palmer, J. (2001). Conflict resolution: Strategies for the elementary classroom. *Social Studies, 92*(2), 65–68.

Palonsky, S.B. (1993). A knowledge base for social studies teachers. *The International Journal of Social Education, 7*(3), 7–23.

Palonsky, S. & Nelson, J. (1980). Political restraint in the socialization of student teachers. *Theory and Research in Social Education, 7*(4), 19–34.

Parker, W.C. (2001). Educating democratic citizens: A broad view. *Theory into Practice, 40*(1), 6–13.

Parker, W.C. (2002). *Education for democracy: Contexts, curricula, assessments.* Greenwich, CT: Information Age Publishing.

Parker, W.C. (2003). *Teaching democracy: Unity and diversity in public life.* New York: Teachers College Press.

Parker, W.C. & Hess, D. (2001). Teaching with and for discussion. *Teaching and Teacher Education, 17,* 273–289.

Parker, J.C., & Rubin, L.J. (1966). *Process as content: Curriculum design and the application of knowledge.* Chicago: Rand McNally.

Parkham, S. (Ed.) (1990). The stakes are too high for government to be a spectatro sport. Quotations by B. Jordan. Cambridge, MA: Harvard University Press.

Patrick, J. J. (Fall, Winter, 2005–2006).Content and process in education for democracy. *International Journal of Social Education 20*(2), 1–12.

Patrick, J.J. (1997). *The National Assessment of Educational Progress in U.S. History.* ERIC/ChESS Digests. Retrieved February 27, 2002 from: http://www.indiana.edu/~ssdc/naephis.htm

Patrick, J.J. (2000). *The National Assessment of Educational Progress in Civics.* ERIC/ChESS Digests. Retrieved February 27, 2002 from: http://www.indiana.edu/~ssdc/naepc2dig.htm

Paxson, F. (1936). Lecture notes taken by Shirley H. Engle at the University of Illinois.

Percoco, J.A.(2003). Primarily, it's serendipity. *Social Education, 67*(7), 401–404.

Pett, J. (1982). *Pet peeves: Political cartoons.* Bloomington, IN: Herald Times Newspaper.

Pohl, F.J. (1986). *The new Columbus.* Rochester, NY: Security Dupont.

Popham, W. (2004). *America's "failing" schools: How parents and teachers can cope with No Child Left Behind.* New York: Routledge Falmer.

Porro, B. (1996). *Talk it out: Conflict resolution in the elementary classroom.* Alexandria, VA: Association for Supervision and Curriculum Development.

Ravitch, D., & Finn, C.E. (1987). *What do our 17-year-olds know?* New York: Harper & Row.

Reich, R. (1983). *The Next American Frontier.* New York:Time Books.

Reich, R. (1992). *Locked in the Cabinet.* New York: Knopf.

Remarque, E. (1929) *All quiet on the western front.* (A.W. Wheen, Trans.). London: G.P. Putnam's Sons.

Riley, K.L. (2005). The state of the debate: History versus social studies—questions of authority and purpose and rigor. *The International Journal of Social Education, 20*(1). ix–xiv.

Riordon, W.L. (1963). *Plunkitt of Tammany Hall.* New York: E.P.Dutton.

Risinger, C.F. (2003). Teaching about war and peace with the internet. *Social Education, 67*(3), 175–176.

Rom, A. (1996). School finance and equal education opportunity. In C.E. Walsh (Ed.), *Education reform and social change: Multicultural voices, struggles, and visions,* Mahwah, NJ: Lawrence Erlbaum Associates, 21–30.

Ross, E.W. (Ed.) (2001). *The social studies curriculum: Purposes, problems, and possibilities.* Albany, NY: State University Press of New York.

Rossi, J.A. & Pace, C. (1995). In-depth study in an issues-oriented social studies classroom, *Theory and Research in Social Education, 23*(2), 88–120.

Rossi, J.A. & Pace, C. (1998). Issues-centered instruction with low achieving high school students: The dilemmas of two teachers. *Theory and Research in Social Education, 26*(3), 380–409.

Rugg, H. (1921, October). On reconstructing the social studies curriculum. *The Historical Outlook, 12*, 249–252.

Sadalla, G., Holmberg, M., & Halligan, J. (1990). *Conflict resolution: An elementary school curriculum.* San Francisco: The Community Board Program.

Sadker, M. & Sadker, D. (1994). *Failing at fairness: How our schools cheat girls.* New York: Touchstone/Simon & Shuster.

Sandwell, R. (2005). School history versus the historian. *The International Journal of Social Education, 20*(1) 9–17.

Schillings, D. (1994). National Council for the Social Studies documents. Teaching the human condition through the social studies. *Social Education, 58*(4), 197–199.

Schug, M.C., Todd, R.J., & Berry, R. (1984). Why kids don't like social studies. *Social Education, 48*(5), 382–387.

Scott Foresman (2003). *Building a nation, Grade 5.* (Elementary series). Glenview, IL: Scott Foresman.

Segall, A. (2003). The impact of state-mandated testing according to social studies teachers. The Michigan Educational Assessment Program (MEAP) as a case study of consequences. *Theory and Research in Social Education, 31*(3), 287–325.

Selman, R. (1976). Social cognitive understanding: A guide to educational and clinical practice. In T. Lickona (Ed.). *Moral development and behavior.* New York: Holt, Rinehart & Winston.

Selman, R.L. (1980). *The growth of interpersonal understanding.* New York: Academic Press.

Selwyn, D. (1995). *Arts and humanities in the social studies.* NCSS Bulletin 92, Silver Springs, MD: National Council for Social Studies.

Senesh, L. (1966). *Organizing a curriculum around social science concepts.* West Lafayette, IN: Social Science Education Consortium.

Senghor, L.S. (1962). *Nationhood and the African road to socialism* (M. Cook, Trans.). Paris: Presence Africaine.

Senghor, L.S. (1965). *Prose and poetry* (J. Reed & C. Wake, Trans). London: Oxford University.

Shaftel, F.R., & Shaftel, G. 1982). *Role playing in the curriculum* (2nd ed.). Englewood Cliffs, NJ: Prentice-Hall.

Shaver, J.P. (1968) *Democracy, pluralism, and the social studies: Readings and commentary; an approach to curriculum decisions in the social studies.* Boston: Houghton Mifflin.

Shaver, J. (1976). Report of the President of the Board of Directors of N.C.S.S. and the House of Delegates of N.C.S.S. Washington, DC. In Previte, M.A. & Sheehan, J. (Eds.). *The N.C.S.S. Presidential Addresses, Vol. 2.* N.C.S.S. ERIC Clearinghouse for Social Studies/Social Science Education. Bloomington, IN: Social Studies Development International Study.

Shaver, J.P. (1977). *Building rationales for citizenship education.* Bulletin 52. Washington, DC: National Council for the Social Studies.

Shaver, J.P. (1977). Needed: A Deweyean rationale for social studies. *High School Journal, 40*(8), 345–352.

Shaver, J. P. (Ed.) (1991). *Handbook of Research on Social Studies Teaching and Learning.* New York: Macmillan.

Shaver, J.P. (1992). Rationales for issues-centered social studies education. *Social Studies, 83*(3), 95–99.

Shaver, J.P., Davis, O.L., & Helburn, S. (1979). The status of social studies education: Impressions from three National Science Foundation studies. *Social Education, 43*(2), 150–153.

Shaver, J.P. & Strong, W. (1982). *Facing value decisions: Rationale-building for teachers.* New York:Teachers College Press.

Shaw, B. (1941). *Pygmalion: A romance in five acts.* Harmondsworth, Middlesex, England: Penguin Books.

Sheehan, N. (1988). *A bright shining lie: John Paul Vann and America in Vietnam.* New York: Random House.

Shenkman, R. (1988). *Legends, lies and cherished myths of American history.* New York: William Morrow.

Shermis, S. & Barth, J.(March, 1985). Indoctrination and the Study of Social Problems: A re-examination of the 1930's debate in The Social Frontier. *Social Education, 44*(5), 190–193.

Shute, N. (1957). *On the beach.* New York: William Morrow.

Singleton, L.R. & Giese J.R. (1996) Preparing citizens to participate in public discourse: the public issues model. In Evans, R.W. and Saxe, D.W. (Eds.), *Handbook for Teaching Social Issues. Bulletin* 93. Washington, DC: National Council for the Social Studies. 59–65.

Sizer, T. S. (1984). *Horace's compromise: The dilemma of the American high school.* Boston: Houghton Mifflin

Skeel, D.J.(1988). Task force reports on early childhood. *Social Studies Professional, 90*(12), 12.

Skeel, D. (1996). An issues-centered elementary curriculum. In R.W. Evans, & D.W. Saxe (Eds.), *Handbook on teaching social issues.* Bulletin 93. Washington, DC: National Council for the Social Studies, 230–235.

Skiba, R., Michael, R., Nardo, A., Carroll, A., & Peterson, R. (2002). The color of discipline: Sources of racial and gender disproportionality in school punishment. *Urban Review. 34*(4), 317–42.

Skiba, R. & Peterson, R. (2003). Teaching the social curriculum: School discipline as instruction. *Preventing School Failure, 47*(2), 66–73.

Slavin, R.E. (1995). *Cooperative learning: Theory, research, and practice* (2nd ed.). Boston: Allyn and Bacon.

Southern Poverty Law Center (2005). *Intelligence report: Ten years of terror, 118,* 33–46.

Stake, R.E., & Easley, J.A., Jr. (1978). *Case studies in science education. Vol. 2: Design, overview and findings.* (University of Illinois, Urbana: Center for Instructional Research and Curriculum Evaluation). Washington, DC: National Science Foundation.

Stavrianos, L. (1998). *A global history: From prehistory to the 21st century.* New York: Prentice Hall.

Steinbeck, J. (1939). *The grapes of wrath.* New York: Viking.

Sterzing vs. Fort Bend School District (1974) S.D. 496 F. Supp 92 (5th Cir.)

Stowe, H.B (1981) *Uncle Tom's Cabin*. New York: Penguin Classics.

Taba, H. (1967). *Teacher's handbook for elementary social studies* Reading, MA: Addison-Wesley.

Thelen, D. (1996). *Becoming citizens in the age of television*. Chicago:University of Chicago Press.

Thornton, S. (2004). *Teaching social studies that matters: curriculum for active learning*. New York: Teachers College Press.

Thornton, S. (2005). History and social studies: A question of philosophy. *The International Journal of Social Education, 20*(1), 1–7.

Tinker vs. Des Moines Independent S.D. (1969). 39 U.S. 503,571

Torney-Purta, J. (2000). Comparative perspectives on political socialization and civic education. *Comparative Education Review, 44*(1), 88–95.

Torney-Purta, J., Lehman, Oswald, & Schulz (2001). *Citizenship and education in twenty-eight countries: Civic knowledge and engagement at age fourteen*. Amsterdam: IEA.

Torney, J., Oppenheim, A., & Farnen, R. (1975). *Civic education in ten countries*. New York: John Wiley & Sons.

Trefousse, H.L. (1975). *Lincoln's decision for emancipation*. New York:J.B. Lippincott.

Torres M.N. (2004). he Role of participatory democracy in the critical praxis of social justice. In O'Donnenn, Pruyo,M. & Chavez Chavez, R., (Eds). *Social justice in these times*. Greenwich:Conn: Information Age Publishing.

U.S. Census (2005). www.U.S.Census.gov. Retrieved June, 2005.

Van Sickle, R. (1996). Questions of motivation for achievement in social studies. In Massialas, B.G. and Allen, R.F., Eds. *Critical Issues in Teaching Social Studies*. Belmont, CA: Wadsworth Publishing Company.

Vidal, G. (2001). *The last empire: essays 1992–2000* (1st ed.). New York: Doubleday.

Vinson, D. & Ross, W.D.(2001). In search of the social studies curriculum:standardization, diversity, and a conflict of appearances. In Stanley, W.B. (Ed.), *Critical issues in social studies research for the 21st century*. Greenwich, CT: Information Age Publishing, 39–71.

Wade, R.C. & Saxe, D. (1996). Community service learning in the social studies: Roots, empirical evidence, critical issues. *Theory and Research in Social Education, 24*(4), 321–354.

Walker, A. (2000). *The way forward is with a broken heart*. New York: Random House.

Walker, A. (1997). *Anything we love can be saved: A writer's activism*. New York: Random House.

Wesley, E.B. (1937). *Teaching social studies in high school*. Boston: D.C. Heath.

West, C. (1993).*Race matters*. Boston: Beacon Press.

West, C. (2004). *Democracy matters: Winning the fight against imperialism*. New York: The Penguin Press.

Whitehead, A.N. (1929*). The aims of education and other essays*. New York: MacMillan.

Wiggins, G. (1989). The futility of trying to teach everything of importance. *Educational Leadership, 47*(3), 44–48, 57–59.

Wilen, W.W. & Clegg, A.A. Jr. (1986). Effective questions and questioning: A research review. *Theory and Research in Social Education, 14*(2), 153–161.

Wilen, W.W., & White, J.J. (1991). Interaction and discourse in social studies class-rooms. In Shaver, J.P. (Ed.), *Handbook of research on social studies teaching and learning.* New York: Macmillan, 483–495.

Wilson, B.P. (1978). *Giants for justice: Bethune, Randolph, and King.* New York: Har-court Brace Jovanovich.

The world almanac and book of facts 2000 (2001). Mahwah, NJ: World Almanac Books.

World Watch Institute. (2001). *State of the world 2001.* New York: W.W. Norton. Childhood Origins.

Zacher, J. C. (2005). Effects of a multicultural literacy curriculum in a racially and socio-economically diverse fifth-grade classroom. In McInerney, D.M. & Van Etten, S., (Eds.) *Focus on Curriculum.* Greenwich, CT: Information Age Publishing.

Zellman & Sears (1977). Childhood Attitudes of Tolerance for Dissent in Tapp, J.L.and Levine, F.J. *Law, Justice, and the individual in society.* New York: Holt, Rine-hart and Winston.

Zinn, H. (2002). *A people's history of the United States, 1492-present* (1st Perennial Classics ed.). New York: Perennial Classics.

Zinn, H. & Arnove, A. (2004). *Voices of a people's history of the United States.* New York: Seven Stories Press.

Zola, E. (1928). *Nana.* New York: The Modern Library.

ABOUT THE AUTHOR

Anna S. Ochoa-Becker has devoted her efforts to social studies education throughout her career. She has taught at the middle and high school level for eleven years and for two years, she taught at the elementary level. She received her undergraduate degree at Wayne State University, her masters degree in History with a minor in Political Science at the University of Michigan and her doctorate in Curriculum and Instruction/Social Studies at the University of Washington. She has written extensively in the field and has served as the President of the National Council for the Social Studies. Her higher education experience was at the University of Wisconsin–Milwaukee, Florida State University, and Indiana University in Bloomington, Indiana.

Greg Mears

Printed in the United States
68376LVS00001B/1-10